Critical Theory Today

Garland Reference Library of the Humanities
Volume 2070

Critical Theory Today
A User-Friendly Guide

Lois Tyson

Garland Publishing, Inc.
A member of the Taylor & Francis Group
New York & London
1999

Library of Congress Cataloging-in-Publication Data

Tyson, Lois.
　　Critical theory today : a user-friendly guide / Lois Tyson.
　　　　　p.　　cm. — (Garland reference library of the
　　humanities ; vol. 2070)
　　　　Includes bibliographical references and index.
　　　　ISBN 0-8153-2880-X (alk. paper) — ISBN 0-8153-2879-6
　　(pkb. : alk. paper)
　　　　　1. Criticism.　　I. Title.　　II. Series.
　　PN81.T97　　1999
　　801'.95—dc21　　　　　　　　　　　　　　　　　98-15427
　　　　　　　　　　　　　　　　　　　　　　　　　　　CIP

Cover design by Robert Van Keirsbilck

*I gratefully dedicate this book
to my students and to my teachers.
I hope I will always have difficulty telling you apart.*

CONTENTS

ACKNOWLEDGMENTS

My most sincere thanks go to the following friends and colleagues for their helpful suggestions and moral support: Hannah Berkowitz, Linda Chown, Gretchen Cline, Diane Griffin Crowder, Michelle DeRose, Milt Ford, David Greetham, Michael Hartnett, Alan Hausman, Roseanne Hoefel, Bill Hoffman, Jay Hullett, Howard Kahane, Stephen Lacey, James Lindesay, Rosalind Srb Mayberry, Joanie Pearlman, James Phelan, Sue William Silverman, Veta Smith Tucker, Brian White, and Sharon Whitehill.

Special thanks also go to Grand Valley State University for its generous financial support of this project and to Phyllis Korper, Kristi Long, Chuck Bartelt, and Susan Chen at Garland for their enthusiasm and patience in guiding me through the labyrinth of publication.

Finally, the deepest gratitude is expressed to Mac Davis, the only braveheart who read every word of every draft of every chapter. Your unflagging support will never be forgotten.

PREFACE FOR INSTRUCTORS

The writing of this textbook was the product of a sense of pedagogical frustration that I suspect many of you may share. In the last decade, critical theory has become a dominant force in higher education. It is now considered an essential part of graduate education, and it plays an increasingly visible role in the undergraduate classroom as well. Yet many college students at all levels, as well as some of their professors, remain confused by much of this jargon-ridden discipline, which seems to defy their understanding. As one colleague said to his students, "Critical theory is a bus, and you're not going to get on it."

Anthologies of essays often used in critical theory courses—which generally include pieces by such frequently arcane theorists as Lacan, Derrida, Spivak, Benjamin, and the like—and books that offer high-tech summaries of these theorists' views, don't help the majority of students who are unfamiliar with the basic principles one must understand in order to understand these texts. Conversely, the very few theory textbooks that are written in accessible language are much too limited in scope to offer an adequate introduction to this complex field.

Critical Theory Today: A User-Friendly Guide attempts to fill this gap by offering an accessible, unusually thorough introduction to this difficult field that will (1) enable readers to grasp heretofore obscure theoretical concepts by relating them to our everyday experience; (2) show them how to apply theoretical perspectives to literary works; and (3) reveal the relationships among theories—their differences, similarities, strengths, and weaknesses—by applying them all to a single literary work: F. Scott Fitzgerald's *The Great Gatsby*.

I've chosen *The Great Gatsby* for this purpose for several reasons. In addition to lending itself readily to the ten theoretical readings I offer, the novel is fairly short, quite readable, and familiar, both in terms of its treatment of common American themes and in terms of readers' prior exposure to the work. In fact, many of my colleagues who teach critical theory have indicated that they would prefer a textbook that uses *The Great Gatsby* for its literary applications because of their *own* familiarity with the novel.

Aimed primarily at newcomers to the field, each chapter explains the basic principles of the theory it addresses, including the basic principles of literary application, in order to enable students to write their own theoretical interpretations of literature and read with insight what the theorists, themselves, have written. Thus, this book can be used as the only text in a course or as a precursor to (or in tandem with) critical theory anthologies. Each chapter has grown out of classroom practice, has been thoroughly field tested, and has demonstrated its capacity to motivate students by showing them what critical theory can offer, not only in terms of their practical understanding of literary texts, but also in terms of their personal understanding of themselves and the world in which they live. In a very real sense, this textbook is a "how-to" manual for readers who will probably come to their study of theory with some anxiety, whether they are first-year theory students or college professors who wish to familiarize themselves with theoretical perspectives with which they have not yet become thoroughly acquainted.

Chapters are sequenced for a specific pedagogical purpose: to demonstrate how critical theories both argue and overlap with one another, sometimes overturning, sometimes building upon the insights of competing theories. Nevertheless, each chapter is self-explanatory and was written to stand on its own. Therefore, this textbook can be customized to fit your own instructional needs by assigning the chapters in any order you choose; by eliminating some chapters entirely; or by assigning only certain sections of particular chapters, for which purpose chapter subtitles should prove helpful. Similarly, the "Questions for Further Practice" (which follow each reading of *The Great Gatsby* and can serve as paper topics) encourage students to apply each theory to other well known, frequently anthologized literary works, but you can have your students apply these questions to any works you select.

However you choose to use *Critical Theory Today,* I hope you will agree that critical theory is a bus our students have every reason to climb aboard. And if this book does its job, they will even enjoy the ride.

Critical Theory Today

CHAPTER 1

Everything You Wanted To Know About Critical Theory But Were Afraid To Ask

Why should we bother to learn about critical theories? Is it really worth the trouble? Won't all those abstract concepts (if I can even understand any of them) interfere with my natural, personal interpretations of literature? These questions, or ones like them, are probably the questions most frequently asked by new students of critical theory, regardless of their age or educational status, and they reveal the two-fold nature of our reluctance to study theory: (1) fear of failure and (2) fear of losing the intimate, exciting, magical connection with literature that is our reason for reading it in the first place. I think both these fears are well founded.

With notable exceptions, most theoretical writing—by the big names in the field and by those who attempt to explain their ideas to novices—is filled with technical terms and theoretical concepts that assume a level of familiarity newcomers simply don't have. And because such writing doesn't seem to connect with our love of literature, let alone with the everyday world we live in, it seems that theory's purpose must be to take us into some abstract, intellectual realm in which we try to impress one another by using the latest theoretical jargon (which we hope our peers haven't heard yet) and dropping the names of obscure theorists (whom we hope our peers haven't read yet). In other words, because knowledge of critical theory has become, over the last decade or so, a mark of status, an educational "property" for which students and professors compete, it has also become a costly commodity, difficult to acquire and to maintain at the state of the art.

Indeed, I think the anxiety that most of us bring to our study of critical theory is due largely to our initial encounters with theoretical jargon or, more accurately, with people who use theoretical jargon to inflate their own status. To cite just one example, a student recently asked me what *"the death of the author"* means. He'd heard the phrase bandied about, but no one explained it to him, so he felt excluded from the conversation. Because the meaning of the phrase wasn't evident in the context in which he'd heard it used, the student felt that it must be a complex concept. Because those who used the phrase acted as though they belonged to an elite club, at the same time as they pretended that everyone knew what it meant, he felt stupid for not knowing the term and, therefore, afraid to ask about it, afraid to reveal his stupidity. In fact, "the death of the author" is a simple concept, but unless someone explains it to you, the phrase makes little sense. "The death of the author" merely refers to the change in attitude toward the role of the author in our interpretation of literary works. In the early decades of the twentieth century, students of literature were taught that the author was our primary concern in reading a literary work: our task was to examine the author's life in order to discover what the author meant to communicate—his or her message, theme, or moral—which is called *authorial intention.* Our focus has changed over the years to the point that, now, among many contemporary critical theorists at least, the author is no longer considered a meaningful object of analysis. We focus, instead, on the reader; on the ideological, rhetorical, or aesthetic structure of the text; or on the culture in which the text was produced, usually without reference to the author. So, for all intents and purposes, the author is "dead." It's a simple idea, really, yet, like many ideas that belong to a particular academic discipline, it can be used to exclude people rather than to communicate with them.

This situation is especially objectionable because it results in the exclusion of those of us who might stand to benefit from critical theory in the most concrete ways: current and future teachers at the elementary and secondary levels; faculty and students at community colleges; and faculty and students, in all departments, at the thousands of liberal arts colleges responsible for the bulk of American education but whose members may not be on the "fast track" to academic stardom.

What are the concrete ways in which we can benefit from an understanding of critical theory? As I hope the following chapters will illustrate, theory can help us learn to see ourselves and our world in valuable new ways, ways that can influence how we educate our children, both as parents and teachers; how we view television, from the nightly news to situation comedies; how we behave as voters and consumers; how we react to others with whom we do not agree on social, religious, and political issues; and how we recognize and deal with our own motives, fears, and desires. And if we believe that human productions—not just literature but also, for example, film, music, art, science, technology, and architecture—are outgrowths of human experience and therefore reflect human desire, conflict, and potential, then we can learn to interpret those productions in order to learn something important about ourselves as a species. Critical theory, I think you will find, provides excellent tools for that endeavor, tools that not only can show us our world and ourselves through new and valuable lenses but also can strengthen our ability to think logically, creatively, and with a good deal of insight.

To that end, each chapter will explain the basic principles of the theory it addresses in order to enable you to read what the theorists, themselves, have written. Each chapter will focus on a critical theory that has had a significant impact on the practice of literary criticism today and will attempt to show the world through the lens of that theory. Think of each theory as a new pair of eyeglasses through which certain elements of our world are brought into focus while others, of course, fade into the background. Did that last idea give you pause, I hope? Why should some ideas have to fade into the background in order to focus on others? Doesn't this suggest that each theory can offer only an incomplete picture of the world?

It seems unavoidable, and part of the paradox of seeing and learning, that in order to understand some things clearly we must restrict our focus in a way that highlights certain elements and ignores others, just as the close-up camera crystallizes whatever it frames and renders the rest a blurred background. Perhaps this is why, for example, science and religion often seem so at odds, not just because they often offer conflicting explanations of the same phenomena but because they focus our vision on different dimensions of our own experience. This is why it seems to me so important that we study a number of theories in succession, not just to remind ourselves that multiple viewpoints are important if we are to see the whole picture but to grasp the very process of understanding that underlies human experience and to thereby increase our ability to see both the value and the limitations of every method of viewing the world. In fact, one of the most important things theory can show us is that methodologies *are* ways of seeing the world, whether we're talking about physics or sociology, literature, or medicine.

Indeed, because they are ways of seeing the world, critical theories compete with one another for dominance in educational and cultural communities. Each theory offers itself as the most (or the only) accurate means of understanding human experience. Thus, competition among theories has always had a strong political dimension in at least two senses of the word *political*: (1) different theories offer very different interpretations of history and of current events, including interpretations of government policies, and (2) advocates of the most popular theories of the day usually receive the best jobs and the most funding for their projects.

Even within the ranks of any given critical theory there are countless disagreements among practitioners that result in the emergence of different schools of thought within a single theory. In fact, the history of every critical theory is, in effect, the history of an ongoing debate among its own advocates as well as an ongoing debate with the advocates of other theories. However, before you can understand an argument, you have to understand the language or languages in which the opponents express their ideas. By familiarizing you with the language each theory speaks—that is, with the key concepts upon which each theory is grounded—this book will prepare you to understand the ongoing debates both within and among critical theories. Learning to use the different languages of theory offered here will also accustom you to "thinking theoretically," that is, to seeing the assumptions, whether stated or not, that underlie every viewpoint.

For example, as you read the following chapters, I hope it will become clear to you that even our "personal," "natural" interpretations of literature and of the world we live in—interpretations "unsullied" by theory—are based on assumptions, on ways of seeing the world, that are themselves theoretical and that we don't realize we've internalized. In other words, there is no such thing as a non-theoretical interpretation. We may not be aware of the theoretical assumptions that guide our thinking, but those assumptions are there nevertheless. For example, why do we assume that the proper way to interpret a story for an English class is to show how images and metaphors convey ideas and feelings or how the story illustrates a theme or reflects some aspect of history or communicates the author's viewpoint? Why isn't the proper response, instead, to do volunteer work at a shelter for the homeless, sculpt a statue, or throw a party? In other words, the interpretations of literature we produce before we study critical theory may seem completely personal or natural, but they are based on beliefs—beliefs about literature, about education, about language, about selfhood—that permeate our culture and that we therefore take for granted.

I hope you will also find, once you've become better acquainted with critical theory, that it increases rather than decreases your appreciation of literature. Think back to your junior-high or high-school experience as a reader. Can you remember a story or two, or a novel or play, that you just loved or just hated, yet when you read it again a few years later your reaction had significantly changed? The more we experience in life, the more we are capable of experiencing in literature. So as you grow in your capacity to understand theory, to think more broadly and more deeply about human experience and the world of ideas, the more you will be capable of appreciating the rich density, the varied texture and shades of meaning, available in literary works. It's possible that an old favorite might fall by the wayside, but you'll have new favorites, and you'll have the capacity to see more and therefore appreciate more in everything you read.

In order to illustrate the various ways in which different critical theories interpret literature, each chapter will include, in addition to short examples drawn from different literary texts, a fully developed reading of the same work: F. Scott Fitzgerald's well-known novel, *The Great Gatsby*, published in 1925.[1] The focus of the following chapters is primarily literary for two reasons: (1) I assume that most readers will be approaching critical theory as students or teachers of literature, and (2) literature, conceived as a "laboratory" of human life, provides examples of human experience presumably common to all readers.

Why *The Great Gatsby* and not some other literary work? I did not choose Fitzgerald's novel because I think you will find it, necessarily, a great work or even an enjoyable work, although many readers consider it both. I chose it because it lends itself well to the critical theories we are studying. Although, hypothetically at least, every literary work can be interpreted using every critical framework, most works lend themselves more readily to some frameworks than to others, and the attempt to read a text using an incompatible framework can be a relatively fruitless endeavor that risks distorting elements of the text, the theory, or both, as we try to make them fit each other. It's a judgment call, of course, and readers will differ as to which theories they are able to fruitfully apply to which literary works. Our task, then, is to know our own strengths and limitations as well as those of the theories we employ, even as we work to increase our ability to use theories.

Another fact to keep in mind as we apply critical theories to *The Great Gatsby* and as you begin to use them to read other literary works is that different theoretical interpretations of the same literary work can bring forth very different views of the work, focusing on different characters and different parts of the plot or generating opposing views of the same characters and events. Theories can also overlap a good deal with one another, producing very compatible, even similar, readings of the same work. Critical theories are not isolated entities, completely different from one another, separable into tidy bins, like the tubs of tulips, daffodils, and carnations we see at the florist. It would be more useful to think of theories, to continue the metaphor, as mixed bouquets, each of which can contain a few of the flowers that predominate in or that serve different purposes in other bouquets.

Thus, for example, while Marxism focuses on the socioeconomic considerations that underlie human behavior, it doesn't exclude the psychological domain of human experience; rather, when it addresses human psychology, it does so in order to demonstrate how psychological experience is produced by socioeconomic factors rather than by the causes usually posited by psychoanalysis. Similarly, while feminist analysis often draws on psychoanalytic and Marxist concepts, it uses them to illuminate feminist concerns, for example, to examine the ways in which women are psychologically and socioeconomically oppressed. And even when critics use the same theoretical tools to read the same literary work, they might produce very different interpretations of that work. Using the same theory doesn't necessarily mean reading the literary work in the same way. If you read other critics' interpretations of *The Great Gatsby*, you will probably find that they agree with my interpretations on some points and disagree on others even when we seem to be using the same critical tools.

At this point, a brief explanation of a few important concepts might be useful. I refer above to other "critics," and it's important to remind ourselves that the terms *critic* and *literary criticism* don't necessarily imply finding fault with literary works. Literary criticism, by and large, tries to explain the literary work to us: its production, its meaning, its design, its beauty. Critics tend to find flaws in one another's interpretations more than in literary works. Unlike movie critics and book reviewers, who tell us whether or not we should see the films or read the books they review, literary critics spend much more time explaining than evaluating, even when their official purpose, like that of the New Critics described in Chapter Five, is to assess the aesthetic quality of the literary work. Of course, when we apply critical theories that involve a desire to change the world for the better—such as feminism, Marxism, African American criticism, and lesbian/gay/queer criticism—we will sometimes find a literary work flawed in terms of its deliberate or inadvertent promotion of sexist, capitalist, racist, or homophobic values. But even in these cases, the flawed work has value because we can use it to understand how these repressive ideologies operate.

Critical theory (or *literary theory*), on the other hand, tries to explain the assumptions and values upon which various forms of literary criticism rest. Strictly speaking, when we interpret a literary text, we are doing literary criticism; when we examine the criteria upon which our interpretation rests, we are doing critical theory. Simply put, literary criticism is the application of critical theory to a literary text, whether or not a given critic is aware of the theoretical assumptions informing her or his interpretation. In fact, the widespread recognition that literary criticism cannot be separated from the theoretical assumptions on which it is based is one reason why the word *criticism* is often used as if it included the word *theory.*

Examples of critical theory include Jacques Derrida's essays on his deconstructive theory of language, Louise Rosenblatt's definitions of *text, reader,* and *poem,* and even my attempt, in the following chapters, to explain the operations of and relationships among theoretical concepts from various critical schools. Examples of literary criticism would include a deconstructive interpretation of Mary Shelley's *Frankenstein* (1818), a Marxist analysis of Toni Morrison's *The Bluest Eye* (1970), a gay reading of the imagery in Walt Whitman's "Song of Myself" (1855), and the various interpretations of *The Great Gatsby* offered in the following chapters.

Despite their tendency to interpret rather than to evaluate literature, literary critics have an enormous effect on the literary marketplace, not in terms of what they say about particular works but in terms of which works they choose to interpret and which works they ignore. And of course, critics tend to interpret works that lend themselves readily to the critical theory they employ. Thus, whenever a single critical theory dominates literary studies, those works that lend themselves well to that theory will be considered "great works" and will be taught in the college classroom, while other works will be ignored. Since most of us who become teachers tend to teach the works we were taught, a popular critical theory can result in the institutionalization, or *canonization,* of certain literary works: those works then are taught to successive generations of students as "great works" with "timeless" appeal.

The last concept I want to discuss with you, before explaining how this book is organized, might be called *reading "with the grain" or "against the grain"* of a literary work. When we read with the grain, we read the work the way it seems to invite us to read it. For example, the Marxist interpretation of *The Great Gatsby* found in Chapter Three reads with the grain of the story to the extent that it clarifies the ways in which the text, itself, explicitly condemns the superficial values that put social status above every other concern. In contrast, that same interpretation reads against the grain of the story when it seeks to show the ways in which the novel, apparently unwittingly, fosters the ideology responsible for the values it condemns. Thus, when we read against the grain, we analyze elements in the text of which the text, itself, seems unaware. To give another example, because *The Great Gatsby* explicitly shows that Tom, Daisy, and Myrtle are hardly ideal spouses, our psychoanalytic interpretation of the novel in Chapter Two reads with the grain when it suggests that these characters are not really in love with their mates. However, because the novel presents Gatsby's love for Daisy in such a traditional romantic manner—Nick says that Gatsby "committed himself" to Daisy as "to the following of a grail" (156; ch. 8), and Gatsby ends up sacrificing his life for her—our psychoanalytic interpretation may be said to read against the grain when it argues that his feelings for Daisy are as far from real love as those of the other characters.

Reading with the grain thus implies seeing what the author intended us to see, while reading against the grain implies seeing something the author didn't intend, something of which he or she was unaware. However, we generally talk about what the text intends, rather than what the author intended. As the New Critics observed, we can't always know what the author intended, and even if authors say what they intended, the literary work might fail to live up to that intention or might go beyond it. Of course, some critics do choose to talk about the author's intention, and they shoulder the burden of providing biographical arguments to try to convince us that they're right. By the same token, talking about what the text intends doesn't guarantee that our analysis is correct; we still must provide evidence from the text to support our view. In any event, any given theory can read with or against the grain of any literary work at any given point in the text. It's usually important to know whether we're reading with or against the grain so that we don't, for example, condemn a literary work for its portrayal of sexist behavior when that very portrayal is given in order to condemn sexism. Like many elements of literary interpretation, this is a sticky one, and critics often disagree about what a work invites us to see and what it does not.

While such issues are important, at this point in time they shouldn't concern you too much. For now, just let them float around in the back of your mind as you read through the chapters that follow. Indeed, I think this book will do its job best if you read it for interest and enjoyment rather than in hopes of becoming a master theoretician who understands everything. For one thing, reading this book won't make you a master theoretician who understands everything. Of course, there's no such creature. And the book you have in your hands is only an introduction to critical theory, a first step into what I hope will be a long and enriching process. While this book will acquaint you with what many of us consider the most well-known and useful theories, there are many other theories not offered here. Having read this book, however, you should be ready to read about additional theories on your own if you're interested, and you should also be ready to read more about the theories covered here if you find you have a particular interest in some of them.

To help you attain that readiness, each chapter begins with a plain-English explanation of the theory in question, drawing on examples from everyday experience and well-known literary works to clarify key points. To help you look at literature the way a theorist might, each chapter also contains a list of general questions such theorists ask about literary works. Then, as a specific illustration, an interpretation of Fitzgerald's novel, through the lens of the theory at hand, follows. Next, you will find a list of questions for further practice, which serves as a guide to applying the theory under consideration to other literature. These questions (which also can function as paper topics) attempt to focus your attention on specific theoretical concepts illustrated in specific literary works. Most of these works are frequently anthologized and appear often on college syllabi, but you or your instructor might want to apply the questions to different pieces of literature. Finally, in case you would like to learn more about a particular theory, each chapter closes with a bibliography of theoretical works, "For Further Reading," that will serve as a useful follow-up to what you have just learned. Chapter Twelve, "Gaining an Overview," offers you a way to clarify and organize your thoughts about the critical theories discussed in this textbook by providing a list of questions—one for each theory—that represent the general focus, a kind of bird's-eye view, of each school of criticism. In addition, Chapter Twelve attempts to explain how theories reflect the history and politics of the culture that produces them and how different theories can be used in conjunction to produce a single interpretation of a literary work.

It might also be helpful to know that the theories we will examine are presented in logical sequence rather than in strict chronological order. We will begin with those theories I think you will find most accessible and most clearly related to our everyday world and then move to others in terms of some logical connection among them, so that you can see theories as overlapping, competing, quarrelling visions of the world rather

than as tidy categories. Thus, we will begin with a chapter on psychoanalytic criticism because most of us have been exposed to some psychoanalytic concepts in our daily lives, albeit as clichéd commonplaces, and because psychoanalysis draws on personal experiences to which most of us
can very readily relate. A chapter on Marxist criticism will immediately
follow because Marxism both overlaps and argues with psychoanalysis.
Feminism follows these theories because it both draws on and argues
with psychoanalytic and Marxist concepts. And so on. Although historical categories will not provide our organizing principle, historical relationships among theories (for example, how New Criticism was a reaction against traditional historicism or how deconstruction was a reaction
against structuralism) will be explained because such relationships can
clarify some of the theoretical concepts we're using and some of the ways
in which, as noted earlier, the struggle for intellectual dominance is also a
struggle for economic, social, and political dominance.

Let me close with a personal anecdote that you might find relevant to
your initial encounter with critical theory. When I first read Jacques
Derrida's "Structure, Sign and Play"—possibly the most widely reprinted
introduction to his theory of deconstruction—I was sitting in my '64
Chevy, stuck in a parking lot during a violent thunderstorm. I was just
beginning to learn about critical theory, and my reaction to the essay was
a burst of tears, not because I was moved by the essay or by the sublime
nature of the thunderstorm but because I couldn't understand what I'd
just read. I'd thought, until then, that I was very intelligent: I'd studied
philosophy diligently in college, and I was a great "decoder" of dense, difficult writing. "So why can't I understand this essay?" I wondered. "Am I a
good deal less intelligent than I'd thought?" (Sound familiar?) I finally
learned that my problem was not with the complexity of Derrida's ideas,
though they are complex, but with their unfamiliarity. There seemed to
be nothing in my experience up to that point to enable me to relate his
ideas to anything I already knew. I had no road map. I was lost. I think
this experience is common for students approaching any new theory, not
just deconstruction. We simply don't know how to get there from here.

In a very real sense, then, what I'm offering you in the following
chapters is a road map. And I think the journey metaphor is appropriate
for our endeavor here. For knowledge isn't something we acquire; it's
something we are or something we hope to become. Knowledge is what
constitutes our relationship to ourselves and to our world, for it is the
lens through which we view ourselves and our world. Change the lens
and you change both the view and the viewer. This principle is what

makes knowledge at once so frightening and so liberating, so painful and so utterly, utterly joyful. If this book can help you discover that the joy is worth the pain and that the pain, itself, is honorable—if it can help you value your initial fear and confusion as signs that you've taken your first big step into an unfamiliar territory worthy of the work required to explore it—then it will have accomplished something important.

Notes

1. References to *The Great Gatsby* are cited parenthetically throughout this textbook and refer to the 1995 edition of the novel published by Simon & Schuster (with notes and preface by Matthew J. Bruccoli). Parenthetical references include chapter as well as page numbers to aid those readers using a different edition of the novel.

Works Cited

Fitzgerald, F. Scott. *The Great Gatsby*. 1925. New York: Simon & Schuster, 1995.

CHAPTER 2

Psychoanalytic Criticism

We're starting our study of critical theory with psychoanalytic criticism because, whether we realize it or not, psychoanalytic concepts have become part of our everyday lives, and therefore psychoanalytic thinking should have the advantage of familiarity. If you've ever told an angry friend "Don't take it out on me!" you were accusing that friend of *displacement*, which is the psychoanalytic name for transferring our anger with one person onto another person (usually one who won't fight back or can't hurt us as badly as the person with whom we are really angry). Psychoanalytic concepts such as sibling rivalry, inferiority complexes, and defense mechanisms are in such common use that most of us feel we know what they mean without ever having heard them defined. The disadvantage of such common usage, however, is that most of us have acquired a very simplistic idea of what these concepts mean, and in their clichéd form they seem rather superficial if not altogether meaningless. Couple this unfortunate fact with our fear that psychoanalysis wants to invade our most private being and reveal us to ourselves and to the world as somehow inadequate, even sick, and the result is very often a deep-seated mistrust of "psycho-babble." Indeed, our common use of the word *psycho-babble* illustrates our belief that psychoanalysis is both impossible to understand and meaningless. Thus, in a culture that uses psychoanalytic concepts in its everyday language we frequently see the wholesale rejection of psychoanalysis as a useful way of understanding human behavior.

I hope this chapter will show you that seeing the world psychoanalytically can be simple without being simplistic. If we take the time to un-

derstand some key concepts about human experience offered by psychoanalysis, we can begin to see the ways in which these concepts are operating in our daily lives in profound rather than superficial ways, and we'll
begin to understand human behaviors that until now may have seemed
utterly baffling. And, of course, if psychoanalysis can help us better understand human behavior, then it must certainly be able to help us understand literary texts, which are about human behavior. The concepts we'll
discuss below are based on the psychoanalytic principles established by
Sigmund Freud (1856–1939). We must remember that Freud evolved his
ideas over a long period of time, and many of his ideas changed as he developed them. In addition, much of his thinking was, as he pointed out,
speculative, and he hoped that others would continue to develop and
even correct certain of his ideas over time. So the attempt in this chapter
is to outline those areas of psychoanalytic theory that are particularly
useful to literary criticism and to show how the psychoanalytic view of
human behavior is relevant to our experience of literature.[1]

The Origins of the Unconscious

When we look at the world through a psychoanalytic lens, we see that it is
comprised of individual human beings, each with a psychological history
that begins in childhood experiences in the family and each with patterns
of adolescent and adult behavior that are the direct result of that early
experience. Because the goal of psychoanalysis is to help us resolve our
psychological problems, often called disorders or dysfunctions (and none
of us is completely free of psychological problems), the focus is on patterns of behavior that are destructive in some way. I say *patterns of behavior* because our repetition of destructive behavior reveals the existence of
some significant psychological difficulty that has probably been influencing us for some time without our knowing it. In fact, it is our not knowing about a problem—or, if we do know we have a problem, not realizing
when it is influencing our behavior—that gives it so much control over
us. For this reason, we must begin our discussion with the concept central
to all psychoanalytic thinking: the existence of the unconscious.

Do you remember the song "You Can't Always Get What You Want"
by the Rolling Stones? The idea expressed is "You can't always get what
you want, but you get what you need." This formulation, with the addition of two words, gives us the key to thinking psychoanalytically: "You
can't always get what you *consciously* want, but you get what you *uncon-*

sciously need." The notion that human beings are motivated, even driven, by desires, fears, needs, and conflicts of which they are unaware—that is, unconscious—was one of Sigmund Freud's most radical insights, and it still governs psychoanalysis today.

The *unconscious* is the storehouse of those painful experiences and emotions, those wounds, fears, guilty desires, and unresolved conflicts we do not want to know about because we feel we will be overwhelmed by them. The unconscious comes into being when we are very young through the *repression*, the expunging from consciousness, of these unhappy psychological events. However, repression doesn't eliminate our painful experiences and emotions. Rather, it gives them force by making them the organizers of our current experience: we unconsciously behave in ways that will allow us to "play out," without admitting it to ourselves, our conflicted feelings about the painful experiences and emotions we repress. Thus, for psychoanalysis, the unconscious isn't a passive reservoir of neutral data, though the word is sometimes used this way in other disciplines and in common parlance, but a dynamic entity that engages us at the deepest level of our being.

Until we find a way to know and acknowledge to ourselves the true cause(s) of our repressed wounds, fears, guilty desires, and unresolved conflicts, we hang onto them in disguised, distorted, and self-defeating ways. For example, if I don't realize that I still long for the love I never received from my long-dead, alcoholic father, I am very liable to select an alcoholic, aloof mate so that I can re-enact my relationship with my father and, "this time," make him love me. In fact, even when I do realize that I have this kind of core issue with my father, it is difficult to recognize when I am "acting it out" with another person. Indeed, I probably won't see the profound similarity between my father and my beloved: I'll focus, instead, on superficial differences (my father has dark hair and my beloved is blond). In other words, I will experience my longing for my neglectful father as longing for my current heart-throb. I will feel that I am in love with my current sweetheart, perhaps even desperately in love, and I will believe that what I really want is for my sweetheart to love me back.

I will not necessarily realize that what I really want in wanting this man is something I never received from my father. The evidence will lie in the similarities between his treatment of me and my father's treatment of me and in the fact that, should I succeed in gaining the kind of attention I want from my current "crush," either it will not be enough (he will never be able to convince me that he really loves me; I will think that my insecurity is proof of his indifference), or if he does convince me that he really loves me, I will lose interest in him because the attentive lover does not fulfill my need to re-experience the abandonment I suffered at the hands of my father. The point is that I want something I don't know I want and can't have: the love of my neglectful father. In fact, even if my father were still alive and had the kind of psychological rebirth that permitted him to give me his love, I would still have to heal the psychological wounds he inflicted over the course of my childhood—my feelings of inadequacy and abandonment, for example—before I could benefit from his love.

As you can see in the above example, the *family* is very important in psychoanalytic theory because we are each a product of the role we are given in the family-complex. In one sense, the "birth" of the unconscious lies in the way we perceive our place in the family and how we react to this self-definition: for example, "I'm the failure"; "I'm the perfect child"; "I must always 'come in second' to my brother"; "I'm unlovable"; or "I'm responsible for my parents' problems." The *oedipal* conflict (competition with the parent of the same gender for the attention and affection of the parent of the opposite gender), and all the commonplace ideas of old-style Freudian theory (for example, sibling rivalry, penis envy, castration anxiety) are merely descriptions of the dominant ways in which family conflicts can be lived. They give us merely starting points for understanding differences among individuals. For example, in some families, *sibling rivalry* (competition with siblings for the attention and affection of parents) can occur, in an important sense, between a parent and child. If I feel jealous of my mate's affection for our child, what may be going on is a re-enactment of my unresolved childhood rivalry with a sibling I believed was more loved by my parents than I. That is, seeing my mate's affection for our child reawakens some or all of the hurt I felt when I saw my parents' affection for the sibling I believed they preferred. And so I now find myself competing with my child for the attention of my mate.

It is important to note that oedipal attachments, sibling rivalry, and the like are considered developmental stages. In other words, we all go through these experiences, and they are a natural and healthy part of maturing and establishing our own identities. It is when we fail to outgrow these conflicts that we have trouble. Here's an example common to many women. If I remain in competition with my mother for my father's love (a competition that can go on in my unconscious long after one or both parents are dead), I will probably be most attracted to men who already have girlfriends or wives because their attachment to another woman will allow me to replay my competition with my mother and, "this time," win. Of course, I might not win the man this time, and even if I do, once I've won him I'll lose interest in him. Although I probably don't realize it consciously, his desirability lies in his attachment to someone else. Once he's mine, he's not so exciting anymore. On the other hand, if as a child I felt that I won my father's affection from my mother (which he may have given me as a way of punishing or avoiding my mother), then I may be attracted to men who already have girlfriends or wives (and who don't seem likely to leave them) because I feel I need to be punished for "stealing" Dad from my mother. Of course, another way to punish myself for stealing Dad from my mother (or for wanting to steal him or, if he sexually molested me, for feeling that it was somehow my fault) is to be unable to respond sexually to my mate.

A common way in which men replay unresolved oedipal attachments involves what is often called the "good-girl/bad-girl" attitude toward women. If I remain in competition (usually unconscious) with my father for my mother's love, I am very liable to deal with my guilt by categorizing women as either "like Mom" ("good girls") or "not like Mom" ("bad girls") and then by being able to enjoy sex only with women who are "not like Mom." In other words, because I unconsciously associate sexual desire with desire for my mother, sexual desire makes me feel guilty and dirty, and for this reason I can enjoy it only with "bad girls," who are themselves guilty and dirty and whom I don't associate with Mom. This view often creates a seduce-and-abandon pattern of behavior toward women. When I seduce a "bad girl," I must abandon her (sooner or later) because I cannot allow myself to be permanently attached to someone so unworthy of marriage, that is, unworthy of being classified with my mother. When I seduce a "good girl," two things happen: (1) she becomes a "bad girl" and, like other "bad girls," unworthy of my permanent commitment, and (2) I feel so guilty for "soiling" her (which is like "soiling" Mom) that I must abandon her to avoid my guilt. The point is that, for both women and men, only by recognizing the psychological motivations for our destructive behavior can we hope to begin to change that behavior.

The Defenses

Our unconscious desire not to recognize or change our destructive behavior—because we have formed our identity around it and because we are afraid of what we will find if we examine it too closely—is served by our *defenses*. Defenses are the processes by which the contents of our unconscious are kept in the unconscious. In other words, they are the processes by which we keep the repressed repressed in order to avoid knowing what we feel we can't handle knowing. Defenses include *selective perception* (hearing and seeing only what we feel we can handle), *selective memory* (modifying our memories so that we don't feel overwhelmed by them or forgetting painful events entirely), *denial* (believing that the problem doesn't exist or the unpleasant incident never happened), *avoidance* (staying away from people or situations that are liable to make us anxious by stirring up some unconscious—i.e., repressed—experience or emotion), *displacement* ("taking it out" on someone or something less threatening than the person who caused our fear, hurt, frustration, or anger), and *projection* (ascribing our fear, problem, or guilty desire to someone else, and condemning them for it, in order to deny that we have it ourselves).

Perhaps one of the most complex defenses is *regression*, the temporary return to a former psychological state, which is not just imagined but relived. Regression can involve a return either to a painful or a pleasant experience. It is a defense because it carries our thoughts away from some present difficulty (as when *Death of a Salesman*'s Willy Loman flashes back to his past in order to avoid the unpleasant realities of his present life). However, it differs from other defenses in that it carries with it the opportunity for *active reversal*, the acknowledgement and working through of repressed experiences and emotions, because we can alter the effects of a wound only when we re-live the wounding experience. This is why regression is such a useful therapeutic tool.

Many psychological experiences can function as defenses, even when not formally defined as such. For example, *fear of intimacy*—fear of emotional involvement with another human being—is often an effective defense against learning about our own psychological wounds because it keeps us at an emotional distance in relationships most likely to bring those wounds to the surface: relationships with lovers, spouses, offspring, and best friends. By not permitting ourselves to get too close to significant others, we "protect" ourselves from the painful past experiences that intimate relationships inevitably dredge up. Having more than one romantic or sexual partner at a time, breaking off romances when they start to evolve past the infatuation stage, and keeping oneself too busy to spend much time with family and friends are just a few of the many ways we can maintain an emotional distance from loved ones without admitting to ourselves what we are doing.

Of course, sometimes our defenses momentarily break down, and this is when we experience *anxiety*. Anxiety can reveal our *core issues* (issues that define our being in fundamental ways and that we carry through life, such as fear of intimacy, fear of abandonment, low self-esteem, fear of betrayal, an insecure or unstable sense of self, confusion about one's sexuality, and the like) because we are anxious in situations in which those issues are in play. For example, I become anxious when one of my friends goes to the movies with another friend because it makes me re-live the abandonment I felt from a neglectful parent whether or not I see the connection between the two events. That is, I feel abandoned now because I was wounded by feeling abandoned as a child, and I am anxious because I don't want to admit to myself that, in some important way, I was abandoned by my parent. So I become hurt and angry with my friend without consciously knowing why. My unconscious knowledge of the reason why is what makes me anxious. In this way, anxiety always involves the *return of the repressed*: I am anxious because something I repressed—some painful or frightening or guilty experience—is resurfacing, and I want to keep it repressed. Psychoanalysis, as a form of therapy, is the controlled working in and with anxiety. Its goal (unlike that of ego psychology, which is a popular form of therapy today) isn't to strengthen our defenses or restore us to social adaptation but to break down our defenses in order to effect a basic change in the structure of our personality and the way we act.

Under ordinary circumstances, however, our defenses keep us unaware of our unconscious experience, and our anxiety, even if it is somewhat prolonged or recurrent, doesn't succeed in breaking through our repression. How then, without the aid of psychotherapy, can we learn about the operations of our own unconscious? As I noted earlier, patterns in our behavior, if we can recognize them, provide clues, especially in the area of interpersonal relations and, within that domain, especially in our romantic or sexual relationships, because it is here that our initial unresolved conflicts within the family are re-enacted. In addition, we have access to our unconscious, if we know how to use it, through our dreams and through any creative activities we engage in because both our dreams and our creativity, independent of our conscious will or desire, draw directly on the unconscious.

Dreams and Dream Symbols

When we sleep, it is believed that our defenses do not operate in the same manner they do when we are awake. During sleep, the unconscious is free to express itself, and it does so in our dreams. However, even in our dreams there is some censorship, some protection against frightening insights into our repressed experiences and emotions, and that protection takes the form of dream distortion. The "message" our unconscious expresses in our dreams, which is the dream's underlying meaning, or *latent content*, is altered, so that we don't readily recognize it, through processes called *displacement* and *condensation*. Dream displacement occurs whenever we use a "safe" person, event, or object as a "stand-in" to represent a more threatening person, event, or object. For example, I may dream that an elementary-school teacher is sexually molesting me in order to express (and at the same time avoid) my unconscious knowledge that one of my parents sexually molested me. *Condensation* occurs during a dream whenever we use a single dream image or event to represent more than one unconscious wound or conflict. For example, my dream that I'm battling a ferocious bear might represent psychological "battles" or conflicts both at home and at work. Or, to expand upon the above example, my dream that I am being sexually molested by an elementary-school teacher might represent my unconscious feeling that my self-esteem is under attack by any number of family members, friends, and colleagues. (A single dream event may thus be a product of both displacement and condensation.)

Because displacement and condensation occur while we dream, these processes are referred to collectively as *primary revision*. What we actually dream, once primary revision has disguised the unconscious message, or the dream's latent content, is the dream's *manifest content*. The dream images described above—images of an elementary-school teacher molesting me and of myself battling a ferocious bear—are examples of manifest content. What these images actually mean is the dreams' latent content, and that is a matter of interpretation. Is the elementary-school teacher a stand-in for one of my parents, or are the images of sexual molestation a stand-in for verbal attacks on my self-esteem? Does the bear represent a psychological conflict, and if so, what is that conflict? In interpreting our dreams, then, our goal is to recall the manifest content and try to uncover the latent content. However, we must remember that, at this conscious stage as well, we're very liable to unconsciously change the dream in order to further protect ourselves from knowing what is too painful to know. For example, we might forget certain parts of the dream or remember those parts somewhat differently from how they actually occurred. This process, which takes place when we are awake, is called *secondary revision*.

It may be helpful to think of the dream's manifest content as a kind of dream symbolism that can be interpreted much the way we interpret symbols of any kind, if we keep in mind that there is no one-to-one correspondence between a given symbol and its meaning. That is, while there are some images that tend to have the same symbolic meaning from dreamer to dreamer, at least if those dreamers are members of the same culture, there are also important individual differences in the ways we represent our unconscious experience in our dreams. So to increase our chances of interpreting our dreams accurately, we must learn, over time, how we tend to represent certain ideas, feelings, and people in our dreams, and we must know the context in which a particular dream image occurred: what happened in the dream before, during, and after a particular dream image appeared?

Certain general principles of dream interpretation tend to apply in most cases, and they are as follows. Because dreamers create all the "characters" in their dreams, there is a real sense in which each person we dream about is really a part of our own psychological experience that we project, during the dream, onto a stand-in. If I dream that my sister gives birth to a stillborn child, for example, I might be dreaming either that *I* have given birth to a stillborn child (a failed relationship? a failed career? a failed artistic endeavor?) or that I *am* a stillborn child (am I feeling abandoned? helpless? depressed?). As this example makes evident, dreams about children almost always reveal something about our feelings toward ourselves, toward the child that is still within us and that is probably still wounded in some way.

Given that our sexuality is such an important reflection of our psychological being, our dreams about our gender roles or about our attitudes toward ourselves and others as sexual beings are also revealing. In order to interpret these dreams, we need to be aware of the male and female imagery that can occur in them. Male imagery, or *phallic symbols*, can include towers, rockets, guns, arrows, swords, and the like. In short, if it stands upright or goes off, it might be functioning as a phallic symbol. For example, if I dream that I am holding my friend at gun point, I might be expressing unconscious sexual aggression toward that friend or toward someone else for whom that friend is a safe stand-in (such as my friend's mate or my own). In addition, my sexual aggression might be interpreted in a number of ways: Is the emphasis on the sexual, on the aggression, or on both? Do I desire my friend's mate, or am I jealous of my friend's mate? Do I want to become more assertive in my sexual relationship with my mate, or do I want to hurt my mate's sexual self-image as my mate has hurt mine? To decide which interpretation is correct requires more data in the form of other similar dreams, patterns in my waking behavior, and an honest analysis of my feelings about the dream and about the people involved. Analogously, if I dream that I am being held at gun point, I might be expressing an unconscious feeling that my sexuality, or my identity in general, is being exploited or endangered.

Female imagery can include caves, rooms, walled-in gardens (like the ones we see in paintings representing the Virgin Mary), cups, or enclosures and containers of any kind. If the image can be a stand-in for the womb, then it might be functioning as female imagery. Thus, if I dream I am trapped or lost in a small, dark room, I might be expressing an unconscious fear of my mother's control over me or an unconscious fear that I have never completely matured as a human being. Perhaps I'm expressing both, for these two problems are certainly related. Female imagery can also include milk, fruit, and other kinds of food as well as the containers in which food is delivered, such as bottles or cups (yes, there is an overlap here with womb imagery)—in other words, anything that can be a stand-in for the breast, which is itself a stand-in for emotional nurturing. So if I dream that I am trying to feed a litter of hungry kittens from a small and rapidly diminishing bottle of milk (a dream that either gender can have), I might be expressing an unconscious feeling that too much is being asked of me by my children or by my spouse or by my employer— or by all of them—or that I am putting too much pressure on myself to take care of others. Analogously, if I dream I am hungry or looking for food, I might be expressing an unconscious need for emotional nurturing.

To move to other kinds of symbols, if I dream about water—which is fluid, changeable, sometimes soothing, sometimes dangerous, and often deeper than it looks—chances are good that I'm dreaming about my sexuality or the realm of the emotions or the realm of the unconscious. So a dream that I'm about to be overwhelmed by a tidal wave probably indicates some fear of being overwhelmed by a repressed emotion that I fear is about to erupt. Of course, water is also related to our experience in the womb, so dreams that involve water, especially immersion in water, might also be about our relationship to our mother. Dreams about buildings may refer to my relationship with myself, with the attic or the basement as the stand-in for the unconscious. Or dreams about buildings may refer to my relationship with some institution that the building represents for me, for example, the church, the school, the company for which I work, or the law (which, because it represents social rules and definitions, might be a stand-in for my superego). Although we might often dream about fears and wounds that we know we have—that are clearly part of our conscious experience—our dreams about these concerns probably indicate that we need to work further on them, that they bite into us in ways we aren't ready to admit. Of course, recurring dreams or recurring dream images are the most reliable indicators of our unconscious concerns.

Regardless of how frightening or disturbing our dreams are, they are relatively safe outlets for unconscious wounds, fears, guilty desires, and unresolved conflicts because, as we have seen, they come to us in disguised form, and we will interpret them only to whatever extent we are ready to do so. In addition, if a dream becomes too threatening, we will wake up, as we most often do during nightmares. However, if my nightmares begin to occur while I'm awake—that is, if the breakdown of my defenses is more than temporary, if my anxiety cannot be abated, if the truth hidden by repression comes out before my conscious self in a manner I can neither disguise nor handle—then I am in *crisis*, or *trauma*.

The Meaning of Death

Crisis brings into the spotlight wounds, fears, guilty desires, or unresolved conflicts that I have failed to deal with and demands action. I am flooded by the past because I can now see what was really going on. This is how I can know myself through crisis. The word *trauma* is also used, of course, to refer to a painful experience that scars us psychologically. Thus, I might experience the childhood trauma of losing a sibling to illness, accidental death, or suicide and, in later life, experience the trauma, or crisis, of being flooded by all the guilt, denial, and conflict I've repressed concerning that death. And I might also see, for example, the ways in which my parents unconsciously encouraged my guilt in order to relieve their own.

In fact, our relationship to death, whether or not we are traumatized by it in childhood, is a principal organizer of our psychological experience. Before we examine how our relationship to death operates in this way, it is important to note that death is the subject which, it seems to me, has given psychoanalytic theorists the most trouble probably because of its importance in their own, as well as everyone else's, psychological experience. There has been some tendency to treat death as an abstraction—that is, to theorize about it in ways that don't allow us to feel its force too intimately—presumably because its force is too frightening. So even when, or especially when, theorists have addressed the subject of death directly, they sometimes have done so in ways that tend to keep it at an emotional distance from themselves and, therefore, from us. I think this is the reason—to cite just one example—behind Freud's theory that death is a biological drive, which he called the *death drive*, or *thanatos*.

In suggesting that human beings have a death drive, Freud's attempt was to account for the alarming degree of self-destructive behavior he saw both in individuals, who seemed bent on destroying themselves psychologically if not physically, and in whole nations, whose constant wars and internal conflicts could be viewed as little other than a form of mass suicide. He concluded that there must be something in our biological make-up as a species to explain this *death work*, this psychological and physical self-destruction. Of course, when we conceptualize our death work as a drive, as something natural and unavoidable, we are off the hook of having to probe too deeply into its workings or to try to change it; after all, nothing we do can alter a biological drive. This is why I call the concept of the death drive an abstraction, an idea that operates only on the conceptual level, with no connection to the concrete world of experience. Although the concept of the death drive rests on biology, which is concrete reality, it takes our thoughts and our feelings out of the everyday world of action and responsibility, just as abstractions do. And this is exactly why I think some theorists have found abstract explanations of death attractive. Such explanations take us out of the everyday world in which our acts of psychological and physical self-destruction occur.

A more useful, and I think more accurate, way of understanding our relationship to death is to examine it in relation to the rest of our psychological experience, of which it is an integral part. If we do this, we will see that death, in particular our fear of death, is intimately connected to a number of other psychological realities. And we will see that individuals respond to death in various ways because of differences in their psychological make-up. In other words, while the processes I am about to describe probably occur in all of us, they will occur to different degrees and with different results in each individual.

First and foremost, for many of us, the thought of our own death keys into our fear of abandonment, our fear of being alone. Death is the ultimate abandonment: no matter how close we are to our loved ones, no matter how important we are in our communities, when we die we die alone. Even if we die in a plane crash with two hundred other people, we each die our own private death. Thus, one of the greatest comforts religious belief can offer us is to assure us that we will not die alone and that after we die we will not be alone: God the Father will be there for us and with us; our Heavenly Father will not abandon his children even when everyone else we know has done so.

Fear of abandonment also plays a role when we fear the death of others. When children lose a parent, when adults lose a spouse, the overwhelming feeling of loss is often a feeling of abandonment. How could you leave me? Don't you love me? What did I do wrong? Sometimes the bereaved feel abandoned even by God. In this context, whether we realize it or not, the death of a loved one pushes our guilt buttons: somehow I must have been inadequate; I must have done something wrong or I wouldn't be punished in this way. In fact, fear of such a loss, of such intense psychological pain, is probably the biggest reason why some of us are afraid to get too close to another person, afraid to love too deeply. If I can hold something back, not give my whole self over to the loved one, then I will be better able to bear the loss when the beloved dies.

Fear of death is thus often responsible—along with other reasons, as we saw earlier—for fear of intimacy. This is one of the ways we can see how fear of death often results in fear of life. That is, our fear of death, of losing our life, can result in our fear of being intimately attached to life. "When you ain't got nothin', you got nothin' to lose," as so many blues and folk songs have pointed out. This fear of life can also be played out as a fear of risk. The ultimate loss, of which I am utterly terrified, is death. Therefore, I can't take any risk that might result in death. But life itself ultimately and inevitably results in death. Therefore I can't risk living my life. I must somehow remove myself from it by doing as little as possible and by feeling as little as possible: I will try to be emotionally dead to avoid being hurt by death. Taken to its logical extreme, this relationship to death will result in suicide. My intense fear of losing my life makes living so painful and frightening that my only escape is death.

If we complicate matters by realizing that our fear of death is not merely fear of biological death but translates for most of us into fear of loss in general—loss of my mate's attention, loss of my children's love, loss of my health, loss of my job, loss of my looks, loss of my money—then we can see how death, emotional death if not biological death, is so attractive, at least on the unconscious level: if I don't feel anything, then I can't be hurt. And if we realize that our first experience of death is not biological at all, but the psychological "death" most of us suffered the first time we felt abandoned by a parent, then we can see the ways in which our early experiences of abandonment created our fear of death. This desire not to feel, this desire to insulate ourselves from life in order to insulate ourselves from pain, is probably the most common form of death work.

Is it any wonder then, given the enormous role that death plays in our lives, that we should be fascinated with it? In fact, I think it's reasonable to conclude that the greater our fear, the greater our fascination. Put another way, the greater the role that death work plays in our psychological being, the greater our attraction, despite the horror that accompanies it, to death in all its forms: we can't see too many violent movies or docudramas about natural disasters; we can't keep our eyes off the roadside car wreck; we can't see too many news reports about child abuse, rape, and AIDS; we can't see too many made-for-television movies about people who kill their spouses or their lovers' spouses, or too many talk shows on which members of dysfunctional relationships display their dysfunctions apparently with no more self-awareness than children displaying their favorite toys. Our fascination with media representations of death and death work is another example of how we project our fears and problems onto people and events outside ourselves. This fascination thus operates as a defense: if I think about the child abuser on the other side of town (or from a different social class or ethnic background from mine) I divert my attention from the ways in which I've been abused or from my abuse of others.

The Meaning of Sexuality

Another area of psychological experience that has tended to elicit abstract explanations—and as we saw above, this points to its frightening power in our lives—is human *sexuality*. For some psychoanalytic theorists, especially in the past, sexuality was a matter of a biological pressure that is discharged in the act of sexual intercourse. Freud called that drive *eros* and placed it in opposition to thanatos, the death drive. However, Freud didn't stop there. For one thing, he realized that our sexuality is part and parcel of our identity and thus relates to our capacity to feel pleasure in ways that are not generally considered sexual. This is why he believed that even infants are sexual beings who pass through stages—oral, anal, and genital—in which pleasure is focused in different parts of the body. (You can imagine the furor, and the misunderstanding, *that* caused in Victorian society!) Theorists have continued to build upon Freud's insights, and psychoanalysis today sees a close connection between our sexuality and our identity because the origin of our sexual being is in the nature of the affirmation or disruption of our sense of self that occurs in child-hood. Therefore, our sexuality is one of the clearest and most consistent barometers of our psychological state in general. For psychoanalysis, our sexuality is an inescapable human reality to which we must live a rela-tionship. Our sexuality is not a matter of biological drive-discharge mechanisms but a matter of meanings. In analyzing sexual behavior, then, the appropriate psychoanalytic question is, "What conscious and unconscious meanings and purposes do I express or enact in my sexual-ity?" Do I use sex to "purchase" something I want from my mate? Do I withhold sex to punish my mate? Do I avoid sexual encounters alto-gether? Do I seek frequent sexual encounters with different people? It is interesting to note that these last two questions both suggest a fear of inti-macy—if I get too close to someone I will lose myself or be emotionally harmed—because varying our sexual partners can protect us from get-ting close to any one person as effectively as avoiding sexual encounters completely.

Of course, sexual behavior is also a product of our culture because our culture sets down the rules of proper sexual conduct and the defini-tions of normal and abnormal sexual behavior. (For psychoanalysis, there is no meaningful difference between normal and abnormal, and the issue isn't one of moral versus immoral behavior; there are merely psychologi-cal differences among individuals, and the issue is one of non-destructive versus destructive behavior.) Society's rules and definitions concerning sexuality form a large part of our *superego*, or the social values and taboos that we internalize (consciously or unconsciously) and experience as our sense of right and wrong. Whereas the word *conscience*, as it is usually used, generally implies something good—as Jiminy Cricket says, "Let your conscience be your guide"—the word *superego* often implies feeling guilty when we shouldn't, feeling guilty only because we are socially pro-grammed (usually through the family) to feel so, as when we feel guilty for taking a lower-paying job even when we know that it is a more satisfy-ing or socially important one, or when we feel guilty, as many of us still do, for having sexual relations with our beloved prior to marriage.

The superego is in direct opposition to the *id*, the psychological res-ervoir of our instincts and our *libido*, or sexual energy. The id is devoted solely to the gratification of prohibited desires of all kinds—desire for power, for sex, for amusement, for food—without an eye to conse-quences. In other words, the id consists largely of those desires regulated or forbidden by social convention. Thus, the superego—or cultural ta-boos—determines which desires the id will contain. The *ego*, or the conscious self that experiences the external world through the senses, plays referee between id and superego, and all three are defined by their relationship: none acts independently of the others; a change in one always involves changes in the other two. In this way, the ego is, to a large degree, the product of conflicts between what society says we can't have and what we (therefore) want. For this reason, the relationship among ego, id, and superego tells us as much about our culture as it does about ourselves.

Indeed, it is the cultural context that has helped us come to a more meaningful understanding of some of Freud's early concepts that seem to contradict our own sense of how the world works. For example, many women, whether they consider themselves feminists or not, have a difficult time believing that little girls, upon realizing that little boys have penises, suffer from *penis envy*, or the desire to have a penis, or that little boys, upon realizing that little girls don't have penises, suffer from *castration anxiety*, or the fear that they will lose their penises. The explanation for these two phenomena becomes clear, however, when we realize the cultural context within which Freud observed them: Victorian society's rigid definition of gender roles, used to oppress females of all ages and to elevate males to positions of dominance in all spheres of human activity. Is it any wonder that a little girl will want (at least unconsciously) to be a little boy when she realizes that little boys have rights and privileges she isn't supposed to even desire? In other words, when you see "penis envy" read "power envy." It's power and all that seems to go with it—self-esteem, fun, freedom, safety from physical violation by the opposite gender—that little girls envy. And what little boy, upon realizing his social superiority to, and power over, little girls, isn't going to have some anxiety about losing it? "You're a girl, you sissy!" has the power to wound little boys (and big boys!) because it threatens them with just such a loss of power. Castration anxiety is thus best understood as fear of demotion to the powerless position occupied by females.

Psychoanalysis and Literature

Of course, there are many more psychoanalytic concepts than the ones discussed above. And as in every field, there is a good deal of disagreement among psychoanalytic theorists concerning, for example, the way in which our personalities are formed and the best way of treating dysfunctional behavior. Among psychoanalytic literary critics, there is much disagreement concerning how psychoanalytic concepts can best be applied to our study of literature. What role should an author's literary output play in our psychoanalysis of his or her life? To what extent is it legitimate to psychoanalyze literary characters as if they were real people? When doing so, which psychoanalytic theorists offer us the best insights? What role do readers play in "creating" the text they're reading by projecting their own desires and conflicts onto the work? As you'll see when you read Chapter Six on reader-response criticism, psychoanalysis and reader-response theory overlap in many ways concerning their attention to the psychological experience of the reader. We'll also see in Chapter Three and Chapter Four some overlap of psychoanalysis with Marxism and feminism as well as some ways in which Marxism and feminism reject the psychoanalytic perspective. Our purpose at this point, however, is simply to cover the main ideas, the basic principles of psychoanalysis to which most other psychoanalytic concepts are in some way related in order to facilitate your reading of psychoanalytic theorists and literary critics with some understanding of the issues they raise.

Of course, you won't find every psychoanalytic concept we've discussed represented in every literary work you read. Our job, when we read psychoanalytically, is to see which concepts are operating in the text in such a way as to enrich our understanding of the work and, if we plan to write a paper about it, to yield a meaningful, coherent psychoanalytic interpretation. We might focus mainly on the work's representation of oedipal dynamics or of family dynamics in general; on what the work can tell us about human beings' psychological relationship to death or to sexuality; on the way the narrator's unconscious problems keep asserting themselves over the course of the story; or on any other psychoanalytic concepts that seem to produce a useful understanding of the text.

Some critics have objected to the use of psychoanalysis to understand the behavior of literary characters because literary characters are not real people and, therefore, do not have psyches that can be analyzed. However, psychoanalyzing the behavior of literary characters is probably the best way to learn how to use the theory. Furthermore, this practice has been defended by many psychoanalytic critics on two important grounds: (1) when we psychoanalyze literary characters, we are not suggesting that they are real people but that they represent the psychological experience of human beings in general; and (2) it is just as legitimate to psychoanalyze the behavior represented by literary characters as it is to analyze their behavior from a feminist, Marxist, or African American critical perspective, or from the perspective of any critical theory that analyzes literary representations as illustrations of real-life issues.

Let's look at a few specific examples to see the kinds of insights produced by psychoanalyzing the behavior represented by literary characters.
A psychoanalytic reading of Arthur Miller's *Death of a Salesman* (1949)
might examine the ways in which Willy Loman's flashbacks to the past are
really regressive episodes brought on by his present psychological trauma:
his own and his son's lack of success in the business world, success Willy
needed in order to assuage the massive insecurity he's suffered since his
abandonment in childhood by his father and older brother. The play is
thus structured by the return of the repressed, for Willy has spent his life
repressing, through denial and avoidance, his psychological insecurity
and the social inadequacy and business failure that have resulted. From a
psychoanalytic perspective, then, *Death of a Salesman* might be read as an
exploration of the psychological dynamics of the family: an exploration
of the ways in which unresolved conflicts about our role within the family
are "played out" in the workplace and "passed down" to our children.

Similarly, a psychoanalytic reading of Toni Morrison's *The Bluest Eye*
(1970) might analyze the ways in which the novel reveals the debilitating
psychological effects of racism, especially when it is internalized by its
victims, which we see in the belief of many of the black characters that
their race has the negative qualities ascribed to it by white America. These
psychological effects are evident, for example, in the Breedloves' conviction that they are ugly simply because they have African features; in Mrs.
Breedlove's devotion to the white family for whom she works, while she
neglects her own family; in the self-hatred of the young black boys who
mercilessly pick on Pecola for having black skin; in the assumption by
black characters as well as white that Maureen Peal, a light-skinned African American girl, is superior in every way to her darker-skinned classmates; and in Geraldine's inability to relax and enjoy her life or let herself
love her husband and son because she fears that the slightest loss of control (whether it be the control of her emotions or of her hair's natural
curl) will make her a "nigger," as she calls any black person who does not
conform to her standard of dress and behavior. As these examples illustrate, the novel shows how internalized racism results in self-contempt on
the part of the black characters and in a projection of that self-hatred
onto other members of their race. We see particularly damaging forms of
this projection in much of the black characters' treatment of Pecola,
whose self-negating desire for blue eyes is the most striking illustration of
the psychological destructiveness of racism. Or we might use psychoanalysis to understand the ways in which the Breedloves illustrate the dynamics of the dysfunctional family, the roots of which can be seen in

Pauline and Cholly's youthful experiences of isolation, abandonment, and betrayal.

Finally, a psychoanalytic reading of Mary Shelley's *Frankenstein* (1818) might reveal the ways in which Victor's creation of a monster responsible for the deaths of his family and friends serves his unconscious need to punish his father and mother (for whom Elizabeth is an obvious surrogate) and play out the intense, unresolved sibling rivalries created by their adoption of Elizabeth, the "perfect" child, when Victor was five years old. The total absence of any normal childhood jealousy on Victor's part, coupled with his frequent protestations of love for the newcomer who dethroned him as the sole object of parental attention and affection, suggest the repression of feelings of abandonment that, because they are kept in the unconscious, are never resolved. We see numerous signs of these unresolved conflicts in Victor's adult life, for example, in his failure to mention subsequent siblings during the narrative of his childhood with Elizabeth (we learn of their existence through Elizabeth's letter to him at the university); in his extremely prolonged absence from his beloved family, including Elizabeth, to whom he is betrothed; in the dream sequence that reveals his psychological merger of Elizabeth and his dead mother and foreshadows the former's death; in his fits of feverish disorientation, which read like dream sequences and include frequent expressions of fear that he is losing his mind or protestations that he is perfectly sane; and in the uncanny way he seems to always make exactly the right move to facilitate the monster's next murder. Furthermore, we might cautiously speculate on the relationship between the representation of psychological abandonment in the novel and the experiences of abandonment Mary Shelley apparently suffered in her own life: her mother died shortly after Mary was born; her father found single parenthood more than he could handle; and the woman her father subsequently wed neglected Mary in favor of her own daughter by a previous marriage.

This might be a good place to pause and answer a frequently asked question concerning psychoanalytic readings of literary works: If we find psychoanalytic concepts operating in a literary text, does it mean that the author has deliberately put them there, and how can an author put them there if he or she lived before Freud or never heard of him? The answer is simple: Freud didn't invent psychoanalytic principles; he discovered them operating in human beings. In other words, Freud named and explained principles of human behavior that were present long before he found them and that would be present even if he didn't describe them. So any literary text that accurately describes human behavior or that is the product of an author's unconscious (which we presume all creative works are, to some extent) will include psychoanalytic principles whether or not the author had any awareness of those principles when writing the work. For psychoanalysis, literature, indeed all art forms, are largely products of unconscious forces at work in the author, in the reader, or, for some contemporary psychoanalytic critics, in our society as a whole.

Our use of psychoanalytic concepts is not limited to one literary genre or to one artistic medium; we can use psychoanalytic criticism to read works of fiction, poetry, drama, folklore, and nonfiction, and we can use it to interpret paintings, sculptures, architecture, film and music. Any human production that involves images, that seems to have narrative content (the way many paintings seem to tell a story), or that relates to the psychology of those who produce or use it (which means just about everything!) can be interpreted using psychoanalytic tools.

Some Questions Psychoanalytic Critics Ask about Literary Texts

The following questions are offered to summarize psychoanalytic approaches to literature. Whatever approach you use, it is customary to note that the psychoanalytic dimension of the text you examine helps drive the narrative (is responsible for a good deal of the plot).

1. How do the operations of repression structure or inform the work? That is, what unconscious motives are operating in the main character(s); what core issues are thereby illustrated; and how do these core issues structure or inform the piece? (Remember, the unconscious consists of repressed wounds, fears, unresolved conflicts, and guilty desires.)

2. Are there any oedipal dynamics—or any other family dynamics—at work here? That is, is it possible to relate a character's patterns of adult behavior to early experiences in the family as represented in the story? How do these patterns of behavior and family dynamics operate and what do they reveal?

3. How can characters' behavior, narrative events, and/or images be explained in terms of psychoanalytic concepts of any kind (for example, regression, crisis, projection, fear of or fascination with death, sexuality—which includes love and romance as well as

sexual behaviors—as a primary indicator of psychological identity or the operations of ego-id-superego)?

4. In what ways can we view a literary work as analogous to a dream? That is, how might recurrent or striking dream symbols reveal the ways in which the narrator or speaker is projecting his or her unconscious desires, fears, wounds, or unresolved conflicts onto other characters, onto the setting, or onto the events portrayed? Symbols relevant to death, sexuality, and the unconscious are especially helpful.

5. What does this work suggest about the psychological being of its author? Although this question is no longer the primary question asked by psychoanalytic critics, some critics still address it, especially those who write psychological biographies (*psychobiographies*). In these cases, the literary text is interpreted much as if it were the author's dream. Psychoanalyzing an author in this manner is a difficult undertaking, and our analysis must be carefully derived by examining the author's entire corpus as well as letters, diaries, and any other biographical material available. Certainly, a single literary work can provide but a very incomplete picture.

6. What might a given interpretation of a literary work suggest about the psychological motives of the reader? Or what might a critical trend suggest about the psychological motives of a group of readers (for example, the tendency of literary critics to see Willy Loman as a devoted family man and ignore or underplay his contribution to the family dysfunction)?

Depending upon the literary work in question, we might ask one or any combination of these questions. Or we might come up with a useful question not listed here. These are just some starting points to get us thinking about literary works in productive psychoanalytic ways. It is important to keep in mind that not all psychoanalytic critics will interpret the same work in the same way, even if they focus on the same psychoanalytic concepts. As in every field, even expert practitioners disagree. Our goal is to use psychoanalysis to help enrich our reading of literary works, to help us see some important ideas they illustrate that we might not have seen so clearly or so deeply without psychoanalysis.

The following psychoanalytic reading of F. Scott Fitzgerald's *The Great Gatsby* is offered as an example of what a psychoanalytic interpretation of that novel might yield. I will argue that fear of intimacy forms a pattern of psychological behavior that is common to all of the novel's main characters and responsible for a good deal of the narrative progression. Through a psychoanalytic lens, then, *The Great Gatsby* becomes a psychological drama of dysfunctional love.

"What's Love Got to Do with It?": A Psychoanalytic Reading of *The Great Gatsby*

One area of human behavior explored in F. Scott Fitzgerald's *The Great Gatsby* (1925) that has important implications for psychoanalytic criticism is found in the romantic relationships portrayed in the novel. Indeed, even for readers not viewing the novel through a psychoanalytic lens, one of the most memorable qualities of the book is the force and endurance of Gatsby's love for Daisy, the emotional magnetism of which, for many fans, renders *The Great Gatsby* one of the great American love stories. For a psychoanalytic reading, however, the interest created by the romance between Gatsby and Daisy lies not in its apparent uniqueness but in the ways in which it mirrors all of the less appealing romantic relationships portrayed in the novel—those between Tom and Daisy, Tom and Myrtle, Myrtle and George, and Nick and Jordan—and thereby reveals a pattern of psychological behavior responsible for a good deal of the narrative progression. As we shall see, this pattern is grounded in the characters' fear of intimacy, the unconscious conviction that emotional ties to another human being will result in one's being emotionally devastated. This psychological problem is so pervasive in the novel that *The Great Gatsby*'s famous love story becomes, through a psychoanalytic lens, a drama of dysfunctional love. For the sake of clarity, let's begin by examining the relationship most obviously based on fear of intimacy: the marriage of Tom and Daisy Buchanan.

Perhaps the clearest indication of fear of intimacy in the novel lies in Tom Buchanan's chronic extramarital affairs, of which Jordan became aware three months after the couple's wedding. Jordan tells Nick,

> I saw them [Tom and Daisy] in Santa Barbara when they came back [from their honeymoon]. . . . A week after I left . . . Tom ran into a wagon on the Ventura road one night and ripped a front wheel off his car. The girl who was with him got into the papers too because her arm was broken—she was one of the chambermaids in the Santa Barbara Hotel. (81–82; ch. 4)

When we meet Tom, he's engaged in his latest affair, this time with Myrtle Wilson. Dividing his interest, time, and energy between two women protects him from real intimacy with either. Indeed, Tom's relationships with women, including his wife, reveal his desire for ego gratification rather than for emotional intimacy. For Tom, Daisy represents social superiority: she's not the kind of woman who can be acquired by a "Mr. Nobody from Nowhere" (137; ch. 7) like Jay Gatsby. Tom's possession of Myrtle Wilson—whom Nick describes as a "sensu[ous]," "smouldering" woman with "an immediately perceptible vitality" (29–30; ch. 2)—reinforces Tom's sense of his own masculine power, which is why he brings her to fashionable restaurants where they are seen by his male acquaintances and why he introduces her to Nick so soon after their reunion at his East Egg home. In fact, Tom's interest in other women is so routine that Daisy has come to expect it. When Tom tells her he wants to eat supper with a group of strangers at Gatsby's party, rather than with her, because he finds one of the men amusing, she immediately realizes that her husband is pursuing another woman: she offers him her "little gold pencil" in case he wants to "take down any addresses," and "[s]he looked around after a moment and told [Nick] that the girl was 'common but pretty'" (112; ch. 6).

Daisy's fear of intimacy, though as intense as Tom's, is not quite as immediately apparent. Indeed, her marital fidelity, until her affair with Gatsby, and her distress over Tom's involvement with Myrtle might suggest to some readers that Daisy desires emotional intimacy with her husband. Jordan's description of Daisy after her honeymoon reinforces this interpretation:

> I'd never seen a girl so mad about her husband. If he left the room for
> a minute she'd look around uneasily and say "Where's Tom gone?"
> and wear the most abstracted expression until she saw him coming
> in the door. She used to sit on the sand with his head in her lap by the
> hour rubbing her fingers over his eyes and looking at him with un-
> fathomable delight. (81–82; ch. 4)

However, the history of Tom and Daisy's relationship suggests psychological motives that point to a different interpretation of Daisy's "delight" in her husband.

It is obvious that Daisy didn't love Tom when she married him: she tried to call off the wedding the evening before when she'd received an overseas letter from Gatsby. In fact, her behavior upon receiving his letter suggests that she married Tom to keep herself from loving Gatsby, to whom she had gotten too attached for her own comfort: she got drunk

for the first time in her life, and "she cried and cried. . . . [W]e . . . got her
into a cold bath. She wouldn't let go of [Gatsby's] letter. . . . [A]nd [she]
only let [Jordan] leave it in the soap dish when she saw that it was coming
to pieces like snow" (81; ch. 4). Why else would she marry Tom, when she
obviously preferred Gatsby, who she believed was "from much the same
strata as herself . . . fully able to take care of her" (156; ch. 8)? Yet just
three months after the wedding she seemed obsessively fond of her new
husband. What happened in this short time to change Daisy's attitude so
dramatically? Given Tom's compulsive pursuit of women, it is probable
that by the time he and Daisy arrived in Santa Barbara, Daisy already sus-
pected him of infidelity. This would explain why she seemed so distracted
whenever Tom was out of sight. She had good reason to fear that, if he
wasn't with her, he might be pursuing another woman, as she believes he
was doing, for example, when she "woke up out of the ether with a totally
abandoned feeling," after giving birth to Pammy, "and Tom was God
knows where" (21; ch. 1). Rather than hate him for such mistreatment,
however, Daisy fell head-over-heels in love with him. Although such a response may not seem to make sense, it can be explained psychologically.

In psychoanalytic terms, a woman who falls in love with a man suffering from severe fear of intimacy probably fears intimacy herself. If she
fears intimacy, nothing can make her feel safer than a man who has no
desire for it. Upon learning that Tom's interest did not focus exclusively
on her, such a woman would have become very capable of loving him intensely because he posed no threat to her protective shell: he wouldn't
have wanted to break through it even if he could have. And this is just
what we see in Daisy's changed attitude toward Tom, though she certainly
wouldn't use this language to describe her feelings, and it is very unlikely
that she was even aware of her psychological motives.

As we learned earlier in this chapter, fear of intimacy with others is
usually a product of fear of intimacy with oneself. Because close interpersonal relationships dredge up the psychological residue of earlier family
conflicts and bring into play aspects of our identity we don't want to deal
with or even know about, the best way to avoid painful psychological self-
awareness is to avoid close interpersonal relationships, especially romantic
relationships. Why not simply avoid romantic relationships altogether? Although this practice may be an effective form of avoidance for some people
who fear intimacy, the psychological wounds responsible for that fear usually demand a stage upon which to re-enact, in disguised form, the original
wounding experience, and romantic relationships provide an excellent
stage. For example, if I was hurt by a parent who was neglectful or abusive, I

will seek a mate who has these same characteristics, unconsciously hoping to fulfill whatever psychological needs were left unfulfilled by that parent. Ironically, choosing a mate who shares my parent's negative qualities almost guarantees that my unmet psychological needs will remain unmet. However, by this time in my life, due to the low self-esteem produced by my psychological wounds, I probably feel I don't deserve to have my needs met. Because the unconscious premise operating here—I wouldn't have these wounds if I were a good person—remains repressed, its illogic remains unchallenged, and I remain in its grasp.

For both Tom and Daisy, fear of intimacy is related to low self-esteem. If Tom were as emotionally secure as his wealth and size make him appear, he wouldn't work as hard as he does to impress others with his money and power, as he does, for example, when he brags about his house and stables to Nick, when he flaunts Myrtle before Nick and others, when he degrades those who don't belong to the "dominant race" (17; ch. 1), and when he toys with George Wilson concerning whether or not he will sell George a car that the poor mechanic might be able to resell at a profit. Even Tom's choice of mistresses—all from the lower class—bespeaks his need to bolster an insecure psyche through power over others.

Daisy's low self-esteem, like her fear of intimacy, is indicated in large part by her relationship with Tom. Falling so much in love with a man who was openly unfaithful to her suggests an unconscious belief that she doesn't deserve better. Furthermore, Daisy's insecurity, like Tom's, frequently requires the ego reinforcement obtained by impressing others, attempts at which we see in her numerous affectations. Nick notes her artifice when she "assert[s] her membership in a rather distinguished secret society to which she and Tom belon[g]" (22; ch. 1):

> "I think everything's terrible anyhow. . . . Everybody thinks so—the most advanced people. And I *know*. I've been everywhere and seen everything and done everything." Her eyes flashed around her in a defiant way, rather like Tom's, and she laughed with thrilling scorn.
> The instant her voice broke off . . . I felt the basic insincerity of what she had said. (22; ch. 1)

We see Daisy's affected behavior almost every time we see her in a group, as the following examples illustrate. When Nick joins the Buchanans and Jordan Baker for the first time at Daisy's Long Island home, Daisy tells him, "'I'm p-paralyzed with happiness.' . . . She laughed . . . as if she said something very witty . . . looking up into my face, promising that there was no one in the world she so much wanted to see. That was a way she had" (13;

ch. 1). At Gatsby's party she tells Nick, "If you want to kiss me any time during the evening . . . just let me know and I'll be glad to arrange it for you. Just mention my name. Or present a green card" (111; ch. 6). When Gatsby visits the Buchanans with Nick and Jordan, Daisy sends Tom out of the room, and then she "got up and went over to Gatsby, and pulled down his face kissing him on the mouth. . . . 'I don't care!' cried Daisy and began to clog on the brick fireplace" (122–23; ch. 7). Affectation is a sign of insecurity, of which Daisy clearly has a good deal.

Tom and Daisy's fear of intimacy is apparent in their relationships with others as well. Neither of them spends time with Pammy. Their daughter is being raised by her nurse, and Daisy's artificial behavior toward the child—"'Bles-sed pre-cious,' she crooned, holding out her arms. 'Come to your own mother that loves you'" (123; ch. 7)—bespeaks, as usual, an eye for the dramatic pose rather than maternal ardor. Neither Tom nor Daisy forms close ties with Nick or Jordan, although the former is Daisy's cousin and the latter, whom Daisy has known since childhood, spends a good deal of time living under their roof. In this light, the couple's frequent relocations—as Nick puts it, they "drifted here and there unrestfully" (10; ch. 1)—are not the cause of their lack of intimacy with others, but the result: they don't stay in one place for any length of time because they don't want to become close to anyone.

It is no surprise, therefore, that Tom's relationship with Myrtle lacks intimacy. He has no desire to be close to his mistress; she is merely the means by which he avoids being close to his wife. And his treatment of Myrtle certainly suggests no deep emotional investment. He calls for her when it suits him, lies to her about Daisy's religious opposition to divorce in order to keep her from becoming inconveniently demanding, and casually breaks her nose with "a short deft movement" (41; ch. 2) when she becomes so anyway. Tom's maudlin account of his final visit to the small apartment he kept for their rendezvous, where he "sat down and cried like a baby" (187; ch. 9), suggests sentimental self-indulgence, not love. The only ballast for Tom's insensitivity to her is Myrtle's lack of real concern for him.

For Myrtle, Tom Buchanan represents a ticket out of George Wilson's garage. Through Tom, Myrtle hopes to acquire permanent membership in a world where she can display the "impressive hauteur" we see her enjoy at the party in the couple's apartment, during which "[h]er laughter, her gestures, her assertions became more violently affected moment by moment" (35; ch. 2). While economic desperation, rather than fear of intimacy, is the only motive given in the novel for Myrtle's pursuit of Tom, her other relationships suggest that she wants to avoid emotional closeness. She was apparently induced to marry George Wilson not by any personal feeling for him but by her mistaken impression that he was from a higher class than the one to which he belongs: she "thought he was a gentleman" who "knew something about breeding," and when she learned that the good suit in which he was married was borrowed, she "cried to beat the band all afternoon" (39; ch. 2). George's complete emotional dependence on Myrtle, like his belief that the billboard eyes of Doctor T. J. Eckleburg are the eyes of God, suggests psychological disorientation rather than emotional intimacy. With a man as lost in space as George, Myrtle need not fear his getting too close. And her artificial behavior toward her sister and the McKees, apparently her only friends, indicates that these relationships provide opportunities for social display, not for intimacy.

The romance between Nick and Jordan reveals that they, too, fear intimacy. Indeed, Nick is first attracted to Jordan by her self-containment, by the image of emotional distance she projects. He refers approvingly to Jordan's apparent "complete self sufficiency" (13; ch. 1) and describes her, along with Daisy, in terms that denote the appeal of their emotional aloofness:

> Sometimes [Daisy] and Miss Baker talked at once, unobtrusively and with a bantering inconsequence that was never quite chatter, that was as cool as their white dresses and their impersonal eyes in the absence of all desire. (16–17; ch. 1)

He frequently uses words such as *insolent, impersonal, cool,* and *contemptuous* to describe what he considers the "pleasing" (23; ch. 1) expression on Jordan's face. And he remains interested in her as long as she seems to belong to a faraway world, the world of "rotogravure pictures of the sporting life at Asheville and Hot Springs and Palm Beach" (23; ch. 1), a world seemingly untouched by emotional realities. However, once the household she shares with the Buchanans becomes too emotionally "untidy," Nick beats a hasty retreat. After returning with her from the scene of Myrtle Wilson's death, he declines Jordan's invitation to keep her company in the Buchanan home: "I'd be damned if I'd go in; I'd had enough of them for one day and suddenly that included Jordan too. She must have seen something of this in my expression for she turned abruptly away and ran up the porch steps into the house" (150; ch. 7).

Nick subsequently avoids Jordan and shortly thereafter ends the relationship in a manner that keeps him emotionally insulated. He represses the memory of breaking up with her on the telephone the day after Myrtle's death—"I don't know which of us hung up with a sharp click" (163; ch. 8)—although he did "throw [her] over" (186; ch. 9), as we learn when Jordan later reminds him of the event. And even when he meets with her to discuss what had happened between them, he admits that he "talked over and around" (185; ch. 9) their shared past, implying that there was a good deal of avoidance of painful issues during the conversation.

That Nick's fear of intimacy is not limited to his relationship with Jordan is suggested by his two previous romances. Although he claims that he "wasn't even vaguely engaged" to "an old friend" (24; ch. 1) back home in Minnesota, he admits that he came East, in part, to escape local rumors to that effect. The only way he could have been, as he puts it, "rumored into marriage" (24; ch. 1) was if the young lady in question didn't consider herself just an "old friend." We learn that she *was* more than a friend when Nick decides that, before getting involved with Jordan, "first [he] had to get [him]self definitely out of that tangle back home" (64; ch. 3). Clearly, this relationship was more serious than he cares to acknowledge, and he wants out. Similarly, in New York City he "had a short affair with a girl . . . who worked in the accounting department" at his place of business, "but her brother began throwing mean looks in [his] direction so when she went on her vacation in July [he] let it blow quietly away" (61; ch. 3). In other words, when the affair became somewhat serious, he dropped her, again in the manner most likely to avoid an emotional scene. In his relationships with women, Nick is a master of avoidance and denial.

As Jordan's "cool insolent smile" (63; ch. 3) suggests, she shares Nick's desire to remain emotionally insulated, and it is no coincidence that her career and the friends she chooses allow her to do so. Her sporting life provides a ready-made glossy image—"the bored haughty face that she turned to the world" (62; ch. 3)—to shield her from intimacy with others. "[S]he was a golf champion and everyone knew her name" (62; ch. 3), but she made sure, through various "subterfuges" (63; ch. 3), that that's all they know about her. Her choice of friends like the Buchanans, who prefer the world of social image to that of genuine emotional engagement, also protects her from intimacy. They don't want to be close any more than she does. And as Nick observes, Jordan "instinctively avoided clever shrewd men" (63; ch. 3) who might see through her charade. Surely, in choosing men like Nick, Jordan is safe from the threat of emotional ties.

Although the intense affair between Gatsby and Daisy seems to be offered as counterpoint to the Buchanans' marriage of psychological convenience, and to all the other emotionally distant relationships in the novel as well, Gatsby and Daisy's romance has striking similarities to the others. For example, Daisy has no more desire for intimacy with Gatsby than she has for intimacy with Tom. Her extramarital affair, like her earlier romance with her lover, would not have occurred had she known that Gatsby does not belong to her social class. Whatever she feels for Gatsby requires the reinforcement of the same social status Tom provides. Indeed, Tom's revelation of Gatsby's social origin during their confrontation in the New York hotel room results in Daisy's immediate withdrawal:

> [Gatsby] began to talk excitedly to Daisy, denying everything, defending his name against accusations that had not been made. But with every word she was drawing further and further into herself, so he gave that up and only the dead dream fought on as the afternoon slipped away . . . struggling . . . toward that lost voice across the room.
>   The voice begged again to go.
>   "*Please*, Tom! I can't stand this any more."
>   Her frightened eyes told that whatever intentions, whatever courage she had had, were definitely gone. (142; ch. 7)

All the years of Gatsby's devotion, as well as Daisy's desire to be part of his life, disappear for her when she learns that Gatsby does not come from "the right side of the tracks." And Daisy, herself, disappears shortly thereafter, as she and Tom pack their bags and leave town directly after Gatsby's death the following day.

Daisy doesn't realize it, but Gatsby and Myrtle function in much the same capacity for the Buchanans: as psychological pawns in their relationship with each other. Just as Tom uses Myrtle to avoid the emotional problems in his marriage, so Daisy uses Gatsby. Gatsby came along again just in time to buffer Daisy from what seems to be a new development in Tom's extramarital activities. The insistent Myrtle intrudes herself, by means of repeated telephone calls, right into Daisy's home. Tom's flaunting Myrtle out of Daisy's sight does not invade his wife's territory as does his accepting his mistress's telephone calls at home. Just because a mate's behavior has psychological pay-offs for us—as Tom's affairs do for Daisy—it does not mean that those behaviors do not also give us pain. That's why psychological problems are so often referred to as *conflicts*: we unconsciously desire a particular experience because it fulfills a psychological need, but because that need is the result of a psychological wound, the experience is often painful.

Daisy's marriage has become painful, and her affair with Gatsby provides a welcome distraction. If she has Gatsby, she can tell herself that she doesn't need Tom, that she doesn't even have to think about Tom (or, better yet, she can think about how her affair with Gatsby is an appropriate punishment for Tom), and she can therefore afford the blasé attitude toward Tom's womanizing that she exhibits at Gatsby's party. Daisy's affair thus functions as a psychological defense, and as such, it underscores the psychological importance of her dysfunctional marriage: if her marriage weren't a powerful force in her life then she wouldn't have to defend against it. In fact, it is the continued unconscious importance of her marriage that finally makes Daisy feel safe enough to be with Gatsby again. As long as she remains psychologically involved with Tom, she need not fear that she will develop the kind of attachment she had to Gatsby before her marriage.

Given that Gatsby and Myrtle are psychological tokens in the Buchanans' marriage, it is symbolically significant that Tom and Daisy, in effect, kill each other's lover. Although it is apparently a genuine accident, Daisy is the driver who kills Myrtle with Gatsby's car. Far less of an accident, surely, is Tom's sending George Wilson, armed and crazed, to Gatsby's house. Even if, from fear for his and Daisy's life, Tom felt he had to tell Wilson that it was Gatsby who killed Myrtle (or so Tom thought), had Tom not hoped Wilson would kill his wife's lover, he could have phoned Gatsby to warn him. That Daisy lets Gatsby take the blame for Myrtle's death, apparently without a second thought, indicates both her conception of him as an emotional buffer between her and the world and, once her knowledge of his social origin renders him useless as her lover, his expendability.

For many readers, perhaps the most difficult case to make for fear of intimacy is the case for Gatsby. How can we say that Gatsby fears intimacy when he is committed to Daisy as to "the following of a grail" (156; ch. 8), when he kept a scrapbook of all news items concerning her, when he remained faithful to her even during the long years of her married life, and when all the money he acquired during that time was acquired only to win Daisy back? We can make the case by examining what it is that Gatsby remains devoted to in remaining devoted to Daisy.

Although Gatsby believes that his ultimate goal is the possession of Daisy—a belief that many readers, as well as Nick, Jordan, Tom, and Daisy, seem to share—Daisy is merely the key to his goal rather than the goal itself. Gatsby had set his sights on the attainment of wealth and social status long before he knew Daisy. The boyhood "schedule" of Jimmy

Gatz (Jay Gatsby's legal name)—in which the young man divided his day, in the self-improvement tradition of Ben Franklin, among physical exercise, the study of electricity, work, sports, the practice of elocution and poise, and the study of needed inventions—suggests that he'd long planned to live the "rags-to-riches" life associated with such self-made millionaires as John D. Rockefeller and Andrew Carnegie.

Gatsby's desire to move up in the world resulted from his unhappy life with his impoverished parents, "shiftless and unsuccessful farm people" (104; ch. 6). And, apparently, the unhappiness of his boyhood resulted from more than his family's poverty, as is hinted when Mr. Gatz tells Nick, "He told me I et like a hog once and I beat him for it" (182; ch. 9). Whatever psychological traumas Gatsby suffered in his youth, they were sufficient to make him completely reject his emotional relationship with his parents: "his imagination had never really accepted them as his parents at all" (104; ch. 6). Thus, from a psychoanalytic perspective, Gatsby's invented past is more than just a ploy to pass himself off as a member of the upper class; it's also a form of denial, a psychological defense to help him repress the memory of his real past. And his claim that his invented family "all died and [he] came into a good deal of money" (70; ch. 4) becomes, in this context, a metaphor for his desire to psychologically kill the parents whose wounding influence still inhabits his own psyche and, paradoxically, receive from those parents the psychological nourishment—the "money"—they'd never given him.

The financial achievements Gatsby planned for himself revealed their ultimate psychological pay-off, however, only upon meeting Daisy. "She was the first 'nice' girl he had ever known. . . . [H]e had come in contact with such people but always with indiscernible barbed wire between" (155; ch. 8). Through Daisy, he could imagine what it would feel like to be part of her world, to be, as he felt she was, "gleaming like silver, safe and proud above the hot struggles of the poor" (157; ch. 8), the struggles he experienced as a youth, which he can't help but associate with the psychological pain of that period of his life. Daisy is, for him, not a flesh-and-blood woman but an emblem of the emotional insulation he unconsciously desires: emotional insulation from himself, from James Gatz and the past to which he belongs. As we saw in the case of Tom and Daisy, the best way to achieve emotional insulation from oneself is to avoid intimacy with others. Gatsby's outrageous idealization of Daisy as the perfect woman—she can do no wrong; she can love no one but him; time cannot change her—is a sure sign that he seeks to avoid intimacy, for it is impossible to be intimate with an ideal. In fact, we can't even know a person we idealize because we substitute the ideal for the real human being, and that's all we see. Even during the years when his only access to her was through the news items he read on the society page, Gatsby's obsession with Daisy protected him from intimacy with other women.

It is significant, then, that Fitzgerald could not imagine what went on emotionally between Gatsby and Daisy during their Long Island affair. As the author notes in a letter to Edmund Wilson, he "had no feeling about or knowledge of . . . the emotional relations between Gatsby and Daisy from the time of their reunion to the catastrophe" (*Letters* 341–42). I think it is clear, from a psychoanalytic perspective, that Fitzgerald was unable to provide us with an account of their emotional relationship because there is none. I'm not suggesting that Gatsby and Daisy don't experience emotions, but that whatever they feel for each other is always a means of avoiding feeling something else, something profoundly disturbing that they want to keep repressed.

Clearly, a psychoanalytic lens reveals a much different love story than the one ordinarily associated with *The Great Gatsby*. As the novel illustrates, romantic love is the stage upon which all of our unresolved psychological conflicts are dramatized, over and over. Indeed, it's the over-and-over, the repetition of destructive behavior, that tells us an unresolved psychological conflict is "pulling the strings" from the unconscious. All of the characters discussed above illustrate this principle, though its operations are, at once, most dramatic and most camouflaged—that is, most repressed—in Gatsby's obsession with Daisy. For Gatsby's repression of his psychological motives outstrips that of all the other characters put together. His famous words, "Can't repeat the past? . . . Why of course you can!" (116; ch. 6), are especially meaningful, in this context, because they betoken the implicit premise upon which the psychoanalytic content of the novel is based: that our repression of psychological wounds condemns us to repeatedly incur them. Gatsby's lonely pursuit of Daisy replays the loneliness of his youth, and he seems to feel as much an outsider in the mansion he bought to receive her—the only room he uses or marks with a personal possession is his bedroom—as he must have felt in the home of his parents. Surely, Gatsby could not have been wounded more severely by his parents than he is by Daisy's abandonment of him, both when she married Tom and when he loses her again to his rival the night of Myrtle Wilson's death. Thus, whether it intends to do so or not, *The Great Gatsby* shows us how effectively romantic relationships can facilitate our repression of psychological wounds and thereby inevitably carry us, as the novel's closing line so aptly puts it, "ceaselessly into the past" (189; ch. 9).

Questions for Further Practice: Psychoanalytic Approaches to Other Literary Works

The following questions are intended as models. They can help you use psychoanalytic criticism to interpret the literary works to which they refer or other texts of your choice.

1. How might an understanding of the return of the repressed help us understand the relationship of the reincarnated Beloved (who might be viewed as the embodiment of the former slaves' unbearable pasts) to Sethe, Paul D, and the black community in Toni Morrison's *Beloved* (1987)?

2. How might an understanding of regression help us interpret Alberto Moravia's "The Chase" (1967)? What seems to be the narrator's core issue?

3. How might an understanding of the ways in which death work can be projected onto the environment help us interpret Marlow in Joseph Conrad's *Heart of Darkness* (1902)?

4. How might an understanding of denial and displacement (in this case, displacement of negative feelings for one's husband onto one's child) help us analyze the narrator's relationship to her troubled daughter in Tillie Olsen's "I Stand Here Ironing" (1956)?

5. How might we use an understanding of repression, the superego, and dream symbolism (especially water as a symbol of the emotions or of sexuality) to help us interpret Emily Dickinson's "I Started Early—Took My Dog" (1862)?

For Further Reading

All of the following works will help you develop your skills as psychoanalytic critics. Texts listed under "Category I" are written in language accessible to most beginners. Texts listed under "Category II" employ more technical language but are well worth the extra effort that may be required of some students new to the field.

Category I

Davis, Walter A. "The Drama of the Psychoanalytic Subject." In *Inwardness and Existence: Subjectivity in/and Hegel, Heidegger, Marx, and Freud*. Madison: U of Wisconsin P, 1989. (See, especially, "The Familial Genesis of the Psyche," 242–50; "Identity and Sexuality," 296–307; and "Love Stories," 307–13.)

Freud, Sigmund. *The Complete Introductory Lectures on Psychoanalysis*. Trans. James Strachey. New York: W. W. Norton, 1966.

———. *The Freud Reader*. Ed. Peter Gay. New York: Norton, 1989.

Jung, Carl. *The Archetypes and the Collective Unconscious*. Vol. 9, Part I of *Collected Works*. 2nd ed. Trans. R. F. C. Hull. Princeton: Princeton UP, 1968.

Schwartz, Murray, and Coppelia Kahn, eds. *Representing Shakespeare: New Psychoanalytic Essays*. Baltimore: Johns Hopkins UP, 1980.

Segal, Hanna. *Introduction to the Work of Melanie Klein*. 2nd ed. New York: Basic Books, 1974.

Winnicott, D. W. *Playing and Reality*. Harmondsworth, England: Penguin, 1977.

Wright, Elizabeth. *Psychoanalytic Criticism: Theory in Practice*. New York: Methuen, 1984.

Category II

Davis, Robert Con, ed. *The Fictional Father: Lacanian Readings of the Text*. Amherst: U of Massachusetts P, 1981.

Davis, Walter A. *Get the Guests: Psychoanalysis, Modern American Drama, and the Audience*. Madison: U of Wisconsin P, 1994.

Freud, Sigmund. *The Interpretation of Dreams*. 1900. Rpt. in *The Basic Writings of Sigmund Freud*. Trans. Dr. A. A. Brill, ed. New York: Modern Library, 1938. 180–549.

Klein, George S. *Psychoanalytic Theory: An Exploration of Essentials*. New York: International Universities, 1976.

Klein, Melanie. *"Envy and Gratitude" and Other Works, 1946–1963*. New York: Delacorte, 1975.

———. *"Love, Guilt, and Reparation" and Other Works, 1921–1945*. New York: Delacorte, 1975.

Lacan, Jacques. *Écrits: A Selection*. Trans. Alan Sheridan. New York: Norton, 1977. (See, especially, "The Mirror Stage as Formative of the Function of the I," 1–7; "The Agency of the Letter in the Unconscious or Reason since Freud," 146–75; and "The Signification of the Phallus," 281–91.

———. *The Four Fundamental Concepts of Psycho-Analysis*. Ed. Jacques-Alain Miller. Trans. Alan Sheridan. New York: Norton, 1978.

Ragland-Sullivan, Ellie. *Jacques Lacan and the Philosophy of Psychoanalysis*. Urbana: U of Illinois P, 1986.

Schafer, Roy. *A New Language for Psychoanalysis*. New Haven: Yale UP, 1976.

Winnicott. D. W. *The Maturational Processes and the Facilitating Environment*. New York: International UP, 1965.

Notes

1. The psychological theories of Carl Jung (1875–1961) and of Jacques Lacan (1901–1981) have generated two schools of psychological literary criticism distinct from the Freudian-based psychoanalytic criticism discussed in this chapter. Indeed, adequate coverage of Jungian criticism (sometimes called archetypal criticism or myth criticism) and Lacanian criticism would require a chapter devoted to each. Jungian criticism is not covered in this textbook because its practice is not widespread enough at this time to warrant its inclusion. Although Lacanian criticism is very influential today, it is an extremely abstract theory that reinterprets Freudian principles within the framework of structural linguistics. It is not generally useful, therefore, to beginning students of critical theory. In any event, students who wish to study Jungian or Lacanian criticism will need to begin with a thorough understanding of Freudian psychoanalysis, to which this chapter offers an introduction. In addition, works that address the theories of Jung and Lacan are listed in "For Further Reading" at the end of this chapter.

CHAPTER 3

Marxist Criticism

Students new to the study of critical theory often ask why we study Marxist criticism now that the Communist Bloc in Europe has failed, thereby proving that Marxism is not a viable theory. In addition to ignoring the existence of China, among other communist countries, such a question overlooks two important facts. First, beyond some relatively small and relatively short-lived communes, there has never been, as far as we know, a true Marxist society on the face of the Earth. Communist societies, though they claim to be based on the principles developed by Karl Marx (1818–1883), have been, in reality, oligarchies in which a small group of leaders controls the money and the guns and forces its policies on a population kept in line through physical intimidation. Second, even if communist countries were true Marxist societies and even if all of them had failed, Marxist theory would still give us a meaningful way to understand history and current events. Indeed, one could use Marxism to interpret the failure of Marxist regimes. However, before we can attempt a Marxist interpretation of such political events, or of events of any kind, we must first, of course, understand Marxist theory.

The Fundamental Premises of Marxism

What, exactly, is Marxist theory? Let's begin to answer that question by answering another: What would Marxist critics say about the preceding chapter on psychoanalytic criticism? They would say that, by focusing our attention on the individual psyche and its roots in the family complex, psychoanalysis distracts our attention from the real forces that create human experience: the economic systems that structure human societies. Indeed, Marxist critics would have the same complaint, more or less, about all the other theories discussed in this book. If a theory does not foreground the economic realities of human culture, then it misunderstands human culture. For Marxism, getting and keeping economic power is the motive behind all social and political activities, including education, philosophy, religion, government, the arts, science, technology, the media, and so on. Thus, economics is the *base* upon which the *superstructure* of social/political/ideological realities is built. Economic power therefore always includes social and political power as well, which is why many Marxists today refer to *socioeconomic class*, rather than economic class, when talking about the class structure.

In Marxist terminology, economic conditions are referred to as *material* circumstances, and the social/political/ideological atmosphere generated by material conditions is called the *historical* situation. For the Marxist critic, neither human events (in the political or personal domain) nor human productions (from nuclear submarines to television shows) can be understood without understanding the specific material/historical circumstances in which those events and productions occur. That is, all human events and productions have specific material/historical causes. An accurate picture of human affairs cannot be obtained by the search for abstract, timeless essences or principles but only by understanding concrete conditions in the world. Therefore, Marxist analysis of human events and productions focuses on relationships among socioeconomic classes, both within a society and among societies, and explains all human activities in terms of the distribution and dynamics of economic power. And Marxist *praxis*, or methodology, dictates that theoretical ideas can be judged to have value only in terms of their concrete applications, that is, only in terms of their applicability to the real world.

From a Marxist perspective, differences in socioeconomic class divide people in ways that are much more significant than do differences in religion, race, ethnicity, and gender. For the real battle lines are drawn, to put the matter simply, between the "haves" and the "have-nots," between the *bourgeoisie*—those who control the world's natural, economic, and human resources—and the *proletariat*, the majority of the global population who live in substandard conditions and who have always performed the manual labor—the mining, the factory work, the ditch-digging, the railroad building—that fills the coffers of the rich. Unfortunately, the prole-

tariat are often the last to recognize this fact; they usually permit differences in religion, race, ethnicity, and gender to separate them into warring factions that accomplish little or no social change. Few Marxists today believe, as Marx did, that the proletariat will one day spontaneously
develop the class consciousness needed to rise up in violent revolution
against their oppressors and create a classless society. However, were the
proletariat of any given country to act as a group, regardless of their differences (for example, were they all to vote for the same political candi-
dates, boycott the same companies, and go on strike until their needs
were met), the current power structure would be radically altered.

The Class System in America

It has become increasingly difficult in the twentieth century to clearly
place people either in the bourgeoisie or the proletariat. How do we classify, for example, the person who employs several workers in a small, fam-
ily-owned business but whose yearly profits are less than the annual
wages of a salesperson working for a big corporation? In other words, in
America, at least, some workers earn more than some owners. To complicate matters further, the words *bourgeoisie* (noun) and *bourgeois* (adjective) have come to refer, in everyday speech, to the middle class in general,
with no distinction between owners and wage-earners. At this point in
history, therefore, it might be more useful to classify Americans according
to socioeconomic lifestyle, without reference to the manner in which
their income is acquired. For the sake of clarity, let's take a moment to do
so now by drawing a simplified sketch of the major socioeconomic divisions in contemporary America.

Whether or not we would agree on which individuals belong to the
bourgeoisie and which to the proletariat, most of us can observe the
striking difference in socioeconomic lifestyle among the following
groups: the homeless, who have few, if any, material possessions and little
hope of improvement; the poor, whose limited educational and career
opportunities keep them struggling to support their families and living in
fear of becoming homeless; the financially established, who own nice
homes and cars and can usually afford to send their children to college;
the well-to-do, who can afford two or more expensive homes, several cars,
and luxury items; and the extremely wealthy, such as the owners of large,
well-established corporations, for whom money (mansions, limousines,
personal airplanes, yachts) is no problem whatsoever. We might loosely

refer to these five groups as America's underclass, lower class, middle class, upper class, and "aristocracy."

Clearly, the underclass and the lower class are economically oppressed: they suffer the ills of economic privation, are hardest hit by economic recessions, and have limited means of improving their lot. In sharp contrast, the upper class and "aristocracy" are economically privileged: they enjoy luxurious lifestyles, are least affected by economic recessions, and have a great deal of financial security. But what about members of the middle class? Are they economically oppressed or economically privileged? Of course, the answer is probably both. Their socioeconomic lifestyle is certainly better than that of the classes below them, but they'll probably never own a mansion; they have more financial stability than the lower classes, yet they are often hard hit by economic recessions and usually have good reason to worry about their financial future; they benefit from institutionalized forms of economic security, such as good medical insurance and pension plans, but they shoulder an enormous (and, many would argue, unfair) tax burden relative to their income.

Why don't the economically oppressed fight back? What keeps the lower classes "in their place" and at the mercy of the wealthy? At least for the poor and homeless in America today, the struggle to survive is certainly a factor in keeping them down. Who has the time to become politically active, or even politically aware, when one is struggling just to stay alive and feed one's children? Other elements oppressing them are the police and other government strong-arm agencies, who, under government orders, have mistreated lower-class and underclass poor perceived as a threat to the power structure, such as the striking workers who were arrested, beaten, or killed in the early days of American labor unions or the homeless who were routed from their cardboard boxes in New York's Central Park a few years ago because their shanties, in effect, "ruined the view" from the windows of the wealthy living in posh apartments nearby. The poor are oppressed even more effectively, however, by ideology.

The Role of Ideology

For Marxism, an *ideology* is a belief system, that is, a product of cultural conditioning. For example, capitalism, communism, Marxism, patriotism, religion, ethical systems, humanism, environmentalism, astrology, and karate are all ideologies. The critical theories we will study in this book are all ideologies. Even our assumption that nature behaves according to the laws of science is an ideology. However, although almost any experience or field of study we can think of has an ideological component, not all ideologies are equally productive or desirable. Undesirable ideologies promote repressive political agendas and, in order to ensure their acceptance among the citizenry, pass themselves off as natural ways of seeing the world instead of acknowledging themselves as ideologies. "It's natural for men to hold leadership positions because their biological superiority renders them more physically, intellectually, and emotionally capable than women" is a sexist ideology that sells itself as a function of nature, rather than a product of cultural belief. "Every family wants to own its own home on its own land" is a capitalist ideology that sells itself as natural by pointing, for example, to the fact that almost all Americans want to own their own property, without acknowledging that this desire is created in us by the capitalist culture in which we live. Many Native American nations, in contrast, don't believe that land is something that can be owned. For them, it's like trying to own the air we breathe.

By posing as natural ways of seeing the world, repressive ideologies prevent us from understanding the material/historical conditions in which we live because they refuse to acknowledge that those conditions have any bearing on the way we see the world. Marxism, a non-repressive ideology, acknowledges that it is an ideology. Marxism works to make us constantly aware of all the ways in which we are products of material/historical circumstances and of the repressive ideologies that serve to blind us to this fact in order to keep us subservient to the ruling power system. Although Marxist theorists differ in their estimation of the degree to which we are "programmed" by ideology, all agree that the most successful ideologies are *not* recognized as ideologies but are thought to be natural ways of seeing the world by the people who subscribe to them. Thus, although we could argue that the economic interests of middle-class America would best be served by a political alliance with the poor in order to attain a more equitable distribution of America's enormous wealth among the middle and lower classes, in political matters the middle class generally sides with the wealthy against the poor.

To cite one simple example, the middle class tends to resent the poor because so much middle-class tax money goes to government programs to help the poor. However, the middle class fails to realize two important socioeconomic realities: (1) that it is the wealthy in positions of power who decide who pays the most taxes and how the money will be spent (in other words, it is the wealthy who make the middle class support the poor), and (2) that the poor receive but a small portion of the funds earmarked for them because so much of it goes, through kickbacks and "creative" bookkeeping, into the pockets of the wealthy who control our social services and the middle-class employees who administer them. What is the ideology that blinds the middle class to the socioeconomic inequities in contemporary America? In large part, the middle class is blinded by their belief in the *American dream*, which tells them that financial success is simply the product of initiative and hard work. Therefore, if some people are poor, it is because they are shiftless and lazy.

In this country, we believe that it is natural to want to "get ahead," to want to own a better house and wear better clothes. The key word here is *better*, which refers not only to "better than I had before" but also to "better than other people have." That is, embedded within the belief in "getting ahead" is the belief in competition as a natural or necessary mode of being. After all, haven't we learned from science that nature demands the "survival of the fittest"? And doesn't this view of human behavior fit perfectly with the belief in rugged individualism upon which America was founded and without which it would not have become the great nation it is today? For that matter, isn't all of the above—getting ahead, competition, and rugged individualism—part and parcel of the American dream, according to which we are all born equal and are free to advance as far as our own "get-up-and-go" will take us?

While this view of human endeavor may seem, to most Americans at least, quite natural and proper—and we can certainly point to the success of self-made men like Benjamin Franklin and Abraham Lincoln to underscore its apparent fairness—Marxist analysis reveals that the American dream is an ideology, a belief system, not an innate or natural way of seeing the world. And like all ideologies that support the socioeconomic inequities of capitalist countries like ours—that is, countries in which the means of production (natural, financial, and human resources) are privately owned and in which those who own them inevitably become the dominant class— the American dream blinds us to the enormities of its own failure, past and present: the genocide of Native Americans, the enslavement of Africans, the virtual enslavement of indentured servants, the abuses suffered by immigrant populations, the widening economic gulf between America's rich and poor, the growing ranks of the homeless and hungry, the enduring socioeconomic barriers against women and people of color, and the like. In other words, the success of the American dream—the acquisition of a wealthy lifestyle for a few—rests on the misery of the many. And it is the power of ideology, of our belief in the naturalness and fairness of this dream, that has blinded us to the harsh realities it masks.

Some of us might want to pause at this point to ask, "But isn't the American dream an ideal? Although our ideals may fail in practice, shouldn't we continue to aspire to them? Should we abandon, for example, the ideal that human life is sacred just because we sometimes fail to live up to it?" For Marxism, when an ideal functions to mask its own failure, it is a false ideal, or *false consciousness*, whose real purpose is to promote the interests of those in power. In the case of the American dream, then, the question for Marxist analysis is, "How does the American dream enlist the support of all Americans, even of those who fail to achieve it, in promoting the interests of those in power?"

The answer, at least in part, is that the American dream, much like the state lotteries or the big-bucks sweepstakes that are its latest incarnation, opens the possibility that anyone can win, and, like gambling addicts, we cling to that possibility. In fact, the less financial security we have, the more we need something to hope for. The American dream also tells us what we want to hear: that we are all "as good as" the wealthiest among us. It's not supposed to matter that the wealthy don't think I'm as good as they are as long as I believe it's true. And it's not supposed to matter that "as good as" doesn't mean entitled to the same health care, material comforts, or social privileges, including the privilege of hiring the best lawyers should the need arise. In my need to "feel good about myself," especially if my life is burdened with financial worries, I will cling to the ego gratification offered by the American dream. Analogously, if I want to avoid the guilt that accompanies my acquisition of a large fortune while so many of my fellow citizens can barely eke out a living, I will be comforted by the assurance I receive from the American dream that I deserve whatever wealth I have the initiative to amass. Indeed, the power of the American dream to mask material/historical reality is such that it can invoke an America for whom class doesn't matter and plunk that ideology down right in the middle of an America whose class system is too complex for me to map, beyond the rough outline provided earlier.

From a Marxist perspective, the role of ideology in maintaining those in power is so important that we should briefly examine a few more examples so that we can see how it works. *Classism*, for example, is an ideology that equates one's value as a human being with the social class to which one belongs: the higher one's social class, the better one is assumed to be because quality is "in the blood," that is, inborn. From a classist perspective, people at the top of the social scale are naturally superior to those below them: more intelligent, more responsible, more trustworthy, more ethical, and so on. People at the bottom of the social scale, it follows, are naturally shiftless, lazy, and irresponsible. Therefore, it is only right and natural that those from the highest social class should hold all the positions of power and leadership because they are naturally suited to such roles and are the only ones who can be trusted to perform them properly.

Patriotism is an ideology that keeps poor people fighting wars against poor people from other countries (one way or another, sufficient money can generally keep one out of the armed forces during war time or, at least, out of the combat units) while the rich on both sides rake in the profits of war-time economy. Because it leads the poor to see themselves as members of a nation, separate from other nations, rather than as members of a world-wide oppressed class, opposed to all privileged classes including those from their own country, patriotism prevents the poor from banding together to improve their condition globally.

Religion, which Karl Marx called "the opiate of the masses," is an ideology that helps to keep the faithful poor satisfied with their lot in life, or at least tolerant of it, much as a tranquilizer might do. The question of God's existence is not the fundamental issue for Marxist analysis; rather, what human beings do in God's name—organized religion—is the focus. For example, while many Christian religious groups work to feed, clothe, house, and even educate the world's poor, the religious tenets that are disseminated along with the food and clothing include the conviction that the poor, if they remain non-violent, will find their reward in heaven. Obviously, the 10 percent (or less) of the world's population who own 90 percent (or more) of the world's wealth have a vested interest in promoting this aspect of Christian belief among the poor, and, historically, have exploited Christianity for just this purpose. Indeed, the bible has been used successfully to justify and promote the enslavement of Africans in America and the subordination of women, gay men, and lesbians.

Rugged individualism, which, as we have seen, is a cornerstone of the American dream, is an ideology that keeps the focus on "me" instead of on "us," thus working against class action and giving us the illusion that we make our own decisions and are not significantly influenced by ideology. *Consumerism*, or shop-'till-you-drop-ism, is another cornerstone of the American dream. Consumerism is an ideology that says I'm only as good as what I buy. Thus, it simultaneously fulfills two ideological purposes: it gives me the illusion that I can be "as good as" the wealthy if I can purchase what they purchase or a reasonable facsimile thereof, albeit on credit, and it fills the coffers of the wealthy who manufacture and sell the consumer products I buy and who reap the 15–20 percent interest on my credit-card purchases.

Of course, there are many more capitalist ideologies we could analyze. These few are intended just to illustrate, in general terms, the Marxist view of repressive ideologies. Our goal, as Marxist critics, is to identify the ideology at work in cultural productions—literature, film, painting, music, television programs, commercial advertisements, education, popular philosophy, religion, forms of entertainment, and so on—and to analyze how that ideology supports or undermines the socioeconomic system (the power structure) in which that cultural production plays a significant role. While Marxists believe that all social phenomena, from child-rearing practices to environmental concerns, are cultural productions—and that culture cannot be separated from the socioeconomic system that produced it—many Marxists are interested in cultural productions in the narrower sense of the word: for example, art, music, film, theatre, literature, and television. For these critics, culture, in this narrower sense, is the primary bearer of ideology because it reaches so many people in what seems to be an innocent form: entertainment. When we are being entertained, our guard is down, so to speak, and we are especially vulnerable to ideological programming.

Consider, for example, this representation of a homeless man I saw recently on a situation-comedy on television. The man sleeps every night in a bus station, where the sitcom is set. We see him in a public phone booth, talking on the phone, when he is interrupted by one of the workers, who gives him his mail. (Big laugh: the guy hangs around the station so much that the post office thinks it's his home!) He inspects his mail and makes a casual comment like, "I wish the post office would do something about all this junk mail!" (Another big laugh: instead of complaining about—or even noticing—the situation he's in, he's complaining about junk mail!) The scene may seem innocent enough, but a Marxist critic would see in it an implied message that serves the capitalist power structure in America: "Don't worry about the homeless; they're doing alright for themselves" or, worse, "The homeless like to live this way; it's as natural to them as our lifestyle is to us."

How does the American dream contribute to just such a view of the homeless? It does so by promoting the myth, which we discussed earlier, that financial success can be achieved in this country merely through initiative and hard work. Therefore, the poor must be shiftless and lazy. We are thus encouraged to forget, for example, that a homeless person can't get a job without an address and can't get an address without a job, that most homeless people become so due to economic circumstances wholly beyond their control, and that many people are homeless today because

they were evicted from the mental health institutions closed during the
Reagan administration and are, therefore, in need of increasingly expensive medication, and/or therapy as well as homes.

Human Behavior, the Commodity,
and the Family

Although the later works of Karl Marx focus on economics, on the workings of society as a whole, rather than on the individual, it is important to
remember that he began as a student of human behavior—we might even
say a social psychologist—in his own right. For example, his concern over
the rise of industrialism in the mid-nineteenth century was a concern for
the effects of factory work on people who were forced to sell their labor to
the industries that were replacing independent artisans and farmers. Because factory workers produced such large quantities of products, none
of which bore their name or any other mark of their individual contribution, Marx observed that they became dissociated not only from the
products they produced but from their own labor as well, and he noted
the debilitating effects of what he called *alienated labor* on the laborer and
on the society as a whole.

Similarly, Marx's concern over the rise of capitalist economy (in
which an object's value is translated into a monetary "equivalent" and determined solely in terms of its relationship to a monetary market) and its
replacement of barter economy (in which labor or goods can be exchanged for other labor or goods, depending upon the abilities and needs
of the individuals involved in the exchange) was a concern for the effects
of capitalism on human values. The focus of many later Marxists on the
ways in which ideology is transmitted through popular culture and operates in our emotional lives is thus compatible with Marx's own interest in
human behavior and experience.

Of course, many Marxist insights into human behavior involve the
damaging effects of capitalism on human psychology, and those damaging effects often appear in our relationship to the *commodity*. For Marxism, a commodity's value lies not in what it can do (*use value*) but in the
money or other commodities for which it can be traded (*exchange value*)
or in the social status it confers on its owner (*sign-exchange value*). An
object becomes a commodity only when it has exchange value or sign-
exchange value, and both forms of value are determined by the society in
which the object is exchanged. For example, if I read a book for pleasure

or for information, or even if I use it to prop up a table leg, the book has use value. If I sell that same book, it has exchange value. If I leave that book out on my coffee table to impress my date, it has sign-exchange value. *Commodification* is the act of relating to objects or persons in terms of their exchange value or sign-exchange value. I commodify a work of art when I buy it as a financial investment, that is, with the intention of selling it for more money, or when I buy it to impress other people with my refined tastes. If I purchase and display costly goods or services excessively in order to impress people with my wealth, I am guilty of *conspicuous consumption*, as when I buy a full-length, white mink coat (or even a pair of $100 designer sunglasses), not just for the object's usefulness or beauty but in order to show the world how much money I have.

Finally, I commodify human beings when I structure my relations with them to promote my own advancement financially or socially. Most of us know what it means to treat a person like an object (for example, a sex object). An object becomes a commodity, however, only when it has exchange value or sign-exchange value. Do I choose my dates based on how much money I think they will spend on me (their exchange value) or how much I think they will impress my friends (their sign-exchange value)? If so, then I'm commodifying them.

From a Marxist perspective, because the survival of capitalism, which is a market economy, depends on consumerism, it promotes sign-exchange value as our primary mode of relating to the world around us. What could be better for a capitalist economy than for its members to be unable to "feel good about themselves" unless they acquire a fashionable "look" that can be maintained only by the continual purchase of new clothing, new cosmetic products, and new cosmetic services? In other words, in economic terms, it's in capitalism's best interests to promote whatever personal insecurities will motivate us to buy consumer goods. (Are my teeth not white enough? Should my hair be blonder? Should my muscles bulge more? Is my breath fresh enough?) And because the kinds of personal insecurities that make us buy consumer products are produced by comparing ourselves with other people (Are my teeth as white as his? Is my hair as blond as hers?), competition is promoted not just among companies who want to sell products but among people who feel they must "sell" themselves in order to be popular or successful.

Capitalism's constant need for new markets in which to sell goods and for new sources of raw materials from which to make goods is also responsible for the spread of *imperialism*: the military, economic, and/or cultural domination of one nation by another for the financial benefit of the dominating nation with little or no concern for the welfare of the dominated. Spain's rule of Mexico, England's domination of India, Belgium's exploitation of the Congo region of Africa, and U.S. efforts to subordinate native populations in North, Central, and South America are but a few examples of imperialist activities. When the imperialist nation establishes communities in an "underdeveloped" country, those communities are called *colonies*, as were the American Colonies before the American Revolution, and it uses those colonies to extend its economic interests. For the motive of all imperialist endeavor, no matter what positive influence the conquering nation claims to have on the local population, is economic gain for the "mother country."

Less clear cut, perhaps, but equally important for our understanding of capitalism today, is the way in which consciousness can be "colonized" by imperialist governments. To *colonize* the *consciousness* of subordinate peoples means to convince them to see their situation the way the imperialist nation wants them to see it, to convince them, for example, that they are mentally, spiritually, and culturally inferior to their conquerors and that their lot will be improved under the "guidance" and "protection" of their new leaders. Antebellum slave owners, for example, tried to convince African slaves that they were uncivilized, godless savages who would revert to cannibalism without the constant vigilance of their white masters. In reality, of course, African slaves came from ancient cultures that could boast many forms of art, music, religion, and ethics. This same attempt to colonize consciousness along racial lines has continued into the twentieth century through, for example, stereotypes of black Americans in the media, the inadequate representation of African American experience in American history books, and the promotion of an Anglo-Saxon ideal of beauty. Thus, the attempt to colonize consciousness can be practiced against us by our own culture. Indeed, the promotion of consumerism discussed earlier is just such another example.

Clearly, Marxism's concern with human psychology overlaps with that of psychoanalysis: both disciplines study human behavior and motivation in psychological terms. However, while psychoanalysis focuses on the individual psyche and its formation within the family, Marxism focuses on the material/historical forces—the politics and ideologies of socioeconomic systems—that shape the psychological experience and behavior of individuals and groups. For Marxism, the family is not the source of the individual's psychological identity, for both the individual and the family are products of material/historical circumstances. The family unconsciously carries out the cultural "program" in raising its children, but that program is produced by the socioeconomic culture within which the family operates. While it is our parents who read us bedtime stories, take us to movies, and, in these and other ways, form our morals, it is our social system that provides the stories, movies, and morals, all of which ultimately serve the economic interests of those in control of that social system. Thus, while psychoanalytic critics examine the family conflicts and psychological wounds that determine individual behavior, Marxist critics examine that same behavior as a product of the ideological forces carried, for example, by film, fashion, art, music, education, and law. Indeed, the Marxist critic will show us the ways in which family dysfunctions are themselves products of the socioeconomic system and the ideologies it promotes.

Marxism and Literature

Of course, the family is a recurrent theme in literature, so let's begin our discussion of Marxism and literature by contrasting Marxist and psychoanalytic readings of Arthur Miller's greatest familial play, *Death of a Salesman* (1949). A psychoanalytic reading of the play would focus on such elements as Willy's abandonment, at a very young age, by his father and older brother; Willy's insecurity and the massive denial of reality that results; Willy's projection of his personal needs onto his son Biff; Happy's sibling rivalry with Biff; the oedipal dimension at work in the family dynamic; and Linda's avoidance and displacement of her problems with Willy. The central scene for such an interpretation would be Biff's confrontation with Willy in the hotel, where he discovers his father with another woman. These aspects of the play would be of interest to psychoanalytic critics because they focus on the individual psyche as the product of the family.

A Marxist reading, in contrast, would focus on the ways in which the psychological problems listed above are produced by the material/historical realities within which the family operates: the ideology of the American dream that tells Willy his self-worth is earned only by economic success and that keeps him looking up to his predatory brother Ben; the rampant consumerism that keeps the Lomans buying on credit what they can't afford; the competitiveness of the business world that puts Willy back on straight commission-work after thirty years of employment with the same firm; the exploitative potential of a socioeconomic system that doesn't require all companies to provide adequate pension coverage for their employees; and the ideology of "survival-of-the-fittest" capitalism that allows Howard to fire Willy with no concern for the latter's deteriorating mental condition. The central scene for such an interpretation would be that in which Howard (after displaying signs of his own economic success) fires Willy, telling him to turn to his sons for financial help.

Clearly, if a Marxist critic uses a psychoanalytic concept, it is used in service of a Marxist interpretation. For example, Willy's denial of reality, and the regressive hallucinations that accompany it, would be viewed as evidence of the American dream's debilitating ideological agenda: the American dream is certainly good for capitalist economics, but it sacrifices the well-being of the many individuals who don't achieve it. Similarly, as you read other Marxist interpretations of culture and cultural productions, you may notice that concepts from other theories we are studying will appear. For example, you may notice that, by revealing the subtle but profound capitalist similarities between, say, Democratic, Republican, Socialist, and Fascist cultural and educational funding policies, a Marxist critic is engaged in a kind of structuralist enterprise. Or you may notice that, by revealing the ways in which a literary work covertly reinforces the capitalist values it criticizes, a Marxist critic is engaged in a deconstructive enterprise. Indeed, many Marxist critics are, among other things, feminists, deconstructors, social psychologists, and cultural anthropologists. In every case, however, you will see that concepts overlapping with or borrowed from other fields are put in service of Marxist goals.

Of course, the Marxist concepts discussed above do not exhaust the field; there are many others. And as in every field, there is a great deal of disagreement among Marxist theorists and literary critics concerning, for example, the formation and role of class solidarity among the proletariat, the role of the media in manipulating our political consciousness, the relationship between ideology and psychology, the compatibility of Marxism with other critical theories, and many other topics. However, the concepts provided here can be considered the basic principles, the main ideas you need to know in order to read Marxist theorists and literary critics with some understanding of the issues they raise. Before we extend these concepts to the realm of literary interpretation, let's take a look at Marxism's view of literature in general.

For Marxism, literature does not exist in some timeless, aesthetic realm as an object to be passively contemplated. Rather, like all cultural manifestations, it is a product of the socioeconomic and hence ideological conditions of the time and place in which it was written, whether or not the author intended it so. Because human beings are themselves products of their socioeconomic and ideological environment, it is assumed that authors cannot help but create works that embody ideology in some form.

The fact that literature grows out of and reflects real material/historical conditions creates at least two possibilities of interest to Marxist critics: (1) the literary work might tend to reinforce in the reader the ideologies it embodies, or (2) it might invite the reader to criticize the ideologies it represents. Many texts do both. And it is not merely the *content* of a literary work—the "action" or the theme—that carries ideology, but the *form* as well or, as most Marxists would argue, the form primarily. Realism, naturalism, surrealism, symbolism, romanticism, modernism, postmodernism, tragedy, comedy, satire, interior monologue, stream of consciousness, and other genres and literary devices are the means by which form is constituted. If content is the "what" of literature, then form is the "how."

Realism, for example, gives us characters and plot as if we were looking through a window onto an actual scene taking place before our eyes. Our attention is drawn not to the nature of the words on the page but to the action those words convey. Indeed, we frequently forget about the words we're reading and the way the narrative is structured as we "get lost" in the story. Part of the reason we don't notice the language and structure, the form, is because the action represented is ordered in a coherent sequence that invites us to relate to it much as we relate to the events in our own lives, and the characters it portrays are believable, much like people we might, ourselves, meet. So we get "pulled into" the story. In contrast, a good deal of postmodern literature (and non-realistic, experimental literature of any kind) is written in a fragmented, surreal style that seems to defy our understanding and serves to distance or estrange us from the narrative and the characters it portrays.

For some Marxists, realism is the best form for Marxist purposes because it clearly and accurately represents the real world, with all its socioeconomic inequities and ideological contradictions, and encourages readers to see the unhappy truths about material/historical reality, for whether or not authors intend it, they are bound to represent socioeconomic inequities and ideological contradictions if they accurately represent the real world. Marxist fans of realist fiction often have been inclined to reject non-realistic, experimental fiction for being inaccessible to the majority of readers and for being too exclusively concerned with the in-

ner workings of an individual mind rather than with the individual's relationship to society. However, many Marxists value non-realistic, experimental fiction because the fragmentation of experience it represents and
the estrangement the reader often experiences constitute a critique of the
fragmented world and the alienated human beings produced by capitalism in the twentieth century.

To see how form affects our understanding of content (or how form
is a kind of content), let's take another brief look at *Death of a Salesman*.
As we have seen, the play has a strong Marxist component in that it invites us to condemn the capitalist exploitation Willy suffers at the hands
of his employer, and it shows us the contradictions inherent in capitalist
ideology, which promotes the interests of big business at the expense of
the "little man" who has "bought into" capitalist values. However, for
many Marxists, this anti-capitalist theme is severely undermined by the
fact that the play is written in the form of a tragedy. You will recall that
tragedy portrays the ruin of an individual human being due to some
character flaw—usually hubris, or excessive pride—in that individual's
personal make-up. The tragic form of *Death of a Salesman* thus encourages us to focus primarily on the character flaws in Willy as an individual
rather than on the society that helped produce those flaws, and we are
thus led to overlook the negative influence of the capitalist ideology that
is, at bottom, responsible for all the action in the play.

Although Marxists have long disagreed about what kinds of works
are most useful in promoting social awareness and positive political
change, many today believe that even those literary works that reinforce
capitalist, imperialist, or other classist values are useful in that they can
show us how these ideologies work to seduce or coerce us into collusion
with their repressive ideological agendas. Mary Shelley's *Frankenstein*
(1818), for example, may be said to reinforce classist values to the extent
that it portrays those born into the upper classes—for example, Alphonse
Frankenstein, Elizabeth Lavenza, and the De Laceys—as morally and intellectually superior to those below them on the social scale. Characters at
the bottom of the social ladder, on the other hand, are often depicted as
rude, insensitive, and easily incensed to mob behavior. In contrast, Toni
Morrison's *The Bluest Eye* (1970) undermines classist values by illustrating the injustices suffered under the class system imposed by American
capitalism in the early 1940s. In addition, by revealing the ways in which
religion and escapist movies encourage the poor to ignore the harsh realities of their lives, rather than fight for their fair share of the pie, this novel
can be said to have a Marxist agenda.

Some Questions Marxist Critics Ask about Literary Texts

The following questions are offered to summarize Marxist approaches to literature.

1. Does the work reinforce (intentionally or not) capitalist, imperialist, or other classist values? If so, then the work may be said to have a capitalist, imperialist, or classist agenda, and it is the critic's job to expose and condemn this aspect of the work.

2. How might the work be seen as a critique of capitalism, imperialism, or classism? That is, in what ways does the text reveal, and invite us to condemn, oppressive socioeconomic forces (including repressive ideologies)? If a work criticizes or invites us to criticize oppressive socioeconomic forces, then it may be said to have a Marxist agenda.

3. Does the work in some ways support a Marxist agenda but in other ways (perhaps unintentionally) support a capitalist, imperialist, or classist agenda? In other words, is the work ideologically conflicted?

4. How does the literary work reflect (intentionally or not) the socioeconomic conditions of the time in which it was written and/or the time in which it is set, and what do those conditions reveal about the history of class struggle?

5. How might the work be seen as a critique of organized religion? That is, how does religion function, in the text, to keep a character or characters from realizing and resisting socioeconomic oppression?

Depending upon the literary work in question, we might ask one or any combination of these questions. Or we might come up with a useful question of our own not listed here. These are just some starting points to get us thinking about literary works in productive Marxist ways. Remember, not all Marxist critics will interpret the same work in the same way, even if they focus on the same Marxist concepts. As always, even expert practitioners disagree. Our goal is to use Marxist theory to help enrich our reading of literary works, to help us see some important ideas they illustrate that we might not have seen so clearly or so deeply without Marxist theory, and, if we use Marxist theory the way it is intended to be used, to help us see the ways in which ideology blinds us to our own participation in oppressive sociopolitical agendas.

The following Marxist reading of F. Scott Fitzgerald's *The Great Gatsby* is offered as an example of what a Marxist interpretation of that novel might yield. It focuses on what I will argue is the novel's critique of American capitalist ideology. In addition, I will try to show the ways in which the novel fails to push its critique far enough, becoming the unwitting prey of the capitalist ideology it attacks.

You Are What You Own:
A Marxist Reading of *The Great Gatsby*

Written and set during the Post-World-War-I economic boom of the 1920s, F. Scott Fitzgerald's *The Great Gatsby* (1925) can be seen as a chronicle of the American dream at a point in this nation's history when capitalism's promise of economic opportunity for all seemed at its peak of fulfillment. "Get rich quick" schemes abounded, and many of them succeeded, for it was a time when stocks could be bought on a 10 percent margin, which means that a dollar's worth of stocks could be purchased, on credit, for ten cents. So even the "little man" could play the stock market and hope to make his fortune there. We see the tenor of the times in the feverish abandon of Gatsby's party guests—confident that their host's abundance of food and drink, like the nation's resources, will never be depleted—and in Gatsby, himself, whose meteoric rise from the son of "shiftless and unsuccessful farm people" (104; ch. 6) to the proprietor of a "colossal" Long Island mansion with "a marble swimming pool and over forty acres of lawn and garden" (9; ch. 1) seems to embody the infinite possibility offered by the American dream.

The Great Gatsby, however, does not celebrate the heady capitalist culture it portrays but, as a Marxist interpretation of the novel makes especially clear, reveals its dark underbelly. Through its unflattering characterization of those at the top of the economic heap and its trenchant examination of the ways in which the American dream not only fails to fulfill its promise but also contributes to the decay of personal values, Fitzgerald's novel stands as a scathing critique of American capitalist culture and the ideology that promotes it. In addition, we will see how a Marxist perspective shows us the ways in which the novel fails to push its critique of capitalism far enough, falling an unwitting prey to the very ideology it tries to undermine.

One of the most effective ways *The Great Gatsby* criticizes capitalist culture is by showing the debilitating effects of capitalist ideology even on those who are its most successful products, and it does so through its representation of commodification. By definition, a commodity has value not in terms of what it can do (use value) but in terms of the money or other commodities for which it can be traded (exchange value) or in terms of the social status its ownership confers (sign-exchange value). An object becomes a commodity only when it has exchange value or sign-exchange value, and neither form of value is inherent in any object. Both are forms of social value: they are *assigned* to objects by human beings in a given social context. Commodification, then, is the act of relating to persons or things in terms of their exchange value or sign-exchange value to the exclusion of other considerations. Of course, commodification is a necessary function of buying and selling, and thus it is a necessary function of capitalism, which depends for its survival upon buying and selling. However, as the novel illustrates, commodification, especially in the form of sign-exchange value, is not merely a marketplace activity that we can leave at the office when we go home at the end of the day. Rather, it is a psychological attitude that has invaded every domain of our existence.

Nowhere in *The Great Gatsby* is commodification so clearly embodied as in the character of Tom Buchanan. The wealthiest man in the novel, Tom relates to the world only through his money: for him, all things, and all people, are commodities. His marriage to Daisy Fay was certainly an exchange of Daisy's youth, beauty, and social standing for Tom's money and power and the image of strength and stability they imparted to him. Appropriately, the symbol of this "purchase" was the $350,000 string of pearls Tom gave his bride-to-be. Similarly, Tom uses his money and social rank to "purchase" Myrtle Wilson and the numerous other working-class women with whom he has affairs, such as the chambermaid with whom he was involved three months after his marriage to Daisy and the "common but pretty" (112; ch. 6) young woman he picks up at Gatsby's party. Tom's consistent choice of lower-class women can also be understood in terms of his commodified view of human interaction: he "markets" his socioeconomic status where it will put him at the greatest advantage—among women who are most desperate for and most easily awed by what he has to sell.

Of course, Tom's acts of commodification are not limited to his relationships with women. Because capitalism promotes the belief that "you are what you own"—that our value as human beings is only as great as the value of our possessions—much of Tom's pleasure in his expensive possessions is a product of their sign-exchange value, of the social status their ownership confers on him. "I've got a nice place here," he tells Nick, adding, "It belonged to Demaine, the oil man" (12; ch. 1), as if the house's "pedigree" could confer a pedigree on him. We see this same desire to flex his socioeconomic muscles, so to speak, when he toys with George Wilson concerning the mechanic's wish to buy Tom's car in order to sell it at a profit. Given that Tom was born into enormous wealth, apparently more than he could ever spend, why should he need the socioeconomic ego-boost provided by such posturing?

One of the ironies of commodification is that it creates desire even as it fulfills it. Because the sense of self-worth it fosters in us is always derived from external standards, such as fashion trends, we can never rest secure in our possessions: something new and better is always being sold, and others may purchase something we don't have, in which case they will be "better" than we are. In Tom's case, this kind of insecurity is increased by his awareness of a type of social status he can never acquire: the status that comes from being born in the East. Although he inherited his wealth from an established Chicago family—so his money is not "new" in the sense of having been earned during his lifetime—an established Chicago family in the 1920s would not have been considered "old" in the East, where America's "blue-bloods" had lived since their English and Dutch forebears' initial immigration. For Easterners, in the 1920s at least, one of the requirements of old money was that it be earned not only in the past but in the East. To be from the Midwest, regardless of the size or age of one's fortune, was to be a latecomer in the eyes of Easterners.

Having attended Yale, Tom must be, as Fitzgerald was, painfully aware of the Eastern social requirement he can never by birth fulfill. Even if he and Daisy return to Europe or the Midwest, Tom carries the knowledge of his social inferiority inside himself. He therefore seeks a status other than the one he can't have, a status that would declare his indifference to the issue of old money versus new. Thus his vulgarity—his lack of discretion with Myrtle Wilson; his loud, aggressive behavior; his rudeness—can be seen as an attempt to reassure himself that his money and power are all that count, an attempt to show that his wealth insulates him from considerations of class or refinement. The pseudoscientific "intellectualism" Tom adopts in referring Nick to a book he'd read about white civilization—as well as the racism endorsed by his reading—might be seen in this same light. He doesn't need to belong to old money because he belongs to a larger and more important group—the Aryan race: "we've produced all the things that go to make civilization—oh, science and art and all that" (18; ch. 1).

A corollary of Tom's commodification of people is his ability to manipulate them very cold-bloodedly to get what he wants, for
commodification is, by definition, the treatment of objects *and people* as
commodities, as *things* whose only importance lies in their benefit to ourselves. In order to get Myrtle Wilson's sexual favors, he lets her think that
he may marry her someday, that his hesitation is due to Daisy's alleged
Catholicism rather than his own lack of desire. And in order to eliminate
his rival for Daisy's affection, he sacrifices Gatsby to George Wilson,
whom he deliberately sends, armed and crazed, to Gatsby's house without
even telephoning Gatsby to warn him. In addition, Tom's sinister capa-
bilities are hinted at through his familiarity with the underworld in the
person of Walter Chase, who was involved in illegal activities with Gatsby.

While a character such as Tom Buchanan is likely to make us sympa-
thize with anyone who is dependent upon him, Daisy is not merely an
innocent victim of her husband's commodification. In the first place,
Daisy's acceptance of the pearls—and of the marriage to Tom they represent—is, of course, an act of commodification: she wanted Tom's sign-
exchange value as much as he wanted hers. And certainly, Daisy is capable, like Tom, of espousing an idea for the status she thinks it confers
on her, as when she commodifies disaffection in order to impress Nick:

> "You see I think everything's terrible anyhow," she went on in a con-
> vinced way. "Everybody thinks so—the most advanced people. And I
> *know*. I've been everywhere and seen everything and done everything."
> Her eyes flashed around her in a defiant way, rather like Tom's. . . .
>   The instant her voice broke off . . . I felt the basic insincerity of
> what she had said. . . . [I]n a moment she looked at me with an abso-
> lute smirk on her lovely face as if she had asserted her membership in
> a rather distinguished secret society to which she and Tom belonged.
> (21–22; ch. 1)

Even Daisy's extramarital affair with Gatsby, like her earlier romance with
him, is based on a commodified view of life. She would never have become interested in him had she known that Gatsby was not from "much
the same strata as herself . . . fully able to take care of her" (156; ch. 8),
and when she learns the truth during the confrontation scene in the hotel
suite, her interest in him quickly fades. The apparent ease with which she
lets Gatsby take the blame for Myrtle's death, while she beats a hasty retreat with Tom, indicates that her commodification of people, like that of
her husband, facilitates the cold-blooded sacrifice of others to her convenience.

The Buchanans' commodification of their world and the enormous wealth that makes it possible for them to "smas[h] up things and creatures and then retrea[t] back into their money" (187–88; ch. 9) are rendered especially objectionable by the socioeconomic contrast provided by the valley of ashes. People like George and Myrtle Wilson don't stand a chance in a world dominated by people like the Buchanans. The valley of ashes—

> a fantastic farm where ashes grow like wheat into ridges and hills and grotesque gardens, where ashes take the forms of houses and chimneys and rising smoke and finally, with a transcendent effort, of men who move dimly and already crumbling through the powdery air (27; ch. 2)

—is a powerfully chilling image of the life led by those who do not have the socioeconomic resources of the Buchanans. Ashes are what's left over after something is used up or wasted, and, indeed, the area is a literal "dumping ground" where "occasionally a line of grey cars . . . comes to rest, and immediately the ash-grey men swarm up with leaden spades and stir up an impenetrable cloud" (27; ch. 2) as they remove the refuse from the cars. It's obviously a human "dumping ground" as well: aside from the men who remove the trash from the train, there is only "a small block of yellow brick" (28; ch. 2) containing a shop for rent, "an all-night restaurant approached by a trail of ashes" (29; ch. 2), and George Wilson's garage.

It is precisely from settings such as this that the American dream is supposed to emerge, that a shaky but persistent business enterprise is supposed to lead to financial security for oneself and one's children. But the language used to describe this scene makes it clear that this is a land of hopelessness, not of dreams likely to be fulfilled: it is a "grey land," "impenetrable," with "spasms of bleak dust . . . drift[ing] endlessly over it" and "bounded . . . by a small foul river" (27–28; ch. 2). And there are no children here, no emblems of hope for a better future, except for the "grey, scrawny Italian child . . . setting torpedoes [firecrackers] in a row along the railroad track" (30; ch. 2), hardly the embodiment of a promising tomorrow. The only way to survive this hell on earth is to let someone like Tom Buchanan exploit you, as George does when he tolerates Tom's humiliating banter in the hope of getting a good price on Tom's car and as Myrtle does when she accepts Tom's mistreatment in the hope of getting out of the valley of ashes for good. But the only way out of capitalism's "dumping ground," as George and Myrtle both finally learn, is in a coffin.

Even the character who seems, at first, to embody the American dream and the hope capitalism thereby offers to all—even Jay Gatsby—

reveals, upon closer inspection, the hollowness of that dream. In true rags-to-riches style, Gatsby has risen from extreme poverty to extreme wealth in a very few years. His boyhood "schedule," in which he divided his time, in the self-improvement tradition of Benjamin Franklin, among such pursuits as the practice of "elocution" and the study of "needed inventions" (181; ch. 9), resonates strongly with the American dream's image of the self-made man. And even his motive for amassing wealth seems pure: he did it to win the woman he loves. If Gatsby is the novel's representative of the American dream, however, the dream must be a corrupt one, for Gatsby achieves it only through criminal activities, a fact that severely deflates the image of the honest, hardworking man that the dream is supposed to foster. And although Gatsby is certainly more charming than Tom and Daisy, and more sympathetically portrayed by Nick, he commodifies his world just as they do. In fact, one might argue that he commodifies it more.

However much the Buchanans' possessions are important to them in terms of sign-exchange value, they also have use value: we see the couple reclining on their sofas and eating at their tables. In contrast, we are told that the only room Gatsby occupies in his magnificently furnished mansion is his simple bedroom, and the only time we see him there his purpose is to show it to Daisy. He almost never uses his library, pool, or hydroplane himself; and he doesn't drink the alcohol or know most of the guests at his lavish parties. It seems that for Gatsby the sole function of material possessions is sign-exchange value: he wants the image their ownership confers on him and nothing more. Furthermore, Gatsby's commodity signs are almost all empty: his Gothic library filled with uncut (and, therefore, unopened) books, his "*imitation* . . . Hôtel de Ville" with its "spanking new" tower "under a *thin beard* of raw ivy" (9; ch. 1, my italics), and his photo of himself at Oxford are all surfaces without interiors, all images without substance. It seems fitting, then, that he acquired them in order to acquire the ultimate image of sign-exchange value he wants to possess: Daisy.

Possession of Daisy would give Gatsby what he really wants: a permanent sign that he belongs to her socioeconomic class, to the same bright, spotless, airy, carefree world of the very rich that Daisy embodied for him when they first met. For Gatsby, her presence gave the house in which she lived a feeling of "breathless intensity,"

> a hint of bedrooms upstairs more beautiful and cool than other bedrooms, of gay and radiant activities taking place through its corri-

dors and of romances that were . . . redolent of this year's shining
motor-cars and of dances whose flowers were scarcely withered. (155–
56; ch. 8)

Possession of Daisy, the ultimate commodity sign, would, in Gatsby's
eyes, "launder" his "new money" and make it "old," would make his
"spanking new" imitation Hôtel de Ville an ancestral seat. Thus, in accu-
mulating material goods in order to win Daisy, he accumulated one kind
of commodity sign in order to acquire another.

Gatsby's commodification of his world is linked, like Tom's, to the
cold-blooded aggression with which he pursues what he wants. The lap of
luxury in which Gatsby lives does not exist in a vacuum. It is supported
by a very dark and sinister world of corruption, crime, and death. The
underworld activities from which his wealth derives include bootlegging
and the selling of fraudulent bonds. This is the underworld of Meyer
Wolfshiem, who has such unlimited criminal connections that he was
able to "fix" the 1919 World Series. And this is the man who takes credit
for giving Gatsby his start.

We get a glimpse of this world in the "villainous" looking servants
(119; ch. 7) Wolfshiem sends to work for Gatsby and in the phone calls
Gatsby receives (and which, after Gatsby's death, Nick receives by accident) from obvious criminal sources. This is a world of predators and
prey in which illegal—and thus often imperfect—liquor is sold over the
counter to anyone with the money to pay for it and in which fake bonds
are passed in small towns to unsuspecting investors. Some of the people
who buy the liquor may become ill from it; some may die. All of the small
investors who buy the fraudulent bonds will lose money that they can't
afford to lose. And when the inevitable mistakes are made and the law
steps in, someone will have to be sacrificed as Gatsby sacrifices Walter
Chase.

Even the protagonist's desire for Daisy is informed by an underworld
perspective. When Gatsby first courted Daisy at her parents' home in
Louisville, he "let her believe that he was a person from much the same
strata as herself" when, in fact, "he had no comfortable family standing
behind him and he was liable at the whim of an impersonal government
to be blown anywhere about the world" (156; ch. 8):

However glorious might be his future . . . he was at present a penniless young [soldier] without a past, and at any moment the invisible
cloak of his uniform might slip from his shoulders. So he made the

most of his time. He took what he could get, ravenously and unscrupulously—eventually he took Daisy one still October night, took her
because he had no real right to touch her hand. (156; ch. 8)

This language—"He took what he could get, ravenously and unscrupulously"—is hardly the language of love. Rather, it is the kind of language that
would be used to describe a hoodlum, the kind of language that resonates
strongly with Gatsby's dubious association with Dan Cody before meeting
Daisy and with his criminal activities subsequent to their initial affair.

Thus Gatsby is not exempt from the novel's unflattering portrait of
the wealthy. Indeed, his characterization suggests that the American
dream does not offer a moral alternative to the commodified world of the
Buchanans but produces the same commodification of people and things
as does Tom and Daisy's inherited wealth. The Great Gatsby's representation of American culture, then, reveals the debilitating effects of capitalism on socioeconomic "winners" such as Tom, Daisy, and Gatsby, as well
as on "losers" such as George and Myrtle.

Operating against The Great Gatsby's powerful critique of capitalism
is the novel's subtle reinforcement of capitalism's repressive ideology.
This counter-movement operates in three ways. First, the unflattering
portraits of George and Myrtle Wilson deflect our attention from their
victimization by the capitalist system in which they both struggle to survive. Second, because Nick is seduced by the American dream Gatsby represents, his narrative romanticizes the protagonist, obscuring the ways in
which Jimmy Gatz's investment in the dream produced the amoral Jay
Gatsby. Third, the lush language used to describe the world of the wealthy
makes it attractive despite people like the Buchanans who populate it.

Perhaps The Great Gatsby's most obvious flaw, from a Marxist perspective, is its unsympathetic rendering of George and Myrtle Wilson, the
novel's representatives of the lower class. George and Myrtle try to improve their lot the only way they know how. George clings to his founder-
ing business, and Myrtle, in a sense, tries to start one of her own by marketing the only commodity she has in stock: she "rents" her body to Tom
Buchanan, hoping he'll want someday to "purchase" it by marrying her.
They are victims of capitalism because the only way to succeed in a capitalist economy is to succeed in a market, and, as neither George nor
Myrtle succeed in the only markets open to them, they are condemned to
the valley of ashes. Their characterizations, however, are so negative that
it is easy to overlook the socioeconomic realities that control their lives.
Indeed, one might argue that George and Myrtle are negative stereotypes

of a lower-class couple: he's not very bright; she's loud, obnoxious, and overtly sexual. We may feel sorry for George, but our sympathy is undercut by his personal failings. That is, instead of feeling sorry (or angry at the system) that he is a victim of class oppression, we feel sorry (or angry at him) that he doesn't have what it takes to "pull himself up by his bootstraps" and better himself, as the American dream tells us he should: we blame the victim instead of the system that victimizes him. Similarly, Myrtle's cruel rejection of George and brazen pursuit of Tom make her an easy target for our disapproval: our awareness of Myrtle's severely limited options is dimmed by the very fact that she does her best to use them.

In a more subtle manner, the novel is flawed, from a Marxist perspective, by Nick's romanticization of Gatsby. Nick may like to think he disapproves of Jay Gatsby—because he knows he *should* disapprove of him for the same reasons he disapproves of the Buchanans—but it is clear from the beginning that the narrator is charmed by him. As Nick tells us, "There was something gorgeous about him, some heightened sensitivity to the promises of life. . . . [I]t was an extraordinary gift for hope, a romantic readiness such as I have never found in any other person and which it is not likely I shall ever find again" (6; ch. 1).

This idealization is foregrounded in Nick's narrative through his focus on romantic images of Gatsby: the rebellious boy, the ambitious young roughneck, the idealistic dreamer, the devoted lover, the brave soldier, the lavish host. Gatsby's criminal connections are acknowledged, but because of Nick's response to them, they don't influence his opinion of the man. For example, Nick's manner of discussing Gatsby's criminal life tends to deflect attention away from the moral implications of Gatsby's underworld activities, as when Nick reports the following conversation he overheard at one of Gatsby's parties: "'He's a bootlegger,' said the young ladies, moving somewhere between his cocktails and his flowers" (65; ch. 4). The rhetoric of this phrase is typical of Nick's defense of Gatsby against his detractors, even when those detractors are right: his statement focuses on Gatsby's generosity and on the willingness to abuse it of those who gossip about him, thereby sidestepping the fact that "his cocktails and his flowers" weren't rightfully his at all: they were purchased with funds obtained from his criminal activities.

Similarly, Nick influences our reaction to Gatsby by his own emotional investment in those events that show Gatsby in a good light. For example, when Gatsby, confronted by Tom, admits in front of everyone that his Oxford experience was provided by a government arrangement for American soldiers who remained in Europe after World War I, Nick

"wanted to get up and slap him on the back" (136; ch. 7). This small concession to reality on Gatsby's part elicits in Nick a renewal "of complete
faith in him" (136; ch. 7). Despite what Nick knows about the underworld
sources of Gatsby's wealth, despite the "unaffected scorn" Nick says he has
for Gatsby's world, Gatsby himself is "exempt" from Nick's disapproba-
tion: "Gatsby turned out all right at the end; it is what preyed on Gatsby,
what foul dust floated in the wake of his dreams" (6; ch. 1) that elicits
Nick's disaffection—and that of many readers. It is easy to be influenced
by the warmth of Nick's feelings because these feelings so strongly inform
the portrait he paints. Following Nick's lead, and typical of the response
of many literary critics to the title character, Tom Burnam says that
Gatsby "survives sound and whole in character, uncorrupted by the corruption which surrounded him" (105), and Rose Adrienne Gallo believes
that Gatsby "maintained his innocence" to the end (43).[1]

Why should Nick deceive himself, and us, about Gatsby? Why should
he foreground all the positive, likable qualities in Gatsby's personality and
shift responsibility for the unpleasant ones onto others' shoulders? I think
it is because the narrator is, himself, seduced by Gatsby's dream. At the
age of thirty, and still being financed by his father while he tries to figure
out what he should do with himself, it is not surprising that Nick wants to
believe life still holds promise because he is afraid that it doesn't. He fears
that all he has to look forward to is, as he puts it, "a thinning list of single
men to know, a thinning brief-case of enthusiasm, thinning hair" (143;
ch. 7). With his summer in New York—his latest in a series of adventures—having ended in disaster, he wants to believe in the possibility of
hope. Nick believes in Gatsby because he wants to believe that Gatsby's
dream can come true for himself: that a young man at loose ends can
make the kind of outrageous financial success of himself that Gatsby has
made, can find the woman of his dreams, and can be so optimistic about
the future. Nick doesn't want to be reminded that Gatsby's glittering
world rests on corruption because he wants that kind of hopeful world
for himself. He is in collusion with Gatsby's desire, and his narrative can
lead readers into collusion with that desire as well.

The appeal to readers of Gatsby's desire to belong to the magical world
of the wealthy—as Andrew Dillon puts it, "Gatsby has possessed what the
reader must also desire: the orgiastic present" (61)—is also a testimonial to
the power of the commodity. Gatsby may not make the best use of his mansion, his hydroplane, his swimming pool, and his library, but many of us
might feel that *we* certainly would. Thus another flaw in the novel, from a
Marxist perspective, is the way in which the commodity's appeal is power-

fully reinforced for the reader by the lush language used to describe this world of leisure and luxury. Consumer goods are invested with magic—with the capacity to transform reality—which suggests that the commodity is *itself* transcendent, beyond earthly limitation. Even the refreshments at Gatsby's parties, for example, seem enchanted: a "tray of cocktails *floated* at us through the twilight" (47; ch. 3, my italics), and on "buffet tables, garnished with glistening hors-d'oeuvre, spiced baked hams crowded against salads of *harlequin* designs and pastry pigs and turkeys *bewitched* to a dark gold" (44; ch. 3, my italics).

The commodity is especially compelling in the following description of the Buchanans' home on East Egg:

> Their house was . . . a cheerful red and white Georgian Colonial mansion overlooking the bay. The lawn started at the beach and ran toward the front door for a quarter of a mile, jumping over sun-dials and brick walks and burning gardens—finally when it reached the house drifting up the side in bright vines as though from the momentum of its run. The front was broken by a line of French windows, glowing now with reflected gold, and wide open to the warm windy afternoon. . . .
>
> [T]he front vista . . . [included] in its sweep a sunken Italian garden, a half acre of deep pungent roses and a snub-nosed motor boat that bumped the tide off shore. . . .
>
> We walked through a high hallway into a bright rosy-colored space, fragilely bound into the house by French windows at either end. . . . A breeze blew through the room, blew curtains in at one end and out the other like pale flags, twisting them up toward the frosted wedding cake of the ceiling—and then rippled over the wine-colored rug, making a shadow on it as wind does on the sea. (11–12; ch. 1)

This passage is a delicious appeal to every one of the five senses, with language so sensual that the house seems to breathe with a life of its own. This setting thus has an existence independent of the characters who inhabit it: the estate doesn't need Tom and Daisy in order to be gorgeous; it was gorgeous before Tom bought it, and it will be gorgeous after the Buchanans are gone. In fact, we could easily, and happily, imagine this place without its occupants. That is, the setting is bigger than the Buchanans—it contains and exceeds them. They neither use it up nor exhaust its possibilities. And it is impervious to their corruption: we are not led to associate the place with the events that occur there. Therefore, it can exert a magnetic appeal on many readers. As much as Fitzgerald is the critic of capitalism, he is also its poet laureate, and his poetry can attract readers to the very thing that, on a more overt level, the novel condemns.

While *The Great Gatsby* offers a significant critique of capitalist ideology, it also repackages and markets that ideology anew. This double movement of the text gives the closing line a special irony: if we do "beat on, boats against the current, borne back ceaselessly into the past" (189; ch. 9), there is in this novel that which strengthens the back-flow, bearing us ceaselessly back under capitalism's spell. In the end, Gatsby fails to realize the American dream, but because the novel falls prey to the capitalist ideology it condemns, many readers will continue to invest in it.

Questions for Further Practice: Marxist Approaches to Other Literary Works

The following questions are intended as models. They can help you use Marxist criticism to interpret the literary works to which they refer or other texts of your choice.

1. How is the rigid class structure evident in William Faulkner's "A Rose for Emily" (1931) responsible for much of the story's action and characterization? Would you say the story does or does not invite us to criticize the classism it represents?

2. What can we learn from Toni Cade Bambara's "The Lesson" (1972) about conspicuous consumption and commodification? How does the story use its representation of these capitalist realities to criticize class oppression?

3. How does John Steinbeck's *The Grapes of Wrath* (1939) qualify as a Marxist critique of American capitalism? How does the novel's form (realism) support that critique? How does the ending of the film version (which is flawed, from a Marxist perspective) undermine the more realistic ending of the novel?

4. Describe the class system operating in the lives of the characters in Kate Chopin's "The Storm" (1898). In what ways does the story fail to criticize, and fail to invite us to criticize, the classism it depicts?

5. How does Langston Hughes' "On the Road" (1952) qualify as a Marxist critique of organized religion?

For Further Reading

All of the following works will help you develop your skills as Marxist critics. Texts listed under "Category I" are written in language accessible to most beginners. Texts listed under "Category II" employ more technical language but are well worth the extra effort that may be required of some students new to the field.

Category I

Eagleton, Terry. *Marxism and Literary Criticism*. Berkeley: U of California P, 1976.
Horkheimer, Max, and Theodor Adorno. *Dialectic of Enlightenment*. 1944. Trans. John Cumming. New York: Continuum, 1982. (See, especially, "The Culture Industry," 120–67.)
Marx, Karl. *Capital: A Critique of Political Economy*. 1867. New York: International Publishers, 1967.
———. *Economic and Philosophic Manuscripts of 1844*. New York: International Publishers, 1964.
Veblen, Thorstein. *The Theory of the Leisure Class: An Economic Study of Institutions*, 1899. New York: Mentor-NAL, 1953.
Weber, Max. *The Protestant Ethic and the Spirit of Capitalism*. New York: Scribner, 1958.
Williams, Raymond. *Marxism and Literature*. Oxford: Oxford UP, 1977.

Category II

Althusser, Louis. *Lenin and Philosophy and Other Essays*. Trans. Ben Brewster. New York: Monthly Review, 1971. (See, especially, "Ideology and Ideological State Apparatuses," 127–86.)
Baudrillard, Jean. *For a Critique of the Political Economy of the Sign*. 1972. Trans. Charles Levin. St. Louis: Telos, 1981.
Benjamin, Walter. *Illuminations*. Trans. Harry Zohn. Ed. Hannah Arendt. New York: Harcourt, Brace and World, 1955.
Bennett, Tony. *Formalism and Marxism*. London: Methuen, 1979. 93–175.
Habermas, Jürgen. *The Philosophical Discourse of Modernity*. Trans. Frederick Lawrence. Cambridge: MIT, 1987.
Jameson, Fredric. *The Political Unconscious: Narrative as a Socially Symbolic Act*. Ithaca: Cornell UP, 1981.
Laclau, Ernesto, and Chantal Mouffe. *Hegemony and Socialist Strategy: Towards a Radical Democratic Politics*. London: Verso, 1985.
Lukács, Georg. *History and Class Consciousness*. 1923. Trans. Rodney Livingstone. Cambridge, Massachusetts: MIT P, 1971.
Macherey, Pierre. *A Theory of Literary Production*. Trans. G. Wall. London: Routledge and Kegan Paul, 1978.
Žižek, Slavoj. *The Sublime Object of Ideology*. London: Verso, 1989.

Notes

1. For similar views of Gatsby, see, for example, Bewley, Cartwright, Chase, Dillon, Hart, Le Vot, Moore, Nash, Stern, and Trilling.

Works Cited

Bewley, Marius. "Scott Fitzgerald's Criticism of America." *Sewanee Review* 62 (1954): 223–46. Rpt. in *Modern Critical Interpretations: F. Scott Fitzgerald's* The Great Gatsby. Ed. Harold Bloom. New York: Chelsea, 1986. 11–27.

Burnham, Tom. "The Eyes of Dr. Eckleburg: A Re-Examination of *The Great Gatsby.*" *College English* 13 (1952). Rpt. in *F. Scott Fitzgerald: A Collection of Critical Essays*. Ed. Arthur Mizener. Englewood Cliffs: Prentice-Hall, 1963. 104–11.

Cartwright, Kent. "Nick Carraway as Unreliable Narrator." *Papers on Language and Literature* 20.2 (1984): 218–32.

Chase, Richard. "*The Great Gatsby.*" *The American Novel and Its Traditions*. New York: Doubleday, 1957. 162–67. Rpt. in The Great Gatsby: *A Study*. Ed. Frederick J. Hoffman. New York: Scribner's, 1962. 297–302.

Dillon, Andrew. "*The Great Gatsby*: The Vitality of Illusion." *Arizona Quarterly* 44.1 (1988): 49–61.

Gallo, Rose Adrienne. *F. Scott Fitzgerald*. New York: Ungar, 1978.

Hart, Jeffrey. "'Out of it ere night': The WASP Gentleman as Cultural Ideal." *New Criterion* 7.5 (1989): 27–34.

Le Vot, André. *F. Scott Fitzgerald: A Biography*. Trans. William Byron. Garden City, New York: Doubleday, 1983.

Moore, Benita A. *Escape into a Labyrinth: F. Scott Fitzgerald, Catholic Sensibility, and the American Way*. New York: Garland, 1988.

Nash, Charles C. "From West Egg to Short Hills: The Decline of the Pastoral Ideal from *The Great Gatsby* to Philip Roth's *Goodbye, Columbus.*" *Philological Association* 13 (1988): 22–27.

Stern, Milton R. *The Golden Moment: The Novels of F. Scott Fitzgerald*. Urbana: U of Illinois P, 1970.

Trilling, Lionel. "F. Scott Fitzgerald." *The Liberal Imagination*. New York: Viking, 1950. 243–54. Rpt. in The Great Gatsby: *A Study*. Ed. Frederick J. Hoffman. New York: Scribner's, 1962. 232–43.

CHAPTER 4

Feminist Criticism

"I'm not a feminist—I like men!"

"I'm not a feminist—I think women should be able to stay at home and raise children if they want to!"

"I'm not a feminist—I wear a bra!"

Contrary to the opinions of many students new to the study of feminist literary criticism, many feminists like men, think that women should be able to stay at home and raise children if they want to do so, and wear bras. Broadly defined, feminist criticism examines the ways in which literature (and other cultural productions) reinforce or undermine the economic, political, social, and psychological oppression of women. However, just as the practitioners of all critical theories do, feminist critics hold many different opinions on all of the issues their discipline examines. In fact, some feminists call their field *feminisms* in order to underscore the multiplicity of points of view of its adherents and offer ways of thinking that oppose the traditional tendency to believe there is a single best point of view. Yet many of us who are new to the study of feminist theory, both male and female, have decided ahead of time that we are not feminists because we don't share whatever feminist point of view we have found the most objectionable. In other words, before we even come to the theory classroom, many of us have reduced feminism to whatever we consider its most objectionable element and, on that basis, have rejected it. This attitude reveals, I think, the oversimplified, negative view of feminism that still persists in American culture today. For it is from the culture at large—the home, the workplace, the media, and so on—that we have gathered the anti-feminist bias we sometimes bring into the classroom.

To see how this negative oversimplification works to blind us to the seriousness of the issues feminism raises, let's briefly examine one of the most maligned feminist claims: that we should not use the masculine pronoun *he* to represent both men and women. For many people, this claim suggests what they see as the trivial, even infantile, nature of feminist demands. What possible difference could it make if we continue to use the "inclusive *he*" to refer to members of both sexes? We know what we mean when we do it: it's simply a convention of language that includes both males and females. Such people believe that feminists should just concentrate on getting women an equal crack at the dough and forget all this nonsense about pronouns! For many feminists, however, the use of the pronoun *he* to refer to members of both sexes reflects and perpetuates a "habit of seeing," a way of looking at life, that uses male experience as the standard by which the experience of both sexes is evaluated. In other words, although the "inclusive *he*" claims to represent both men and women, in reality it is part of a deeply-rooted cultural attitude that ignores women's experiences and blinds us to women's points of view. The damaging effects of this attitude can be seen in a number of areas.

For example, before the centuries-old struggle for women's equality finally emerged in literary studies in the late 1960s, the literary works of (white) male authors describing experience from a (white) male point of view was considered the standard of universality—that is, representative of the experience of all readers—and universality was considered a major criterion of greatness. Because the works of (white) female authors (and of all authors of color) do not describe experience from a (white) male point of view, they were not considered universal and hence did not become part of the literary canon. It is interesting to note that popularity was not necessarily considered evidence of universality, for many women writers who enjoyed widespread fame during their lives were not "canonized" in literary histories, which focused primarily on male writers. Of course, those holding up this standard of greatness did not believe they were being unfairly discriminatory; they simply believed that they were rejecting literary texts that were not universal, that were not great. Even when (white) women authors began to appear more frequently in the canon and on college syllabi in the mid–1970s, they were not represented on an equal basis with (white) male authors.

Even today, unless the critical or historical point of view is feminist, there is a tendency to under-represent the contribution of women writers. For example, in Matthew J. Bruccoli's preface to the 1992 Scribner's edition of *The Great Gatsby*, he notes that the 1920s was "an age of achievement . . . in American literature" (x) and lists the names of twelve authors to support his claim. Only one of those authors—Willa Cather—is a woman. What about Ellen Glasgow, Susan Glaspell, Nella Larsen, Edna St. Vincent Millay, Rolla Lynn Riggs, Gertrude Stein, Djuna Barnes, Elizabeth Maddox Roberts, H. D. (Hilda Doolittle), or Marianne Moore? That many students probably recognize only a few of these names illustrates the marginalization of many women writers by literary history, though not necessarily by the reading public at the time they wrote. Similarly, in most Hollywood films, even today, the camera eye (the point of view from which the film is shot) is male: the female characters, not the male, are the objects gazed upon by the camera and often eroticized as if a male eye were viewing them, as if the point of view of the "universal" movie-goer were male.

Perhaps the most chilling example of the damaging effects of this "habit of seeing" is found in the world of modern medicine, where drugs prescribed for both sexes often have been tested on male subjects only. In other words, in laboratory tests to determine the safety of prescription drugs before marketing them, men's responses frequently have been used to gather statistical data on the medications' effectiveness and possible side-effects. As a result, women may experience unexpected side-effects while male users are unaffected. How could medical scientists not have anticipated this problem? Surely, the cultural habit of seeing male experience as universal played a role.

Traditional Gender Roles

I offer the above examples up front because I think they show some of the ways in which all of us have been programmed to see—or to be blind—myself included. I consider myself a recovering patriarchal woman. By *patriarchal woman* I mean, of course, a woman who has internalized the norms and values of *patriarchy*, which can be defined, in short, as any culture that privileges men by promoting traditional gender roles. *Traditional gender roles* cast men as rational, strong, protective, and decisive; they cast women as emotional (irrational), weak, nurturing, and submissive. These gender roles have been used very successfully to justify such inequities, which still occur today, as excluding women from equal access to leadership and decision-making positions (in the family as well as in politics, academia, and the corporate world), paying men higher wages than women for doing the same job (if women are even able to obtain the job), and convincing women that they are not fit for careers in such areas as mathematics and engineering. Many people today believe such inequities are a thing of the past because anti-discriminatory laws have been passed, such as the law that guarantees women equal pay for equal work. However, these laws are frequently side-stepped. For example, an employer can pay a woman less for performing the same work as a man (or more work than a man) simply by giving her a different job title. So women still are paid only about seventy cents for every dollar earned by men.

Patriarchy is thus, by definition, *sexist*, which means it promotes the belief that women are innately inferior to men. This belief in the inborn inferiority of women is called *biological essentialism* because it is based on biological differences between the sexes that are considered part of our unchanging essence as men and women. A striking illustration is the word *hysteria*, which derives from the Greek word for womb (*hystera*) and refers to psychological disorders deemed peculiar to women and characterized by over-emotional, extremely irrational behavior. Feminists don't deny the biological differences between men and women; in fact, many feminists celebrate those differences. But they don't agree that such differences as physical size, shape, and body chemistry make men naturally superior to women: for example, more intelligent, more logical, more courageous, or better leaders. Feminism therefore distinguishes between the word *sex*, which refers to our biological constitution as female or male, and the word *gender*, which refers to our cultural programming as feminine or masculine, which are categories created by society rather than by nature.

The belief that men are superior to women has been used, feminists have observed, to justify and maintain the male monopoly of positions of economic, political, and social power, in other words, to keep women powerless by denying them the educational and occupational means of acquiring economic, political, and social power. That is, the inferior position long occupied by women in patriarchal society has been culturally, not biologically, produced. For example, it is a patriarchal assumption, rather than a fact, that more women than men suffer from hysteria. But because it has been defined as a female problem, hysterical behavior in men won't be diagnosed as such. Instead, it will be ignored or given another, less damaging name, for example, shortness of temper. Of course, not all men accept patriarchal ideology, and those who don't—those who don't believe, for example, that because men generally have been endowed by nature with stronger muscles, they have been endowed with any other natural superiority—are often derided, by both patriarchal men and women, as weak and unmanly, as if the only way to be a man were to be a patriarchal man.

I call myself a patriarchal woman because I was socially programmed, as are most women and men, *not* to see the ways in which women are oppressed by traditional gender roles. I say that I'm recovering because I learned to recognize and resist that programming. For me, such recognition and resistance will always require effort—I'm recovering rather than recovered—not just because I internalized patriarchal programming years ago but because that program continues to assert itself in my world: in movies, television shows, books, magazines, and advertisements as well as in the attitudes of salespeople who think I can't learn to operate a simple machine, repair technicians who assume I won't know if they've done a shoddy job, and male drivers who believe I'm flattered by sexual offers shouted from passing cars (or, worse, who don't give a moment's thought to how I might feel or, worse yet, who hope I feel intimidated so that they can feel powerful). The point here is fairly simple: patriarchy continually exerts forces that undermine women's self-confidence and assertiveness, then points to the absence of these qualities as proof that women are naturally, and therefore correctly, self-effacing and submissive.

To cite a similar example of patriarchal programming, little girls have been (and some still are) told early in their educational careers that they can't do math. If not told so explicitly in words (by parents, teachers, or friends), they are told so by the body language, tone of voice, and facial expression of adults and peers. Because it is often assumed that little girls can't do math and, furthermore, that their deficiency doesn't really matter because most of them won't need math in later life, girls are not called upon by the teacher as frequently as boys to perform mathematical operations. In fact, girls are often "rewarded" for failing at math: they receive ready sympathy, coddling, and other debilitating though enticing payoffs for being feminine. If girls manage to do well in math despite these obstacles, they are considered exceptions to the rule (which, from a child's point of view, usually means they are considered "freaks"). In short, girls are programmed to fail. Then the patriarchal mind-set points to girls' lower test scores in math and their failure to become math majors as proof that they are biologically ill-suited to mathematical studies, which, given the close relationship between math and logic, suggests that females are less logical than males. In other words, patriarchy creates the failure which it then uses to justify its assumptions about women.

Because I'm a recovering patriarchal woman, I am also very aware of the ways in which patriarchal gender roles are destructive for men as well as women. For example, because traditional gender roles dictate that men are supposed to be strong (physically powerful and emotionally stoic), they are not supposed to cry because crying is considered a sign of weakness, a sign that one has been overpowered by one's emotions. For similar reasons, it is considered unmanly for men to show fear or pain or to express their sympathy for other men. Expressing sympathy (or any loving feeling) for other men is especially taboo because patriarchy assumes that only the most mute and stoic (or boisterous and boyish) forms of male bonding are free of homosexual overtones. In addition, men are not permitted to fail at anything they try because failure in any domain implies failure in one's manhood.

Failure to provide adequate economic support for one's family is considered the most humiliating failure a man can experience because it means that he has failed at what is considered his biological role as provider. The imperative for men to succeed economically has become an extremely pressurized situation in contemporary America because the degree of success men are expected to achieve keeps increasing: to be a "real" man in this day and age one must have a more expensive house and car than one's father, siblings, and friends, and one must send one's children to a more expensive school. If men can't achieve the unrealistic economic goals set for them in contemporary America, then they must increase the signs of their manhood in some other area: they must be the most sexually active (or make others believe that they are) or be able to hold the most liquor or display the most anger. It is not surprising, in this context, that anger and other violent emotions are the only emotions permitted, even encouraged, in men, for anger is a very effective means of blocking out fear and pain, which are not permitted, and anger usually produces the kind of aggressive behaviors associated with manhood.

I refer to male programming, at this point, for two reasons, both of which reflect my personal feminist biases. I want the men reading this chapter to see in feminism the potential for learning a good deal about themselves as well as about women. And I want readers of both genders to see that, even when we think we're talking about men, we're also talking about women because, in a patriarchy, everything that concerns men usually implies something (usually negative) about women. For example, it is important to note that all the behaviors described in the preceding two paragraphs—behaviors forbidden to men—are considered "woman-ish," that is, inferior, beneath the dignity of manhood. Men, and even little boys, who cry are called "sissies." *Sissy* sounds very much like *sister*, and it means "cowardly" or "feminine," two words which, in this context, are synonyms. Clearly, one of the most devastating verbal attacks to which a man can be subjected is to be compared to a woman. Thus, being a "real" man in patriarchal culture requires that one hold feminine quali-ties in contempt. Homosexuality is included on the list of "feminine" be-haviors, at least for American men, because despite the plentiful example of very masculine homosexual men, the American stereotype of the ho-mosexual male is an extremely feminine one. This phenomenon implies that whenever patriarchy wants to undermine a behavior, it portrays that behavior as feminine. It is important to note, too, that the patriarchal concept of femininity—which is linked to frailty, modesty, and timid-ity—disempowers women in the real world: it is not feminine to succeed in business, to be extremely intelligent, to earn big bucks, to have strong opinions, to have a healthy appetite (for anything), or to assert one's rights.

To briefly illustrate the debilitating effects of patriarchal gender roles on both women and men, consider the story of "Cinderella." Feminists have long been aware that the role of Cinderella, which patriarchy im-poses upon the imagination of young girls, is a destructive role because it equates femininity with submission, encouraging women to tolerate fa-milial abuse, wait patiently to be rescued by a man, and view marriage as the only desirable reward for "right" conduct. By the same token, how-ever, the role of Prince Charming—which requires men to be wealthy res-cuers responsible for making their women happy "ever after"—is a de-structive role for men because it promotes the belief that men must be unflagging super-providers without emotional needs.

Unfortunately, the notion of a feminist critique of fairy tales has been the target of mockery by social commentators who offer absurdly humor-ous and what they claim are politically correct versions of classic fairy tales in order to show us the allegedly ridiculous extremes to which femi-nists and other "malcontents" would lead us. However, feminist readings of fairy tales can, in fact, provide a wonderful means for illustrating the ways in which patriarchal ideology informs what appear to be even the most innocent of our activities. Consider, for example, the similarities among the ever popular "Snow White and the Seven Dwarfs," "Sleeping Beauty," and, of course, "Cinderella." In all three tales, a beautiful, sweet young girl (for females must be beautiful, sweet, and young if they are to

be worthy of romantic admiration) is rescued (for she is incapable of res-
cuing herself) from a dire situation by a dashing young man who carries
her off to marry him and live happily ever after. The plot thus implies that
marriage to the right man is a guarantee of happiness and the proper reward for a right-minded young woman. In all three tales, the main female
characters are stereotyped as either "good girls" (gentle, submissive, virginal, angelic) or "bad girls" (violent, aggressive, worldly, monstrous).
These characterizations imply that if a woman does not accept her patriarchal gender role, then the only role left her is that of a monster. In all
three tales, the "bad girls"—the wicked queen in "Snow White," the
wicked fairy in "Sleeping Beauty," and the wicked stepmother and stepsis-
ters in "Cinderella"—are also vain, petty, and jealous, infuriated because
they are not as beautiful as the main character or, in the case of the
wicked fairy, because she wasn't invited to a royal celebration. Such motivations imply that even when women are evil, their concerns are trivial.
In two of the stories, the young maiden is awakened from a death-like
slumber by the potent (after all, it brings her to life) kiss of the would-be
lover. This ending implies that the proper patriarchal young woman is
sexually dormant until "awakened" by the man who claims her. We could
analyze these tales further, and we could analyze additional tales, but the
point here is to see how pervasive patriarchal ideology is and how it can
program us without our knowledge or consent.

I refer in the above paragraph to "good girls" and "bad girls," and this
concept deserves more attention because it's another way in which sexist
ideology continues to influence us. As we saw above, patriarchal ideology
suggests that there are only two identities a woman can have. If she accepts her traditional gender role and obeys the patriarchal rules, she's a
"good girl"; if she doesn't, she's a "bad girl." These two roles—also referred to as "madonna" and "whore" or "angel" and "bitch"—view women
only in terms of how they relate to the patriarchal order. Of course, how
"good girls" and "bad girls" are specifically defined will alter somewhat
according to the time and place in which they live. But it is patriarchy that
will do the defining because both roles are projections of patriarchal male
desire: for example, the desire to own "valuable" women suited to be
wives and mothers, the desire to control women's sexuality so that men's
sexuality cannot be threatened in any way, and the desire to dominate in
all financial matters. This last desire is well served by the patriarchal ideology that deems certain kinds of work improper for "good girls," an ideology that forced many women writers in Victorian England to publish
their work under male pseudonyms and that required women writers on

both sides of the Atlantic to accommodate their art to patriarchal expectations or face the consequences (as Kate Chopin did at the turn of the twentieth century when her work was buried due to its feminist content, not to be reprinted until it was rediscovered by feminists in the late 1960s).

According to a patriarchal ideology in full force through the 1950s, versions of which are still with us today, "bad girls" violate patriarchal sexual norms in some way: they're sexually forward in appearance or behavior, or they have multiple sexual partners. Men sleep with "bad girls," but they don't marry them. "Bad girls" are used and then discarded because they don't deserve better, and they probably don't even expect better. They're not good enough to bear a man's name or his legitimate children. That role is appropriate only for a properly submissive "good girl." The "good girl" is rewarded for her "good" behavior by being placed on a pedestal by patriarchal culture. To her are attributed all the virtues associated with patriarchal femininity and domesticity: she's modest, unassuming, self-sacrificing, and nurturing. She has no needs of her own, for she is completely satisfied by serving her family. At times, she may be sad about the problems of others, and she frequently worries about those in her care—but she is never angry. For Victorian culture in England she was the "angel in the house." She made the home a safe haven for her husband, where he could spiritually fortify himself before resuming the daily struggles of the workplace, and for her children, where they could receive the moral guidance needed to eventually assume their own traditional roles in the adult world.

What's wrong with being placed on a pedestal? For one thing, pedestals are small and leave a woman very little room to do anything but fulfill the prescribed role. For example, to remain on her Victorian pedestal, the "good girl" had to remain uninterested in sexual activity, except for the purpose of legitimate procreation, because it was believed unnatural for women to have sexual desire. In fact, "good" women were expected to find sex frightening or disgusting. For another thing, pedestals are shaky. One can easily fall off a pedestal, and when a woman does, she is often punished. At best, she suffers self-recrimination for her inadequacy or "unnaturalness." At worst, she suffers physical punishment from the community or from her husband, which until relatively recently was encouraged by law and custom and which is still too often tacitly condoned by an ineffectual or complicit justice system.

In upwardly mobile middle-class American culture today, the woman on the pedestal is the woman who successfully juggles a career and a family, which means she looks great at the office and over the breakfast table, and she's never too tired after work to fix dinner, clean house, attend to all her children's needs, and please her husband in bed. In other words, patriarchal gender roles have not been eliminated by modern women's entrance into the male-dominated workplace, even if some of those women now hold what used to be traditionally male jobs. For many of those same women are still bound by patriarchal gender roles in the home, which they must now fulfill in addition to their career goals.

Furthermore, the persistence of repressive attitudes toward women's sexuality is still visible in our language today. For example, we use the negative word *slut* to describe a woman who sleeps with a number of men while we use the positive word *stud* to describe a man who sleeps with a number of women. And though women's fashions have radically changed since the nineteenth century, the most "feminine" clothing still promotes patriarchal ideology. For example, the extremely tight corsets worn by nineteenth-century women prevented them from getting enough oxygen to be physically active or to experience emotion without getting "the vapors": shortness of breath or slight fits of fainting, which were considered very feminine and proved that women were too fragile and emotional to participate in a man's world. Analogously, one of the most "feminine" styles of clothing for today's woman is the tight skirt and high heels, which create a kind of "feminine" walk (while precluding running) symbolically akin both to the restrained physical capability imposed by nineteenth-century women's clothing and to the male sexual access to women's bodies such attire allows.

A Summary of Feminist Premises

So far, we've been examining how patriarchal ideology works to keep women and men in traditional gender roles and thereby maintain male dominance. That patriarchal ideology functions in this way is a belief shared by all feminists even if they disagree about other issues. In fact, feminists share several important assumptions, which might be summarized as follows.

1. Women are oppressed by patriarchy economically, politically, socially, and psychologically; patriarchal ideology is the primary means by which they are kept so.
2. In every domain where patriarchy reigns, woman is *other*: she is marginalized, defined only by her difference from male norms

and values, which means defined by what she (allegedly) lacks that men (allegedly) have.

3. All of western (Anglo-European) civilization is deeply rooted in patriarchal ideology, as we see, for example, in the biblical portrayal of Eve as the origin of sin and death in the world (not to mention the rest of the female crew of "good girls" and "bad girls" that populates the bible); the numerous patriarchal women and female monsters of Greek and Roman literature and mythology; the representation of woman as a non-rational creature by traditional Western philosophy; and the reliance on *phallogocentric* thinking (thinking that is male oriented in its vocabulary, rules of logic, and criteria for what is considered objective knowledge) by educational, political, legal, and business institutions. As we saw earlier, even the development of the Western canon of great literature, including traditional fairy tales, was a product of patriarchal ideology.

4. While biology determines our sex (male or female), culture determines our gender (masculine or feminine). That is, for most English speaking feminists, the word *gender* refers not to our anatomy but to our behavior as socially programmed men and women. I behave "like a woman" (for example, submissively) not because it is natural for me to do so but because I was taught to do so. In fact, all the traits we associate with masculine and feminine behavior are learned, not inborn.

5. All feminist activity, including feminist theory and literary criticism, has as its ultimate goal to change the world by promoting gender equality. Thus, all feminist activity can be seen as a form of *activism*, although the word is usually applied to feminist activity that directly promotes social change through political activity such as public demonstrations, boycotts, voter education and registration, the provision of hot-lines for rape victims and shelters for abused women, and the like. Although frequently falsely portrayed in opposition to "family values," feminists continue to lead the struggle for better family policies such as nutrition and health care for mothers and children; parental leave; and high-quality, affordable day care.

6. Gender issues play a part in every aspect of human production and experience, including the production and experience of literature, whether we are consciously aware of these issues or not.

Of course, the assumptions listed above are related, overlapping ideas, and, together, they imply that patriarchal ideology has a pervasive, deeply rooted influence on the way we think, speak, see ourselves, and view the world in which we live. The pervasiveness of patriarchal ideology raises some important questions for feminist theory. For example, if patriarchal ideology influences our identity and experience so strongly, how can we ever get beyond it? If our modes of thinking and our language are patriarchal, how can we ever think or speak differently? In other words, if the fabric of our existence is patriarchal, how can we ever become non-patriarchal?

Getting Beyond Patriarchy

Feminists have long puzzled over the problem of getting beyond patriarchal programming and have offered many different solutions. For example, French feminists, who generally have focused more strongly than British and American feminists on the philosophical dimension of women's issues, have suggested that women (and men) may maintain a connection to their pre-verbal relationships with their mothers and that this connection generates a capacity for a kind of writing (*écriture féminine*) and thinking that is different from patriarchal modes of writing and thinking. Patriarchal modes generally require prescribed, "correct" methods of organization, rationalist rules of logic (logic that stays "above the neck," relying on narrow definitions of cognitive experience and discrediting many kinds of emotional and intuitive experience), and linear thinking (x precedes y, which precedes z). In contrast, *écriture féminine* is fluidly organized and freely associative. Thus, it has the capacity to both reflect and create human experience beyond the control of patriarchy. Such writing can be found, for example, in Toni Morrison's *Beloved*, Virginia Woolf's *Mrs. Dalloway*, James Joyce's *Ulysses*, and William Faulkner's *Absalom, Absalom!*

Another way to deal with our apparent entrapment within patriarchal ideology is to consider the possibility that no ideology succeeds in fully programming all of the people all of the time. Every ideology has points of self-contradiction, of illogic, that permit us to understand its operations and decrease its influence, for example, as Mary Wollstonecraft did in 1792 when she wrote *A Vindication of the Rights of Woman*, as Virginia Woolf did in 1929 when she wrote *A Room of One's Own*, as Simone de Beauvoir did in 1949 when she wrote *The Second Sex*, and as feminist theorists continue to do today. Perhaps the difficulty in theorizing our way out of patriarchal ideology arises when we think of our immersion in it as an all-or-nothing situation: if we're not completely beyond patriarchy, then we must be completely programmed by it. I think it might be more useful to look at our relationship to patriarchal ideology as a dynamic situation: we must constantly struggle to understand and resist the various ways in which patriarchy dictates our lives, although we can't always see all the ways in which it does so. Individually and collectively, we will move forward in some areas even as we remain static or backslide in others, but we must continue to move forward—to understand and resist patriarchal ideology—wherever and whenever we can.

Given the difficulties involved in resisting patriarchal programming, many feminist theorists and literary critics believe we should be especially cautious about using frameworks that are themselves patriarchal, such as psychoanalysis and Marxism. Such frameworks are considered patriarchal because they embody various elements of patriarchal ideology. For example, because he used male experience as the standard against which he measured female experience, Freud believed that women suffer from what he called "penis envy" and that they tend to see their first-born sons as "penis substitutes" to make up for their own lack. Despite Marx's insights into the ways in which economic forces determine the lives of both genders, he failed to realize the ways in which women have been oppressed by men no matter what their economic class.

Nevertheless, many feminists draw on elements of psychoanalytic and Marxist theory as well as other critical theories because they find them useful in examining issues relevant to women's experience. For example, psychoanalysis can be used to help us understand the psychological effects of patriarchal ideology as well as how and why women and men internalize it. Marxism can be used to help us understand how economic forces have been manipulated by patriarchal law and custom to keep women economically, politically, and socially oppressed as an underclass. Structuralist principles can be used to study similarities in the experience and production of women from various cultures as well as similarities in the ways they are oppressed. And deconstruction can be used to find the ways in which a literary work covertly reinforces the patriarchal ideology it criticizes, which some feminist literary critics were doing in America before the theory of deconstruction reached American shores.

Deconstruction is also useful to feminists in helping us see the ways in which patriarchal ideology is often based on the false opposition of categories. For example, in refuting the sexist belief that men are naturally rational while women are naturally emotional, a feminist might do more than argue, for example, that women have been programmed to be more emotional or that both categories apply equally to both genders. Using deconstructive principles, she might argue that we are mistaken to separate the rational and the emotional into such diametrically opposed categories. Aren't our rational reasons for subscribing to a particular philosophical view or theoretical framework based, consciously or unconsciously, on how that viewpoint or framework makes us feel? Don't the rational and the emotional, properly understood, often work in tandem in our lives?

To my mind, one of feminism's strengths is the freedom with which it borrows ideas from other theories and adapts them to its own rapidly evolving needs. This is one reason why I believe that feminist theory will never become stale: it constantly incorporates new ideas from other fields and finds new ways to use old ideas. This is also why feminism can be seen as an interdisciplinary theory that can help us learn to make connections among seemingly divergent schools of thought. While all of the theories addressed in this book overlap with one another in various ways, few acknowledge that fact or use it to broaden or deepen their theoretical explorations to the extent that feminism does.

Of course, the question of how we can get beyond any ideology that dominates the way we think is a question relevant to any theory that purports to be new, which means it's a question relevant to all theories, though few directly address it. In fact, many of the unsolvable theoretical problems that feminist thinkers continue to engage are unsolvable problems for every theory, though these problems either remain unacknowledged by practitioners in those fields or are considered solved by earlier thinkers. For example, related to the problem of the possibility (or impossibility) of getting beyond any ideology that dominates the way we think is the problem of one's own *subjectivity*: one's own selfhood, the way one views oneself and others, which develops from one's own individual experiences. Given that we can't be aware of all the ways in which our own subjectivity determines how we interpret the world, how can we ever know that our speculations about human experience, or about anything else for that matter, are anything but an expression of our own subjectivity?

As we'll see in subsequent chapters, deconstruction and new historicism engage this problem, but most of the other theories do not directly address it. For feminism, as for deconstruction and new historicism, all perception, therefore all acts of interpretation, are unavoidably subjective.

We cannot leave ourselves out of the picture when describing what we see because what we see is a product of who we are: our gender, our politics, our religion, our race, our socioeconomic class, our sexual orientation, our education, our family background, our problems, our strengths, our weaknesses, our theoretical framework, and so on. To claim that we are objective, as patriarchy encourages men to do, is merely to blind ourselves to the ways in which we are not so.

From a feminist perspective, when we interpret texts, or anything else, the way to deal with our subjectivity is not to try to avoid it but to be as aware of it as possible, to include it in our interpretation as fully as possible, so that others will be able to take it into account when evaluating our viewpoint. This is why it's especially appropriate that I refer in this chapter, as you may have noticed, to my own experience and biases. My experience as a middle-aged, middle-class, heterosexual, white American woman with a Ph.D. in English and a lovingly dysfunctional family is bound to affect my interpretation of feminism as well as the feminist reading of *The Great Gatsby* I offer at the end of this chapter. Unavoidably, I'll see some things differently from other theorists and literary critics, and many of those differences can probably be accounted for by differences in the personal data I listed above. By knowing a little bit about me, it is hoped that my readers will be on the lookout for the ways in which my point of view is just that: what I see from where I'm standing.

Multicultural Feminism

Awareness of one's own subjectivity has become especially important as white, middle-class, heterosexual feminists, who have always held the most visible positions of leadership in women's movements in America, are finally recognizing the ways in which their policies and practices have reflected their own experiences while ignoring the experiences of women of color, lesbians, and poor, undereducated women both in America and throughout the world. While all women are subject to patriarchal oppression, each woman's specific needs, desires, and problems are greatly shaped by her race, socioeconomic class, sexual orientation, educational experience, religion, and nationality.

For one thing, patriarchy operates differently in different countries: there are significant differences between patriarchy in the United States and patriarchy in, say, India, Mexico, or Iran. Furthermore, even within the borders of a single country, cultural differences affect women's experience of patriarchy. In the United States, for example, the experience of patriarchy for women of color is inseparable from their experience of racism (see Chapter Eleven); lesbians' experience of patriarchy is inseparable from their experience of heterosexism (see Chapter Ten); poor women's experience of patriarchy is inseparable from their experience of classism (see Chapter Three); and so forth. And you can imagine the complex operations of oppression in the lives of women who belong to three or more of these categories. Therefore, the promotion of *sisterhood*—psychological and political bonding among women based on the recognition of common experiences and goals—must include respect for and attention to individual differences among women as well as an equitable distribution of power among various cultural groups within feminist leadership.

African American feminists have been especially helpful in revealing the political and theoretical limitations inherent in white mainstream feminists' neglect of cultural experience different from their own. For example, black feminists have analyzed the ways in which gender oppression cannot be understood apart from racial oppression. A black woman is oppressed by patriarchy, black feminists observe, not just because she's a woman but because she's a black woman, a category that has been defined historically in America as less valuable than the white woman. The Victorian ideal of the "true woman" as submissive, fragile, and sexually pure, which still influences patriarchal thinking today, excluded by definition black women and poor women of all races, whose survival demanded hard physical labor and who were vulnerable to rape and to sexual exploitation in the workplace. The logic was circular and deadly: a woman whose racial or economic situation forced her into hard labor and made her the victim of sexual predators was defined as unwomanly and therefore unworthy of protection from those who exploited her. This view was widely held by men, both white and black, and by white women as well. Black women, therefore, were in a double bind. They could expect neither gender solidarity from white women nor racial solidarity from black men, the two groups on whom they should have been able to count for help.

Unfortunately, this dilemma persists today. White mainstream feminism, while it has tended to marginalize black women because of their race, nevertheless encourages them to prioritize gender issues over racial issues, arguing that black women are oppressed more by sexism than by racism. At the same time, the black male community, while it has tended to marginalize black women because of their gender, nevertheless encourages them to prioritize racial issues over gender issues, arguing that black women are oppressed more by racism than by sexism. As Lorraine Bethel observes, an understanding of this double oppression forms the basis of African American feminist criticism:

> Black feminist literary criticism offers a framework for identifying the common socio-aesthetic problems of authors who attempt to fashion a literature of cultural identity in the midst of racial/sexual oppression. It incorporates a political analysis that enables us to comprehend and appreciate the incredible achievements Black women . . . made in establishing artistic and literary traditions of any sort, and to understand their qualities and sensibilities. Such understanding requires a consciousness of the oppression these artists faced daily in a society full of institutionalized and violent hatred for both their Black skins and their female bodies. Developing and maintaining this consciousness is a basic tenet of Black feminism. (178)

On the other hand, some black women feel that feminism is a divisive force in the black community. As a result, some have either abandoned feminism or sought ways to reconcile it with the concerns of the black community, as Alice Walker did when she called herself a *"womanist"* (xi) because she works for the survival and wholeness of her people, men and women both, and for the promotion of dialogue and community as well as for the valorization of women and of all the varieties of work women perform. Similarly, as Carolyn Denard points out, many African American women "advocate what may be called ethnic cultural feminism" (172), which is "concerned more with the particular female cultural values of their own ethnic group rather than with those of women in general" (171). Drawing on the novels of Toni Morrison to illustrate this approach, Denard explains that ethnic cultural feminism acknowledges the damaging effects of sexism on women of color, both inside and outside their ethnic community, but it "does not advocate as a solution to their oppression [a] . . . political feminism that alienates black women from their ethnic group" (172). Furthermore, ethnic cultural feminism "celebrat[es] the unique feminine cultural values that black women have developed in spite of and often because of their oppression" (172).

Whatever theoretical preferences black feminist critics bring to their analyses of literature, their interpretations often demonstrate the importance of understanding gender issues in cultural context. Given that some cultural groups have their own categories of literary criticism and that some women may find their concerns addressed in more than one category, it might be useful to pause here and note what those categories are.

Depending on its theoretical orientation, literary criticism that addresses women's issues may fall under one or more different headings. Among them are feminist criticism, African American criticism (which studies, among other things, works by African Americans within the context of African American experience, history, and literary traditions), lesbian criticism, Marxist criticism, and post-colonial criticism (which studies, among other things, works that have emerged from cultures that developed in response to colonial domination, for example, works by writers from India, which was controlled by Britain until 1947). Of course, women's issues will also be addressed in any literary criticism that focuses on women writers from a particular ethnic group: for example, to name a few we haven't mentioned, Chicanas, Latinas, Native American women, and Asian American women. Although all of these categories may address women's experience, generally speaking it is only when a feminist perspective helps guide the interpretation that a piece of criticism is referred to as feminist. Clearly, these categories easily overlap, and it is not unusual to find literary critics who consider themselves hybrids of a sort, for example, Marxist-feminist or lesbian-feminist-Chicana critics.

Of course, there are many more feminist issues than the ones discussed in this chapter. And as in every field, there is a great deal of disagreement among feminist theorists and literary critics concerning, for example, how (and how much) women are programmed by patriarchal ideology, whether or not there is a distinctive way of writing that might be called feminine, whether or not the work of female writers should be interpreted along different lines than that of male writers, and as we have just seen, the ways in which various cultural factors intersect with gender in creating women's experience. Our purpose here is merely to introduce you to the main ideas, the general principles you need to know in order to read feminist theorists and literary critics with some understanding of the issues they raise.

Feminism and Literature

Naturally, some literary works will lend themselves more readily than others to feminist analysis or at least to certain kinds of feminist analysis. For students new to the field, I think it useful to examine the ways in which literary texts reinforce patriarchy because the ability to see when and how patriarchal ideology operates is crucial to our ability to resist it in our own lives. This approach, applied to literary works in the male canon, was the dominant mode of feminist literary analysis in America during the 1970s, and it usually requires reading "against the grain" of the text's apparent intention, for patriarchal literature is usually unconscious of the sexist ideology it promotes, or perhaps more precisely, patriarchal literature sees nothing wrong with its own sexism.

A feminist analysis of the patriarchal ideology operating in Arthur Miller's *Death of a Salesman* (1949), for example, might examine three related areas: (1) the ways in which the female characters (Biff's and Happy's various "conquests," the woman Willy meets in the Boston hotel room, and Linda Loman) function as tokens of male status; (2) the ways in which the "good-girl"/"bad-girl" view of women validates the Loman men's sexism; and (3) the ways in which Linda Loman has internalized patriarchal ideology. A feminist reading would also note that the play reinforces patriarchal ideology through its sympathetic portrayal of Willy and apparent approval of Linda's support for his patriarchal attitude. Such a reading would also relate the play's patriarchal ideology to the period in which it was written and is set: Post-World-War-II America. This was a time when American patriarchy was attempting to counteract the wartime freedom of women who took on the jobs and family responsibilities of their absent men by re-establishing the belief that "the (good) woman's place is in the home."

Of course, it is also important to be able to recognize when a literary work depicts patriarchal ideology in order to criticize it or invite us to criticize it. For example, a feminist reading of Toni Morrison's *The Bluest Eye* (1970) might examine the ways in which the novel invites us to criticize the sexist behaviors and attitudes it portrays. A striking illustration of the novel's insight into patriarchal psychology is its depiction of women as the site upon which men's pain and anger are displaced, a memorable example of which we see in the young Cholly's hatred of Darlene, upon whom he displaces his hatred of the white hunters who humiliate them. In addition, the novel's feminist agenda is revealed in its appreciation of strong women—such as Aunt Jimmy, M'Dear, and Mrs. MacTeer—and of the importance of sisterhood to women's survival. *The Bluest Eye* also shows us how gender issues intersect with race, for Cholly's hatred of Darlene is a direct result of the black youngster's powerlessness in the face of the white hunters' racism, and the importance of sisterhood to women's survival becomes especially acute when the women are victims of the combined forces of sexism and racism.

Finally, many literary works have a conflicted response to patriarchal ideology, as we see, for example, in Mary Shelley's *Frankenstein* (1818).

On the one hand, the text undermines patriarchy's belief in female weakness through its portrayal of women's strength: Caroline is the sole financial and moral support of her ruined father; Justine bears up bravely and nobly under the community's unjust condemnation of her, which includes the penalty of death; and Safie defies her patriarchal father and successfully undertakes a dangerous journey in pursuit of her own goals. The Monster, too, can be read as an indirect advocate for women's rights. In many ways, the monster occupies the woman's position in eighteenth-century European society: it is considered inferior to men and therefore denied the rights and comforts men enjoy. Nevertheless, it acquires an education on its own, is clearly very intelligent and articulate, and wants only to be accepted as an equal member of the human family, to which it will willingly contribute its share (as we see it do when it anonymously helps the De Lacey family).

On the other hand, the novel reinforces patriarchal ideology through its admiration of the way in which Caroline, Elizabeth, Justine, and Agatha conform to traditional gender roles. Three of these "madonnas" devote themselves to nurturing others to the point, whether they realize it or not, of sacrificing their lives for them. Caroline dies as a dutiful mother, tending Elizabeth; Justine dies as a dutiful servant and surrogate mother, when it should be Victor who dies; and Elizabeth dies as a dutiful wife and surrogate mother, trusting her husband's judgement and catering to his needs, when, again, it should be Victor who dies. Even Safie's independent behavior is in service of the traditional woman's desire to secure herself a husband. In addition, the novel does not seem to invite us to criticize the *misogyny* (hatred of women) or *gynophobia* (fear and loathing of women as sexual and reproductive beings) clearly evident in Victor's murderous rage against the female monster and more subtly suggested by his prolonged avoidance of Elizabeth. This reading of *Frankenstein* might also examine the ways in which the novel's conflicted response to patriarchal ideology is reflected in Mary Shelley's own conflicts concerning her personal experience of patriarchy: for example, she was an ardent admirer of the anti-patriarchal essays of her late mother, Mary Wollstonecraft; she violated patriarchal values when she eloped with a married man, Percy Shelley; yet she seemed extremely dependent upon, even submissive to, her husband.

Because feminist issues range so widely across cultural, social, political, and psychological categories, feminist literary criticism is wide ranging, too. Whatever kind of analysis is undertaken, however, the ultimate goal of feminist criticism is to increase our understanding of women's experience, both in the past and present, and promote our appreciation of women's value in the world.

Some Questions Feminist Critics Ask about Literary Texts

The questions that follow are offered to summarize feminist approaches to literature. Approaches that attempt to develop a specifically female framework for the analysis of women's writing (such as #4 and #5 below) are often referred to as *gynocriticism*.

1. What does the work reveal about the operations (economically, politically, socially, or psychologically) of patriarchy? How are women portrayed? How do these portrayals relate to the gender issues of the period in which the novel was written or is set? In other words, does the work reinforce or undermine patriarchal ideology? (In the first case, we might say that the text has a patriarchal agenda. In the second case, we might say that the text has a feminist agenda. Texts that seem to both reinforce and undermine patriarchal ideology might be said to be ideologically conflicted).

2. What does the work imply about the possibilities of sisterhood as a mode of resisting patriarchy and/or about the ways in which women's situations in the world—economic, political, social, or psychological—might be improved?

3. What does the work suggest about the ways in which race, class, and/or other cultural factors intersect with gender in producing women's experience?

4. What does the work suggest about women's creativity? In order to answer this question, biographical data about the author and historical data about the culture in which she lived will be required.

5. What might an examination of the author's style contribute to the ongoing efforts to delineate a specifically feminine form of writing (*écriture féminine*)?

6. What does the history of the work's reception by the public and by the critics tell us about the operations of patriarchy? Has the literary work been ignored or neglected in the past? Why? Or, if

recognized in the past, is the work ignored or neglected now?
Why?

7. What role does the work play in terms of women's literary history
   and literary tradition?

Depending upon the literary work in question, we might ask one or
any combination of these questions. Or we might come up with a useful
question not listed here. These are just some starting points to get us
thinking about literary works in productive feminist ways. Keep in mind
that not all feminist critics will interpret the same work in the same way
even if they focus on the same feminist concepts. As in every field, even
expert practitioners disagree. Our goal is to use feminist theory to help
enrich our reading of literary works; to help us see some important ideas
they illustrate that we might not have seen so clearly or so deeply without
feminist theory; and to help us see the ways in which patriarchal ideology
blinds us to our own participation in, or at least complicity with, sexist
agendas.

The following feminist reading of F. Scott Fitzgerald's *The Great
Gatsby* is offered as an example of what a feminist interpretation of that
novel might yield. It focuses on what I will argue is the novel's sexist
agenda as revealed through the text's characterizations of women, the
ideological content of which should be fairly easy for you to see at this
point. In addition, I will situate the novel's patriarchal ideology in terms
of the changing role of American women during the 1920s because most
feminists have come to realize the importance of seeing how specific historical circumstances foster particular ideologies. The historical component of my argument is not complex, however, but rather draws on historical information with which most of you are probably somewhat
familiar.

"...next they'll throw everything overboard...": A Feminist Reading of *The Great Gatsby*

In a sudden panic over his discovery that his wife has taken a lover, Tom
Buchanan, from F. Scott Fitzgerald's *The Great Gatsby* (1925), exclaims,
"Nowadays people begin by sneering at family life and family institutions
and next they'll throw everything overboard and have intermarriage between black and white" (137; ch. 7). In addition to Tom's double standard

for his own and his wife's behavior (as well as his racism), this statement reveals Tom's assumptions that the moral structure of society rests on the stability of the patriarchal family and that the stability of the patriarchal family rests on the conformity of women to patriarchal gender roles. Of course, through the vehicle of Nick Carraway's narration, the novel clearly ridicules Tom's position: "Flushed with his impassioned gibberish," Nick observes, "[Tom] saw himself standing alone on the last barrier of civilization" (137; ch. 7). Nevertheless, I think it can be shown that *The Great Gatsby* also shares Tom's view of patriarchal gender roles.

The novel was written and is set in the decade following World War I, which ended in November 1918. The Roaring Twenties, or the Jazz Age, a term coined by Fitzgerald, was a period of enormous social change in America, especially in the area of women's rights. Before World War I, American women did not enjoy universal suffrage. In 1920, two years after the end of the war (and after seventy-two years of organized political agitation), they were finally given the vote. Before the war, standard dress for women included long skirts, tightly-laced corsets, high-buttoned shoes, and long hair demurely swept up onto the head. A few years after the war, skirts became shorter (in some cases, much shorter), laced corsets began to disappear (indeed, the most bold and unconventional young women wore few, if any, restraining undergarments), modern footwear frequently replaced high-buttoned shoes, and "bobbed" hair (cut short and worn loosely) became the fashion for young women.

Perhaps most alarming for proponents of the old ways, women's behavior began to change. Women could now be seen smoking and drinking (despite Prohibition), often in the company of men and without chaperons. They could also be seen enjoying the sometimes raucous night life offered at night clubs and private parties. Even the new dances of the era, which seemed wild and overtly sexual to many, bespoke an attitude of free self-expression and unrestrained enjoyment. In other words, as we often see during times of social change, a "Modern Woman" emerged in the 1920s. And, again as usual, her appearance on the scene evoked a good deal of negative reaction from conservative members of society, both male and female, who felt, as they generally do at these times, that women's rejection of any aspect of their traditional role inevitably results in the destruction of the family and the moral decline of society as a whole.

This view of women as the standard-bearers of traditional values, whose presence as non-wage-earning supervisors of hearth and home was deemed necessary to maintain the moral structure of society, became the dominant patriarchal ideology of the industrialized nineteenth century as the home ceased to be the place where the family worked together to earn their living and men went off to earn the family bread at various occupations in the towns. That is, as women's economic role in the home disappeared, a spiritualized domestic role was created for her in order to keep her, among other things, from competing with men on the job market. Thus, although most Americans believed the survival of America's moral structure depended on traditional gender roles, it was really the nation's economic structure, which gave economic dominance to men, that depended upon the axiom, "a woman's place is in the home." Of course, another advantage of keeping women at home, modestly dressed and quietly behaved, was that it reaffirmed men's ownership of women's sexual and reproductive capacities. The threat posed by the Modern Woman of the 1920s, then, had repercussions on many levels of public consciousness.

Literary works often reflect the ideological conflicts of their culture, whether or not it is their intention to do so, because, like the rest of us, authors are influenced by the ideological tenor of the times. Even a writer like F. Scott Fitzgerald, who cut a dashing figure among the avant-garde social set of the 1920s and who was himself married to a Modern Woman, was subject to the ideological conflicts that characterized his age. One might speculate that it was precisely his experience of "life in the fast lane" that created some (conscious or unconscious) misgivings about the changes occurring in America during the 1920s. Or one might speculate that he was able to accept the Modern Woman only as long as he could view her as psychologically troubled and in need of his help, a situation illustrated in his semi-autobiographical novel, *Tender Is the Night* (1934), as well as in his turbulent life with his wife Zelda. However, it's not my intention to examine Fitzgerald's life but to examine the ways in which *The Great Gatsby*, his most enduring work, embodies its culture's discomfort with the Post-World-War-I Modern Woman.

We see this discomfort in the novel's representation of its minor female characters, and we see it in more complex ways in the novel's characterizations of Daisy Buchanan, Jordan Baker, and Myrtle Wilson, who, despite their numerous differences, are all versions of the Modern Woman. We can assume that Nick's descriptions of these characters represent the novel's ideological biases, and not merely his own, because the text portrays Nick sympathetically, unlike Tom Buchanan. In addition to the sympathy Nick evokes by the author's use of first-person narration—because we see the narrative events through Nick's eyes, we are able to more or less "walk in his shoes"—Nick also gains our sympathy because he tells his story in a sensitive and engaging manner, sharing with the reader his personal feelings: his desires, dislikes, fears, doubts, and affections. Finally, as the only character who is consistently aware of ethical considerations, Nick functions as the moral center of the novel. It is therefore reasonable to conclude that, whether or not Fitzgerald intended Carraway as a reliable narrator, many readers will be strongly influenced by Nick's perspective.

The novel abounds in minor female characters whose dress and activities identify them as incarnations of the Modern Woman, and they are portrayed as clones of a single, negative character type: shallow, exhibitionist, revolting, and deceitful. For example, at Gatsby's parties we see insincere, "enthusiastic meetings between women who never knew each other's names" (44; ch. 3), as well as numerous narcissistic attention-seekers in various stages of drunken hysteria. We meet, for example, a young woman who "dumps" down a cocktail "for courage" and "dances out alone on the canvass to perform" (45; ch. 3); "a rowdy little girl who gave way upon the slightest provocation to uncontrollable laughter" (51; ch. 3); a drunken woman who "was not only singing, she was weeping too," her face lined with "black rivulets" created when her "tears . . . came into contact with her heavily beaded eyelashes" (55–56; ch. 3); a drunken young girl who has her "head stuck in a pool" (113; ch. 6) to stop her from screaming; and two drunken young wives who refuse to leave the party until their husbands, tired of the women's verbal abuse, "lifted [them] kicking into the night" (57; ch. 3). Then there are Benny McClenahan's "four girls":

> They were never quite the same ones in physical person but they were so identical one with another that it inevitably seemed they had been there before. I have forgotten their names—Jaqueline, I think, or else Consuela or Gloria or Judy or June, and their last names were either the melodious names of flowers and months or the sterner ones of the great American capitalists whose cousins, if pressed, they would confess themselves to be. (67; ch. 4)

In other words, all of these look-alike women who accompanied McClenahan to Gatsby's parties invented names and biographies for themselves to impress their new acquaintances. We should not be too surprised, then, to hear Nick say, "Dishonesty in a woman is a thing you never blame deeply" (63; ch. 3), implying that women don't seem able to help it: perhaps it's just a natural failing, like so many other feminine weaknesses.

The only minor female characters we get to know a little better, both of whom fit the category of the Modern Woman, are Mrs. McKee—who is described as "shrill, languid, handsome, and horrible" (34; ch. 2)—and Myrtle's sister Catherine, who perfectly fits the negative stereotype outlined above. The novel gives Catherine a good deal of attention for such a minor character, perhaps because she has been chosen to represent the physical unattractiveness of her type, which is only hinted at in the descriptions of the other minor female characters.

> The sister . . . was a slender, worldly girl of about thirty with a solid sticky bob of red hair and a complexion powdered milky white. Her eyebrows had been plucked and then drawn on again at a more rakish angle but the efforts of nature toward the restoration of the old alignment gave a blurred air to her face. When she moved about there was an incessant clicking as innumerable pottery bracelets jingled up and down upon her arms. She came in with such proprietary haste and looked around so possessively at the furniture that I wondered if she lived here. But when I asked her she laughed immoderately, repeated my question aloud and told me she lived with a girl friend at a hotel. (34; ch. 2)

This is the description of a rather revolting, loud, vulgar young woman whose opening words to Nick are an obvious lie. And Catherine fulfills the expectations such a description raises by the vulgar nature of her conversation with Nick concerning Myrtle and her "sweetie" (39; ch. 2) and by her claim that she doesn't drink, which we learn is a lie when she turns up drunk at George Wilson's garage the night of Myrtle's death. Her vulgarity, as well as her foolishness, is further revealed in her description of her and her girlfriend's experience in Monte Carlo: "We had over twelve hundred dollars when we started but we got gypped out of it all in two days in the private rooms. We had an awful time getting back, I can tell you. God, how I hated that town!" (38; ch. 2).

One could argue that the novel's bias here is not sexist, but classist, for all the women described above belong to the lower socioeconomic strata of society. However, there are several male characters from these same strata who are described sympathetically. For example, George Wilson is portrayed as a simple, hardworking man who, despite his other limitations, is devoted to his wife. Mr. Michaelis, who owns a coffee shop in the Valley of Ashes, is kind to George and tries to take care of him after Myrtle's death. And even the two party-going husbands mentioned earlier, themselves sober, tolerate their wives' drunken abuse with admirable patience. Thus it is these women's violation of patriarchal gender roles, not their socioeconomic class, that elicits the novel's condemnation.

The novel's discomfort with the Modern Woman becomes evident, in a more complex fashion, in the characterizations of Daisy, Jordan, and Myrtle. Despite their striking differences in class, occupation, marital status, personal appearance, and personality traits, these three characters are all versions of the Modern Woman. Like the minor female characters who embody the Modern Woman in appearance and social freedom, Daisy, Jordan, and Myrtle look and act their part. Their hair and clothing are very modern, and they don't feel, as their mothers and grandmothers surely did, that they must behave modestly in public by avoiding hard liquor, cigarettes, and immodest dancing. In addition, all three women display a good deal of modern independence. Only two are married, and they don't keep their marital unhappiness a secret, although secrecy about such matters is one of the cardinal rules of patriarchal marriage. Jordan has a career of her own, and on top of that, it's in the male-dominated field of professional golf. They all prefer the excitement of night life to the more traditional employments of hearth and home. There is only one child among them, Daisy's daughter Pammy, and while Pammy is well looked after by her nurse and affectionately treated by her mother, Daisy's life does not revolve exclusively around her maternal role. Finally, all three women violate patriarchal sexual taboos: Jordan engages in premarital sex, and Daisy and Myrtle are engaged in extramarital affairs.

That the novel finds this freedom unacceptable in women is evident in its unsympathetic portrayals of those who exercise it. Daisy Buchanan is characterized as a spoiled brat and a remorseless killer. She is so used to being the center of attention that she can think of no one's needs but her own. Although Myrtle's death is accidental, Daisy doesn't stop the car and try to help the injured woman. On the contrary, she speeds off and lets Gatsby take the blame. (One can't help but wonder if some readers, at least in decades past, have said to themselves, "See what happens when you let a woman get behind the wheel of a car?") Once she learns that Gatsby doesn't come from the same social stratum as herself, she retreats behind the protection of Tom's wealth and power, abandoning her lover to whatever fate awaits him. Indeed, much of our condemnation of Daisy issues from her failure to deserve Gatsby's devotion. Although she lets Gatsby believe she will leave her husband for him, Nick observes during the confrontation scene in the New York hotel room that "[h]er eyes fell on Jordan and me with a sort of appeal, as though she . . . had never, all along, intended doing anything at all" (139; ch. 7). Even her way of speaking is frequently so affected—"I'm p-paralyzed with happiness" (13; ch. 1); "You remind me of a—of a rose, an absolute rose" (19; ch. 1); and "Bles-sed precious. . . . Come to your own mother that loves you" (123; ch. 7)—as to make it difficult to take anything she says seriously. Thus, on top of all her other sins, she's a phony.

Jordan Baker is characterized as a liar and a cheat. Nick catches her lying about having left a borrowed car out in the rain with its top down, and apparently she was caught cheating during a golf tournament, though she managed to get away with it under circumstances that imply the use of bribery or coercion: "The thing approached the proportions of a scandal—then died away. A caddy retracted his statement and the only other witness admitted that he might have been mistaken" (62–63; ch. 3). Like Daisy, she exhibits a lack of concern for others that manifests itself in a refusal to take responsibility for herself, as we see when Nick reports that she drove her car "so close to some workmen that our fender flicked a button on one man's coat" (63; ch. 3). Her response to Nick's admonition that she should drive more carefully or not drive at all is a careless remark that "They'll [other people will] keep out of my way. . . . It takes two to make an accident" (63; ch. 3). When Nick says, "Suppose you met somebody just as careless as yourself" (63; ch. 3), Jordan's manipulativeness is revealed in her response: "I hope I never will. . . . I hate careless people. That's why I like you" (63; ch. 3). And her manipulation works: "for a moment I thought I loved her," Nick admits (63; ch. 3). Of course, the fact that Jordan must cheat to succeed at golf also implies that women can't succeed in a man's field purely on their own ability. And her physical description completes the stereotype that women who invade the male domain are rather masculine: "She was a slender, small-breasted girl with an erect carriage which she accentuated by throwing her body backward at the shoulders like a young cadet" (15; ch. 1). The word most frequently used to describe her appearance is *jaunty*. In other words, Jordan looks like a boy.

Surely, the most unsympathetic characterization of the three is that of Myrtle Wilson. She's loud, obnoxious, and phony, as we see in her "violently affected" (35; ch. 2) behavior at the party in the small flat Tom keeps for their rendezvous. She cheats on George, who is devoted to her—so she doesn't even have the excuse Daisy has of an unfaithful husband—and she bullies and humiliates him as well. She has neither the youth nor the beauty of Daisy and Jordan: "She was in the middle thirties, and faintly stout. . . . Her face . . . contained no facet or gleam of beauty"

(29–30; ch. 2). And unlike the other two women, she is overtly sexual: "[S]he carried her surplus flesh sensuously" (29; ch. 2), and "there was an immediately perceptible vitality about her as if the nerves of her body were continually smouldering" (30; ch. 2). In addition, she's much more sexually aggressive than Daisy or Jordan. When Tom and Nick show up unexpectedly at Wilson's Garage,

> [s]he smiled slowly and walking through her husband as if he were a ghost shook hands with Tom, looking him flush in the eye. Then she wet her lips and without turning around spoke to her husband in a soft, coarse voice:
>   "Get some chairs, why don't you, so somebody can sit down."
>   "Oh sure," agreed Wilson. . . . A white ashen dust veiled his dark suit and his pale hair as it veiled everything in the vicinity—except his wife, who moved close to Tom. (30; ch. 2)

In fact, Myrtle is the only woman in the novel we "see" having sex: when Nick returns to their flat after his errand to buy cigarettes, she and Tom have disappeared into the bedroom and emerge only as the rest of their company begins to arrive. Furthermore, Myrtle's interest in Tom is clearly mercenary. She was first attracted to him by the expensive quality of his clothing, she begins spending his money the instant they meet in town, and she wants him to divorce Daisy and marry her so that she can move out of the garage apartment she's shared with George for the past eleven years.

It is important to note that, in all three cases, the transgressive woman is punished by the progression of narrative events. That Daisy gets stuck with Tom in a loveless marriage seems, at that point in the narrative, only right and proper: she doesn't deserve any better, and we can be relatively certain, given Tom's proclivity toward other women, that her punishment will fit her crime. Tom will continue to be unfaithful to her just as she has been unfaithful to him and, more important, unfaithful to Gatsby. Jordan is punished when Nick "throw[s] [her] over" (186; ch. 9) during a telephone conversation just before Gatsby's murder. Later, at the end of Nick's farewell visit to Jordan, he says, "[S]he told me without comment that she was engaged to another man. I doubted that though there were several she could have married at a nod of her head" (185–86; ch. 9). Jordan adds, "I don't give a damn about you now but [being rejected] was a new experience for me and I felt a little dizzy for a while" (186; ch. 9). The way in which Jordan insists she doesn't care merely underscores the fact that she is finally "brought down a peg or two."

The most severe punishment, however, is meted out to the woman who threatens patriarchy the most: Myrtle Wilson. I say she threatens patriarchy the most because she violates patriarchal gender roles so unabashedly and because, despite the powerlessness of her situation as a woman from the lower strata of society, her sexual vitality is portrayed as a form of aggressiveness, a personal power much greater than that of Daisy or Jordan. Her husband all but disappears in her presence, and her "intense vitality" (35; ch. 2) makes her the only thing in the garage to stand out from the "cement color of the walls" into which her husband "mingl[es] immediately" (30; ch. 2). Even as Nick speeds past Wilson's garage on his way to town with Gatsby, he can't help but notice "Mrs. Wilson straining at the garage pump with panting vitality" (72; ch. 4). As Michaelis observes, "Wilson was his wife's man and not his own" (144; ch. 7). Indeed, Michaelis believes "there was not enough of him for his wife" (167; ch. 8). Myrtle even stands up to Tom, insisting that she has a right to "mention Daisy's name": "'Daisy! Daisy! Daisy!' shouted Mrs. Wilson. 'I'll say it whenever I want to!'" (41; ch. 2).

Her punishment for saying Daisy's name is swift and merciless: "Making a short deft movement Tom Buchanan broke her nose with his open hand" (41; ch. 2). But Nick quickly trivializes the incident, effectively forestalling any sympathy we might feel for Myrtle. "Then there were bloody towels upon the bathroom floor and women's voices scolding" (41; ch. 2), he reports. Mr. McKee is so unimpressed by the event that he slowly rambles out the door, and Nick follows him, leaving Mrs. McKee "and Catherine scolding and consoling as they stumbled here and there among the crowded furniture with articles of aid" (41–42; ch. 2). In other words, the breaking of Myrtle's nose is no big deal, just another mess for women to clean up, nothing important enough to concern men, and what's more, Myrtle had it coming.

Of course, Tom's abuse of Myrtle is slight in comparison to the novel's punishment of her: as Myrtle flees her husband and attempts to flag down the car she believes carries her lover, she is hit by that car and killed. It is important to note that her death includes sexual mutilation—"when they had torn open her shirtwaist still damp with perspiration they saw that her left breast was swinging loose like a flap" (145; ch. 7)—which underscores the notion that Myrtle's sexual vitality, that is, her aggressiveness, was her real crime. Indeed, the description of her death closes with a reference to her vitality: "The mouth was wide open and ripped at the corners as though she had choked a little in giving up the tremendous vitality she had stored so long" (145; ch. 7). Thus, although

Myrtle's misconduct is much less serious than that of Daisy or Jordan—she doesn't, like Daisy, commit vehicular homicide and then let her lover take the blame; and she is not, like Jordan, fundamentally dishonest—her punishment is by far the most severe. Obviously, the novel finds aggressiveness, especially sexual aggressiveness, the most unattractive and unforgivable quality a woman can have. Daisy and Jordan may be "bad girls" from time to time, but Myrtle's sexual aggressiveness makes her a "bad girl" all the time.

The Great Gatsby's discomfort with the Post-World-War-I Modern Woman, which, I have argued, is responsible for its negative characterizations and punitive treatment of the modern women it portrays, persists in some of the patriarchal ideology still operating in American culture today. Certainly, women are no longer generally condemned for wearing their hair or their skirts short, for dancing wild dances, or for frequenting raucous night clubs (unless violence is perpetrated against them under these circumstances, in which case they may be blamed for "bringing it on themselves"). But women are still often looked at askance for other violations of patriarchal gender roles, such as opting to have children out of wedlock and raise them on their own, being sexually assertive, being "too" success-oriented on the job, or putting career before marriage and family, all of which behaviors are frequently considered "too aggressive" for women and are often satirized by the television and movie industries. Like Myrtle Wilson, American women today are often punished for what is perceived as their aggressiveness. Indeed, some Americans want to blame women's increased aggressiveness, or at least what is perceived as such, for the increase in crimes of violence against women in this country. At the same time, however, the public doesn't want to admit that women's gender is a factor in the crimes of violence committed against them.

Although, finally, laws have been passed to protect women from sexual harassment on the job, to protect them from sexual abuse and other forms of domestic violence in the home, and to censure rape as a crime of violence rather than tacitly condone it as a crime of passion, public awareness and willingness to support the victims of such mistreatment still lag far behind the legislation. For example, there is the lingering belief that the victim must somehow be responsible: "How low-cut was her dress?" "Did she aggravate her husband before he beat her?" This is called *blaming the victim*: we want to believe that it is women's aggressive or inappropriate or foolish behavior, not their gender, that can get them into trouble. Even the FBI's definitions of crime categories, quoted in my university's pamphlet on campus security, ignores the role of gender in its definition of hate crimes, which it describes as "crimes that manifest evidence of prejudice based on race, religion, sexual orientation [homosexuality], or ethnicity" ("Campus Security Information," Grand Valley State University, 1995).

Yet when the women engineering students were lined up against a classroom wall at a Canadian university several years ago and shot by a male intruder, wasn't that a hate crime against women? And when, shortly thereafter, women engineering students at an American university began to receive anonymous threatening letters, wasn't that a hate crime against women? Aren't rape, sexual harassment, and wife-beating hate crimes against women? Yes, of course they are, but they are still not generally recognized as such. In other words, the patriarchal ideology responsible for the oppression of women can't be effectively addressed until there is public as well as legal recognition that it still exists.

I can understand very well the difficulty involved in recognizing patriarchal ideology because I've had difficulty learning to recognize it myself, even when I've been its victim. In the white, working-class household in which I was raised, the emphasis was on economic survival, on issues of class rather than gender. My parents taught me to see the ways in which political leaders, and our social system as a whole, favored the rich and penalized the middle classes, especially the middle-middle and lower-middle classes. While I was very strongly encouraged to go to college and not to feel that marriage was an inevitable goal, my parents nevertheless believed that it would be to my best advantage to be trained as a schoolteacher because the hours and the nature of the work would not interfere with my future duties as a wife and mother should I choose to marry. Perhaps the absence of a focus on gender issues, combined with a very strong focus on other political issues, helped blind me to the operations of patriarchy.

I'm sure, however, that I was also blinded by my own desire to avoid pain: I didn't want to know all the ways in which I was oppressed because I didn't think there was anything I could do about it. So when I was fired from a job after twice turning down a date with my married boss, I simply thought he had no more use for my services. When I didn't receive a job offer from the man whose hand I removed from my left breast during the job interview, I simply felt sorry for whatever poor woman might end up working for him. And when I noticed that one of my professors seemed extremely uncomfortable whenever I approached him and would quickly leave whatever group he was talking with when I came near, it didn't occur to me that it might have something to do with my being the only woman in the graduate program in philosophy, at that time, or with my being a head taller than he was.

It should come as no surprise, therefore, that when I first read *The Great Gatsby* in my early twenties and found the female characters—especially Myrtle—heartless, amoral, and unsympathetic, it didn't occur to me that the novel had a patriarchal agenda. I didn't see any connections between the novel's portrayals of women and the countless sexist portrayals of women I'd seen in the other male-authored works I loved (works I still value highly, for different reasons, today) because I didn't see how sexist these portrayals really are. The process of "opening my eyes" has been a long and painful one, and it's still in progress. I know from talking with numerous students, friends, and colleagues that my experience has been shared by many women and by some men as well.

Clearly, there is an important connection between our ability to recognize patriarchal ideology and our willingness to experience the pain such knowledge is liable to cause us. Perhaps this is one reason why feminism is still regarded so suspiciously by many women and men today: it holds a mirror not just to our public lives but to our private lives as well, and it asks us to re-assess our most personal experiences and our most entrenched and comfortable assumptions. For this reason, works like *The Great Gatsby* can be very helpful to new students of feminist criticism. By helping us learn to see how patriarchal ideology operates in literature, such works can prepare us to direct our feminist vision where we must eventually learn to focus it most clearly: on ourselves.

Questions for Further Practice: Feminist Approaches to Other Literary Works

The following questions are intended as models. They can help you use feminist criticism to interpret the literary works to which they refer or other texts of your choice.

1. How does Charlotte Perkins Gilman's "The Yellow Wallpaper" (1892) critique patriarchal ideology, specifically as it manifested itself in nineteenth-century marriage and medical practices?

2. How does Joseph Conrad's *Heart of Darkness* (1902) reflect patriarchal ideology through Marlow's comments about and attitude toward women and through his sexist representations of

the numerous minor female characters that populate the novel (including his aunt, Kurtz's intended, the "savage" woman, the native laundress, and the women in black at company headquarters in Europe)? Does the novel invite us to accept or criticize Marlow's sexism? Is the novel even aware of his sexism?

3. How does Toni Morrison's *Beloved* (1987) reveal the ways in which race intersects with gender in creating women's experience? How does the work underscore the importance of sisterhood, of women's community?

4. When Kate Chopin's "The Storm" was written in 1898, it was generally considered unnatural for women to have sexual desire. How does Chopin's story critique this patriarchal belief? What other patriarchal ideology does the story critique? What does the story suggest about the intersection of patriarchy, religion, and socioeconomic class?

5. How does Langston Hughes' "Thank You, Ma'am" (1958) celebrate women's strength, perseverance, and generosity? What does the story imply about the intersection of patriarchal, racial, and class oppression?

For Further Reading

All of the following works will help you develop your skills as feminist critics. Texts listed under "Category I" are written in language accessible to most beginners. Texts listed under "Category II" employ more technical language but are well worth the extra effort that may be required of some students new to the field.

Category I

Frye, Marilyn. *Willful Virgin: Essays in Feminism.* Freedom, CA: Crossing, 1992.

Gates, Jr., Henry Louis, ed. *Reading Black, Reading Feminist: A Critical Anthology.* New York. Meridian, 1990.

Gilbert, Sandra M., and Susan Gubar. *Madwoman in the Attic: The Woman Writer and the Nineteenth-Century Literary Imagination.* New Haven: Yale UP, 1979.

hooks, bell. *Ain't I a Woman: Black Women and Feminism.* Boston: South End Press, 1981.

Mohanty, Chandra Talpade, Ann Russo, and Lourdes Torres, eds. *Third World Women and the Politics of Feminism.* Bloomington: Indiana UP, 1991.

Moi, Toril. *Sexual/Textual Politics: Feminist Literary Theory*. New York: Methuen, 1985.

Moraga, Cherríe, and Gloria Anzaldúa. *This Bridge Called My Back: Writings by Radical Women of Color*. 2nd ed. New York: Kitchen Table: Women of Color Press, 1983.

Showalter, Elaine. *A Literature of Their Own: British Women Novelists from Brontë to Lessing*. Princeton: Princeton UP, 1977.

Todd, Janet. *Feminist Literary History*. New York: Routledge, 1988.

Woolf, Virginia. *A Room of One's Own*. London: Hogarth, 1929.

Category II

Abel, Elizabeth, ed. *Writing and Sexual Difference*. Chicago: U of Chicago P, 1982.

Allen, Paula Gunn. *The Sacred Hoop: Recovering the Feminine in American Indian Traditions*. Boston: Beacon, 1986.

Beauvoir, Simone de. *The Second Sex*. 1949. Trans. H. M. Parshley. Harmondsworth: Penguin, 1972.

Boone, Joseph A., and Michael Cadden, eds. *Engendering Men: The Question of Male Feminist Criticism*. New York: Routledge, 1990.

Cixous, Hélène, and Catherine Clément. *The Newly Born Woman*. Trans. Betsy Wing. Minneapolis: U of Minnesota P, 1986.

Collins, Patricia Hill. *Black Feminist Thought: Knowledge, Consciousness, and the Politics of Empowerment*. New York: Routledge, 1990.

Irigaray, Luce. *This Sex Which Is Not One*. 1977. Trans. Catherine Porter with Carolyn Burke. Ithaca: Cornell UP, 1985.

Kristeva, Julia. *The Kristeva Reader*. Ed. Toril Moi. Oxford: Blackwell, 1986.

Marks, Elaine, and Isabelle de Courtivron, eds. *New French Feminisms*. Brighton: Harvester, 1980.

Mitchell, Juliet. *Psychoanalysis and Feminism*. Harmondsworth: Penguin, 1974.

Showalter, Elaine, ed. *The New Feminist Criticism: Essays on Women, Literature, and Theory*. New York: Pantheon, 1985.

Spivak, Gayatri Chakravorti. *In Other Worlds: Essays in Cultural Politics*. New York: Routledge, 1987.

Warhol, Robyn R., and Diane Price Herndl, eds. *Feminisms: An Anthology of Literary Theory and Criticism*. 2nd ed. New Brunswick: Rutgers UP, 1997.

Works Cited

Bethel, Lorraine. "'This Infinity of Conscious Pain': Zora Neale Hurston and the Black Female Literary Tradition." *All the Women Are White, All the Blacks Are Men, But Some of Us Are Brave*. Eds. Gloria T. Hull, Patricia Bell Scott, and Barbara Smith. Old Westbury, New York: The Feminist Press, 1982. 176–88.

Bruccoli, Matthew J. Preface. *The Great Gatsby*. F. Scott Fitzgerald. New York: Simon and Schuster, 1995. vii-xvi.

Denard, Carolyn. "The Convergence of Feminism and Ethnicity in the Fiction of Toni Morrison." *Critical Essays on Toni Morrison*. Ed. Nellie Y. McKay. Boston: G. K. Hall, 1988. 171–78.

Walker, Alice. *In Search of Our Mothers' Gardens*. San Diego: Harcourt Brace
    Jovanovich, 1984.

CHAPTER **5**

New Criticism

New Criticism occupies an unusual position, both in this textbook and in the field of literary studies today. On the one hand, it's the only theory covered in this book that is no longer practiced by literary critics, so it can't really be called a contemporary theory. On the other hand, New Criticism, which dominated literary studies from the 1940s through the 1960s, has left a lasting imprint on the way we read and write about literature. Some of its most important concepts concerning the nature and importance of textual evidence—the use of concrete, specific examples from the text itself to validate our interpretations—have been incorporated into the way most literary critics today, regardless of their theoretical persuasion, support their readings of literature. In fact, if you're an English major, you probably take for granted the need for thorough textual support for your literary interpretations because this practice, which the New Critics introduced to America and called "close reading," has been a standard method of high-school and college instruction in literary studies for the past several decades. So in this sense, New Criticism is still a real presence among us and probably will remain so for some time to come.

Few students today, however, are aware of New Criticism's contribution to literary studies or of the theoretical framework that underlies the classroom instruction it has fostered. For this reason, I think we should give New Criticism the same kind of attention we give to the other theories in this textbook. In addition, we need to understand New Criticism in order to understand those theories that have developed in reaction against it. As we'll see in subsequent chapters, reader-response criticism opposes New Criticism's definition of the literary text and method of interpreting it, and structuralism rejects New Criticism's focus on the individual literary work in isolation from other literature and from other cultural productions. In addition, deconstruction's theory of language and new historicism's view of objective evidence are directly opposed to New Critical assumptions about language and objectivity.

"The Text Itself"

To fully appreciate New Criticism's contribution to literary studies today, we need to remember the form of criticism it replaced: the biographical-historical criticism that dominated literary studies in the nineteenth century and the early decades of the twentieth. At that time, it was common practice to interpret a literary text by studying the author's life and times to determine *authorial intention*, that is, the meaning the author intended the text to have. The author's letters, diaries, and essays were combed for evidence of authorial intention as were autobiographies, biographies, and history books. In its most extreme form, biographical-historical criticism seemed, to some, to examine the text's biographical-historical context *instead* of examining the text. As one of my former professors described the situation, students attending a lecture on Wordsworth's "Elegiac Stanzas" (1805) could expect to hear a description of the poet's personal and intellectual life: his family, friends, enemies, lovers, habits, education, beliefs, and experiences. "Now you understand the meaning of 'Elegiac Stanzas,'" they would be told, without anyone in the room, including the lecturer, having opened the book to look at the poem itself. Or, in a similar manner, scholars viewed the literary text merely as an adjunct to history, as an illustration of the "spirit of the age" in which it was written, not as an art object worthy of study for its own sake. For New Critics, however, the poem itself was all that mattered.

"*The text itself*" became the battle cry of the New Critical effort to focus our attention on the literary work as the sole source of evidence for interpreting it. The life and times of the author and the spirit of the age in which he lived are certainly of interest to the literary historian, New Critics argued, but they do not provide the literary critic with information that can be used to analyze the text itself. In the first place, they pointed out, sure knowledge of the author's intended meaning is usually unavailable. We can't telephone William Shakespeare and ask him how he intended us to interpret Hamlet's hesitation in carrying out the instructions of his father's ghost, and Shakespeare left no written explanation of his intention. More important, even if Shakespeare had left a record of his intention, as some authors have, all we can know from that record is what he wanted to accomplish, not what he did accomplish. Sometimes a literary text doesn't live up to the author's intention. Sometimes it is even more meaningful, rich, and complex than the author realized. And sometimes the text's meaning is simply different from the meaning the author wanted it to have. Knowing an author's intention, therefore, tells us nothing about the text itself, which is why New Critics coined the term *intentional fallacy* to refer to the mistaken belief that the author's intention is the same as the meaning of the text.

Just as we cannot look to the author's intention to find the meaning of a literary text, neither can we look to the reader's personal response to find it. Any given reader may or may not respond to what is actually provided by the text itself. Readers' feelings or opinions about a text may be produced by some personal association from past experience rather than by the text. I may, for example, respond to Hamlet's mother based solely on my feelings about my own mother and nevertheless conclude that I have correctly interpreted the literary character. Such a conclusion would be an example of what New Critics called the *affective fallacy*. While the intentional fallacy confuses the text with its origins, the affective fallacy confuses the text with its affects, that is, with the emotions it produces. The affective fallacy leads to impressionistic responses (if a reader doesn't like a character, then that character must be evil) and relativism (the text means whatever any reader thinks it means). The final outcome of such a practice is chaos: we have no standards for interpreting or evaluating literature, which is therefore reduced to the status of the ink-blot upon which psychiatric patients project their own meanings.

Although the author's intention or the reader's response is sometimes mentioned in New Critical readings of literary texts, neither one is the focus of analysis. For the only way we can know if a given author's intention or a given reader's interpretation actually represents the text's meaning is to carefully examine, or "closely read," all the evidence provided by the language of the text itself: its images, symbols, metaphors, rhyme, meter, point of view, setting, characterization, plot, and so forth, which, because they form, or shape, the literary work are called its *formal elements*. But before we discuss how this method of close reading operates, we need to understand just what New Critics meant by "the text itself" because their definition of the literary work is directly related to their beliefs concerning the proper way to interpret it.

For New Criticism, a literary work is a *timeless, autonomous (self-suffi-*

cient) verbal object. Readers and readings may change, but the literary text stays the same. Its meaning is as objective as its physical existence on the page, for it is constructed of words placed in a specific relationship to one another—specific words placed in a specific order—and this one-of-a-kind relationship creates a complex of meaning that cannot be reproduced by any other combination of words. A New Critical reading of Robert Hayden's "Middle Passage" (1966) can help us appreciate the poem by explaining how the poem's complex of meaning works, but it cannot replace that complex of meaning: only "Middle Passage" is "Middle Passage," and it will always be "Middle Passage." This is why New Criticism asserted that the meaning of a poem could not be explained simply by paraphrasing it, or translating it into everyday language, a practice New Critics referred to as the *heresy of paraphrase.* Change one line, one image, one word of the poem, they argued, and you will have a different poem.

Literary Language and Organic Unity

The importance of the formal elements of a literary text is a product of the nature of *literary language,* which, for New Criticism, is very different from scientific language and from everyday language. Scientific language, and a good deal of everyday language, depends on denotation, the one-to-one correspondence between words and the objects or ideas they represent. Scientific language doesn't draw attention to itself, doesn't try to be beautiful or emotionally evocative. Its job is to point not to itself but to the physical world beyond it, which it attempts to describe and explain. Literary language, in contrast, depends on connotation: on the implication, association, suggestion, and evocation of meanings and of shades of meaning. (For example, while the word *father* denotes *male parent,* it connotes *authority, protection,* and *responsibility.*) In addition, literary language is expressive: it communicates tone, attitude, and feeling. While everyday language is often connotative and expressive, too, in general it is not deliberately or systematically so, for its chief purpose is practical. Everyday language wants to get things done. Literary language, however, organizes linguistic resources into a special arrangement, a complex unity, to create an aesthetic experience, a world of its own.

Unlike scientific and everyday language, therefore, the form of literary language—the word choice and arrangement that create the aesthetic experience—is inseparable from its content, its meaning. Put more simply, *how* a literary text means is inseparable from *what* it means. For the form and meaning of a literary work, at least of a great literary work, develop together, like a complex living organism whose parts cannot be separated from the whole. And indeed, the work's *organic unity*—the working together of all the parts to make an inseparable whole—is the criterion by which New Critics judged the quality of a literary work. If a text has an organic unity, then all of its formal elements work together to establish its theme, or the meaning of the work as a whole. Through its organic unity, the text provides both the *complexity* that a literary work must have, if it is to adequately represent the complexity of human life, and the *order* that human beings, by nature, seek. For New Criticism, then, the explanation of literary meaning and the evaluation of literary greatness became one and the same act, for when New Critics explained a text's organic unity they were also establishing its claim to greatness. Let's take a closer look at each of the criteria of literary value embodied in organic unity: complexity and order.

For New Criticism, the complexity of a text is created by the multiple and often conflicting meanings woven through it. And these meanings are a product primarily of four kinds of linguistic devices: paradox, irony, ambiguity, and tension. Briefly, *paradox* is a statement that seems self-contradictory but represents the actual way things are. For example, it is a biblical paradox that you must lose your life in order to gain it. On the surface, that phrase seems self-contradictory: how can you gain an object by losing it? However, the phrase means that by giving up one kind of life, the transitory life of the flesh, you gain another, more important kind of life: the eternal life of the soul. Similarly, a paradox of everyday experience can be seen in the old saying Joni Mitchell uses so effectively in her song "You Take Paradise and Put Up a Parking Lot": "You don't know what you've got 'till it's gone." Not unlike the biblical reference above, this old adage tells us that you have to lose something (physically) before you can find it (spiritually). Many of life's spiritual and psychological realities are paradoxical in nature, New Critics observed, and paradox is thus responsible for much of the complexity of human experience and of the literature that portrays it.

Irony, in its simple form, means a statement or event undermined by the context in which it occurs. The following description of a wealthy husband's sense of moral rectitude, from Edith Wharton's *House of Mirth* (1905), is an example of an ironic statement.

> Once in the winter the rector would come to dine, and her husband
> would beg her to go over the list and see that no *divorcées* were in-

cluded, except those who had showed signs of penitence by being re-
married to the very wealthy. (57)

Part of the ironic implication of this passage is that the husband is a
hypocrite: he condemns divorce only if it is not followed by the acquisition of equal or greater wealth, so what he really condemns, under the
guise of moral principles, is financial decline. An example of an ironic
event can be seen in Toni Morrison's *The Bluest Eye* (1970) when Pecola
finally receives the blue eyes she has wished for so desperately. Her wish
has been "fulfilled" only because she has lost touch with reality so completely that she believes her brown eyes are blue.

New Criticism, however, primarily valued irony in a broader sense of
the term, to indicate a text's inclusion of varying perspectives on the same
characters or events. We see this kind of irony, for example, when Jane
Austen's *Sense and Sensibility* (1811) offers us perspectives from which we
may utterly condemn Willoughby for his treachery to Maryanne; forgive
him because his behavior resulted from a combination of love, financial
desperation, and a weakness of character which he himself laments; sympa-
thize with him for the severity of the punishment his behavior has brought
upon him; and see the ways in which Maryanne's willful foolishness contributed to her own heartbreak. Such a variety of possible viewpoints is
considered a form of irony because the credibility of each viewpoint undermines to some extent the credibility of the others. The result is a complexity
of meaning that mirrors the complexity of human experience and increases
the text's believability. In contrast, had Willoughby been portrayed as
purely and uncomplicatedly evil, Maryanne would have been idealized as a
completely innocent victim, and the text would have become vulnerable to
the reader's skepticism, which would put the reader at an ironic distance
from the text. Thus the text's own internal irony, or awareness of multiple
viewpoints, protects it from the external irony of the reader's disbelief.

Ambiguity occurs when a word, image, or event generates two or
more different meanings. For example, in Toni Morrison's *Beloved*
(1987), the image of the tree produced by the scar tissue on Sethe's back
implies, among other things, suffering (the "tree" resulted from a brutal
whipping, which is emblematic of all the hardships experienced under
slavery), endurance (trees can live for hundreds of years, and the scar tissue, itself, testifies to Sethe's remarkable ability to survive the most trau-
matic experiences), and renewal (like the trees that lose their leaves in the
fall and are "reborn" every spring, Sethe is offered, at the novel's close, the
chance to make a new life). In scientific or everyday language, ambiguity

is usually considered a flaw because it's equated with a lack of clarity and precision. In literary language, however, ambiguity is considered a source of richness, depth, and complexity that adds to the text's value.

Finally, the complexity of a literary text is created by its *tension*, which, broadly defined, means the linking together of opposites. In its simplest form, tension is created by the integration of the abstract and the concrete, of general ideas embodied in specific images. For example, in Arthur Miller's *Death of a Salesman* (1949), the concrete image of Willy's tiny house, bathed in blue light and surrounded by enormous apartment buildings that emanate an angry orange glow, embodies the general idea of the underdog, the victim of forces larger and more numerous than itself. Similarly, the concrete image of Linda Loman singing Willy to sleep embodies the general idea of the devoted wife, the caretaker, the nurturer. Such *concrete universals*—or images and fictional characters that are meaningful on both the concrete level, where their meaning is literal and specific, and the symbolic level, where they have universal significance—are considered a form of tension because they hold together the opposing realms of physical reality and symbolic reality in a way characteristic of literary language. In other words, the Loman home and the character of Linda Loman represent both themselves and something larger than themselves.

Tension is also created by the dynamic interplay among the text's opposing tendencies, that is, among its paradoxes, ironies, and ambiguities. For example, we might say that the action of *Death of a Salesman* is structured by the tension between reality and illusion: between the harsh reality of Willy Loman's life and the self-delusion into which he keeps trying to escape. Ideally, the text's opposing tendencies are held in equilibrium by working together to make a stable and coherent meaning. For example, the tension between harsh reality and self-delusion in *Death of a Salesman* is held in equilibrium by the following meaning: so great is Willy's desire to succeed as a salesman and a father that his only defense against the common man's inevitable failures in a dog-eat-dog world is self-delusion, but that self-delusion only increases his failure. Thus, the play shows us how harsh reality and self-delusion feed off each other until the only escape is death.

As noted earlier, the complexity of the text, to which all of these linguistic devices contribute, must be complemented by a sense of order if a literary work is to achieve greatness. Therefore, all of the multiple and conflicting meanings produced by the text's paradoxes, ironies, ambiguities, and tensions must be resolved, or harmonized, by their shared contribution to the theme. The text's *theme,* or complete meaning, is not the same thing as its topic. Rather the theme is what the text does with its topic. For example, adultery is the topic of both Kate Chopin's "The Storm" (1898) and Alberto Moravia's "The Chase" (1967), but the meaning of adultery—its moral and psychological implications—is quite different in each story. In Chopin's tale, a single, spontaneous act of adultery seems to improve the emotional health and marriages of the two participants. The theme of "The Storm," we might say, is that individual circumstances, not abstract rules, determine what is right and wrong, healthy and unhealthy. In Moravia's story, in contrast, the young wife's extramarital affair seems to both result from and contribute to the emotional distance between her husband and herself. The theme of "The Chase," it might be argued, is that adultery is a form of emotional distance, and, as such, it signals the end of emotional intimacy in a marriage. Thus, the theme is, itself, an interpretation of human experience, and if the text is a great one, the theme serves as a commentary on human values, human nature, or the human condition. In other words, great literary works have themes of universal human (moral and/or emotional) significance.[1] They tell us something important about what it means to be human. We may not like or agree with the theme a story offers, but we can still see what that theme is and, most important for New Criticism, we can judge whether or not that theme is established by the text's formal elements in a way that produces an organic unity.

Close reading, the scrupulous examination of the complex relationship between a text's formal elements and its theme, is how the text's organic unity was established by the New Critic. Because of New Criticism's belief that the literary text can be understood primarily by understanding its form (which is why you'll sometimes hear it referred to as a type of *formalism*), a clear understanding of the definitions of specific formal elements is important. In addition to the formal elements discussed above—the linguistic devices of paradox, irony, ambiguity, and tension—we should also take a moment to briefly define a few of the most frequently used kinds of figurative language: images, symbols, metaphors, and similes.

Figurative language is language that has more than, or other than, a strictly literal meaning. For instance, "It's raining cats and dogs" is a figurative expression used to indicate that it's raining very heavily. If it were taken literally, then the phrase would mean, of course, that actual cats and dogs were falling from the sky. Broadly defined, an *image,* as illustrated by our use of the word earlier, consists of a word or words that refer to an object perceived by the senses or to sense perceptions themselves: colors, shapes, lighting, sounds, tastes, smells, textures, temperatures, and so on. More narrowly defined, and most common in the practice of analyzing literary texts, imagery is visual, consisting of descriptions of objects, characters, or settings as they are seen by the eye. Although images always have literal meaning—a description of clouds means that the weather is cloudy—they can evoke an emotional atmosphere as well: for example, a description of clouds can be used to evoke sadness.

If an image occurs repeatedly in a text, it probably has symbolic significance. A *symbol* is an image that has both literal and figurative meaning, a concrete universal, such as the swamp in Ernest Hemingway's "Big, Two-Hearted River" (1925). The swamp is a literal swamp—it's wet, it contains fish and other forms of aquatic life, one needs boots and special equipment to fish in it—but it also "stands for," or "figures," something else: the emotional problems the protagonist does not feel quite ready to face. Public symbols are usually easy to spot. For example, spring is usually a symbol of rebirth or youth; autumn is usually a symbol of death or dying; a river is usually a symbol of life or of a journey. Thus a symbol has properties similar to those of the abstract idea it stands for. For example, a river can symbolize life because both a river and life are fluid and forward moving; both have a source and an end-point. In addition, a river literally nurtures life: some life forms live in it; others drink from it.

The context provided by the text also helps us figure out a symbol's meaning. To use the example of Hemingway's swamp again, in addition to the similarities between a swamp and emotional problems—both are difficult to deal with because both involve unknown pitfalls that may be dangerous and are certainly challenging—the protagonist manifests the same attitude toward the swamp that he manifests toward his emotional problems: he avoids them. And this similarity tips us off to the swamp's symbolic content. Sometimes, the context provided by the text is all we have to go on because some symbols are private, or meaningful only to the author, and therefore more difficult to figure out. We may suspect, for example, that the image of a purple felt hat has symbolic significance in a story because it recurs frequently or plays a role that seems to reverberate with some abstract quality such as love or loneliness or strength, but we'll have to figure out what that symbolic significance is by studying how the hat operates within the overall meaning of the text. Of course, how something operates within the overall meaning of the text was always the bottom line for New Criticism, so it does not matter whether or not our analysis of the text's private symbolism matches the author's intention. What matters is that our analysis of the text's private symbolism, like our analysis of all its formal elements, supports what we claim is the text's theme.

In contrast with the double dimension of the symbol—its inclusion of both literal and figurative meaning—a *metaphor* has only figurative meaning. A metaphor is a comparison of two dissimilar objects in which the properties of one are ascribed to the other. For example, the phrase "my brother is a gem" is a metaphor. Obviously, it has no literal meaning. If it did, it would mean that my mother gave birth to a crystalline stone, for which feat she'd be on the cover of every tabloid in the nation. The figurative meaning of the phrase, which is the only meaning it has, is of course that my brother shares certain properties with a gem: for example, he is of great worth. Thus "he's a gem" is generally used to mean "he's a great guy." To get from metaphor to *simile* requires one small step: add *like* or *as*. "My brother is like a gem" or "my brother is as valuable as a gem" are similes that make the same comparison as the metaphor from which I derived them, though one might argue that the simile is softer because the connection between the idea of "brother" and the idea of "gem" is less direct or less forceful.

I think it's time we put these New Critical tools to work in order to see the New Critical method in action. So let's do a close reading of Lucille Clifton's "There Is a Girl Inside" (1977).

A New Critical Reading of "There Is a Girl Inside"

There Is a Girl Inside

there is a girl inside.
she is randy as a wolf.
she will not walk away
and leave these bones
to an old woman.

she is a green tree
in a forest of kindling.
she is a green girl
in a used poet.

she has waited
patient as a nun
for the second coming,
when she can break through gray hairs
into blossom

and her lovers will harvest
honey and thyme
and the woods will be wild
with the damn wonder of it.

The poem's title, "There Is a Girl Inside," which also serves as the opening line, and the final two lines of the first stanza, which refer to the "bones" of an "old woman," tell us immediately that the speaker is an old woman who still feels young and vital inside. So we know that the central tension in the poem is probably the tension between youth and age, between what the speaker feels like on the inside and what she looks like on the outside. And indeed, we can see that this tension structures the poem as a whole through the alternation of the language of youthful vitality ("girl," "randy"—sexually free or assertive—"green tree," "green girl," "blossom") with the language of aging and decay ("bones," "old woman," "kindling"—old, dried up sticks used for starting fires—"used poet," "gray hairs"). In addition, the narrative dimension of the poem, or the "story" the poem tells, reveals an old woman dreaming about the miraculous rejuvenation, the "second coming" of youth, that she feels awaits the "girl inside" herself, the girl that she is still, despite "these bones" and "gray hairs." Thus we might hypothesize, at this point, that the theme of the poem probably involves the paradox of timeless youth. (Timeless youth is a paradox because, on the literal level of biology, time and youth are mutually exclusive: the passage of time inevitably results in aging.) To discover the specific nature of the theme, and to understand how the poem establishes it, we need to closely examine the poem's formal elements.

The first thing we might notice, looking at the poem as a whole, is that the alternation of images of youth with images of age ends with the fourth line of the third stanza. The final five lines of the poem, which include the entire last stanza, consist of images of youth, fertility, and sexuality, and they evoke the youthfulness the speaker believes can overpower age: "blossom," "lovers," "harvest," "honey and thyme," "woods," "wild," and "wonder." Does anything else in the poem reinforce this emphasis on the triumph of youth over age? Still looking at the poem as a whole, note the decrease in punctuation as the poem progresses, which is literally a decrease in stops and pauses. There are a total of five periods (full stops) in the first two stanzas, but there is only one comma (pause) in the third stanza and no punctuation at all in the final stanza until we get to the period that ends the poem. In fact, counting from the comma in stanza three, there is no punctuation in the final six lines of the poem. This dramatic decrease in punctuation, or decrease in stops and pauses, suggests acceleration, excitement, and power, thus reinforcing the emphasis on the triumph of youth in the final stanza.

As we are already engaged in examining the grammatical elements of the poem, let's see what the use of verbs can tell us. First, we might note the speaker's use of powerful verbs in the active voice: the girl inside "will not walk away," she "can break through," and "her lovers will harvest." These powerful, active verbs reinforce the idea that this girl is powerful and active, strong enough to get what she wants. I think the use of "has waited" in the third stanza reinforces the idea that the girl inside is ready to emerge. The line does not read "she is waiting," which would imply that the waiting will go on for an indeterminate length of time, but "she has waited," which suggests that her waiting is over or should be over soon. In this context, we should also mention the simile "she is randy as a wolf," for a wolf is a powerful animal that fights for what it wants and usually gets what it fights for. ("Randy as a rabbit," for example, would certainly not carry the same implication.)

Are there any other images associated with the girl inside, and if so, do they contribute to the theme we're trying to formulate? The metaphor "she is a green tree" is useful for our purposes because it invokes the growing seasons, spring and summer, the seasons of rebirth and plenitude. And because "green tree" is a nature image, it carries with it the inevitability of rejuvenation. The tree that has been a mere skeleton all winter, like the old woman's "bones," and as dead looking as "kindling," has blossomed. The rejuvenating power of the "green tree" inside the winter tree is thus linked to the rejuvenating power of the "green girl" two lines down. If the green tree can "break through . . . / into blossom," then so can the green girl who waits inside the old woman.

Of course "green girl" also implies that the girl is inexperienced, naive, unused to the world. And this aspect of the image fits nicely with the simile in the second line of the next stanza: "patient as a nun." As most of us know, nuns take a vow of chastity, poverty, and obedience, which means, in short, that they renounce the material world, the world of the flesh. The image of the nun thus forms a bridge between the inexperi-

enced girl and the old woman, for all three are cut off, in one way or another, from the world of the flesh. And just as a nun waits patiently for
her reward—the second coming of Christ—so the old woman and the
girl inside have both waited patiently for theirs: the second coming of
youth.

Is there anything else in the poem that reinforces the link between
the aging speaker and the young girl inside? Let's look again at the language of the final stanza, where youth, which has "blossom[ed]" at the
end of the previous stanza, will be "harvest[ed]." Closing lines are always
very important, and these seem to have especially rich images. We said
earlier that this is the stanza where youth triumphs over age, and indeed
it does, for this is the stanza in which the speaker imagines the newly
emerged girl consummating her sexual desire in the woods. However, the
words "harvest," "honey," and "thyme" have an ambiguity that also reinforces the bond between youth and age. For in addition to their connota-
tions of youthful sexual vitality, "harvest," "honey," and "thyme" can refer
to activities associated with autumn and therefore with the old woman.

A harvest occurs in the fall, at the end of the growing season, when
the plants are fully mature, not when they are "green," or young, like the
"green girl" inside. Honey and thyme, in that they are crops that are harvested, carry the same meaning. For honey is the product bees make from
flower pollen after the pollen is harvested; beekeepers, in turn, harvest the
honey from the hive after it is made. And thyme, a fragrant herb used to
season food, is used primarily after it has dried up. Metaphorically, then,
the stanza implies a merger of age and youth. The word "kindling" in the
second stanza has an ambiguity that is useful in this context, too. As
noted earlier, "kindling" refers to old, dried up sticks used to start fires.
But the very fact that kindling catches fire so easily associates it with the
quality of passion, which also "catches fire" easily. In this sense, we might
say that, in passion, youth and age are one.

Let's see what we can learn about the relationship between youth and
age from the poem's *tone,* which it might be helpful to think of as the
speaker's tone of voice, for it expresses the speaker's attitude toward what
he or she is saying and toward the reader. We know that the speaker is an
old woman. Is her tone somber or lighthearted? Weary or energetic? Formal or informal? How would we characterize it? Right away, her use of
slang—"randy" to indicate sexual hunger in the second line of the poem
and "damn" in the final stanza—tells us that the tone is somewhat playful
and irreverent, a tone often associated with youth. And so is her play on
words in the third stanza: the "second coming" for which the "nun" has

waited can refer to both the second coming of Christ and the speaker's second "coming," or second round of orgasms.

The informality created by the speaker's use of slang and humor is reinforced by the poem's short lines, which make it seem as if she were speaking to us conversationally, and by the absence of traditional features such as capital letters, rhyme, and meter. We might say, then, that in the playful irreverence and informality of the speaker's tone, we have the merger of youth and age: the young person who disdains formality and the old woman who has grown beyond it. Or to put it another way, we know that the girl inside the speaker is an important presence in her life because we can hear her youthful voice in the voice of the old woman. And surely the tone of voice in the last line is the voice of both girl and woman, the voice in which we can almost hear them raise their hands to their hips as they refer to "the damn wonder of it."

Perhaps, then, we can formulate our theme in the following manner. The theme of "There Is a Girl Inside" is not merely a restatement of the old adage "Hope springs eternal in the human breast," but a transformation of that adage into a new one of equally universal importance: Youth springs eternal in the human breast. For the poem suggests that age brings with it a special "harvest" of its own, which is the capacity to appreciate the gifts of youth that remain within us as seeds remain within a ripened fruit and, as a result, to feel young even when we are old. Thus the theme of the poem resolves the tension between youth and age that structures it. And we can conclude that the poem has an organic unity because, as we have seen, its theme is carried by all of its formal elements; that is, its form and content are inseparable. Furthermore, although the poem appears to be charmingly, and disarmingly, simple, our analysis of its organic unity reveals a surprising complexity in the operations of its formal elements. We would be justified in arguing, then, that from a New Critical perspective, "There Is a Girl Inside" is a finely wrought literary text, a unified, complex art object the theme of which has universal human significance.

New Criticism as Intrinsic, Objective Criticism

As I hope this reading of Clifton's poem illustrates, New Criticism asked us to look closely at the formal elements of the text to help us discover the poem's theme and to explain the ways in which those formal elements establish it. For New Critics believed that this was the only way to determine the text's value. By staying within the poem in this manner, New Critics believed they allowed the literary work itself to provide the context within which we interpret and evaluate it. To use an obvious example, in analyzing Clifton's poem my discussion of the word *randy* focused only on the slang meaning of the term because only that meaning makes sense in terms of the context of the poem as a whole. Other meanings of the word found in *Webster's New Universal Unabridged Dictionary* include "crude" or "vulgar," "a quarrelsome woman," and "a threatening beggar." Had any of these meanings enriched our reading of the poem by bringing another dimension to the theme, I would have analyzed it as part of the word's ambiguity. But because none of these meanings seemed appropriate in terms of the poem's theme, I ignored them. Thus, although most words can be found to have more than one dictionary definition, a word's ambiguity is determined not by the dictionary but by the context of the poem as a whole, in terms of which alone the word's meaning or meanings must be judged.

Similarly, I did not mention that Clifton is an African American poet, and there is nothing in my reading that would indicate the author's race. Although an African American critic would most probably include some mention of the ways in which the poem participates in the African American literary tradition, from a New Critical perspective such information, while of historical interest, is irrelevant to our evaluation of the poem's organic unity and universal significance. (See Chapter Eleven, "Postcolonial and African American Criticism," for a discussion of the discriminatory properties of the concept of "universalism.")

Finally, I did not try to analyze the speaker's psychological state—though a psychoanalytic reading might have analyzed "wolf," "bones," "kindling," "used," "break," and "wild" in order to argue that a fear of violence and self-destruction lies beneath the poem's sexual imagery—because there doesn't seem to be anything in the poem itself to warrant such an analysis. The speaker's psychology is not involved in the theme of the poem, and it is not relevant to our understanding of the theme of the poem. Sometimes New Critics did believe that the text warranted a discussion of its psychological, sociological, or philosophical elements because those elements were obviously integral to the work's characterization or plot, as we might find psychological elements integral to characterization or plot in William Faulkner's "A Rose for Emily" (1931) or Edgar Allan Poe's "The Tell-Tale Heart" (1843). In such cases, New Critics addressed these elements, but they did so for the purpose of examining how such elements operate to establish the text's theme (or to undermine it, if the text is flawed). In other words, New Critics didn't ignore the obvious psychological, sociological, or philosophical dimensions of the text; they aestheticized them. That is, they treated psychological, sociological, and philosophical content the same way they treated the text's formal elements: to learn what these elements contribute to the aesthetic experience created by the work's organic unity. In this way, New Critics claimed, their interpretation stayed within the context created by the text itself.

Because New Critics believed their interpretations were based solely on the context created by the text and the language provided by the text, they called their critical practice *intrinsic criticism*, to denote that New Criticism stayed within the confines of the text itself. In contrast, forms of criticism that employ psychological, sociological, or philosophical frameworks—in other words, all criticism other than their own—they called *extrinsic criticism* because it goes outside the literary text for the tools needed to interpret it. New Critics also called their approach *objective criticism* because their focus on each text's own formal elements insured, they claimed, that each text—each object being interpreted—would itself dictate how it would be interpreted.

The Single Best Interpretation

Given that the text was thus seen as an independent entity with a stable meaning of its own, New Critics believed that a single best, or most accurate, interpretation of each text could be discovered that best represents the text itself, that best explains what the text means and how it means it, that is, that best explains its organic unity. This is why, during New Criticism's heyday, essays interpreting a literary text frequently began with a survey of other critics' interpretations of the same text in order to show that everyone else's reading fell short—that important scenes or images were unaccounted for, that tensions structuring the text were not resolved—often because a proper understanding of the text's theme was lacking. In other words, in order to establish that yours was the best reading of a literary work, you would have to begin by establishing that all former readings were in some way inadequate.

In light of the scrupulous attention paid to textual details by the New Critics, it is understandable that their method worked best on short poems and stories because, the shorter the text, the more of its formal elements could be analyzed. When longer works were examined, such as long poems, novels, and plays, New Critical readings usually confined themselves to the analysis of some aspect (or aspects) of the work, for example, its imagery (or perhaps just one kind of imagery, such as nature imagery), the role of the narrator or of the minor characters, the function of time in the work, the pattern of light and dark created by settings, or some other formal element. Of course, whatever formal element was analyzed, it had to be shown to play an important role in the text's advancement of its theme and thus contribute to the unity of the work as a whole.

Through your own familiarity or unfamiliarity with the New Critical principles discussed in this chapter, you can probably form some idea of New Criticism's lasting contribution to literary studies. Some of its principles and terminology seem to have fallen by the wayside. For example, few literary critics today assert that a literary text is independent of the history and culture that produced it or that it has a single, objective meaning. And almost no one uses the word *tension* to refer to the symbol's integration of concrete images and abstract ideas. Nevertheless, New Criticism's success in focusing our attention on the formal elements of the text and on their relationship to the meaning of the text is evident in the way we study literature today, regardless of our theoretical perspective. For whatever theoretical framework we use to interpret a text, we always support our interpretation with concrete evidence from the text that usually includes attention to formal elements, and with the notable exception of some deconstructive and reader-response interpretations, we usually try to produce an interpretation that conveys some sense of the text as a unified whole.

It's rather ironic, then, that New Criticism's gift to critical theory—its focus on the text itself—was responsible for its downfall. For New Criticism was eclipsed in the late 1960s by the growing interest, among almost all other schools of critical theory, in the ideological content of literary texts and the ways in which that content both reflects and influences society, an interest that could not be served by the New Critical insistence on analyzing the text as an isolated aesthetic object with a single meaning.

The Question New Critics Asked about Literary Texts

Given New Criticism's focus on the single meaning of the text and its single method of establishing that meaning, it should not be surprising that our list of questions New Critics asked about literary texts should consist of only one complex question:

What single interpretation of the text best establishes its organic unity? In other words, how do the text's formal elements, and the multiple meanings those elements produce, all work together to support the theme, or overall meaning, of the work? Remember, a great work will have a theme of universal human significance. (If the text is too long to account for all of its formal elements, apply this question to some aspect or aspects of its form, such as imagery, point of view, setting, or the like.)

Regardless of the literary text at hand, this is the question we ask in order to produce a New Critical interpretation. It is interesting to note that, despite their belief in the text's single, objective meaning, New Critics rarely agreed about what that meaning was or how the text worked to produce it. Instead, different interpretations of the same texts abounded. As in every field, even expert New Critical practitioners disagreed about the meaning of specific works. Our goal is to use New Criticism to help enrich our reading of literary texts, to help us see and appreciate in new ways the complex operations of their formal elements and how those elements function to create meaning.

The following interpretation of F. Scott Fitzgerald's *The Great Gatsby* is offered as an example of what a New Critical reading might yield. I discovered what I believe is the novel's topic—human longing—by analyzing the text's imagery, the beauty and emotional force of which make it the most memorable and revealing dimension of the novel. Then I examined other formal elements in the text—specifically, characterization, setting, and elements of style—to determine what I claim is the novel's theme: that unfulfilled longing is an inescapable part of the human condition. As a practitioner of New Criticism, I was interested in the historical time and place described in the novel only as they manifest a theme that transcends historical time and place, a theme that has universal human significance.

The "deathless song" of Longing: A New Critical Reading of *The Great Gatsby*

Few readers of F. Scott Fitzgerald's *The Great Gatsby* (1925) will fail to notice the breathtaking beauty of its imagery. Indeed, the haunting, wistful quality of the novel's images evokes the melancholy lyricism of the author's favorite poet, John Keats. Yet there has been little analysis of how the imagery in Fitzgerald's powerfully poetic novel structures the meaning of the text as a whole.

It might be argued that this oversight has resulted from the critical focus on *The Great Gatsby* as the chronicle of the Jazz Age—as a social commentary on a specific period in America's past—which has diverted attention onto historical issues and away from the text's formal elements. Most critics agree that Fitzgerald's novel offers a scathing critique of American values in the 1920s, the corruption of which is represented by Wolfshiem's exploitativeness, Daisy's duplicity, Tom's treachery, Jordan's dishonesty, Myrtle's vulgarity, and the shallowness of an American populace—embodied in Gatsby's parasitical party guests—whose moral fiber had declined with each passing year. This is a world run by men like Tom Buchanan and Meyer Wolfshiem, and despite their positions on opposite sides of the law, both characters are predators consumed by self-interest, capable of rationalizing their way around any ethical obstacle to get what they want. It's an empty world where selfishness, drunkenness, and vulgarity abound, where the graceful social art of dancing has become "old men pushing young girls backward in eternal graceless circles" and "superior couples holding each other tortuously, fashionably and keeping in the corners" (51; ch. 3). And it's a world of impermanence and instability. The Buchanans are forever "drift[ing] here and there unrestfully wherever people played polo and were rich together" (10; ch. 1). Jordan is always on the move among hotels, clubs, and other people's homes. And even George Wilson, with the scant means he has at his disposal, thinks he can solve his problems by pulling up stakes and moving west. Anonymity and isolation are the rule rather than the exception, and superficial values put the pursuit of social status and good times above every other consideration. Indeed, one could say that the valley of ashes is a metaphor for the spiritual poverty of this world:

> a fantastic farm where ashes grow like wheat into ridges and hills and grotesque gardens, where ashes take the forms of houses and chimneys and rising smoke and finally . . . of men who move dimly and already crumbling through the powdery air. (27; ch. 2)

Because Jay Gatsby is clearly portrayed as a romantic figure of rather mythic proportions, a good deal of critical attention has been given to the narrative tension between the corrupt world of the novel and its title character. And for most critics, Gatsby's capacity to dream and to devote himself to the woman who embodies that dream, including his blindness to the fact that she doesn't deserve his devotion, give him an "innocence" that he "maintain[s]" to the end (Gallo 43). Indeed, there is considerable critical consensus with Marius Bewley's opinion that Gatsby represents "the energy of the spirit's resistance" and "immunity to the final contamination" of "cheapness and vulgarity" (13). As Tom Burnam puts it, Gatsby "survives sound and whole in character, uncorrupted by the corruption which surrounded him" (105).[2] For these critics, the protagonist's innocence serves to indict further the society that destroys him.

This critical focus, however, overlooks a more central tension in the novel than that between Gatsby and the world in which he lives. For we cannot ignore the obvious textual evidence, even if we want to contrast Gatsby with the society he inhabits, that he shares at least some of its corruption: for example, he was Wolfshiem's protégé and has made his fortune by selling bootlegged liquor and fake bonds.[3] It seems to me that the text's central tension is, instead, that between the world of corrupt, vulgar materialism portrayed in the novel and the lyric imagery—the wistful beauty and emotional force of which make it the most memorable and revealing dimension of the novel—so frequently used to describe that world. This tension structures the narrative regardless of how we measure the relative innocence or corruption of any particular character, and it is resolved by a theme of universal human significance that transcends the historical period in which the novel is set: the theme that unfulfilled longing is part of the human condition, common to all and inescapable. As we'll see, the imagery of unfulfilled longing is used to describe characters and settings regardless of the wealth or poverty, refinement or vulgarity, corruption or innocence they represent. In addition, the imagery of unfulfilled longing is often linked with nature imagery, which suggests that unfulfilled longing is as inevitable as, for example, the change of the seasons. Finally, the imagery of unfulfilled longing often has a static, timeless quality in the novel, which underscores both its universality and its inevitability: unfulfilled longing has always been and will always be a part of the human condition.

Let's begin by examining how the imagery of unfulfilled longing weaves a common thread through characters who represent very different elements of society. To accomplish this task, we'll analyze Fitzgerald's lyric imagery in terms of the three ways in which it informs characterization in the novel: (1) as nostalgia for a lost past; (2) as dreams of future fulfillment; and (3) as vague, undefined longing that has no specific goal.

We see the imagery of longing for a lost past in the idyllic description of Daisy and Jordan's "beautiful white . . . girlhood" (24; ch. 1) in Louisville, where Jordan "first learned to walk upon golf courses on clean, crisp mornings" (55; ch. 3). This is a romantic past where, Jordan recalls, she walked on "soft ground" in her "new plaid skirt . . . that blew a little in the wind" and where Daisy dressed in white and had a little white roadster and all day long the telephone rang in her house and excited young officers from Camp Taylor demanded the privilege of monopolizing her that night, "anyways for an hour!" (79; ch. 4)

This is a world of virginal romance: clean, crisp mornings, soft ground, new skirts, white dresses, white roadsters, ringing telephones, and hand-some young officers. Even the dust on the ground has a magical glow: "a hundred pairs of golden and silver slippers shuffled the *shining* dust" (158; ch. 8, my italics).

Similarly, Nick's description of the Midwest of his youth is filled with nostalgic images of an idyllic past. Remembering his Christmas train-rides back home from boarding school and college, he says,

> When we pulled out into the winter night and the real snow, our snow, began to stretch out beside us and twinkle against the win-dows, and the dim lights of small Wisconsin stations moved by, a sharp wild brace came suddenly into the air. We drew in deep breaths of it . . . unutterably aware of our identity with this country. . . .
>
> That's my middle-west . . . the thrilling, returning trains of my youth and the street lamps and sleigh bells in the frosty dark and the shadows of holly wreaths thrown by lighted windows on the snow. (184; ch. 9)

Like the "clean, crisp mornings," "soft ground," and "shining dust" of Daisy and Jordan's girlhood, the nature imagery in this passage evokes a fresh, clean, virginal past, untouched by the corrupt world. Phrases such as "the real snow, our snow, began to stretch out beside us and twinkle" and "a sharp wild brace came suddenly into the air" evoke open spaces— clean, white, and shining—that invigorate not just the body but the spirit as well. "[T]he real snow" refers, of course, to the enormous quantity of clean, white snow that falls in Wisconsin and lasts all winter, as contrasted with the sooty snow that becomes slush under the wheels of New York City traffic. But the phrase "real snow" also suggests that life in the Mid-west of Nick's youth was more real, more genuine, than the artificial at-mosphere he associates with his adult life. This idea is underscored by the homey images of street lamps, sleigh bells, holly wreaths, and lighted windows, whose festive, inviting quality evoke the security and stability of a happy childhood.

In *The Great Gatsby*, even brief images of longing for the past carry emotional force. For example, the image of the young Gatsby revisiting

Louisville after Daisy's departure, "stretch[ing] out his hand desperately as if to snatch only a wisp of air, to save a fragment of the spot that she had made lovely for him" (160; ch. 8), and of Tom Buchanan, "drift[ing] on forever seeking a little wistfully for the dramatic turbulence of some irrecoverable football game" (10; ch. 1), are haunting and painful because they bespeak an emptiness that can never be filled. Like the imagery used to describe the youth of Daisy, Jordan, and Nick, these images of Gatsby and Tom evoke a world that is forever lost because it is forever past. We can never be young again, and the world of the past, as Gatsby finally learns, inevitably changes with time.

Perhaps the most powerfully nostalgic images of an idyllic past forever vanished are those that close the novel. As Nick sits on the beach the evening before his return to Wisconsin, he muses on

> the old island here that flowered once for Dutch sailors' eyes—a fresh green breast of the new world. Its vanished trees, the trees that had made way for Gatsby's house, had once pandered in whispers to the last and greatest of all human dreams; for a transitory enchanted moment man must have held his breath in the presence of this continent, compelled into an aesthetic contemplation he neither understood nor desired, face to face for the last time in history with something commensurate to his capacity for wonder. (189; ch. 9)

In this passage, Nick's nostalgic longing is universalized in global historical proportions: all of our individual longing for the dreams of lost youth and lost love—which, just like America, "flowered once," "fresh" and "green," while we "held [our] breath"—is absorbed in and expressed by a longing for the "enchanted . . . wonder" of a pristine American continent forever gone. And the repetition of words associated with this loss—"once," "vanished," "once," "last," "transitory," and "for the last time in history"—underscore its utter, heartbreaking finality.

The imagery of unfulfilled longing also weaves a common thread through characterization in the form of dreams of future fulfillment. Early in the novel, for example, Nick dreams about his successful future in the bond business, embodied in the books he bought on banking and investments, the description of which is immediately preceded by, and wedded to, nature imagery:

> And so with the sunshine and the great bursts of leaves growing on the trees . . . I had that familiar conviction that life was beginning over again with the summer.

> There was so much to read for one thing and so much fine health to be pulled down out of the young breath-giving air. I bought a dozen volumes on banking and credit and investment securities and they stood on my shelf in red and gold like new money from the mint, promising to unfold the shining secrets that only Midas and Morgan and Maecenas knew. (8; ch. 1)

The language used to describe the books—"new," "promising to unfold," and "shining"—links Nick's longing for success with the longing for new life awakened in the spring by the "sunshine," "great bursts of leaves," and "breath-giving air." Furthermore, the inclusion of financier J. P. Morgan's name with the names of mythical figures Midas and Maecenas imbues the passage with an ambience of myth, of fantasy, reinforcing the idea that Nick's success is not guaranteed but dreamed of, longed for with a visionary hopefulness that merges with, and is as natural as, the aching beauty of spring.

Though certainly developed on a less grand scale, the imagery of un-fulfilled longing nevertheless ties the depictions of Myrtle and George Wilson to those of the other characters who dream of future fulfillment. As Nick and Gatsby head to New York City for their lunch appointment, they drive through the valley of ashes:

> We passed Port Roosevelt, where there was a glimpse of red-belted ocean-going ships, and sped along a cobbled slum lined with the dark, undeserted saloons of the faded gilt nineteen-hundreds. Then the valley of ashes opened out on both sides of us, and I had a glimpse of Mrs. Wilson straining at the garage pump with panting vitality as we went by. (72; ch. 4)

We are prepared for our glimpse of the valley of ashes by the two neigh-borhoods—neither of them wealthy residential areas—that precede it. The first contains wharves; the second is a slum. Yet in both we see images of unfulfilled longing. In Port Roosevelt we see "red-belted ocean-going ships," which evoke the possibility of future adventure, enjoyment, profit, or at least change. In the slum we see "undeserted saloons of the faded gilt nineteen-hundreds," which evoke past glamor and excitement. Then we see Myrtle Wilson, whose posture at this moment, "straining at the garage pump," embodies longing for future fulfillment, presumably in the form of marriage to Tom Buchanan, who will rescue her from the valley of ashes and deliver her into a world of, from her perspective, paradisal hap-piness. That she is "panting with vitality" underscores her connection with life, with springtime, with nature, in direct opposition to the "deso-late area of land" (27; ch. 2) in which she lives, where people and objects alike appear "ash-grey" in the "powdery air" (27; ch. 2).

Although George Wilson is one of those "ash-grey" people, who "mingl[es] . . . with the cement color" (30; ch. 2) of his garage, even he is energized by longing for future fulfillment: when he sees Tom and Nick pull into his garage, "a damp gleam of hope spr[ings] into his light blue eyes" (29; ch. 2). This is the only time a lively verb is used to describe George, and it's the only time that color, or at least a healthy color, is associ-ated with him. Notably, it's the color the novel frequently associates with Gatsby's hopefulness: the mansion he bought in order to be near Daisy has "blue gardens" (43; ch. 3) and a "blue lawn" (189; ch. 9); his trees have "blue leaves" (159; ch. 8); and when he and Daisy reunite, "a damp streak of hair lay like a dash of blue paint across her cheek" (90). In addition, the "*damp gleam* of hope" in George's eyes resonates with the "*wet light*" with which the moon "soaked" young Gatsby's "tangled clothes upon the floor" (105; ch. 6, my italics) as he dreamed of the future in his bed at night.

Of course, the imagery of unfulfilled longing finds some of its most poetic expression when it evokes Gatsby's dreams of the future. For ex-ample, the young protagonist, in love with Daisy Fay and longing to pos-sess her, is fascinated by everything about her, including the house in which she and her family live.

> [W]hat gave [her house] an air of breathless intensity was that Daisy lived there. . . . There was a ripe mystery about it, a hint of bedrooms upstairs more beautiful and cool than other bedrooms, of gay and radiant activities taking place through its corridors and of romances that were not musty and laid away in lavender but fresh and breath-ing and redolent of this year's shining motor cars and of dances whose flowers were scarcely withered. (155–56; ch. 8)

Because, in this passage, Gatsby dreams of a lifestyle that is largely un-known to him and seems unattainable, he idealizes it just as Daisy, Jordan, Nick, and Tom idealize their irretrievable youth. The phrases "breathless in-tensity," "ripe mystery," and "hint of bedrooms" create, simultaneously, an air of sensuality and a feeling that Gatsby is a little boy with his face pressed against the window of a candy store, longing for the sweets he sees dis-played inside, which is, metaphorically, precisely what he is doing. The im-agery here also creates a sense of fecundity, of a fruition so longed for that it seems about to happen, as we see in the words "ripe," "radiant," "fresh and breathing and redolent," and "flowers." In fact, such is the power of Gatsby's longing that it can turn "motor cars" into natural objects: the romances that occur in Daisy's house are "redolent"—that is, sweet-smelling, usually of flowers—of "this year's shining motor cars." It should be no surprise, then, that such a longing as this can disconnect itself from its human source and live on its own, as it does when Daisy withdraws from Gatsby during his confrontation with Tom in the New York hotel room: "only the dead dream fought on as the afternoon slipped away, trying to touch what was no longer tangible, struggling unhappily, undespairingly toward that lost voice across the room" (142; ch. 7).

One of the more frequently noted images of Gatsby's longing for future fulfillment is that of the protagonist standing alone on the beach before his Long Island mansion, "trembling" (26; ch. 1) under the "silver pepper of the stars" (25; ch. 1) with his arms outstretched toward the "single green light, minute and far away" (26; ch. 1) at the end of Daisy's dock. This image recalls one discussed earlier: that of Gatsby in Louisville after Daisy's departure, his hand outstretched toward his lost past. But this time, the image of Gatsby's outstretched arms merges longing for the past with longing for the future, which, for him, have become one and the same: the fulfillment of his love for Daisy that he has come to Long Island to gain. The light at the end of her dock is green, carrying with it the hope of new beginnings that the green verdure of spring brings with it. And though the green light seems "minute and far away," Gatsby is, paradoxically, geographically and financially closer to Daisy than he has been since he lost her.

Perhaps the densest imagery used to describe Gatsby's longing for future fulfillment occurs in the description of the young protagonist walking down a Louisville street with Daisy, dreaming of greatness to come:

> Now it was a cool night with that mysterious excitement in it which comes at the two changes of the year. The quiet lights in the houses were humming out into the darkness and there was a stir and bustle among the stars. Out of the corner of his eye Gatsby saw that the blocks of the sidewalk really formed a ladder and mounted to a secret place above the trees—he could climb to it, if he climbed alone, and once there he could suck on the pap of life, gulp down the incomparable milk of wonder.
>
> His heart beat faster and faster as Daisy's white face came up to his own. He knew that when he kissed this girl, and forever wed his unutterable visions to her perishable breath, his mind would never romp again like the mind of God. So he waited, listening for a moment longer to the tuning fork that had been struck upon a star. Then

he kissed her. At his lips' touch she blossomed for him like a flower
and the incarnation was complete. (117; ch. 6)

In this remarkable passage, the imagery of unfulfilled longing performs at
least two important functions. First, as we saw in the case of Nick's longing for future success, the imagery here links human dreams to the concerns of nature: the "stir and bustle among the stars" seem in sympathy
with the "mysterious excitement" the characters feel because of the
change of seasons, which is linked, in turn, to the threshold of the future
at which they stand and which Gatsby longs to cross. In other words, the
imagery suggests that human longing is as natural and inevitable as the
seasons. Second, the imagery weds the cosmic quality of Gatsby's longing—his "unutterable visions" of the future in which his mind
"romp[s] . . . like the mind of God" and he dreams of "gulp[ing] down
the incomparable milk of wonder"—to the mortal "incarnation" of that
longing: Daisy. In other words, even when human longing is attached to
something as specific and ordinary as the desire for a woman, it is really
the incarnation of a cosmic force larger than we are.

To put the matter in slightly different terms, even when we think we
long for a specific person, event, or object, our longing is fed by something
greater than our individual selves, by something inherent in the condition
of being human. And indeed, the most frequent images of unfulfilled longing used to depict characters are those in which the longing is vague and
undefined, not attached to any specific goal. For example, the vague quality
of Nick's longing is expressed in his comment upon crossing from Long Island into New York City: "The city seen from the Queensboro Bridge is always the city seen for the first time, in its first wild promise of all the mystery and the beauty in the world" (73; ch. 4). We're not told what kind of
mystery and beauty are promised because Nick doesn't know. His longing
is non-specific. All he knows is that he wants something new and fresh
("seen for the first time"), exciting ("first wild promise"), and extravagant
("all the mystery and the beauty in the world").

We see the same kind of vague longing in the novel's numerous images of people looking through windows. For example, on Nick's frequent
evening walks along Fifth Avenue, he gazes in the windows of

throbbing taxi cabs, bound for the theatre district. . . . Forms leaned
together in the taxis as they waited, and voices sang, and there was
laughter from unheard jokes, and lighted cigarettes outlined unintel-
ligible gestures inside. (62; ch. 3)

Of course, Nick longs to be a part of what he sees, to belong, to share in the excitement visible through the cab windows. But he experiences the same kind of longing when he is one of the people inside the window, looking out. As he looks from the window of Tom and Myrtle's apartment during their party, he muses,

> high over the city our line of yellow windows must have contributed their share of human secrecy to the casual watcher in the darkening streets, and I was him too, looking up and wondering. I was within and without, simultaneously enchanted and repelled by the inexhaustible variety of life. (40; ch. 2)

I'm not suggesting that the gathering at Tom and Myrtle's apartment should satisfy Nick or make him feel less lonely. As this passage indicates, it makes him feel, yet again, that he is on the outside looking in. My point is simply that, in his thirty years of life, Nick has yet to meet people for whom he can sustain the desire to belong. His longing is a form of loneliness, but he doesn't quite know what it is he's lonely for. He knows only that he is like the young clerks in one of the novel's most touching images of vague, unfulfilled longing: "poor young clerks who loitered in front of windows waiting until it was time for a solitary restaurant dinner—young clerks in the dusk, wasting the most poignant moments of night and life" (62; ch. 3). Furthermore, the image of Nick looking out of Tom and Myrtle's apartment window and imagining that he is "the casual watcher in the darkening streets . . . looking up" at its yellow light, universalizes the image. Nick is not merely describing his own vague, unfulfilled longing, but the vague, unfulfilled longing of an "Everyman" figure, as well—the "casual watcher"—thus evoking the vague, unfulfilled longing experienced by us all.

It is interesting to note that the novel closes with an image of non-specific longing. The image of outstretched arms, which, as we have seen, embodies the longing for both past and future, occurs a third time, as an image of non-specific longing, at the end of the novel.

> Gatsby believed in the green light, the orgastic future that year by year recedes before us. It eluded us then, but that's no matter—tomorrow we will run faster, stretch out our arms farther. . . . And one fine morning—
>
> So we beat on, boats against the current, borne back ceaselessly into the past. (189; ch. 9)

Here the novel insists on the universal nature of Gatsby's longing. Gatsby's green light and outstretched arms become ours: The future "recedes before *us*," "eluded *us*," but "*we* will run faster" and "stretch out *our* arms farther." And in becoming universal, Gatsby's longing also becomes non-specific: for the protagonist, the green light represents Daisy; for us it could represent anything. But whatever it represents, we will pursue it despite the fact that our longing will never be fulfilled. Although we're longing toward the future, with the prow of our boat facing forward, we are in fact, like Gatsby, "borne back ceaselessly into the past." For in the timelessness of human longing, past and future are one, and our own unfulfilled longing is the "current" against which we "beat on" in vain. Thus, while few of the characters in *The Great Gatsby* are sympathetically portrayed, their unfulfilled longing—the experience they have in common with one another and, as this final passage underscores, with us—is portrayed with great poignancy.

The imagery of unfulfilled longing is also pervasive in the novel's evocation of setting, and here, too, it weaves a common thread through disparate social strata. The first notable example occurs in the description of Gatsby's mansion, "a colossal affair by any standard—it was a factual imitation of some Hôtel de Ville in Normandy, with a tower on one side, spanking new under a thin beard of raw ivy" (9; ch. 1). Before we even meet Gatsby, the setting in which he lives suggests the unfulfilled longing that is at the core of his existence. Like Gatsby, the mansion is larger than life, "a colossal affair," that is trying to be something it's not, something it can only imitate—a Hôtel de Ville in Normandy—just as the "thin beard of raw ivy" evokes the image of an adolescent boy trying to be a man. The tower, reaching toward the sky, also suggests a yearning for something beyond the immediately available. Furthermore, the mansion looks out over the bay, again as if yearning for something beyond itself, and as we saw earlier, it faces the green light at the end of Daisy's dock, the novel's icon of unfulfilled longing.

More frequently, an atmosphere of unfulfilled longing is created in the novel by settings that evoke a romantic ambience opposite that experienced by the characters who populate those settings. For example, in the midst of the tension and strife at the Buchanans' home during Nick's first visit there—Tom and Daisy have obviously been fighting, insistent phone calls from Myrtle intrude during lunch, Jordan shamelessly tries to overhear the Buchanans' quarrel in the next room, Tom pontificates about his racist views—the setting is described with keen appreciation for the idyllic fulfillment promised, though not delivered, by the setting.

> We walked through a high hallway into a bright rosy-colored space,
> fragilely bound into the house by French windows at either end. The
> windows were ajar and gleaming white against the fresh grass outside
> that seemed to grow a little way into the house. A breeze blew through
> the room, blew curtains in at one end and out the other like pale
> flags, twisting them up toward the frosted wedding cake of the ceil-
> ing—and then rippled over the wine-colored rug making a shadow
> on it as wind does on the sea. (12; ch. 1)

Everything about this setting suggests newness, hopefulness, and fulfillment. The space Nick enters is "rosy-colored," the traditional ambience of
romantic fulfillment. The "gleaming white" open windows, the "fresh
grass," and the description of the ceiling as a "frosted wedding cake" evoke
the hopefulness of new beginnings: virginity, springtime, weddings. In
addition, the references to wedding cake and wine suggest celebration,
the fulfillment of hopes. The net result of the dissonance between the fulfillment promised by the setting and the dissatisfaction experienced by
the characters within that setting is an atmosphere of unfulfilled longing,
such as Coleridge's Ancient Mariner describes, though far less romantically, on his becalmed boat: "Water, water every where, / Nor any drop to
drink" (ll. 121–22).

Settings described with images of harmony, refinement, and plenitude
imbue even the most vulgar scenes with a sense of unfulfilled longing that
yearns toward a paradisal beauty ironically at odds with the action occurring. For example, the apartment Tom keeps for his adulterous trysts with
Myrtle, where the couple also entertains Myrtle's noisy, vulgar, hard-drink-
ing friends, is in a "long white cake of apartment houses" (32; ch. 2) and
filled with tapestried furniture displaying "scenes of ladies swinging in the
gardens of Versailles" (33; ch. 2). When Nick accompanies Tom and Myrtle
to their apartment, he notes that Fifth Avenue looks "so warm and soft, almost pastoral, on the summer Sunday afternoon that I wouldn't have been
surprised to see a great flock of white sheep turn the corner" (32; ch. 2).
"[L]ong white cake," "ladies" on swings, "gardens," "Versailles," "warm and
soft," "pastoral," "summer Sunday afternoon," "great flock of white
sheep"—this is an idyllic language, a language of plenitude, fulfillment,
pleasure, and harmony. Again, the dissonance between the drunken, violent
vulgarity of the party scene—guests stumble about; Myrtle and Mrs.
McKee make anti-Semitic, elitist, and obscene remarks; Tom and Myrtle
quarrel; Tom breaks Myrtle's nose—and the pastoral plenitude of the descriptive language noted above creates an ambience of unfulfilled longing
for life the way it should be, life the way we want it to be, life the way it isn't.

The sense of unfulfilled longing created by the dissonance between vulgar characters and a setting that bespeaks harmony, refinement, and plenitude is especially interesting in the description of Gatsby's parties. Like the money with which he bought his mansion, the money that pays for Gatsby's extravagant parties comes from criminal activities associated with Meyer Wolfshiem, the novel's most sinister and one of its most vulgar characters. And as Nick points out, Gatsby's guests "conducted themselves," in extremely vulgar fashion, "according to the rules of behavior associated with amusement parks" (45; ch. 3). Almost everyone is rude and obnoxious. They gossip mercilessly about their host, whom few have met or care to meet. And the crowd, itself in varying degrees of drunken hysteria, is frequently treated to a drunken display by one or another of its members. There is, for example, a young woman who "dumps" down a cocktail "for courage" and "dances out alone on the canvass to perform" (45; ch. 3); "a rowdy little girl who gave way upon the slightest provocation to uncontrollable laughter" (51; ch. 3); a driver so drunk that, when his car winds up in a ditch beside the driveway, "violently shorn of one wheel" (58; ch. 3), he doesn't realize it has stopped moving; and a drunken young girl who has to have her "head stuck in a pool" (113; ch. 6) to stop her from screaming.

The setting is described, however, in an intensely romantic fashion: "There was music from my neighbor's house through the summer nights. In his blue gardens men and girls came and went like moths among the whisperings and the champagne and the stars" (43; ch. 3). The "premature moon" is "produced like the supper, no doubt, out of a caterer's basket" (47; ch. 3), and even the refreshments seem enchanted: a "tray of cocktails floated at us through the twilight" (47; ch. 3), and on "buffet tables garnished with glistening hors-d'oeuvre, spiced baked hams crowded against salads of harlequin designs and pastry pigs and turkeys bewitched to a dark gold" (44; ch. 3). The setting is thus described as if it were a quiet pastoral scene—"blue gardens," "whisperings," "stars"—in a mythical kingdom where the moon is somehow magically produced "premature[ly]"; where cocktails "floa[t]" toward those who desire them; and where food is "bewitched."

Of course, we must remember that Nick is our narrator. We see the settings in the novel through his eyes. Therefore, it would not be unreasonable to conclude that, in those scenes in which setting and action are at odds, the unfulfilled longing evoked is Nick's. He yearns for a world of pastoral beauty, like the world he knew as a youth in Wisconsin, but that world is gone. The combined effects of adulthood, World War I, and his own lack of purpose have wiped it out for him. But opulence creates romantic possibilities. What Nick said of Gatsby is also true of himself: he "was overwhelmingly aware of the youth and mystery that wealth imprisons and preserves" (157; ch. 8). Nick longs for the romantic possibilities he sees in the world of the wealthy although most of the people who inhabit that world seem blind to, or take for granted, its idyllic quality.

As these examples illustrate, *The Great Gatsby*'s haunting imagery tells us that unfulfilled longing is universal and inevitable. No matter who we are or what we have, we cannot be long content: we will inevitably long for something else. We may attach that longing to an object and believe that we are longing *for* something, whether that something lie in our past or in our future. Or we may not attach that longing to an object, in which case we will experience it as a vague restlessness, the kind of restlessness that sends Melville's Ishmael to sea "whenever it is a damp, drizzly November in [his] soul" (21). But unfulfilled longing, in one form or another, is inescapable. Even on that afternoon when Gatsby finally reunites with Daisy and "glow[s]" with "well-being" (94; ch. 5) because he has learned that she still loves him, "there must have been moments . . . when Daisy tumbled short of his dreams—not through her own fault but because . . . [n]o amount of fire or freshness can challenge what a man will store up in his ghostly heart" (101; ch. 5).

This sense of inescapability, this feeling that unfulfilled longing is inherent in the human condition, is reinforced in the novel by the static quality of its imagery of unfulfilled longing. Each of the images we've analyzed—indeed, most of the imagery in the novel—seems to exist in a timeless present, a fixed tableau, frozen forever like the lovers carved on the Grecian urn in Keats's famous Ode: "Bold Lover, never, never canst thou kiss, / Though winning near the goal—yet, do not grieve; / She cannot fade, though thou hast not thy bliss, / For ever wilt thou love, and she be fair!" (ll. 17–20). For just as wealth "imprisons and preserves" forever "youth and mystery" (157; ch. 8), unfulfilled longing imprisons and preserves forever that for which it longs. Let's take a look at two images of unfulfilled longing that illustrate this quality of timelessness with particular clarity.

When Tom and Daisy finally attend one of Gatsby's parties, Daisy is attracted, at the beginning of the evening, by the sight of a "celebrity of the movies," a "gorgeous, scarcely human orchid of a woman who sat in state under a white plum tree" with her director "bending over her" (111; ch. 6). At the end of the evening, Nick notices that "the moving picture director and his Star" are "still under the white plum tree . . . their faces . . . touching except for a pale thin ray of moonlight between" (113; ch. 6). He says, "It occurred to me that he had been very slowly bending toward her all evening to attain this proximity" (113; ch. 6). This is an image of longing—literally, a physical leaning toward the object of desire—that seems to exist in a dimension beyond time, like the moment frozen forever on Keats's urn. The characters seem barely to move over the course of an entire evening, and the timeless quality of the image is increased by the otherworldliness of the pictorial details: the woman is a "scarcely human orchid," the only vegetation in sight is a "white plum tree," and the only light is a "pale thin ray of moonlight."

A similar tableau of unfulfilled longing is presented when Tom, Nick, and Gatsby, waiting outside the Buchanan's house to drive Daisy and Jordan to New York City, see a single sailboat in the distance.

> On the green Sound, stagnant in the heat, one small sail crawled slowly toward the fresher sea. . . . Our eyes lifted over the rosebeds and the hot lawn and the weedy refuse of the dog days along shore. Slowly the white wings of the boat moved against the blue cool limit of the sky. Ahead lay the scalloped ocean and the abounding blessed isles. (124; ch. 6)

The unfulfilled longing represented here is the longing for paradisal fulfillment, the longing to escape the real world. The extremely slow movement of the boat, insisted on twice in this short passage (it "crawled slowly" and "[s]lowly the white wings of the boat moved"), the great distance the boat seems to be from land (from where the characters stand, it looks like "one small sail"), and the classic colors of the seascape (white sails against blue sky) freeze this image as it would be frozen by paint on canvas. The sense of timelessness this image evokes is increased by its mythical quality: the "fres[h]," "cool" world in which the boat sails is contrasted sharply with the real world in which Tom, Nick, and Gatsby stand, with its "stagnant . . . heat," "hot lawn," and "weedy refuse of the dog days along shore"; the boat's sail turns into "white wings"; and its destination is some mythical never-never land, "the abounding blessed isles."

It is interesting to note, in this context, that time seems almost literally to stand still at the very center of the novel, when Gatsby and Daisy, whose relationship embodies unfulfilled longing, reunite. The clock on Nick's mantlepiece—which Gatsby leans his head against, knocks over, and catches in his hands—is "defunct" (91; ch. 5): time has stopped. As the scene progresses, Gatsby's existence in time stops, too: he "run[s] down like an overwound clock" (97; ch. 5). And as he and Daisy sit silently together in the gathering dusk, "remot[e]" (102; ch. 5) from the real world in which time passes, the timeless dimension they inhabit is foregrounded by its sharp contrast with the bustle of the real world outside: "Outside the wind was loud and . . . [a]ll the lights were going on in West Egg now; the electric trains, men-carrying, were plunging home" (101; ch. 5).

It is the universal theme of unfulfilled longing, so powerfully carried by the novel's magnificent imagery, that has made *The Great Gatsby* the enduring masterpiece it is. As publisher Charles Scribner III said of the novel in 1992, "to the present day its place at the top of Scribner bestsell[ing paperbacks] has never been challenged" (205). *The Great Gatsby* doesn't have this kind of enduring value because of its social commentary on the Jazz Age, though an excellent social commentary it surely is. The novel has maintained its "hallowed place in American literature" (Scribner 205) because it speaks to something deep in the heart of human experience: the unfulfilled longing that is at the core of the human condition. Like Daisy's voice, which "held [Gatsby] most with its fluctuating, feverish warmth because it couldn't be over-dreamed," the lyric melancholy of unfulfilled longing is a "deathless song" (101; ch. 5), and Fitzgerald's superb novel has captured that song as none other has.

Questions for Further Practice: New Critical Approaches to Other Literary Works

The following questions are intended as models. They can help you use New Criticism to interpret the literary works to which they refer or other texts of your choice.

1. In Kate Chopin's "The Storm" (1898), how do nature imagery and point of view support the theme that individual circumstances, not abstract rules, determine what is right and wrong, healthy and unhealthy?

2. In Alberto Moravia's "The Chase" (1967), how does the characterization of the narrator, the story's opening and closing scenes, and the use of nature imagery support the theme that adultery is a form of emotional distance that signals the end of intimacy in a marriage?

3. How does Langston Hughes's "The Negro Speaks of Rivers" (1926) use geographical, historical, and biblical allusion, as well as

nature imagery, to forward his theme about the negro race? How
would you state that theme?

4. In Arthur Miller's *Death of a Salesman* (1949), how does setting
   work to create sympathy for Willy as the victim of forces beyond
   his control, thus contributing to the theme that the needs of the
   individual are often sacrificed to the demands of society?

5. In Toni Cade Bambara's "The Lesson" (1972), how is the topic of
   initiation suggested by the point of view from which the story is
   told, the narrator's tone of voice and use of slang, and the
   imagery used to describe the toy store and the children's response
   to it? What theme do you think is implied by your analysis of
   these formal elements? Is that theme borne out by the story's
   characterization of the narrator? How? (If not, try to find a theme
   that is supported by all of these formal elements.)

For Further Reading

All of the following works will help you develop your skills as New Critics. Texts listed under "Category I" are written in language accessible to
most beginners. Texts listed under "Category II" employ more technical
language but are well worth the extra effort that may be required of some
students new to the field.

Category I

Brooks, Cleanth. *The Well-Wrought Urn: Studies in the Structure of Poetry*. New York:
    Reynal & Hitchcock, 1947. (See, especially, "Gray's Storied Urn," 96–113; "Keats'
    Sylvan Historian: History without Footnotes," 139–52; and "The Heresy of
    Paraphrase," 176–96.)

Brooks, Cleanth, and Robert Penn Warren. *Understanding Fiction*. 1943. 2nd ed. New
    York: Appleton-Century-Crofts, 1959. (See, especially, "Letter to the Teacher,"
    xi–xx, and "What Theme Reveals," 272–78.)

———. *Understanding Poetry*. 1938. 4th ed. New York: Holt, Rinehart and Winston,
    1976. (See, especially, "Poetry as a Way of Saying," 1–16; "Tone," 112–15; and
    "Theme, Meaning, and Dramatic Structure," 266–70.)

Wellek, René, and Austin Warren. *Theory of Literature*. 1949. 2nd ed. New York:
    Harcourt, Brace and World, 1956. (See, especially, "Image, Metaphor, Symbol,
    Myth," 175–201.)

Wimsatt, W. K., Jr. *The Verbal Icon: Studies in the Meaning of Poetry*. Lexington: U of
    Kentucky P, 1954. (See, especially, "The Intentional Fallacy," 3–18; "The
    Affective Fallacy," 21–39; "The Structure of Romantic Nature Imagery," 103–16;
    and "Explication as Criticism," 235–51.)

Category II

Blackmur, R. P. *The Lion and the Honeycomb: Essays in Solicitude and Critique*. New York: Harcourt Brace, 1955.

Eliot, T. S. *Selected Prose of T. S. Eliot*. Ed. Frank Kermode. New York: Harcourt Brace Jovanovich, 1975. (See, especially, "Tradition and the Individual Talent," 37–44, and "*Hamlet*," 45–49.)

Empson, William. *Seven Types of Ambiguity*. New York: Noonday, 1955.

Krieger, Murray. *The New Apologists for Poetry*. Minneapolis: U of Minnesota P, 1956.

Ransom, John Crowe. *The New Criticism*. New York: New Directions, 1941.

Richards, I. A. *Coleridge on Imagination*. New York: W. W. Norton, 1950.

Wimsatt, W. K., Jr., ed. *Explication as Criticism: Selected Papers from the English Institute, 1941–1952*. New York: Columbia UP, 1963. (See, especially, Cleanth Brooks's "Literary Criticism: Marvell's 'Horatian Ode,'" 100–130; Douglas Bush's "John Milton," 131–45; and Lionel Trilling's "Wordsworth's 'Ode': Intimations of Immortality," 175–202.)

Notes

1. Most literary critics today, regardless of their theoretical orientation, acknowledge that New Criticism's concept of "universal significance" was bogus, even harmful, because a text's "universality" was determined by, and thus too often limited to, white male American experience.

2. For similar arguments, see, for example, Cartwright, Chase, Dillon, Gross, Hart, Le Vot, Moore, Nash, Stern, and Trilling.

3. The view that Gatsby shares the corruption of his world is held, for example, by Bruccoli, Dyson, and Fussell.

Works Cited

Bewley, Marius. "Scott Fitzgerald's Criticism of America." *Sewanee Review* 62 (1954): 223–46. Rpt. in *Modern Critical Interpretations: F. Scott Fitzgerald's* The Great Gatsby. Ed. Harold Bloom. New York: Chelsea, 1986. 11–27.

Bruccoli, Matthew J. *Some Sort of Epic Grandeur: The Life of F. Scott Fitzgerald*. New York: Harcourt, 1981.

Burnam, Tom. "The Eyes of Dr. Eckleburg: A Re-Examination of *The Great Gatsby*." *College English* 13 (1952). Rpt. in *F. Scott Fitzgerald: A Collection of Critical Essays*. Ed. Arthur Mizener. Englewood Cliffs: Prentice-Hall, 1963. 104–11.

Cartwright, Kent. "Nick Carraway as Unreliable Narrator." *Papers on Language and Literature* 20.2 (1984): 218–32.

Chase, Richard. "*The Great Gatsby*." *The American Novel and Its Traditions*. New York: Doubleday, 1957. Rpt. in The Great Gatsby: *A Study*. Ed. Frederick J. Hoffman. New York: Scribner's, 1962. 297–302.

Coleridge, Samuel Taylor. "The Rime of the Ancient Mariner." *Romantic and Victorian Poetry*. 2nd ed. Ed. William Frost. Englewood Cliffs: Prentice-Hall, 1961. 122–39.

Dillon, Andrew. "*The Great Gatsby*: The Vitality of Illusion." *Arizona Quarterly* 44.1 (1988): 49–61.

Dyson, A. E. "*The Great Gatsby*: Thirty-Six Years After." *Modern Fiction Studies* 7.1 (1961). Rpt. in *F. Scott Fitzgerald: A Collection of Essays*. Ed. Arthur Mizener. Englewood Cliffs: Prentice-Hall, 1963. 112–24.

Fussell, Edwin. "Fitzgerald's Brave New World." *ELH, Journal of English Literary History* 19 (1952). Rpt. in *F. Scott Fitzgerald: A Collection of Critical Essays*. Ed. Arthur Mizener. Englewood Cliffs: Prentice-Hall, 1963. 43–56.

Gallo, Rose Adrienne. *F. Scott Fitzgerald*. New York: Ungar, 1978.

Gross, Barry Edward. "Jay Gatsby and Myrtle Wilson: A Kinship." *Tennessee Studies in Literature* 8 (1963): 57–60. Excerpted in *Gatsby*. Ed. Harold Bloom. New York: Chelsea House, 1991. 23–25.

Hart, Jeffrey. "'Out of it ere night': The WASP Gentleman as Cultural Ideal." *New Criterion* 7.5 (1989): 27–34.

Keats, John. "Ode on a Grecian Urn." *Romantic and Victorian Poetry*. 2nd ed. Ed. William Frost. Englewood Cliffs: Prentice-Hall, 1961. 236–37.

Le Vot, André. *F. Scott Fitzgerald: A Biography*. Trans. William Byron. Garden City, New York: Doubleday, 1983.

Melville, Herman. *Moby Dick*. 1851. New York: Signet, 1980.

Moore, Benita A. *Escape into a Labyrinth: F. Scott Fitzgerald, Catholic Sensibility, and the American Way*. New York: Garland, 1988.

Nash, Charles C. "From West Egg to Short Hills: The Decline of the Pastoral Ideal from *The Great Gatsby* to Philip Roth's *Goodbye, Columbus*." *Philological Association* 13 (1988): 22–27.

Scribner, Charles III. "Publisher's Afterword." *The Great Gatsby*. F. Scott Fitzgerald. New York: Simon & Schuster, 1995. 195–205.

Stern, Milton R. *The Golden Moment: The Novels of F. Scott Fitzgerald*. Urbana: U of Illinois P, 1970.

Trilling, Lionel. "F. Scott Fitzgerald." *The Liberal Imagination*. New York: Viking, 1950. 243–54. Rpt. in The Great Gatsby: *A Study*. Ed. Frederick J. Hoffman. New York: Scribner's, 1962. 232–43.

CHAPTER 6

Reader-Response Criticism

As its name implies, reader-response criticism focuses on readers' responses to literary texts. Many new students of critical theory are relieved and happy when they get to the unit on reader-response criticism, perhaps because they enjoy the idea that their responses are important enough to become the focus of literary interpretation. Or perhaps they assume that reader-response criticism means "I can't be wrong because any way I interpret the text is my response, so the professor can't reject it." Let me break the bad news to you up front. Depending on the kind of reader-response theory we're talking about, your response to a literary text can be judged insufficient or less sufficient than others. And even when a given reader-response theory does assert that there is no such thing as an insufficient (or inaccurate or inappropriate) response, your job as a practitioner of that theory isn't merely to respond but to analyze your response, or the responses of others, and that analysis can be found wanting.

The good news, however, is that reader-response criticism is a broad, exciting, evolving domain of literary studies that can help us learn about our own reading processes and how they relate to, among other things, specific elements in the texts we read, our life experiences, and the intellectual community of which we are a member. In addition, for those of you who plan on teaching or are already doing so, reader-response theory offers ideas that can help you in the classroom, whether that classroom is in an elementary school or on a college campus.

If you're getting the feeling that reader-response criticism covers a good deal of diverse ground, you're right. In fact, any time an essay ana-

lyzes the act of reading or readers' responses, one could classify that essay
as reader-response criticism. For example, psychoanalytic criticism, when
it investigates the psychological motives for certain kinds of interpretations of a literary text, is also a form of reader-response criticism. Feminist criticism, when it analyzes how patriarchy teaches us to interpret
texts in a sexist manner, is also a form of reader-response criticism. Structuralist criticism, when it examines the literary conventions a reader must
have consciously or unconsciously internalized in order to be able to read
a particular literary text, is also considered a form of reader-response
criticism.[1] And lesbian and gay criticism, when it studies how our homophobic culture suppresses our ability to see homoeroticism in literary
texts, is also a form of reader-response criticism.

Attention to the reading process emerged during the 1930s as a reaction against the growing tendency to reject the reader's role in creating
meaning, a tendency that became a fixed principle of the New Criticism
that dominated critical practice in the 1940s and 1950s. As we saw in
Chapter Five, the New Critics believed that the timeless meaning of the
text—what the text *is*—is contained in the text alone. Its meaning is not a
product of the author's intention and does not change with the reader's
response. As you may remember, New Critics claimed that attention to
the reader's response confuses what the text *is* with what the text *does*.
Reader-response theory, which didn't receive much attention until the
1970s, maintains that what a text is cannot be separated from what it
does. For despite their divergent views of the reading process, which we'll
examine a little later, reader-response theorists share two beliefs: (1) that
the role of the reader cannot be omitted from our understanding of literature and (2) that readers do not passively consume the meaning presented to them by an objective literary text; rather they actively make the
meaning they find in literature.

This second belief, that readers actively make meaning, suggests, of
course, that different readers may read the same text quite differently. In
fact, reader-response theorists believe that even the same reader reading
the same text on two different occasions will probably produce different
meanings because so many variables contribute to our experience of the
text. Knowledge we've acquired between our first and second reading of a
text, personal experiences that have occurred in the interim, a change in
mood between our two encounters with the text, or a change in the purpose for which we're reading it can all contribute to our production of
different meanings for the same text.

To get a clear idea of just how much the nature of the reader's involvement with a text can alter its meaning, let's look at the following passage. As you read it, imagine that you're a home buyer and circle any detail, positive or negative, that you think would be important if you were considering buying the house described in the passage.

The House Passage[2]

The two boys ran until they came to the driveway. "See, I told you today was good for skipping school," said Mark. "Mom is never home on Thursday," he added. Tall hedges hid the house from the road so the pair strolled across the finely landscaped yard. "I never knew your place was so big," said Pete. "Yeah, but it's nicer now than it used to be since Dad had the new stone siding put on and added the fireplace."

There were front and back doors and a side door which led to the garage which was empty except for three parked 10-speed bikes. They went in the side door, Mark explaining that it was always open in case his younger sisters got home earlier than their mother.

Pete wanted to see the house so Mark started with the living room. It, like the rest of the downstairs, was newly painted. Mark turned on the stereo, the noise of which worried Pete. "Don't worry, the nearest house is a quarter of a mile away," Mark shouted. Pete felt more comfortable observing that no houses could be seen in any direction beyond the huge yard.

The dining room, with all the china, silver and cut glass, was no place to play so the boys moved into the kitchen, where they made sandwiches. Mark said they wouldn't go to the basement because it had been damp and musty ever since the new plumbing had been installed.

"This is where my Dad keeps his famous paintings and his coin collection," Mark said as they peered into the den. Mark bragged that he could get spending money whenever he needed it since he'd discovered that his Dad kept a lot in the desk drawer.

There were three upstairs bedrooms. Mark showed Pete his mother's closet which was filled with furs and the locked box which held her jewels. His sisters' room was uninteresting except for the color TV, which Mark carried to his room. Mark bragged that the bathroom in the hall was his since one had been added to his sisters' room for their use. The big highlight in his room, though, was a leak in the ceiling where the old roof had finally rotted.

Many readers probably would produce a list of positive and negative qualities something like the following:

Positive Qualities	Negative Qualities
tall hedges (privacy)	damp, musty basement
finely landscaped yard	new plumbing amiss
stone siding	rotting roof
fireplace	leak in bedroom ceiling
garage	
newly painted downstairs	
nearest house 1/4 mi. away (privacy)	
den	
3 upstairs bedrooms	
new bathroom added to bedroom	

Now reread the passage and underline any detail, positive or negative, that you think would be important if you were casing the house in order to rob it. Many readers probably would produce a list of positive and negative qualities something like the following:

Positive Qualities	Negative Qualities
tall hedges (safe from observation)	
no one home on Thursdays	
finely landscaped yard (these folks have money)	
3 10-speed bikes in garage	
side door always left open	
nearest house 1/4 mi. away (safe from observation)	
many portable goods: stereo, china, silver, cut glass, paintings, coin collection, furs, box of jewels, tv set	
cash kept in desk drawer	

During our second reading of this passage, because we're thinking of robbing the house, we focus on very different details, and even when we focus on the same details, they have a very different meaning for us. For example, the privacy that, for many home buyers, is an asset becomes a liability in terms of the home's vulnerability to burglars. Merely changing the purpose for which we read a passage can radically alter the passage we read. Of course, some home-buying readers might immediately see the negative aspect of the home's privacy because their experience has made them more aware of crime, illustrating reader-response theory's assertion that readers draw on their personal experiences to create meaning.

As the above exercise illustrates, a written text is not an object, despite its physical existence, but an event that occurs within the reader, whose response is of primary importance in creating the text. Theorists disagree, however, about how our responses are formed and what role, if any, the text plays in creating them. Opinions range from the belief that the literary text is as active as the reader in creating meaning to the belief that the text doesn't exist at all except as it is created by readers.

Let's take a look at a representative sample of this range of approaches, which may be loosely organized under five headings: transactional reader-response theory, affective stylistics, subjective reader-response theory, psychological reader-response theory, and social reader-response theory. It is important to remember that these categories are somewhat artificial: the dividing lines are often fluid and indistinct because practitioners in different schools will hold some ideas in common while practitioners within each school will differ on some points. In addition, as we saw earlier, any attempt to classify reader-response approaches will inevitably include some theories whose practitioners may not call themselves reader-response critics and omit some theories that a different system of classification would include. However, it is precisely because the fabric of reader-response theory is woven of so many diverse and controversial threads that some method of classification is necessary, at least at this stage of the game. The method I've chosen is the one I think will give you the clearest sense of the reader-response enterprise in general and prepare you to read the work of theorists in this field.

Transactional Reader-Response Theory

Often associated with the work of Louise Rosenblatt, who formulated many of its premises, transactional reader-response theory analyzes the

transaction between text and reader. Rosenblatt doesn't reject the importance of the text in favor of the reader; rather she claims that both are
necessary in the production of meaning. She differentiates among the
terms *text*, which refers to the printed words on the page; *reader*; and
poem, which refers to the literary work produced by the text and the
reader together.

How does this transaction take place? As we read a text, it acts as a
stimulus to which we respond in our own personal way. Feelings, associations, and memories occur as we read, and these responses influence the
way in which we make sense of the text as we move through it. Literature
we've encountered prior to this reading, the sum total of our accumulated knowledge, and even our current physical condition and mood will
influence us, as well. At various points while we read, however, the text
acts as a *blueprint* that we can use to correct our interpretation when we
realize it has traveled too far afield of what is written on the page. This
process of correcting our interpretation as we move through the text usually results in our going back to reread earlier sections in light of some
new development in the text. Thus, the text guides our self-corrective
process as we read and will continue to do so after the reading is finished
if we go back and reread portions, or the entire text, in order to develop
or complete our interpretation. Thus the creation of the poem, the literary work, is a product of the transaction between text and reader, both of
which are equally important to the process.

In order for this transaction between text and reader to occur, however,
our approach to the text must be, in Rosenblatt's words, aesthetic rather
than efferent. When we read in the *efferent* mode, we focus just on the information contained in the text, as if it were a storehouse of facts and ideas
that we could carry away with us. "Arthur Miller's *Death of a Salesman*
(1949) is a play about a travelling salesman who kills himself so that his son
will receive his life-insurance money" is an example of an efferent stance
toward the text. In contrast, when we read in the *aesthetic* mode, we experience a personal relationship to the text that focuses our attention on the
emotional subtleties of its language and encourages us to make judgments.
"In *Death of a Salesman*, Willy Loman's plight is powerfully evoked by the
contrast between his small house, bathed in soft blue light, and the large,
orange-colored apartment buildings that surround it" is an example of an
aesthetic stance toward the text. Without the aesthetic approach, there
could be no transaction between text and reader to analyze.

Followers of Wolfgang Iser[3] might explain what Rosenblatt refers to
as the blueprint and stimulus functions of the text in terms of two kinds

of meaning every text offers: determinate and indeterminate meaning. *Determinate meaning* refers to what might be called the facts of the text, certain events in the plot or physical descriptions clearly provided by the words on the page. In contrast, *indeterminate meaning*, or *indeterminacy*, refers to "gaps" in the text—such as actions that are not clearly explained or that seem to have multiple explanations—which allow or even invite readers to create their own interpretations. (Thus, Rosenblatt's efferent approach depends entirely upon determinate meaning, while her aesthetic approach depends upon both determinate and indeterminate meaning.) In *Death of a Salesman* we might say, for example, that the text's determinate meaning includes the fact that Willy habitually lies to Linda about his success on the job, about how well liked he is, and about how important his role in the company has been. The play's indeterminacy includes issues such as how much (or how little) of the truth Linda knows about her husband's career, at what point she realizes the truth (if she ever does), and why she doesn't let Willy tell her the truth about his shortcomings when he tries to do so. Of course, the burden is on us to support our claim that a given textual meaning is determinate or indeterminate.

The interplay between determinate and indeterminate meanings, as we read, results in a number of ongoing experiences for the reader: retrospection, or thinking back to what we've read earlier in the text; anticipation of what will come next; fulfillment or disappointment of our anticipation; revision of our understanding of characters and events; and so on. For what at one point in the work appears to be determinate meaning will often, at a later point in the work, appear to be indeterminate, as our point of view shifts among the various perspectives provided by, for example, the narrator, the characters, and the events of an unfolding plot. Thus, for Iser, though the reader projects meaning onto the text, the reading activities through which we construct that meaning are *prestructured* by, or built into, the text. In other words, Iser believes that the text, itself, guides us through the processes involved in interpreting (projecting meaning onto) it.

According to transactional theorists, different readers come up with different acceptable interpretations because the text allows for a range of acceptable meanings, that is, a range of meanings for which textual support is available. However, because there is a real text involved in this process to which we must refer to justify or modify our responses, not all readings are acceptable and some are more so than others. Even authors' stated intentions in writing their texts, as well as any interpretations they may offer afterwards, are but additional readings of the text, which must be submitted for evaluation to the text-as-blueprint just as all other readings are. Thus, transactional analysis relies a good deal on the authority of the text, insisted upon by the New Critics, while also bringing the reader's response into the limelight. In addition, transactional analysis accounts for the range of successful readings produced even by the New Critics themselves, despite their belief that every text authorizes a single best reading.[4]

Affective Stylistics

Affective stylistics is derived from analyzing further the notion that a literary text is an event that occurs in time—that comes into being as it is read—rather than an object that exists in space. The text is examined closely, often line by line or even word by word, in order to understand *how* (stylistics) it *affects* (affective) the reader in the process of reading. Although there is thus a great deal of focus on the text, which is why some theorists consider this approach transactional in nature, many practitioners of affective stylistics do not consider the text an objective, autonomous entity—it does not have a fixed meaning independent of readers—because the text consists of the results it produces, and those results occur within the reader. For example, when Stanley Fish describes how a text is structured, the structure he describes is the structure of the reader's response as it occurs from moment to moment, not the structure of the text as we might assemble it—like puzzle pieces all spread out at once before us—after we've finished reading. Nevertheless, affective stylistics is not a description of the reader's impressionistic responses but a cognitive analysis of the mental processes produced by specific elements in the text. Indeed, it is the "slow-motion," phrase-by-phrase analysis of how the text structures the reader's response for which affective stylistics is perhaps best known.

Some of the finest examples of this procedure have been produced by Fish. To see how this approach works, let's take a look at his analysis of the following sentence.

> That Judas perished by hanging himself, there is no certainty in Scripture: though in one place it seems to affirm it, and by a doubtful word hath given occasion to translate it; yet in another place, in a more punctual description, it maketh it improbable, and seems to overthrow it. ("Literature" 71)

According to Fish, the question "What does this sentence mean?" or "What does this sentence say?" yields little because the sentence provides us with no facts with which we could answer the question. Even if we notice that the sentence does say something—it says that Scripture gives us no clear indication of whether or not Judas hanged himself—his point is that the sentence tells us only that it is unable to tell us anything. In contrast, he notes, the question "What does the sentence do to the reader?" or "How does the reader of this sentence make meaning?" yields something quite useful.

What this passage about Judas *does*, Fish notes, is move the reader from certainty to uncertainty. The first clause, "that Judas perished by hanging himself" (which, as most of us know, is a kind of shorthand for "the fact that Judas perished by hanging himself"), is an assertion we accept as a statement of fact. We thus begin with a feeling of certainty that leads us, without our being quite conscious of it, to anticipate a number of possible ways the sentence might end, all of which would confirm our certainty that Judas hanged himself. Fish offers these three examples of the kinds of endings the first clause leads us to expect.

1. That Judas perished by hanging himself, *is* (an example for us all).
2. That Judas perished by hanging himself, *shows* (how conscious he was of the enormity of his sin).
3. That Judas perished by hanging himself, *should* (give us pause). ("Literature" 71)

These expectations narrow the possible meanings of the next three words in the passage: "there is no." At this point, the reader expects to see "there is no doubt," but is given instead "there is no certainty." Now the fact of Judas's hanging himself, upon which our understanding of the sentence has rested, becomes uncertain. Now the reader is involved in a completely different kind of activity. As Fish puts it, "Rather than following an argument along a well-lighted path (a light, after all, has gone *out*), [the reader] is now looking for one" ("Literature" 71). In such a situation, the reader will tend to read on in hopes of finding clarification. But as we continue to read the passage, our uncertainty only increases as we move back and forth between words that seem to promise clarity—"place," "affirm," "place," "punctual," "overthrow"—and words that seem to withdraw that promise: "Though," "doubtful," "yet," "improbable," "seems." Uncertainty is further increased by the excessive use of the pronoun *it* because, as the sentence progresses, the reader has more and more difficulty figuring out what *it* refers to.

Such analyses are performed by reader-response critics in order to map the pattern by which a text structures the reader's response while reading. This response is then used to show that the meaning of the text does not consist of the final conclusion we draw about what the text *says*; rather, the meaning of the text consists of our experience of what the text *does* to us as we read it. For a text is an event that occurs in time: it acts upon us as we read each word and phrase. As we just saw, Fish's passage first reinforces a belief about Judas the reader probably already holds and then takes that reinforcement away, leading the reader on in hopes of finding an answer that is never provided. If the kind of experience created in this passage is repeated throughout the text from which the passage is taken, then a reader-response critic might say that the text teaches us, through a pattern of raised expectations disappointed, how to read that text and, perhaps, how to read the world: we must expect to have our expectation of acquiring sure knowledge raised and disappointed. We desire sure knowledge. We pursue it, and we expect to get it. But this text teaches us that we cannot be certain of anything. In other words, for a reader-response critic, this text isn't primarily about Judas or Scripture but about the experience of reading.

In addition to an analysis of the reading activities that structure the reader's response, other kinds of evidence are usually gathered to further support the claim that the text is about the experience of reading. For example, most practitioners of affective stylistics will cite the responses of other readers—of other literary critics, for example—to show that their own analysis of the reading activities provided by a particular text is valid for readers other than just themselves. A critic might even cite an extreme divergence of critical opinion about the text to support, for example, the contention that the text provides an unsettling, decentering, or confusing reading experience. This wouldn't mean that the text is flawed but that by unsettling the reader it demonstrates, say, the fact that interpretation of written texts, and perhaps of the world, is a problematic endeavor from which we should not expect to achieve certainty.

Thematic evidence from the text itself is also usually provided to show that the text is about the experience of reading. For example, the reader-response critic shows how the experiences of characters and descriptions of settings mirror the reader's experience reading the text. If I were to claim that Joseph Conrad's *Heart of Darkness* (1902) provides a reading experience that keeps the reader off balance, unsure of how to interpret the characters and events unfolded by the plot, I would start, as we've just seen, by analyzing the reading activities that produce the uncertainty. Then I would show that the reader's experience of uncertainty is mirrored in Marlow's uncertainty—his inability to interpret Kurtz—and in the recurring references to darkness and obscurity (which are metaphors for uncertainty) that occur in the descriptions of the jungle, the company headquarters in Europe, and the deck of the ship on which Marlow tells his story. I would also look for images described in the text that serve as emblems of the reading experience I've described. Of course, reading materials or acts of reading described in the story work especially well for this purpose. For example, the tattered book that Marlow finds abandoned in the jungle, which he is unable to read, is emblematic of his, and our, inability to decipher what we see before us. Marlow doesn't even know what language the book is written in: he thinks it's some form of code language; he later learns that it's written in Russian.

As noted above, the textual evidence at this point is thematic: the critic shows that the theme of the text is a particular kind of reading experience, such as the difficulties involved in reading, the processes involved in making sense of the text, or the inevitability of misreading. Although many practitioners of affective stylistics believe that the text, as an independent object, disappears in their analysis and becomes what it really is—an experience that occurs within the reader—their use of thematic evidence, as we've just seen, underscores the important role played by the text in establishing what the reader's experience is.

Subjective Reader-Response Theory

In stark contrast to affective stylistics and to all forms of transactional reader-response theory, subjective reader-response theory does not call for the analysis of textual cues. For subjective reader-response critics, led by the work of David Bleich, readers' responses *are* the text, both in the sense that there is no literary text beyond the meanings created by readers' interpretations and in the sense that the text the critic analyzes is not the literary work but the written responses of readers. Let's look at each of these two claims more closely.

To understand how there is no literary text beyond the meanings created by readers' interpretations, we need to understand how Bleich defines the literary text. Like many other reader-response critics, he differentiates between what he calls *real objects* and *symbolic objects*. Real objects are physical objects, such as tables, chairs, cars, books, and the like. The printed pages of a literary text are real objects. However, the experience created when someone reads those printed pages, like language itself, is a symbolic object because it occurs not in the physical world but in the conceptual world, that is, in the mind of the reader. This is why Bleich calls reading—the feelings, associations, and memories that occur as we react subjectively to the printed words on the page—*symbolization*: our perception and identification of our reading experience create a conceptual, or symbolic, world in our mind as we read. Therefore, when we interpret the meaning of the text, we are actually interpreting the meaning of our own symbolization: we are interpreting the meaning of the conceptual experience we created in response to the text. He thus calls the act of interpretation *resymbolization*. Resymbolization occurs when our experience of the text produces in us a desire for explanation. Our evaluation of the text's quality is also an act of resymbolization: we don't like or dislike a text; we like or dislike our symbolization of it. Thus, the text we talk about isn't really the text on the page: it's the text in our mind.

Because the only text is the text in the mind of the reader, this is the text analyzed by subjective reader-response critics, for whom the text is equated with the written responses of readers. Bleich, whose primary interest is pedagogical, offers us a method for teaching students how to use their responses to learn about literature or, more accurately, to learn about literary response. For contrary to popular opinion, subjective criticism isn't an anything-goes free-for-all. It's a coherent, purposeful methodology for helping our students and ourselves produce knowledge about the experience of reading.

Before we look at the specific steps in that methodology, we need to understand what Bleich means by *producing knowledge*. Subjective criticism, and what he calls the subjective classroom, are based on the belief that all knowledge is subjective—the perceived can't be separated from the perceiver—which is a belief held today by many scientists and historians as well as by many critical theorists. What is called "objective" knowledge is simply whatever a given community believes to be objectively true. For example, western science once accepted the "objective" knowledge that the earth is flat and the sun revolves around it. Since that time, western science has accepted several different versions of "objective" knowledge about the earth and the sun. The most recent scientific thinking suggests that what we take to be objective knowledge is actually produced by the questions we ask and the instruments we use to find the answers. In other words, "truth" isn't an "objective" reality waiting to be discovered; it's constructed by communities of people to fulfill specific needs produced by specific historical, sociological, and psychological situations.

Treating the classroom as a community, Bleich's method helps students learn how communities produce knowledge and how the individual member of the community can function as a part of that process. To summarize Bleich's procedure, students are asked to respond to a literary text by writing a response statement and then by writing an analysis of their own response statement, both of which tasks are performed as efforts to contribute to the class's production of knowledge about reading experiences. Let's look at each of these two steps individually.

Although Bleich believes that, hypothetically, every *response statement* is valid within the context of some group of readers for whose purpose it is useful, he stresses that, in order to be useful to the classroom community, a response statement must be *negotiable* into knowledge about reading experiences. By this he means that it must contribute to the group's production of knowledge about the experience of reading a specific literary text, not about the reader or the reality outside the reader. Response statements that are *reader oriented* substitute talk about oneself for talk about one's reading experience. They are confined largely to comments about the reader's memories, interests, personal experiences, and the like, with little or no reference to the relationship between these comments and the experience of reading the text. Reader-oriented response statements lead to group discussions of personalities and personal problems that may be useful in a psychologist's office but, for Bleich, do not contribute to the group's understanding of the reading experience at hand.

Analogously, response statements that are *reality oriented* substitute talk about issues in the world for talk about one's reading experience. They are confined largely to the expression of one's opinions about politics, religion, gender issues, and the like, with little or no reference to the relationship between these opinions and the experience of reading the text. Reality-oriented response statements lead to group discussions of moral or social issues, which members claim the text is about, but such response statements do not contribute to the group's understanding of the reading experience at hand.

In contrast, the response statements Bleich promotes are *experience oriented*. They discuss the reader's reactions to the text, describing exactly how specific passages made the reader feel, think, or associate. Such response statements include judgments about specific characters, events, passages, and even words in the text. The personal associations and memories of personal relationships that are woven throughout these judgments allow others to see what aspects of the text affected the reader in what ways and for what reasons. Bleich cites one student's description of the ways in which particular characters and events in a text reminded her of her sexuality as a young girl. Her response statement moved back and forth between her reactions to specific scenes in the text and the specific experiences they recalled in her adolescence.

A group discussion produced by this student's subjective response could go in any number of directions, some of them quite traditional. For example, the group might discuss whether or not one's opinion of this particular text depends on feelings one has left over from one's adolescent experiences. Or the group might discuss whether or not the text is an expression of the author's adolescent feelings or of the repressive sexual mores of the culture in which the author lived. Even in the case of these last two examples, for which students would have to seek biographical and historical data, the questions themselves would have been raised by a reader's response and by the group's reaction to that response, so there probably would be a higher degree of personal engagement than would occur ordinarily for students upon whom such an assignment had been imposed. The point is that response statements are used within a context determined by the group. The group decides, based on the issues that emerge from experience-oriented response statements, what questions they want answered and what topics they want to pursue.

In addition, the experience-oriented response statement is analyzed by the reader in a *response-analysis statement*. Here the reader (1) characterizes his or her response to the text as a whole; (2) identifies the various responses prompted by different aspects of the text, which, of course, ultimately led to the student's response to the text as a whole; and (3) determines why these responses occurred. Responses may be characterized, for example, as enjoyment, discomfort, fascination, disappointment, relief, or satisfaction, and may involve any number of emotions, such as fear, joy, and anger. A student's response-analysis statement might reveal that certain responses resulted, for example, from identification with a particular character, from the vicarious fulfillment of a desire, from the relief of (or increase of) a guilty feeling, or the like. The goal here is for students to understand their responses, not merely report them or make excuses for them. Thus, a response-analysis statement is a thorough, detailed explanation of the relationship among specific textual elements, specific personal responses, and the meaning the text has for the student as a result of his or her personal encounter with it.

It is interesting to note that, as Bleich points out, students using the subjective approach probably focus on the same elements of the text they would select if they were writing a traditional "objective" essay. To test this hypothesis, Bleich had his students respond to a literary text, not by writing a response statement and a response-analysis statement but by writing a meaning statement and a response statement. The meaning statement explained what the student thought was the meaning of the text, without reference to the student's personal responses. In contrast, the response statement, just like the one discussed above, recorded how the text produced specific personal reactions and memories of personal relationships and experiences. Bleich found that students' response statements clearly revealed the personal sources of their meaning statements, whether or not students were aware of the relationship between the two. In other words, even when we think we're writing traditional "objective" interpretations of literary texts, the sources of those interpretations lie in the personal responses evoked by the text. One of the virtues of the subjective approach is that it allows students to understand why they choose to focus on the elements they do and to take responsibility for their choices.

In addition, by writing detailed response statements, students often learn that more was going on for them during their reading experience than they realized. Some students discover that they benefitted from a reading experience that they would have considered unpleasant or worthless had they not put forth the effort to think carefully and write down their responses. Students can also learn, by comparing their response statements to those of classmates or by contrasting their current response to a text with a response they remember having at an earlier age, how diverse and variable people's perceptions are, how various motives influence our likes and dislikes, and how adult reading preferences are shaped by childhood reading experiences.

From group discussions of response statements and from their own response-analysis statements, students can also learn how their own taste and the taste of others operate. As Bleich notes, one's announcement that one likes or dislikes a text, character, or passage is not enough to articulate taste. Rather, students must analyze the psychological pay-offs or costs the text creates for them and describe how these factors create their likes and dislikes. There's a big difference between knowing what you like and understanding your taste, and it is the latter goal that is, for Bleich, the appropriate goal for the classroom. Indeed, he believes that the organized examination of taste promoted in the subjective classroom is a natural place for students to begin their study of language and literature. The focus on self-understanding is extremely motivating for most students, and Bleich's subjective method fosters a kind of critical thinking that should prove useful to students throughout their lives because it shows that knowledge is created collaboratively, not just "handed down," and that its creation is motivated by personal and group concerns.

Psychological Reader-Response Theory

Psychoanalytic critic Norman Holland also believes that readers' motives strongly influence how they read. Despite his claim, at least in his early work, that an objective text exists (indeed, he calls his method *transactive* analysis because he believes that reading involves a transaction between the reader and a real text), Holland focuses on what readers' interpretations reveal about themselves, not about the text. Given his analyses of the subjective experiences of readers, he is sometimes referred to as a subjective reader-response critic. However, because Holland employs psychoanalytic concepts and focuses on the psychological responses of readers, many theorists think of him as a psychological reader-response critic, which is probably the most useful way for us to think of him, too.

Holland believes that we react to literary texts with the same psychological responses we bring to events in our daily lives. The situations that cause my defenses to emerge in my interpersonal life will cause my defenses to emerge when I read. To use a simple example, if I am quick to dislike new acquaintances who remind me of my alcoholic father, then I probably will be quick to dislike any fictional character who reminds me of him. Or if my overriding psychological trait is my need to control my world, then I probably will be threatened by literary texts that undermine my sense of control, for example, texts in which I can't find a powerful character with whom I can identify or in which I can't find the kind of orderly, logical world in which I feel comfortable. My defense in these situations might be to dislike the text, misunderstand it, or stop reading it altogether. Given that virtually all literary texts will in some way arouse my defenses by tapping some unconscious fear or forbidden desire, I must have a way to cope with texts if I am going to read them at all. According to Holland, that coping process is interpretation.

The immediate goal of interpretation, like the immediate psychological goal of our daily lives, is to fulfill our psychological needs and desires. When we perceive a textual threat to our psychological equilibrium, we must interpret the text in some way that will restore that equilibrium. Imagine, for example, two readers who, at some point in their lives, have felt victimized—perhaps "picked on" by siblings, rejected by peers, or neglected by a parent—for reasons beyond their control. These readers' defenses probably would be raised by the character of Pecola in Toni Morrison's *The Bluest Eye* (1970) because they would perceive her as a victim as they themselves had been. In other words, reading about Pecola would probably remind them of their own painful childhood isolation. The first reader might cope with this textual threat by interpreting the novel in a way that condemns Pecola instead of the characters who torment her: for example, Pecola instigates her own victimization by behaving in such a passive manner and refusing to stand up for herself. In this way, the reader identifies with the aggressor, rather than with the victim, and temporarily relieves his own psychological pain. The second reader for whom victimized characters threaten to stimulate painful childhood memories might cope with Pecola by minimizing the character's suffering, focusing instead on some positive quality Pecola retains intact: for example, Pecola is the only character in the novel who never hurts anyone, and she will remain forever in a state of childlike innocence. This reader denies Pecola's psychological pain in order to deny her own. Other readers upon whom victim figures have a personal psychological impact would have to cope with Pecola, too, and they would do so in the same ways they cope with their relationship to victimization in their own lives.

Holland calls the pattern of our psychological conflicts and coping strategies our *identity theme*. He believes that in our daily lives we project that identity theme onto every situation we encounter and thus perceive the world through the lens of our psychological experience. Analogously, when we read literature, we project our identity theme, or variations of it, onto the text. That is, in various ways we unconsciously re-create in the text the world that exists in our own mind. Our interpretations, then, are products of the fears, defenses, needs, and desires we project onto the text. Interpretation is thus primarily a psychological process rather than an intellectual one. A literary interpretation may or may not reveal the meaning of the text, but to a discerning eye it always reveals the psychology of the reader.

The reason why the psychological dimension of our interpretations is not readily apparent to ourselves and others is that we unconsciously couch it in aesthetic, intellectual, social, or moral abstractions to relieve the anxiety and guilt our projections arouse in us. For example, the two hypothetical readers who react to Pecola as described above, might interpret the character—respectively, as the representative of self-destructive human frailty, like the biblical Eve, or in contrast, as the representative of spiritual innocence—without realizing that their interpretations emerged from their own unconscious psychological conflicts.

Holland's definition of interpretation can thus be summarized as a process consisting of three stages or modes that occur and recur as we read. (1) In the *defense* mode, our psychological defenses are raised by the text (for example, we find Pecola threatening because she reminds us of our own experience of victimization). (2) In the *fantasy* mode, we find a way to interpret the text that will tranquilize those defenses and thus fulfill our desire to be protected from threats to our psychological equilibrium (for example, we minimize Pecola's pain by focusing on the childlike innocence that will remain forever hers). (3) In the *transformation* mode, we transform steps #1 and #2 into an abstract interpretation so that we can get the psychological satisfaction we desire without acknowledging to ourselves the anxiety-producing defenses and guilt-producing fantasies that underlie our assessment of the text (for example, we decide that Pecola represents spiritual innocence). Thus, in the transformation mode, we focus on an intellectual interpretation of the text in order to avoid our own emotional response to it, and we ignore the fact that our intellectual interpretation grew out of our emotional response.

Of course, the possible value of Holland's method seems evident for facilitating therapeutic psychological self-knowledge. But with adequate training, one might also use it as a biographical tool for the study of an author. Holland provides an example of such an application in a brief analysis of Robert Frost. Holland doesn't analyze Frost the writer, but Frost the reader. That is, the focus of analysis is Frost as a person reading the world in which he lives, reacting to and interpreting it. Holland studied the poet's informal remarks; his letters; his tastes in literature; his personality traits; and his expressed attitudes towards science, politics, his own poetry, and himself in order to discover Frost's identity theme. According to Holland, Frost related to himself and to the world in terms of his need to "manage" the "huge unknown forces of sex and aggression" through the means of "smaller symbols: words or familiar objects" (127). Once this identity theme was established, Holland notes, it could be traced, as well, in Frost's poetry, which might itself be taken as the poet's interpretation of his world.

The purpose of such an analysis is, for Holland, an empathic merger with the author. Whether we're analyzing a person or a literary text, every act of interpretation takes place within the context of the interpreter's identity theme, which, as we have seen, sets up defenses against as well as desire for such a merger. It is therefore the interpreter's task to break through the psychological barriers that separate self from other. Understanding an author's identity theme, Holland believes, allows us to fully experience, as a "mingling of self and other" (132), the gift the artist offers us.

Social Reader-Response Theory

While the individual reader's subjective response to the literary text plays the crucial role in subjective reader-response theory, for social reader-response theory, usually associated with the later work of Stanley Fish, there is no purely individual subjective response. According to Fish, what we take to be our individual subjective responses to literature are really products of the *interpretive community* to which we belong. By interpretive community, Fish means those who share the interpretive strategies we bring to texts when we read, whether or not we realize we're using interpretive strategies and whether or not we are aware that other people share them. These interpretive strategies always result from various sorts of institutionalized assumptions (assumptions established, for example, in high schools, churches, and colleges by prevailing cultural attitudes and philosophies) about what makes a text a piece of literature—instead of a letter or a legal document or a church sermon—and what meanings we are supposed to find in it.

An interpretive community can be as sophisticated and aware of its critical enterprise as the community produced by the followers of a specific Marxist critical theorist. Or an interpretive community can be as unsophisticated and unaware of its interpretive strategies as the community produced by a high-school teacher who instructs his students that it is natural to read literature in search of static symbols that tell us the "hidden meaning" of the story. Of course, interpretive communities aren't static; they evolve over time. And readers can belong, consciously or unconsciously, to more than one community at the same time, or they can change from one community to another at different times in their lives. In any case, all readers come to the text already predisposed to interpret it in a certain way based on whatever interpretive strategies are operating for them at the time they read. Thus, while Bleich believes his students produce communal authority through a negotiation that occurs after they've read the text, Fish claims that a multiplicity of communal authorities, based on the multiplicity of interpretive communities to which students already belong, determines how students read the text in the first place.

In other words, for Fish, readers do not interpret poems; they create them. He demonstrated this point rather dramatically when he was teaching two college courses back to back. At the end of his first class he wrote an assignment on the board that consisted of the following list of linguists' names his students were studying. (The question mark after the final name was to indicate Fish's uncertainty about the spelling.)

Jacobs—Rosenbaum
Levin
Thorne
Hayes
Ohman (?)   (*Is There a Text* 323)

When his second class entered the room, he told them that the writing on the board was a seventeenth-century religious poem like the ones they'd been studying and asked them to analyze it.

In the discussion that ensued, his students concluded that the poem celebrated God's love and mercy in giving his only begotten son for our redemption. Their interpretation accounted beautifully for every word in the poem, including, among other evidence, the following points: the poem is in the shape of a cross or an altar; "Jacobs" suggests Jacob's ladder, a reference to the Christian ascent into heaven; "Rosenbaum" literally means rose tree and refers to the Virgin Mary, the rose without thorns, whose son Jesus is the means by which human beings can climb to heaven; "Thorne" thus refers to Jesus's crown of thorns, a symbol of the sacrifice he made to redeem us; and the letters that occur most frequently in the poem are S, O, N (*Is There a Text* 322–29).

I don't need to recount the students' argument in its entirety for you to see Fish's point: every literary judgment we make, including the judgment that a particular piece of writing is a poem, results from the interpretive strategies we bring with us when we read the text. A list of linguists' names, or anything else, can become a poem if a reader or group of readers uses the interpretive strategies required to make it one. That is, the qualities that make a poem a poem do not reside in the text but in the interpretive strategies we've learned, consciously or unconsciously, before we ever encountered the text.

Social reader-response theory doesn't offer us a new way to read texts. Nor does it promote any form of literary criticism that already exists. After all, its point is that no interpretation, and therefore no form of literary criticism, can claim to reveal what's *in* a text. Each interpretation will simply find whatever its interpretive strategies put there. This doesn't mean, however, that we are left with the anarchy of unconstrained interpretation. As Fish notes, interpretations will always be controlled by the relatively limited repertoire of interpretive strategies available at any given point in history. By understanding the principles of social reader-response theory, however, we can become more aware of what it is we're doing when we interpret a text and more aware of what our peers and students are doing, as well. Such awareness could be especially useful to teachers by helping them analyze their students' interpretive strategies; helping them decide if and when to try to replace those strategies with others; and helping them take responsibility for the strategies they choose to teach instead of hiding behind the belief that certain ways of reading are natural or inherently right because they represent what's in the text.

Defining Readers

Before we turn to the uses of reader-response theory in literary criticism, there's one final concept we need to discuss that relates to all the approaches discussed above. You may have noticed that some reader-response theorists refer to "readers" while others refer to "the reader." When theorists discuss actual readers whose responses they analyze, as Norman Holland and David Bleich do, for example, they refer to them as "readers" or "students" or call them by some other name that denotes real people. Many theorists, however, analyze the reading experience of a hypothetical ideal reader encountering a specific text, as we saw, for example, in our examination of affective stylistics. In these cases, references to "the reader" are really references to the critic analyzing his or her own carefully documented reading experience of a specific text according to specific reader-response principles. Because the experience of hypothetical readers may or may not correspond to the experience of actual readers, some hypothetical readers have been given names that describe the reading activity they represent. Thus, in Fish's practice of affective stylistics, he refers to the *informed reader*: the reader who has attained the *literary competency* necessary to experience the text as Fish himself does, in the fullness of its linguistic and literary complexity, and who conscientiously tries to suppress the personal or idiosyncratic dimension of his or her response. Of course, there is a variety of informed readers because the informed reader of, say, Emily Dickinson's poetry may or may not be the informed reader of Richard Wright's fiction. Other terms you may run across that refer to similar hypothetical readers include the *educated reader*, the *ideal reader*, and the *optimal reader*.

Analogously, Wolfgang Iser uses the term *implied reader*, by which he means the reader that the text seems to be addressing, whose characteristics we can deduce by studying the style in which the text is written and the apparent "attitude" of the narrative toward the reader. Thus, the implied reader of a Harlequin romance is quite different from the implied reader of a philosophical novel like Thomas Mann's *Doctor Faustus* (1947) or the implied reader of a psychologically intense, historical novel like Toni Morrison's *Beloved* (1987). Other terms you may encounter that refer to readers implied by the text include the *intended reader* and the *narratee*. The point here is that critics who use hypothetical readers are trying to show us what particular texts require of readers or how particular texts work to position readers in order to guide their interpretation. Whether or not readers accept that guidance or are even aware of it is another matter.

Of course, there are many more reader-response concepts than the ones discussed above. Our purpose here is merely to introduce you to the main ideas, the general principles you need to know in order to read reader-response theorists and literary critics with some understanding of the issues they raise. Naturally, some literary works will seem to lend themselves more readily than others to reader-response analysis or at least to certain kinds of reader-response analysis. And unlike many other theories addressed in this textbook, a reader-response analysis of a literary text is often an analysis not of the text itself but of the responses of actual readers.

Mary Lowe-Evans, for example, analyzed the oral and written responses of college juniors and seniors in her literature class in order to learn how students today form attitudes toward a specific literary text and how those attitudes determine their interpretation of it. The text she used was Mary Shelley's *Frankenstein*, and she mapped the ways in which the following factors influenced students' interpretations of the novel: film versions of the novel (which created students' preconceptions of the text), her own interpretive prompts (Whose story is this? What does the novel mean? Is the narrator reliable?), and the determinate and indeterminate meanings in the text itself. Among other findings, Lowe-Evans confirmed the reader-response notion that interpretation is an ongoing process that evolves as readers use different interpretive strategies to actively work their way through a text. She also learned that preconceptions created by film versions of the novel, in which the monster is very different from Shelley's monster, facilitated certain interpretations of the story while frustrating others. Analogously, particular textual elements, such as the formal style of the tale's "Preface" and the epistolary format that opens the narrative (the story is presented as a series of letters from the narrator to his sister), counteracted the students' expectations of a superficial, entertaining monster story.

Whatever kind of analysis is undertaken, however, the ultimate goal of reader-response criticism is to increase our understanding of the reading process by investigating the activities in which readers engage and the effects of those activities on their interpretations.

Some Questions Reader-Response Critics Ask about Literary Texts

The questions that follow are offered to summarize reader-response approaches to literature or, more accurately, to the reading of literature. Questions #1 draws on transactional reader-response theory. Question #2 and #3 relate to affective stylistics. Question #4 draws on psychological reader-response theory. Question #5 relates to social or psychological reader-response theory. And Question #6 draws on subjective reader-response theory.

1. How does the interaction of text and reader create meaning? How, exactly, does the text's indeterminacy function as a stimulus to interpretation? (For example, what events are omitted or unexplained? What descriptions are omitted or incomplete? What images might have multiple associations?) And how, exactly, does the text lead us to correct our interpretation as we read?

2. What does a phrase-by-phrase analysis of a short literary text, or of key portions of a longer text, tell us about the reading experience prestructured by (built into) that text? How does this analysis of what the text *does* to the reader differ from what the text "says" or "means"? In other words, how might the omission of the temporal experience of reading this text result in an incomplete idea of the text's meaning?

3. How might we interpret a literary text to show that the reader's

response is, or is analogous to, the topic of the story? In other words, how is the text really about readers reading, and what, exactly, does it tell us about this topic? To simplify further, how is a particular kind of reading experience an important theme in the text? Of course, we must first establish what reading experience is created by the text (see question #2) in order to show that the topic of the story is analogous to it. Then we must cite textual evidence—for example, references to reading materials, to characters reading texts, and to characters interpreting other characters or events—to show that what happens in the world of the narrative mirrors the reader's situation decoding it.

4. Drawing on a broad spectrum of thoroughly documented biographical data, what seems to be a given author's identity theme, and how does that theme express itself in the sum of his or her literary output?

5. What does the body of criticism published about a literary text suggest about the critics who interpreted that text and/or about the reading experience produced by that text? You might contrast critical camps writing during the same period, writing during different periods, or both. What does your analysis suggest about the ways in which the text is created by readers' interpretive strategies or by their psychological or ideological projections?

6. If you have the resources to do it, what can you learn about the role of readers' interpretive strategies or expectations, about the reading experience produced by a particular text, or about any other reading activity by conducting your own study using a group of real readers (for example, your students, classmates, or fellow book-club members)? For example, can you devise a study to test Bleich's belief that students' personal responses to literary texts are the source of their formal interpretations?

Depending on the literary work in question, we might ask one or any combination of these questions. Or we might come up with a useful question not listed here. These are just some starting points to get us thinking about literature in productive reader-response ways. Keep in mind that not all reader-response critics will interpret the same text, or even the same readers' responses, in the same way, even if they focus on the same reader-response concepts. As in every field, even expert practitioners disagree. Our goal is to use reader-response theory to help enrich our reading of literary works, to help us see some important ideas they illustrate that we might not have seen so clearly or so deeply otherwise, and to help us understand the complexities and varieties of the reading experience.

The following reader-response analysis of F. Scott Fitzgerald's *The Great Gatsby* is offered as an example of what a reader-response interpretation of that novel might yield. Using the principles of affective stylistics, Iser's notion of indeterminacy, and Holland's notion of projection, I will examine the way the novel continually problematizes our evolving perception of Jay Gatsby as we read, creating an indeterminacy that invites us to project our own beliefs and desires onto the protagonist. In addition, I will show how the novel's thematic content (what the novel "is about") mirrors the reader's experience reading it, that is, how the topic of the novel is the impossibility of establishing determinate meaning.

Projecting the Reader: A Reader-Response Analysis of *The Great Gatsby*

> "Somebody told me they thought he killed a man once."
> A thrill passed over all of us. The three Mr. Mumbles bent forward and listened eagerly.
> "I don't think it's so much *that*," argued Lucille skeptically; "it's more that he was a German spy during the war."
> One of the men nodded in confirmation.
> "I heard that from a man who knew all about him, grew up with him in Germany," he assured us positively.
> "Oh no," said the first girl, "it couldn't be that, because he was in the American army during the war." As our credulity switched back to her she leaned forward with enthusiasm. "You look at him sometime when he thinks nobody's looking at him. I'll bet he killed a man." (48; ch. 3)

The speculation Jay Gatsby inspires in his gossip-hungry party guests, who have an obvious desire to be shocked, is, in two important ways, a prototype of the speculation he inspires in the reader of F. Scott Fitzgerald's *The Great Gatsby* (1925). Our credulity, like that of Gatsby's party guests, is continually "switched" in different directions as we make our way through Nick Carraway's narration; and the final outcome of our speculation—our interpretation of Gatsby and therefore of the meaning of the novel as a whole—is largely a product of our own beliefs and desires, which the tale's indeterminacy invites us to project. In other words, *The Great Gatsby* dramatizes reader-response theory's concept of reading as the making of meaning, and the novel reproduces within the action of the story the reader's experience while reading it.

With Jay Gatsby as the "text" they decode, the characters in the novel model a reading experience that could be described by the following formula: projection + data gathered = confirmation of projection. In other words, the data that interpreters gather from the environment have one primary function: to validate for them the interpretation they've already projected or are in the process of projecting. For example, as we just saw, Gatsby's party guests perform all three steps of the formula in a single conversation. Although the outlandish rumors they rely on are inaccurate, rumors are the only data available, and they are hardly more shocking than the truth about Gatsby's criminal activities. More important, outlandish rumors fulfill the desire for scandal that prompts them to interpret Gatsby in the first place: it hardly matters, in terms of their enjoyment of the "text" that is Gatsby, which of the rumors they believe, as long as it's sufficiently outrageous or provokes further shocking speculations. In other words, the party guests interpret Gatsby in order to be shocked, and their interpretations fulfill their desire.

Analogously, Tom Buchanan wants to believe that Gatsby is a crook with no respectable family background, and he hires private investigators to provide him with the evidence he needs to prove it. Daisy wants to believe Gatsby is her upper-class knight in shining armor, so she conveniently doesn't see through his veneer of wealth and status, which is as thin as the "thin beard of raw ivy" (9; ch. 1) covering the tower of his mansion. Wolfshiem wants to believe that Gatsby is "a man of fine breeding" (76; ch. 4) so he can "use him good" (179) in his underworld activities, and therefore he doesn't see the contradiction in a finely bred man, "an Oggsford," being "so hard up he had to keep on wearing his uniform because he couldn't buy some regular clothes" (179; ch. 9). George Wilson wants to believe that Gatsby seduced and murdered his wife because this belief will permit Wilson to avenge Myrtle's seduction and death and achieve the emotional closure he needs. So Wilson readily believes the first story he hears: he asks no questions and has no doubts about Tom's explanation despite having seen Tom himself driving the "death" car earlier that day and despite Tom's unfulfilled promises to Wilson in the recent past. Finally, Mr. Gatz wants to believe that his son "had a big future before him": "If he'd of lived he'd of been a great man. A man like [railroad tycoon] James J. Hill. He'd of helped build up the country" (176; ch.

9). Mr. Gatz therefore interprets his son's boyhood "schedule" as proof that "Jimmy was bound to get ahead" (182; ch. 9), having swallowed completely whatever improbable lies Gatsby surely told him about the source of his wealth.

I'm not suggesting that these characters have the ability or the opportunity to acquire more accurate information about Gatsby. My point is simply that the eagerness with which they embrace the information they acquire and the readiness with which they use it to construct what they choose to regard as the complete picture of Gatsby are products of the degree to which the information fulfills their own desires concerning the man.

It might be reasonable to conclude that the amount of inaccuracy produced by this sort of interpretation teaches the reader to try another method, that the novel discredits the subjective, self-serving interpretation represented by these characters. However, as we shall see, Nick Carraway—whose first-person narration guides us through the morally ambiguous world of the novel—interprets Gatsby through the lens of his own projections as well. Furthermore, he does so because, in the indeterminate world of the novel, there is no other way to interpret Gatsby. As we follow Nick through his "now-I-like-Gatsby; now-I-don't" narration, we are thrust, along with him, back and forth between opposing perceptions of the protagonist. Nick's opening evaluation of the character—in which he says that Gatsby "represents everything . . . [Nick] . . . scorns" and yet is "exempt from [Nick's negative] reaction" (6; ch. 1) to his Long-Island friends—announces the paradoxical experience of Gatsby he will share with us as his narrative unfolds.

Nick's narrative creates an intricate pattern of reader sympathy for and criticism of Gatsby that would require an essay of its own to trace in detail, but a rough sketch of its contours should demonstrate the sense of indeterminacy this pattern promotes. After the paradoxical evaluation of Gatsby with which Nick introduces us to the character, noted above, the narrator takes us back to the beginning of his tale, or before the beginning, to a description of his own "prominent, well-to-do" (7; ch. 1) family in Wisconsin and his decision to go to New York and learn the bond business. Throughout the rest of Chapter One the only feeling about Gatsby Nick shares with us is his curiosity about the man, which is revealed through his description of "Gatsby's mansion. Or rather, as [Nick] didn't know Mr. Gatsby it was a mansion inhabited by a gentleman of that name" (9; ch. 1). In other words, we travel back in time with Nick and experience events as he experienced them unfolding in time. The

"Gatsby" introduced on page 6 has become "Mr. Gatsby" on page 9 because Nick has taken us back to a point in time when he hadn't yet met the protagonist.

Our curiosity is raised when Jordan mentions Gatsby, a man she met at West Egg, and Daisy demands, "Gatsby? . . . What Gatsby?" (15; ch. 1), but Nick and the reader don't meet Gatsby until the middle of Chapter Three, when the narrator attends one of Gatsby's parties. Having excited our curiosity, and revealed his own, by his minute observations of what he can see of Gatsby's parties from the porch of his cottage, Nick's initial meeting with his neighbor initiates the pattern of conflicting interpretations of Gatsby that will characterize his experience, and ours, throughout the novel. Gatsby introduces himself to Nick, then smiles, and the narrator is charmed. Nick says,

> It was one of those rare smiles with a quality of eternal reassurance in it. . . . [I]t had precisely the impression of you that, at your best, you hoped to convey. Precisely at that point it vanished—and I was looking at an elegant young rough-neck . . . whose elaborate formality of speech just missed being absurd. (53; ch. 3).

In other words, Nick's positive impression that Gatsby is a charming gentleman is immediately followed by a negative impression that Gatsby is a phony.

This pattern is repeated until Nick leaves the party at the end of the evening. The narrator, catching a glimpse of Gatsby "standing alone on the marble steps," says, "I could see nothing sinister about him" (54; ch. 3). But in the very next sentence Nick wonders if Gatsby's innocent appearance is an illusion produced by "the fact that [Gatsby] was [the only one] not drinking . . . for it seemed to me that he grew more correct as the fraternal hilarity increased" (54; ch. 3). Again, as Nick bids Gatsby goodnight he implies that his host is insincere. Gatsby calls Nick "old sport," but "[t]he familiar expression held no more familiarity than the hand which reassuringly brushed my shoulder" (57; ch. 3). Then a few seconds later Gatsby smiles, and Nick likes him again—"suddenly there seemed to be a pleasant significance in having been among the last to go, as if he had desired it so all the time" (58; ch. 3)—and Gatsby's "Good night, old sport. . . . Good night" (58; ch. 3) feels warm and sincere. Finally, as Nick glances back at Gatsby from across the lawn as he heads home, he describes the protagonist in a way that underscores the ambiguity of his own response to him: "A sudden *emptiness* seemed to flow now from the windows and the great doors, endowing with complete *isolation* the figure of the host who stood on the porch, his hand up in a *formal gesture* of farewell" (60; ch. 3, my italics). Does this language emphasize Gatsby's coldness, which would decrease our sympathy for him, or his loneliness, which would increase it? Nick doesn't clarify his own attitude—perhaps he's not sure—so the reader is left, after a series of conflicting responses to Gatsby, to project his or her personal experience onto the protagonist.

Our next encounter with Gatsby occurs at the beginning of Chapter Four, when the protagonist drives Nick to New York. During this scene, our attitude toward Gatsby is again shifted back and forth between positive and negative poles. Nick starts us off with the following account of his change in attitude toward Gatsby prior to their drive to New York, based on the half dozen conversations he'd had with his neighbor during the month since they'd met:

> [T]o my disappointment . . . he had little to say. So my first impression, that he was a person of some undefined consequence, had gradually faded and he had become simply the proprietor of an elaborate road-house next door. (69; ch. 4)

Then, as Nick puts it, "came that disconcerting ride" (69; ch. 4). As Gatsby tells Nick the story about his wealthy family, "all dead now" (69; ch. 4), and his Oxford education, Nick says,

> He looked at me sideways. . . . [And] [h]e hurried the phrase 'educated at Oxford.' . . . And with this doubt his whole statement fell to pieces and I wondered if there wasn't something a little sinister about him after all. (69; ch. 4)

Of course, Nick now believes nothing Gatsby says about his jewel collecting, "chiefly rubies" (70; ch. 4), big-game hunting, and painting, and only "[w]ith an effort" does Nick "manag[e] to restrain [his] incredulous laughter" (70; ch. 4). Gatsby's war story, which he tells next, sounds just as exaggerated as the rest of his tale, and Nick feels as though he is "skimming hastily through a dozen magazines" (71; ch. 4). However, Gatsby then shows Nick a war medal with his name on it, and "[t]o [Nick's] astonishment the thing had an authentic look" (71; ch. 4). When Gatsby produces a snapshot of himself with a group of fellow students at Oxford, Nick concludes, "Then it was all true" (71; ch. 4).

Nick's belief in Gatsby is quickly submerged under his annoyance, however, when Gatsby says that Jordan Baker is going to make a request of Nick on Gatsby's behalf: "I was sure the request would be something utterly fantastic and for a moment I was sorry I'd ever set foot upon his overpopulated lawn" (72; ch. 4). When Nick notes that Gatsby's "correctness grew on him as we neared the city" (72; ch. 4), he seems to be implying again that Gatsby is a phony. Yet the scene ends with an incident that seems to leave Nick's sympathies, and ours, again mired in ambiguity. When Gatsby is pulled over for speeding, he produces a piece of paper that not only gets him out of a ticket but causes the officer who pulled him over to apologize. Gatsby explains, "I was able to do the commissioner a favor once, and he sends me a Christmas card every year" (73; ch. 4). While this incident certainly underscores Gatsby's importance and therefore supports the story he just told Nick, how should we feel about the touch of corruption hinted at here? Nick's response doesn't help— "Even Gatsby could happen [in a place like New York] without any particular wonder" (73; ch. 4)—so we're once more left on our own.

An analysis of the scenes that shape the reader's evolving view of Gatsby through the rest of the novel reveals a similar pattern of opposing influences, as we see in the following summary of those scenes.

1. *Nick, Gatsby, and Wolfshiem have lunch* (73–79; ch. 4)—Our impression of Gatsby is shaped *negatively* due to Nick's description of Gatsby's close association with Wolfshiem, who is very negatively portrayed, and Nick's suspicious comments about Gatsby.

2. *Jordan tells Nick about Gatsby and Daisy* (79–85; ch. 4)—Our impression of Gatsby is shaped *positively* due to Gatsby's faithful devotion to Daisy, his fear of offending Jordan and Nick, and Nick's sympathetic response to Gatsby's plight.

3. *Nick and Gatsby arrange Gatsby's reunion with Daisy* (86–88; ch. 5)—Our impression of Gatsby is shaped *negatively* due to Nick's consistently cool responses to Gatsby's attempts at friendliness, especially after Gatsby "obviously and tactlessly"(88) offers him a chance to make some easy money in exchange for arranging the reunion with Daisy.

4. *Gatsby and Daisy reunite* (88–94; ch. 5)—Our sympathy for Gatsby is shaped *positively* by Nick's description of the protagonist's total emotional investment in Daisy—his nervous apprehension before the meeting, his intense anxiety during the initial awkwardness with Daisy, and his overwhelming joy when

he realizes she still loves him—and by Nick's vicarious experience of the protagonist's embarrassment and happiness.

5. *Nick and Gatsby wait for Daisy on Nick's lawn* (95; ch. 5)—Our impression of Gatsby is shaped *negatively* by Nick's catching Gatsby in an apparent lie about where he got the money to build his house and by Gatsby's rude and defensive reply—"That's my affair" (95)—when Nick asks him what business he's in.

6. *Gatsby shows his house to Daisy and Nick* (96–102; ch. 5)—Our response to Gatsby is moved between *positive and negative* poles as Nick's sympathetic description of Jay's devotion to Daisy is interrupted in the middle by an ominous phone call that hints strongly at Gatsby's hidden criminal life.

7. *Nick relates the real story of Gatsby's youth* (104–107; ch. 6)—Our response to Gatsby is moved between *positive and negative* poles as Nick's sympathetic description of Gatsby's impoverished youth, boyhood dreams, hard work, and sobriety is interrupted twice by Nick's observations that Gatsby's dreams were in "the service of a vast, vulgar and meretricious beauty" (104) and that they inhabited a "universe of ineffable gaudiness" (105). At the end of the scene Nick says, "[Gatsby] told me all this very much later . . . when I had reached the point of believing everything and nothing about him" (107), thus reinforcing our uncertainty for some time to come.

8. *Tom and friends on horseback stop at Gatsby's house* (107–10; ch. 6)—Our response to Gatsby is moved between *positive and negative* poles as Nick's sympathetic description of Gatsby's politeness in the face of his visitors' rudeness is interrupted by his description of Gatsby's "almost aggressiv[e]" attempts to push Tom into talking in order to learn more about him.

9. *Nick, Tom, and Daisy attend Gatsby's party* (110–18; ch. 6)—Our response to Gatsby is shaped *positively* by Nick's sympathetic descriptions of Gatsby's attentions to Daisy, by his angry defense of Gatsby against Tom's insinuations, and by his extremely poetic rendition of Gatsby's account of his early days with Daisy, though that rendition is somewhat undercut by Nick's *negative* reference to Gatsby's "appalling sentimentality" (118).

10. *Nick learns about Gatsby's new servants* (119–20; ch. 7)—Our response to Gatsby is *negatively* shaped by Nick's description of

Gatsby's association with Wolfshiem's people and the
protagonist's apparent failure to notice their sinister quality.

11. *Nick and Gatsby lunch with the Buchanans and Jordan* (121–28;
ch. 7)—Our response to Gatsby is shaped *positively* by Nick's
description of Gatsby's quiet good manners in the face of Tom's
aggressiveness and Daisy's open displays of affection for her lover.
This response is undercut somewhat at the end of the scene by
Nick's *negative* observation, which hints at the protagonist's dark
side, that "an undefinable expression . . . passed over Gatsby's
face" (127) when Tom makes a veiled reference to Gatsby's
criminal activities.

12. *Tom confronts Gatsby in the New York hotel suite* (133–42; ch. 7)—
Our sympathy for Gatsby is shaped *positively* by Nick's description of Gatsby's honesty about his Oxford experience and his
description of Gatsby's desperate and pathetic attempt to hold
Daisy in the face of Tom's ruthlessness and her withdrawal.

13. *Nick meets Gatsby outside the Buchanans' house after Myrtle's
death* (150–53; ch. 7)—Our response to Gatsby is moved *from the
negative to the positive* by the change in Nick's behavior toward
Gatsby after he learns that Daisy, not Gatsby, drove the hit-and-
run car and Gatsby is taking the blame for her.

14. *Nick and Gatsby talk at Gatsby's house the morning after Myrtle's
death* (154–62; ch. 8)—Our response to Gatsby is moved between
positive and *negative* poles as Nick's sympathetic description of
Gatsby's devotion to Daisy is interrupted by his statement that
Gatsby "took" Daisy, "ravenously and unscrupulously" (156),
under false pretenses.

15. *Nick makes Gatsby's funeral arrangements* (171–83; ch. 9)—Our
response to Gatsby is moved several times between *positive and
negative* poles as Nick's "feeling of . . . scornful solidarity" with
Gatsby "against them all" (173) is repeatedly interrupted by
reminders of the protagonist's criminal activities.

16. *Nick walks on Gatsby's beach the night before he heads back to
Wisconsin* (189; ch. 9)—Our sympathy for Gatsby is *positively*
shaped by Nick's poetic comparison of Gatsby's "wonder when he
first picked out the green light at the end of Daisy's dock" (189)
with the wonder inspired by the virgin American continent, the
"fresh, green breast of the new world" (189).

Thus, while the text actively shapes the reader's response to Gatsby in each of these scenes, as we move through the tale we experience a significant degree of indeterminacy. For we gradually learn that the text will support two opposing interpretations of Gatsby: (1) Gatsby the criminal, who will hurt anyone and do anything to get what he wants, and (2) Gatsby the romantic hero, who has pulled himself out of poverty and devoted his life to Daisy as "to the following of a grail" (156; ch. 8). In other words, the novel gives us a protagonist who uses wholly corrupt means, including bootlegging and fraudulent bonds, to achieve pure ends— Gatsby's "incorruptible dream" (162; ch. 8) of winning Daisy and living the good life—and then asks us to decide if the ends justify the means. But the novel doesn't provide the kind of unequivocal evidence we need to answer the question.

A simple "no," the obvious "right" answer from an abstract moral perspective, does not adequately respond to the complexities of the question, given the wretched poverty of Gatsby's childhood and the novel's portrayal of the Valley of Ashes as the only alternative to the life lived by the rich and famous. Our perception of the contrast between wealth and poverty is reinforced throughout the novel by alternating descriptions of, on the one hand, the exciting world of Nick and his crowd and, on the other hand, the dreary world of the Wilsons, the McKees, Myrtle's sister Catherine, and such random characters as Gatsby's freeloading, vulgar party guests and the "poor young clerks who loitered in front of windows . . . in the dusk, wasting the most poignant moments of night and life" (62; ch. 3).

The simple conclusion that Gatsby's ends do not justify his means does not work for Nick, either. But neither does the narrator simply conclude that Gatsby's ends do justify his means. As we have seen, it's through Nick that we learn about Gatsby's dark side: his criminal activities, his deception of Daisy, his invented identity, his association with Wolfshiem, and his insensitivity to the welfare of anyone but Daisy and himself. Yet it's Nick who is also Gatsby's chief defender, who experiences, for example, one of many "renewals of complete faith in him" (136; ch. 7) simply because Gatsby makes a small concession to reality by admitting that his Oxford experience was provided by a government arrangement for American soldiers after World War I. And it's Nick who concludes that Gatsby is "worth the whole damn bunch [of Nick's crowd] put together" (162; ch. 8). In fact, Nick's warm and frequent defense of the protagonist should, on the whole, tend to elicit our sympathy for Gatsby, even while the dark side of his characterization reminds us that Gatsby is not one of the good guys in the white hats. That is, without answering the question the novel poses, without suggesting that Gatsby's ends justify his means, Nick nevertheless sees Gatsby as the only person he met in the East who "turned out all right at the end" (6; ch. 1).

Why should Nick finally interpret Gatsby in such a one-sided manner, given the knowledge he has of him? The enthusiastic tone of Nick's frequent "renewals of complete faith" (136; ch. 7) in Gatsby suggests that, like so many other characters in the novel, Nick projects his own desires onto Gatsby. At the age of thirty, and still being financed by his father while he tries to figure out what he should do with himself, it is not surprising that Nick wants to believe life still holds promise because he is afraid that it doesn't. He fears that all he has to look forward to is, as he puts it, "a thinning list of single men to know, a thinning briefcase of enthusiasm, thinning hair" (143; ch. 7). With one failed romance back home and one in New York, Nick wants to believe that the possibility of romance still exists. With his summer in New York—his latest in a series of adventures—having ended in disaster, he wants to believe in the possibility of fulfilled hope he sees in Gatsby: hope that a young man at loose ends can make the kind of outrageous financial success of himself that Gatsby has made, can fall so completely in love with a woman, and can feel so optimistic about the future. Indeed, as we see throughout the second half of the novel, Nick is so emotionally invested in Gatsby that, without hesitation and despite his own conservative upbringing, he facilitates Gatsby's adulterous affair with Daisy, Nick's own relative.

Nick's tendency to project his own desire into his interpretation of Gatsby seems unavoidable and feels natural given that his, and our, experience of the protagonist develops within a setting that is, itself, full of unanswered questions, contradictions, and multiple possible interpretations. The affective thrust of the novel as a whole thus invites us to project, like Nick, our own meanings onto the world of the novel in order to interpret it at all.

Even the briefest list of the text's indeterminacies would include the following unanswered questions, which my students frequently find disturbing. Why does Daisy marry Tom after receiving Gatsby's letter from Europe? As Gatsby returned to Louisville within three months of Daisy's wedding, didn't his letter tell her that she could expect him soon? Why is Daisy "so mad about her husband" (81; ch. 4) after only three months of marriage, given that she didn't want to marry him the night before the wedding? Given Tom's chronic infidelity, the couple's frequent relocations, and their apparent dissatisfaction with the marriage, what keeps

CHAPTER 6: READER-RESPONSE CRITICISM

Tom and Daisy together? What is Gatsby and Daisy's relationship like after their reunion? (Fitzgerald wrote that he, himself, "had no feeling
about or knowledge of . . . the emotional relations between Gatsby and
Daisy from the time of their reunion to the catastrophe." *Letters* 341–42.)
What's the real story of Nick's relationship with the young woman he left
behind in his home town? How do Nick and Jordan really feel about each
other? What kind of person is Jordan? Given the novel's obvious rejection
of Tom's sexist and racist attitudes, what are we to make of Nick's sexist
and racist remarks, which the text offers without comment and seems to
invite us to accept? (See, for example, Nick's remark in Chapter Three,
page 63, that "[d]ishonesty in a woman is a thing you never blame
deeply" and his reference in Chapter Four, page 73, to three black characters in a limousine as "two bucks and a girl" at whom he "laughed aloud
as the yolks of their eyeballs rolled toward [Gatsby and him] in haughty
rivalry.") Given the text's unflattering portraits of the poor as well as the
rich, is the novel anti-elitist or merely misanthropic? What are the "grotesque and fantastic conceits" that "haunted [Gatsby] in his bed at night"
(105; ch. 6)? (Nick doesn't tell us.) And which definition of *conceits* is operating here and elsewhere: "concepts," "visions," "affectations of style or
speech," or "self-flattering opinions"? What are we to make of the eyes of
Doctor T. J. Eckleburg, which hold such a prominent position in the
novel's imagery but could be taken to represent so many different ideas?

The eyes of Doctor T. J. Eckleburg are, in fact, only one of many ambiguous images in a novel dense with vague, evocative descriptions that
encourage readers to project their own meanings in interpreting them.
For example, what is a "pale gold odor" or a "sparkling odor" (96; ch. 5)?
What does it mean that a "gleam of hope" is "damp" (29; ch. 2)? What
should we make of Gatsby's "blue gardens" (43; ch. 3) or the hair that lies
across Daisy's cheek "like a dash of blue paint" (90; ch. 5)? How can
Daisy's voice, "struggl[ing] through the heat," "moul[d] its senselessness
into forms" (125; ch. 7), and what forms are thus produced? In addition,
Nick's descriptions often acknowledge their own inability to provide concrete, specific details by their frequent use of the words *indefinable,*
uncommunicable, unutterable, ineffable, and *inexplicable,* an evocative dic-
tion that reaches the height of its ambiguity in such phrases as "[t]hat unfamiliar yet recognizable look was back again in Gatsby's face" (141; ch.
7). If Nick can't define, communicate, utter, or explain what he has in
mind, then readers must imagine for themselves what he means, and such
gaps in the text invite us to project our own experience and desires in order to make meaning.

That *The Great Gatsby* easily supports the many different theoretical readings contained in this textbook is a testimony to the novel's indeterminacy. In short, there is so little determinate meaning in the novel that if we don't project our own beliefs and desires onto the text, the only interpretation left us would be that *The Great Gatsby* portrays the indeterminacy of meaning in a morally ambiguous world. While I think that's a useful interpretation of the novel, most readers, including myself, desire more closure than such an interpretation provides. It is interesting to note, in this context, a trend in critical response to Jay Gatsby. Despite the novel's two-sided characterization of the title character, a significant proportion of critical response casts Gatsby as a romantic hero, as we see in the following examples. According to Marius Bewley, Gatsby is "all aspiration and goodness" (25); he's "an heroic personification of the American romantic hero" (14) who represents "the energy of the spirit's resistance" and "immunity to the final contamination" of "cheapness and vulgarity" (13). Jeffrey Hart agrees that Gatsby is "a representative American hero" (34), and Charles C. Nash claims that "Emerson's 'Infinitude of the Private Man'" is "best represented by Jay Gatsby, for whom all things are possible" (23). Andrew Dillon believes Gatsby is imbued with a "sacred energy" (61), and Kent Cartwright says that Gatsby's "dream . . . ennobles him" (229). For Tom Burnam, Gatsby "survives sound and whole in character, uncorrupted by the corruption which surrounded him" (105). Similarly, Rose Adrienne Gallo believes that Gatsby "maintained his innocence" to the end (43), or as André Le Vot puts it, Gatsby never loses his "fundamental integrity, his spiritual intactness" (144). Even when the protagonist's darker side is acknowledged, it is excused. As Cartwright argues, "Gatsby can be both criminal and romantic hero because the book creates for him a visionary moral standard that transcends the conventional and that his life affirms" (232). Or as Andrew Dillon sums up what he sees as the protagonist's merger of worldliness and spirituality, Gatsby is "a sensual saint" (50).[5]

Of course, Nick's defense of Gatsby encourages readers to respond sympathetically to the protagonist. However, given the amount and kind of negative data about Gatsby that Nick himself provides, some additional factors probably influenced the response of those critics who see only the good in Gatsby. In other words, although Nick clearly wants us to exempt Gatsby, as he does, from our condemnation of Gatsby's world, the narrator nevertheless provides us with more than enough data to problematize the sympathetic judgment of the protagonist he promotes. In fact, the critical controversy over whether or not Nick is a reliable narrator underscores this dimension of the novel's indeterminacy.[6]

One possible explanation for a critical trend that ignores so much material in the novel, focusing only on the admirable elements in Gatsby's characterization, is that the protagonist taps some personal belief or desire that many readers have in common and that encourages them to see Gatsby in a wholly positive light. And indeed, I found that most of the critics who idealize Gatsby also idealize what they see as America's uncorrupted past, which they believe Gatsby represents. For these readers, Gatsby stands for a pristine America that was destroyed, as they believe he was, by the selfishness and vulgarity of people like Meyer Wolfshiem and Tom Buchanan.

Richard Chase, for example, sees Gatsby as part of "an earlier pastoral ideal," in that he shares, with Natty Bumppo, Huck Finn, and Ishmael, an "ideal of innocence, escape, and the purely personal code of conduct" (301). Similarly, Marius Bewley argues that the "young dandy of the frontier, dreaming in the dawn and singing to the morning," such as that described by Davy Crockett in 1836, "is a progenitor of Gatsby. It is because of such a traditional American ancestry that Gatsby's romanticism transcends the limiting glamor of the Jazz Age" (128). Thus, Gatsby is seen as "the true heir of the American dream" (Bewley 128) before that dream was corrupted by the influence of the moral wasteland that continues to extend its borders farther into the core of American society. Indeed, one might argue that the American ideology of the "rugged individual"— variations of which include, among other types, the loner, the nonconformist, and the maverick—predispose many readers to see only the admirable side of Gatsby's characterization.

Most of those critics who do not contrast the Jazz-Age world of the novel with an earlier, pristine period of American history interpret Gatsby in non-idealized terms. Edwin Fussell, for example, believes that the novel represents Fitzgerald's deliberate and scathing criticism of the American dream and of Jay Gatsby, the representative American. Neither Matthew Bruccoli nor A. E. Dyson idealizes Gatsby, and like Fussell, they recognize that the protagonist does not transcend the corruption of the world he lives in: rather, he shares it. In other words, many critics seem to interpret Gatsby largely according to their own assumptions about America's past. Perhaps the belief that America was once uncorrupted contributes to the vision of Gatsby as the representative of that pristine past, now gone forever. In any case, the degree to which the critics who idealize Gatsby completely ignore or actively excuse Gatsby's darker side suggests that the projection of our own beliefs and desires, at least when powerfully invited by the text, is stronger than the correctives to interpretation the text provides.

The resistance of many critics to the correctives provided by the novel—the negative data about Gatsby—is mirrored in the text's numerous references to reading materials that don't accomplish anything, that remain unread or unfinished, that fail to impose their reality on their readers. For example, the books in Gatsby's library are uncut, revealing that no one ever has read them. The magazine story Jordan reads to Tom Buchanan is unfinished, "to be continued in our very next issue" (22; ch. 1), and apparently doesn't succeed in entertaining her as it is supposed to do, for she reads it in a "murmurous and uninflected" tone (22; ch. 1). The popular novel Nick reads while waiting for Tom and Myrtle to emerge from the bedroom of their apartment "didn't make any sense" to him (34; ch. 2). Gatsby's letter to Daisy from overseas, which was intended to prevent her marriage to Tom, fails its mission entirely and crumbles in her bath. Neither does Nick's letter to Wolfshiem, entreating him to attend Gatsby's funeral, achieve its purpose. Gatsby has a whole collection of newspaper clippings about the Buchanans despite which "he doesn't know very much about Tom" (84; ch. 4). Nick has bought a whole set of books on banking to help him learn the bond business, but they do him no good: he admits to Gatsby that he's not making much money (87; ch. 5), and he winds up quitting his job when he returns to Wisconsin at the end of the summer. Gatsby's boyhood "schedule" for self-improvement, which he wrote at the back of his book on Hopalong Cassidy, a western icon of the American "good guy," implies a future dedicated to hard work and clean living, yet Gatsby grew up to be a criminal. And ironically, the only text that does the job for which it is intended doesn't have any job to do: Tom is a bigot long before he reads *The Rise of the Coloured Empires*, so the book merely confirms the racist attitude he already has.

As these examples illustrate, the novel shows us what little power texts have to achieve their intended purposes. Even if texts do have meaning independent of readers, that meaning often cannot compete with the meanings we, ourselves, project. In a novel with the degree of indeterminacy we experience in *The Great Gatsby*, the power of readers' projections in the creation of meaning is especially foregrounded, both in the novel's thematic content and in the active reading experience the text promotes. Thus, Fitzgerald's novel illustrates a theory of reading-as-projection as it simultaneously invites us to project our beliefs and desires upon it. And as a good deal of critical response to the novel suggests, this theory of reading, at least in terms of *The Great Gatsby*, seems quite accurate.

Questions for Further Practice: Reader-Response Approaches to Other Literary Works

The following questions are intended as models. They can help you use reader-response criticism to interpret the literary works to which they refer or other texts of your choice.

1. As the reader moves through each of the five sections of Kate Chopin's "The Storm" (1898), what reading experience is produced by the story's indeterminacy (for example, actions, characters, and images that are not clearly explained or that could have multiple meanings)? How is this reading experience reflected in the story's thematic content (for example, characters "reading," or decoding, other characters or situations)?

2. What does a line-by-line analysis of Robert Hayden's "Those Winter Sundays" (1975), or any other poem you would like to use, reveal about the ways in which the poem structures the reader's response as an event that occurs in time?

3. What does the history of critical response to Joseph Conrad's *Heart of Darkness* (1902) reveal about the interpretive communities that have analyzed the novel? You might, for example, differentiate and analyze interpretive communities by determining the interpretive strategies used, the assumptions upon which those strategies were based, and the readings that were thereby produced.

4. Using a narrative with a strong focus on issues of gender, race, and/or socioeconomic class—for example, Toni Morrison's *The Bluest Eye* (1970)—collect a series of brief response statements from your students (or classmates or book-club members). Response statements should focus on sections of the narrative (selected by you) in which these issues are clearly foregrounded. Use these written responses and what you learn from group discussions to analyze the possible relationships between one's own gender, race, and/or socioeconomic background and one's responses to the narrative's representations of gender, race, and/or socioeconomic background. Although this exercise is speculative rather than scientific, what inferences can you derive from it that might be worth putting into experimental practice in the teaching of literature?

5. Select a text you loved (or hated) as a youngster but that you haven't reread in years. Relying on memory and on any diary entries, letters, or the like that you may have available, summarize the story as you remember it, and write a thorough response statement from the perspective of your initial encounter with the book, including the personal experiences and relationships that helped you relate to the book at the time. Now read the book again, and write a current response statement. What does a response-analysis statement, comparing and contrasting your two encounters with the text, reveal about the role of subjective factors and interpretive strategies in the way readers make meaning? How might you apply what you've learned to improve the way literature is taught?

For Further Reading

All of the following works will help you develop your skills as reader-response critics. Texts listed under "Category I" are written in language accessible to most beginners. Texts listed under "Category II" employ more technical language but are well worth the extra effort that may be required of some students new to the field.

Category I

Bleich, David. *Readings and Feelings: An Introduction to Subjective Criticism.* Urbana, Illinois: NCTE, 1975.

Buckler, Patricia Prandini. "Combining Personal and Textual Experience: A Reader-Response Approach to Teaching American Literature." *Practicing Theory in Introductory College Literature Courses.* Eds. James M. Cahalan and David B. Downing. Urbana, Illinois: NCTE, 1991. 36–46.

Fish, Stanley. *Is There a Text in This Class?—The Authority of Interpretive Communities.* Cambridge: Harvard UP, 1980. (See, especially, "Literature in the Reader: Affective Stylistics," 21–67, and "Is There a Text in This Class?" 303–21.)

Freund, Elizabeth. *The Return of the Reader: Reader-Response Criticism.* London: Methuen, 1987.

Holland, Norman. "*Hamlet*—My Greatest Creation." *Journal of the American Academy of Psychoanalysis* 3 (1975): 419–27. Rpt. in *Contexts for Criticism.* Donald Keesey. 2nd ed. Mountain View, California: Mayfield, 1994. 160–65.

———. "Unity Identity Text Self." *PMLA* 90 (1975): 813–22. Rpt. in *Reader-Response Criticism: From Formalism to Post-Structuralism.* Ed. Jane P. Tompkins. Baltimore: Johns Hopkins UP, 1980. 118–33.

Mailloux, Steven J. "Reader-Response Criticism?" *Genre* 10 (Fall 1977): 413–31.

Rosenblatt, Louise. "The Poem as Event." *The Reader, the Text, the Poem: The Transactional Theory of the Literary Work*. Carbondale: Southern Illinois University Press, 1978. 6–21.

Tompkins, Jane P. "An Introduction to Reader-Response Criticism." *Reader-Response Criticism: From Formalism to Post-Structuralism*. Ed. Jane P. Tompkins. Baltimore: Johns Hopkins UP, 1980. ix–xxvi.

Category II

Bleich, David. *Subjective Criticism*. Baltimore: Johns Hopkins UP, 1978.

Booth, Stephen. *An Essay on Shakespeare's Sonnets*. New Haven, Yale UP, 1969.

———. "On the Value of *Hamlet*." *Reinterpretations of Elizabethan Drama*. Ed. Norman Rabkin. New York: Columbia UP, 1969. 77–99.

Fish, Stanley. *Surprised by Sin: The Reader in* Paradise Lost. New York: St. Martin's, 1967.

Holland, Norman. *5 Readers Reading*. New Haven: Yale UP, 1975.

Iser, Wolfgang. *The Act of Reading: A Theory of Aesthetic Response*. Baltimore: Johns Hopkins UP, 1978.

———. *The Implied Reader: Patterns of Communication in Prose Fiction from Bunyan to Beckett*. Johns Hopkins UP, 1974.

Mailloux, Steven. *Interpretive Conventions: The Reader in the Study of American Fiction*. Ithaca, New York: Cornell UP, 1982.

Richards, I. A. *Practical Criticism: A Study of Literary Judgement*. 1929. New York: Harcourt Brace, 1935.

Tompkins, Jane, ed. *Reader-Response Criticism: From Formalism to Post-Structuralism*. Baltimore: Johns Hopkins UP, 1980.

Notes

1. For example, reader-response anthologies often include an essay from Jonathan Culler's *Structuralist Poetics: Structuralism, Linguistics and the Study of Literature* because of Culler's interest in the way readers use interpretive strategies to make meaning. However, Culler's goal is to map the structures that underlie the interpretive strategies we use, just as structural linguistics seeks to map the structures that underlie the languages we speak. For Culler, underlying structures, not readers, are the ultimate objects of analysis, which is why we'll examine his work in Chapter Seven, "Structuralist Criticism."

2. This passage, and the hypothesis that the reader's purpose in reading it will influence his or her perception of the passage, is taken from a psychological study conducted by J. A. Pichert and R. C. Anderson. My thanks to Brian White, my colleague at Grand Valley State University, for showing me how it can be used to teach reader-response theory.

3. Although Iser is generally classified as a phenomenological critic (one who studies the activity of reading as an interaction between the author's consciousness and the reader's), his work has a good deal in common with that of Rosenblatt.

4. An emerging form of transactional reader-response theory that is growing in popularity has recently taken the name rhetorical reader-response theory. Key texts are Wayne Booth's *The Rhetoric of Fiction,* James Phelan's *Narrative as Rhetoric,* and Peter Rabinowitz's *Before Reading.*
5. For similar readings of Gatsby, see, for example, Chase, Gross, Moore, Stern, and Trilling.
6. Critics who believe Nick's viewpoint is trustworthy include, for example, Baxter, Dillon, and Nash. Critics who believe the narrator's perceptions cannot be trusted include, for example, Cartwright, Chambers, and Scrimgeour.

Works Cited

Baxter, Charles. "De-faced America: *The Great Gatsby* and *The Crying of Lot 49.*" *Pynchon Notes* 7 (1981): 22–37.

Bewley, Marius. "Scott Fitzgerald's Criticism of America." *The Sewanee Review* 62 (1954): 223–46. Rpt. in *Modern Critical Interpretations: F. Scott Fitzgerald's* The Great Gatsby. Ed. Harold Bloom. New York: Chelsea, 1986. 11–27.

Bleich, David. *Subjective Criticism.* Baltimore: The Johns Hopkins UP, 1978.

Booth, Wayne C. *The Rhetoric of Fiction.* Chicago: U of Chicago P, 1961.

Bruccoli, Matthew J. "*The Great Gatsby* (April 1925)." *Some Sort of Epic Grandeur: The Life of F. Scott Fitzgerald.* New York: Harcourt Brace Jovanovich, 1981. 220–24.

———. "Preface." *The Great Gatsby* (1925). New York: Simon & Schuster, 1995. vii–xvi.

Burnam, Tom. "The Eyes of Dr. Eckleburg: A Re-Examination of *The Great Gatsby.*" *College English* 13 (1952). Rpt. in *F. Scott Fitzgerald: A Collection of Critical Essays.* Ed. Arthur Mizener. Englewood Cliffs: Prentice-Hall, 1963. 104–11.

Cartwright, Kent. "Nick Carraway as an Unreliable Narrator." *Papers on Language and Literature* 20.2 (1984): 218–32.

Chambers, John B. "*The Great Gatsby.*" *The Novels of F. Scott Fitzgerald.* London: Macmillan, 1989. 91–126.

Chase, Richard. "*The Great Gatsby.*" *The American Novel and Its Traditions.* New York: Doubleday, 1957. 162–67. Rpt. in The Great Gatsby: *A Study.* Ed. Frederick J. Hoffman. New York: Scribner's, 1962. 297–302.

Culler, Jonathan. *Structuralist Poetics: Structuralism, Linguistics and the Study of Literature.* Ithaca: Cornell UP, 1975.

Dillon, Andrew. "*The Great Gatsby*: The Vitality of Illusion." *Arizona Quarterly* 44.1 (1988): 49–61.

Dyson, A. E. "*The Great Gatsby*: Thirty-Six Years After." *Modern Fiction Studies* 7.1 (1961). Rpt. in *F. Scott Fitzgerald: A Collection of Critical Essays.* Ed. Arthur Mizener. Englewood Cliffs: Prentice-Hall, 1963. 112–24.

Fish, Stanley. *Is There a Text in this Class? The Authority of Interpretive Communities.* Cambridge, MA: Harvard UP, 1980.

———. "Literature in the Reader: Affective Stylistics." *New Literary History* 2.1 (1970): 123–62. Rpt. in *Reader-Response Criticism: From Formalism to Post-Structuralism.* Ed. Jane P. Tompkins. Baltimore: The Johns Hopkins UP, 1980. 70–100.

Fitzgerald, F. Scott. *The Letters of F. Scott Fitzgerald*. Ed. Andrew Turnbull. New York: Scribner's, 1963.

Fussell, Edwin. "Fitzgerald's Brave New World." *ELH, Journal of English Literary History* 19 (1952). Rpt. in *F. Scott Fitzgerald: A Collection of Critical Essays*. Ed. Arthur Mizener. Englewood Cliffs: Prentice-Hall, 1963. 43–56.

Gallo, Rose Adrienne. *F. Scott Fitzgerald*. New York: Ungar, 1978.

Gross, Barry Edward. "Jay Gatsby and Myrtle Wilson: A Kinship." Excerpted in *Gatsby*. Ed. Harold Bloom. New York: Chelsea House, 1991. 23–25.

Hart, Jeffrey. "'Out of it ere night': The WASP Gentleman as Cultural Ideal." *New Criterion* 7.5 (1989): 27–34.

Holland, Norman. "Unity Identity Text Self." *PMLA* 90 (1975): 813–22. Rpt. in *Reader-Response Criticism: From Formalism to Post-Structuralism*. Ed. Jane P. Tompkins. Baltimore: The Johns Hopkins UP, 1980. 118–33.

Iser, Wolfgang. *The Act of Reading: A Theory of Aesthetic Response*. Baltimore: The Johns Hopkins UP, 1978.

Le Vot, André. *F. Scott Fitzgerald: A Biography*. Trans. William Byron. Garden City, New York: Doubleday, 1983.

Lowe-Evans, Mary. "Reading with a 'Nicer Eye': Responding to *Frankenstein*." *Case Studies in Contemporary Criticism*. Mary Shelley's *Frankenstein*. Ed. Johanna M. Smith. Boston: Bedford, 1992. 215–29.

Moore, Benita A. *Escape into a Labyrinth: F. Scott Fitzgerald, Catholic Sensibility, and the American Way*. New York: Garland, 1988.

Nash, Charles C. "From West Egg to Short Hills: The Decline of the Pastoral Ideal from *The Great Gatsby* to Philip Roth's *Goodbye, Columbus*." *Philological Association* 13 (1988): 22–27.

Phelan, James. *Narrative as Rhetoric: Technique, Audiences, Ethics, Ideology*. Columbus: Ohio State UP, 1996

Pichert, J. A., and R. C. Anderson. "Taking Different Perspectives on a Story." *Journal of Educational Psychology* 69.4 (1977): 309–15.

Rabinowitz, Peter J. *Before Reading: Narrative Conventions and the Politics of Interpretation*. Ithaca: Cornell UP, 19871

Rosenblatt, Louise. *The Reader, the Text, the Poem: The Transactional Theory of the Literary Work*. Carbondale: Southern Illinois UP, 1978.

Scrimgeour, Gary J. "Against *The Great Gatsby*." *Criticism* 8 (1966): 75–86. Rpt. in *Twentieth Century Interpretations of* The Great Gatsby. Ed. Ernest Lockridge. Englewood Cliffs: Prentice-Hall, 1968. 70–81.

Stern, Milton R. *The Golden Moment: The Novels of F. Scott Fitzgerald*. Urbana: U of Illinois P, 1970.

Trilling, Lionel. "F. Scott Fitzgerald." *The Liberal Imagination*. New York: Viking, 1950. 243–54. Rpt. in The Great Gatsby: *A Study*. Ed. Frederick J. Hoffman. New York: Scribner's, 1962. 232–43.

CHAPTER 7

Structuralist Criticism

The first thing you have to get used to when you begin to study structuralism is that common uses of the word *structure* do not necessarily imply structuralist activity. For example, you are *not* engaged in structuralist activity if you examine the physical structure of a building to discover if it is physically stable or aesthetically pleasing. However, you are engaged in structuralist activity if you examine the physical structures of all the buildings built in urban America in 1850 to discover the underlying principles that govern their composition, for example, principles of mechanical construction or of artistic form. You are also engaged in structuralist activity if you examine the structure of a single building to discover how its composition demonstrates the underlying principles of a given structural system. In the first example of structuralist activity, you're generating a structural system of classification; in the second, you're demonstrating that an individual item belongs to a particular structural class.

In terms of literary study, the same model of structuralist activity holds true. You are *not* engaged in structuralist activity if you describe the structure of a short story to interpret what the work means or evaluate whether or not it's good literature. However, you are engaged in structuralist activity if you examine the structure of a large number of short stories to discover the underlying principles that govern their composition, for example, principles of narrative progression (the order in which plot events occur) or of characterization (the functions each character performs in relation to the narrative as a whole). You are also engaged in structuralist activity if you describe the structure of a single literary work to discover how its composition demonstrates the underlying principles of a given structural system.

In other words, structuralists are not interested in individual buildings or individual literary works (or individual phenomena of any kind) except in terms of what those individual items can tell us about the structures that underlie and organize all items of that kind. For structuralism sees itself as a human science whose effort is to understand, in a systematic way, the fundamental structures that underlie all human experience and, therefore, all human behavior and production. For this reason, structuralism shouldn't be thought of as a field of study. Rather, it's a method of systematizing human experience that is used in many different fields of study: for example, linguistics, anthropology, sociology, psychology, and literary studies.

For structuralism, the world as we know it consists of two fundamental levels—one visible, the other invisible. The visible world consists of what might be called *surface phenomena*: all the countless objects, activities, and behaviors we observe, participate in, and interact with every day. The invisible world consists of the structures that underlie and organize all of these phenomena so that we can make sense of them. For example, the English language consists of over a million words, each of which can be pronounced in any number of different ways by different speakers, resulting in millions of different utterances of individual words. How is it possible that native speakers of English master enough of this overwhelming collection of linguistic items to communicate effectively with one another at a rather advanced level of sophistication and at a rather early age?

The answer is fairly simple: while there are millions of individual linguistic surface phenomena (individual words and all the different ways people pronounce them), there is a relatively simple structure underlying all these words, and it is that structure we master. The structure of English vocabulary consists of approximately thirty-one phonemes (fundamental units of sound recognized as meaningful by native speakers of a language) and the rules of their combination. Most of us are not aware of these phonemes and could not describe the rules of their combination, but our ability to use English vocabulary demonstrates that we have unconsciously internalized these structures. Similarly, our ability to construct simple sentences depends upon our internalization, whether or not we are aware of it, of the grammatical structure subject-verb-object. Without a structural system to govern communication, we would have no language at all. Analogously, without the structuring principles that allow us to organize and understand the natural world, the data provided by our five senses would be overwhelming and meaningless. Structuring principles, whether or not we are aware of them, allow us, for example, to differentiate vegetables (they grow in soil; they reproduce; they're edible) from stones (they don't grow; they don't reproduce; they're not edible) and from all other kinds of physical matter. Structuring principles also allow us to differentiate among groups within a given domain, for example, we might differentiate plant life with medicinal properties from plant life with harmful properties from plant life with neutral properties.

As these examples illustrate, the world we live in consists of innumerable events and objects, that is, innumerable surface phenomena. However, the structures that underlie and organize these phenomena are relatively few. Without these structures our world would be chaos.

Where do these structures come from? Structuralists believe they are generated by the human mind, which is thought of as a structuring mechanism. This is an important and radical idea because it means that the order we see in the world is the order we impose on it. Our understanding of the world does not result from our perception of structures that exist in the world. The structures we think we perceive in the world are actually innate (inborn) structures of human consciousness, which we project onto the world in order to be able to deal with the world. It's not that there is no factual reality; it's that there are too many facts to be perceived without conceptual systems to limit and organize them. And those conceptual systems originate within human consciousness. Thus, structuralism sees itself as a science of humankind, for its efforts to discover the structures that underlie the world's surface phenomena—whether we place those phenomena, for example, in the domain of mathematics, biology, linguistics, religion, psychology, or literature—imply an effort to discover something about the innate structures of human consciousness.

Before we go any further, we should take a moment to consider how structuralism defines the word *structure*. First of all, as we noted earlier, structures aren't physical entities; they're conceptual frameworks that we use to organize and understand physical entities. A structure is any conceptual system that has the following three properties: (1) wholeness, (2) transformation, and (3) self-regulation. *Wholeness* simply means that the system functions as a unit; it's not merely a collection of independent items. The whole is different from the sum of its parts because the parts working together create something new. To use a physical example, water is a whole that is different from its component parts (hydrogen and oxygen). *Transformation* means that the system is not static; it's dynamic, capable of change. The system is not merely a structure (a noun); it also structures (a verb). In other words, new material is always being structured by the system. For example, language, a structural system, is capable of transforming its basic components (phonemes) into new utterances (words and sentences). *Self-regulation* means that the transformations of which a structure is capable never lead beyond its own structural system. The elements engendered by transformations (for example, new linguistic utterances) always belong to the system and obey its laws.

Structuralism assumes that all surface phenomena belong to some structural system, whether or not we are consciously aware of what that system is. The relationship of surface phenomena to structure might be illustrated by the following simplified diagram.

Surface Phenomena:

	dog	runs	happily
	tree	appears	green
(words)	Susan	is	tall
	clouds	roll	ominously
	wisdom	comes	slowly

Structure:

(parts of speech)   Noun   Verb   Descriptor

(rules of combination)   Subject   +   Predicate

If you read the rows of surface phenomena from left to right, you have a list of individual utterances, such as "dog runs happily" and "tree appears green." However, if you read the columns of the whole diagram from top to bottom, you can see that the surface phenomena, which consist of fifteen different items but could consist of many more, are governed by a structure that consists, in this case, of only three parts of speech and two rules of combination. Thus, the utterance "dog runs happily" (or any utterance that follows the same grammatical pattern) is a surface phenomenon governed by the following structure.

Subject (Noun) + *Predicate* (Verb + Descriptor)

The components of a structure (in this example, parts of speech and rules of combination) are always fewer in number than the surface phenomena they underlie because their purpose is to organize, classify, and simplify.

So far, most of my examples have come from language. This is not surprising because language is considered the most fundamental structure of humankind and the one upon which most other structures depend. In fact, the field of structural linguistics is the source of most of structuralism's terminology. So let's take a brief look at that field now.

Structural Linguistics

Structural linguistics was developed by Ferdinand de Saussure between 1913 and 1915, although his work wasn't translated into English and popularized until the late 1950s. Before Saussure, language was studied in terms of the history of changes in individual words over time, or *diachronically*, and it was assumed that words somehow imitated the objects for which they stood. Saussure realized that we need to understand language, not as a collection of individual words with individual histories but as a structural system of relationships among words as they are used at a given point in time, or *synchronically*. This is the structuralist focus. Structuralism doesn't look for the causes or origins of language (or of any other phenomenon). It looks for the rules that underlie language and govern how it functions: it looks for the structure.

In order to differentiate between the structure that governs language and the millions of individual utterances that are its surface phenomena, Saussure called the structure of language *langue* (the French word for *language*), and he called the individual utterances that occur when we speak *parole* (the French word for *speech*). For the structuralist, of course, *langue* is the proper object of study; *parole* is of interest only in that it reveals *langue*. And these terms are used, as well, by structuralists who study literature: as we'll see later, structuralist critics look for the *langue* that structures individual literary works and that structures the system of literature as a whole.

As we saw above, the components of a structure are not merely a collection of independent items: they form a working unit because they exist in relation to one another. They interact. And we are able to perceive those components, as Saussure noted in terms of the structure of language, only because we perceive their difference from one another. *Differ-ence* simply means that our ability to identify an entity (such as an object, a concept, or a sound) is based on the difference we perceive between it and all other entities. For example, if we believed that all objects were the same color, we wouldn't need the word *red* (or *blue* or *green*) at all. Red is red only because we perceive it to be different from blue and green. According to structuralism, the human mind perceives difference most readily in terms of opposites, which structuralists call *binary oppositions*: two ideas, directly opposed, each of which we understand by means of its opposition to the other. For example, we understand up as the opposite of down, female as the opposite of male, good as the opposite of evil, black as the opposite of white, and so on.

Furthermore, unlike his predecessors, Saussure argued that words do not simply refer to objects in the world for which they stand. Instead, a word is a linguistic *sign* consisting, like the two sides of a coin, of two in-separable parts: signifier + signified. A *signifier* is a "sound-image" (a mental imprint of a linguistic sound); the *signified* is the concept to which the signifier refers. Thus, a word is not merely a sound-image (sig-nifier); nor is it merely a concept (signified). A sound-image becomes a word only when it is linked with a concept. Furthermore, the relationship between signifier and signified, Saussure observed, is arbitrary: there is no necessary connection between a given sound-image and the concept to which it refers. There is no reason why the concept of a tree should be represented by the sound-image "tree" instead of by the sound-image "arbre"; the concept of a book is just as well represented by the sound-image "livre" as the sound-image "book." The relationship between signi-fier and signified is merely a matter of social convention: it's whatever the community using it says it is.

The idea that signifiers, or linguistic sound-images, do not refer to things in the world but to concepts in our mind is crucial for structural-ism. As we noted earlier, structuralists believe that our perceptions of the world result from the conceptual framework that is an innate feature of human consciousness. We don't discover the world; we "create" it accord-ing to innate structures within the human mind. Given that language is the most fundamental of these structures, and the one through which our beliefs are passed on from one generation to the next, it makes sense that it is through language that we learn to conceive and perceive the world the way we do. This is why learning a new language carries with it the potential to learn to see the world in new ways.

If native speakers of English learn to speak an Eskimo language, for example, they may learn to see snow quite differently, for they will learn that there are many different words for what English calls *snow*, depending on the size and texture of the flake, the density of the snowfall, the angle at which it falls, the direction from which the storm originates, and so on. Similarly, if native speakers of English learn to speak Spanish, they may learn a new way to view the idea of human existence, for they will learn that Spanish has two different verbs for the English verb *to be*: *ser* and *estar*. *Ser* means "to be" in the sense of what one permanently considers oneself. One uses *ser* to say "I am a human being," "I am a woman," "I am Mexican," and the like. One uses *estar* to make statements about one's changeable state of being, such as "I am at the supermarket" or "I am a cab driver." And one uses neither *ser* nor *estar* to say "I am hungry" or "I am sleepy," for in Spanish these are not considered states of being. In Spanish one *has* hunger or sleepiness—*tengo hambre* or *tengo sueno*—but these are not states of being. Thus, when speaking a particular language, our attention is drawn to particular aspects of our experience, or more precisely, particular experiences are generated by that language. In other words, our language *mediates* our experience of our world and ourselves: it determines what we see when we look around us and when we look at ourselves.

The belief in the primacy of language in structuring human experience is of great interest to many students of human culture. Before we examine structuralist approaches to literature, let's take a brief look at two related areas of cultural study in which structuralist thought plays an important role: structural anthropology, which is the comparative study of human cultures, and semiotics, which is the study of sign systems, especially as they apply to the analysis of popular culture. Examples of structuralist activity in both these areas can help us grasp the structuralist enterprise as a whole and prepare us to better understand its applications to literature.

Structural Anthropology

Structural anthropology, created by Claude Lévi-Strauss in the late 1950s, seeks the underlying common denominators, the structures, that link all human beings regardless of the differences among the surface phenomena of the cultures to which they belong. Despite the very different ritual forms in which different cultures express important aspects of community life, it seems that all human cultures have some codified process of, for example, mate selection, kinship ties, and initiation into adulthood. While trial by ordeal (for example, being expected to survive on one's own in the wilderness for a specified period of time without the provision of food, clothing, or weapons) certainly appears different from, say, a twenty-first birthday party at a college dormitory, structural anthropologists would argue that the differences are only at the level of surface phenomena or, as structural linguists would put it, at the level of *parole*. For as rites of initiation, both cultural practices have the same underlying structures, the same *langue*. Both involve some sort of ritual ceremony: being bathed by members of the community upon one's return from the wilderness or blowing out candles and being toasted by assembled friends. Both involve some special form of personal decoration: special markings painted on the body or party hats and wet t-shirts. And both involve eating some sort of special food at the end of the ritual: perhaps the heart of a powerful animal or birthday cake and beer.

The existence of structural similarities among seemingly different myths of different cultures was one of Lévi-Strauss's particular areas of interest. His goal was to discover when "different" myths are actually different versions of the same myth in order to show that human beings from very different cultures share structures of consciousness that project themselves in the formation of structurally similar myths. These structural similarities, he claimed, reveal that certain human concerns cross cultural boundaries, and they include such practical questions as how to define kinship ties (in order to determine rights of inheritance and incest taboos) and such philosophical questions as how to account for the origin of the human race. An illustration of the latter question occurs in Lévi-Strauss's analysis of the Oedipus myth, which he believed embodies the conflict between our knowledge that we are born of sexual union and the persistent belief among many cultures that we are born of the earth, as the Spartoi spring from the soil in the Oedipus myth (or, we might add, as Adam is fashioned from clay in the Bible). Lévi-Strauss argued that there is no "true" or "original" version of any myth. Each version of a given myth is equally valid because each embodies the attempt of all structures to make sense out of an otherwise chaotic world.

When examined from a structuralist perspective, he found that the enormous number of myths from various cultures reduces itself to a rather limited number of what he called *mythemes*, the fundamental units of myths. A mytheme is analogous to a sentence in that it represents a relationship between two or more concepts, often in the form of a subject-verb relationship. A hero killing a monster is an example of a mytheme, as is a hero violating a moral law. Lévi-Strauss defines mythemes as "bundles" of relations because a mytheme consists of all its variants. For example, the mytheme "the hero kills a monster" includes a variety of different kinds of heroes (rich, poor, orphaned, of good family) killing different kinds of monsters (male, female, half human, sedentary, mobile, land-bound, seafaring, articulate, mute) for different reasons (to win a wife, to save a community, to prove himself). The point is that a structural approach to myth shows us that there is a relatively limited, knowable *langue* (underlying structure) by means of which we can order and understand the otherwise overwhelming number of different myths produced all over the world.

Of course, myths are forms of narrative, and mythemes are therefore narrative structures. So the structural analysis of myths has obvious implications for the structural study of literature. Indeed, as we'll see later in this chapter, in the section entitled "The Structure of Literary Genres," some literary critics believe that all literature consists of the retelling, in various guises, of the same myths.

Semiotics

Just as structural anthropology applies structuralist insights to the comparative study of human cultures, semiotics applies structuralist insights to the study of what it calls sign systems. A *sign system* is a non-linguistic object or behavior (or collection of objects or behaviors) that can be analyzed as if it were a language. In other words, semiotics examines the ways non-linguistic objects and behaviors "tell" us something. For example, the picture of the reclining blond beauty in the skin-tight, black velvet dress on the billboard advertising a particular brand of whiskey "tells" us that those who drink this whiskey (presumably male) will be attractive to seductive, beautiful women like the one displayed here. As this example illustrates, semiotics is especially interested in analyzing popular culture. Other examples of the kinds of pop-culture sign systems semioticians tend to examine might include pictorial ads in magazines, popular dances, Disneyland, roller derby, Barbie dolls, Cadillacs, and, to use two examples analyzed by the famous semiotician Roland Barthes, professional wrestling and the striptease.

Here's a simplified summary of Barthes' semiotic analysis of professional wrestling. He argues that professional wrestling (the brand of wrestling in which the contestants use pseudonyms like Gorgeous George or Haystacks Calhoun, dress in costume, and orchestrate the match in advance) can be viewed as a sign system. It can be interpreted as a language with a very specific purpose: to provide the audience with the cathartic satisfaction of watching justice triumph in a situation that (unlike life) makes it very clear who is good and who is evil. This purpose is revealed in the structural similarities of the matches, regardless of who the contestants are: for example, (1) each wrestler is a clear type (clean-cut All-American, mean-tempered slob, barbarous evildoer, and so on); (2) each match contains contestants who, by their type, their behavior during a particular match, or both, can be clearly identified as the "good guy" and the "bad guy"; and (3) each match ends with the triumph of goodness over evil.

The match, Barthes further observes, greatly resembles the spectacle of ancient Greek theatre, as the wrestlers act out their pain, despair, or triumph with exaggerated gestures and grimaces. The exhibition of suffering, defeat, and justice is thus the purpose of the spectacle. The signs we read in order to come to this conclusion include the names, physiques, and costumes of the contestants; their body language in the ring (strutting, cowering, swaggering, menacing, placating, and the like); and their facial expressions (smug, outraged, proud, horrified, triumphant, defeated, and so on). It doesn't matter that the contest is rigged because its purpose is not to determine who is the better wrestler but to enact the kind of spectacle different versions of which have for centuries provided the public with the vicarious release of anger, fear, and frustration.

Now let's take a look at some of the theoretical concepts underlying semiotic analyses like the one just summarized. Semiotics recognizes language as the most fundamental and important sign system. As we saw in our discussion of structural linguistics, a linguistic sign is defined as a union of signifier (sound-image) and signified (concept to which the signifier refers). For semiotics, too, *sign* = signifier + signified. However, as we just saw, semiotics expands the signifier to include objects, gestures, activities, sounds, images—in short, anything that can be perceived by the senses. Clearly, semiotics gives the signifier a wide range of possibilities. However, of the three recognized classes of signs—index, icon, and symbol—semiotics limits its study to signs that function as symbols. Let's pause briefly to examine why this is the case.

An *index* is a sign in which the signifier has a concrete, causal relationship to the signified. For example, smoke signifies fire; a knock on the door signifies that someone is there. An *icon* is a sign in which the signifier physically resembles the signified. For example, a painting is an icon to the extent that the picture resembles the subject it represents. A realistic painting of President Kennedy is an icon. A *symbol* is a sign in which the relationship between signifier and signified is neither natural nor necessary, but arbitrary, that is, decided upon by the conventions of a community, by the agreement of some group.

As we saw earlier, language is an example of a symbolic sign system. The sound-image "tree" refers to the idea of a tree only because speakers of English have agreed to use it that way. While smoke is an index of fire, and a realistic painting of fire is an icon of fire, the word *fire* is a symbol of fire. There is no quality of fire inherent in the word *fire*. Any other sound-image agreed upon by a group could be used to represent fire. Let's consider a different example. Ice crystals on your living room window are an index of winter. A photograph of a frozen landscape is an icon of winter. However, that same photograph of a frozen landscape or a written description of it in a story (such as Jack London's "To Build a Fire") would function for most English majors as a symbol of death.

Thus, of the three kinds of signs, only the symbol is a matter of interpretation. A group of people doesn't decide that fire produces smoke (an index). It is simply the case that fire produces smoke. A group of people doesn't decide that a realistic portrait of President Kennedy (an icon) will have the same color hair, eyes, skin, and other physical features that the late president had. If the portrait didn't have these physical features, it wouldn't be an icon. But a group of people does have to decide that the color white symbolizes virginity, that the color red symbolizes sexuality, that horns and a pitchfork symbolize Satan, and that the cross symbolizes Christianity.

It is the business of semiotics, then, to isolate and analyze the symbolic function of sign systems, although the objects or behaviors under investigation will often have other functions as well. For example, food and clothing have obvious biological functions (they keep us nourished and protected from the elements) and economic functions (fluctuations in the price of food and clothing influence a society's standard of living). But a semiotician will be interested in food and clothing only to the extent to which they function as sign systems, only to the extent to which they have symbolic content. Furthermore, as a structuralist enterprise, semiotics will analyze a sign system by focusing on a group of similar objects (for example, billboards or pictorial magazine ads or restaurant menus) synchronically (at a given moment in time). To analyze the semiotics of food as it is expressed in restaurant menus, for example, one would not examine menus from a single restaurant as they have changed over time. Instead, one would examine a large number of menus produced by different restaurants at the same point in time in order to discover their *semiotic codes*, the underlying structural components that carry a non-verbal cultural message of some sort.

What might a semiotic analysis of restaurant menus reveal? In other words, besides the concrete data about the five food groups communicated by the words on the menu, what non-linguistic messages are these menus sending? By examining such signs as the menus' color, size, decoration, type of print, size of margins, amount and distribution of blank space, prices, names of dishes (not words like *steak* or *baked potato*, but "tags" like *à la Parisienne* or *Pioneer's*), and the predominance or absence of foods that carry symbolic value (such as hamburger or caviar), we would probably be able to discover a "fashion industry" of food in which, for example, messages about patrons' self-images are communicated. The semiotics of some menus will send the message, "If you're a well-bred, well-educated person of distinction with an extremely discriminating palate and the wallet to back it up, you will slip into your Guccis, slide into your BMW, and dine with us." Other menus will send the message, "If you're a down-to-earth non-phony who doesn't want to waste time or hard-earned dough on sissified showing off, come on in." Still other menus will send the message, "If you're a patriotic American who still believes in God and Grandma's apple pie, you'll celebrate your family values by eating here." For semioticians, anything can be a sign. The whole world is a "text" waiting to be "read," and structuralism provides the theoretical framework to do it.

Structuralist Approaches to Literature

For our purposes as students of literature, structuralism has very important implications. After all, literature is a verbal art: it is composed of language. So its relation to the "master" structure, language, is very direct. In addition, structuralists believe that the structuring mechanisms of the human mind are the means by which we make sense out of chaos, and literature is a fundamental means by which human beings explain the world to themselves, that is, make sense out of chaos. So there seems to be a rather powerful parallel between literature as a field of study and structuralism as a method of analysis.

Our discussion of structuralist approaches to literature will focus on the narrative dimension of literary texts because structuralist criticism deals mainly with narrative. This focus is not as narrow as it may seem at first glance, however, if we remember that narrative includes a long history and broad range of texts, from the simple myths and folk tales of the ancient oral tradition to the complex mélange of written forms found in the postmodern novel. In addition, most drama and a good deal of poetry, though not classified as narrative, nevertheless have a narrative dimension in that they tell a story of some sort. In any event, as we'll see, narratives provide fertile ground for structuralist criticism because, despite their range of forms, narratives share certain structural features, such as plot, setting, and character.

We must keep in mind, however, that structuralism does not attempt to interpret what individual texts mean or even whether or not a given text is good literature. Issues of interpretation and literary quality are in the domain of surface phenomena, the domain of *parole*. Structuralism seeks instead the *langue* of literary texts, the structure that allows texts to make meaning, often referred to as a *grammar* because it governs the rules by which fundamental literary elements are identified (for example, the hero, the damsel in distress, and the villain) and combined (for example, the hero tries to save the damsel in distress from the villain). In short, structuralism isn't interested in what a text means, but in *how* a text means what it means. Thus, *The Great Gatsby*'s Jay Gatsby, Daisy Buchanan, and Tom Buchanan are surface phenomena that draw their meaning from the ways in which they relate to the structures underlying them: respectively, hero, damsel in distress, and villain.

As you may remember from Chapter Six, reader-response critics also focus on how a text means rather than what it means. Indeed, there is some overlap between the two disciplines, for structuralists and reader-response critics would agree that there is a relationship between the underlying structure of the text and the reader's response to it. After all, structuralism believes that the structures we perceive in literature, as in everything else, are projections of the structures of human consciousness. However, you'll recall that the final goal of reader-response criticism is to understand the reader's experience, which structuralists would call a surface phenomenon. In contrast, the final goal of structuralism is to understand the underlying structure of human experience, which exists at the level of *langue*, whether we are examining the structures of literature or speculating on the relationship between the structures of literature and the structures of human consciousness. In other words, reader-response criticism does not seek a universal science that would link innate structures of human consciousness to all human experience, behavior, and production. Structuralism seeks precisely that.

Structuralist approaches to literature have tended to focus on three specific areas of literary studies: the classification of literary genres, the description of narrative operations, and the analysis of literary interpretation. For the sake of clarity, we'll discuss these three areas separately.

The Structure of Literary Genres

Let's begin our discussion of structuralist approaches to genre with a simplified summary of one of its most complex and sweeping examples: what Northrop Frye calls his *theory of myths*, which is a theory of genres that seeks the structural principles underlying the Western literary tradition.[1] *Mythoi* (plural of *mythos*) is a term Frye uses to refer to the four narrative patterns that, he argues, structure myth. These mythoi, he claims, reveal the structural principles underlying literary genres: specifically, comedy, romance, tragedy, and irony/satire.

According to Frye, human beings project their narrative imaginations in two fundamental ways: in representations of an ideal world and in representations of the real world. The ideal world, which is better than the real world, is the world of innocence, plenitude, and fulfillment. Frye calls it the *mythos of summer*, and he associates it with the genre of *romance*. This is the world of adventure, of successful quests in which brave, virtuous heroes and beautiful maidens overcome villainous threats to the achievement of their goals. Examples of romance you may be familiar with include the chivalrous adventures in Sir Thomas Malory's *Morte Darthur* (1470), Edmund Spenser's *The Faerie Queene* (1596), John Bunyan's *The Pilgrim's Progress* (1678), and "Sleeping Beauty."

In contrast, the real world is the world of experience, uncertainty, and failure. Frye calls it the *mythos of winter*, and he associates it with the double genre of *irony/satire*. Irony is the real world seen through a tragic lens, a world in which protagonists are defeated by the puzzling complexities of life. They may try to be heroic, but they never achieve heroic stature. They may dream of happiness; but they never attain it. They're human, like us, and so they suffer. Examples of ironic texts you may have read include Shakespeare's *The Tempest* (1611), Edith Wharton's *Age of*

Innocence (1920), Richard Wright's *Native Son* (1940), and John Steinbeck's *Of Mice and Men* (1937).

Analogously, satire is the real world seen through a comic lens, a world of human folly, excess, and incongruity. In the world of satire, human frailty is mocked, sometimes with biting, merciless humor. Examples of satire you may be acquainted with include Jonathan Swift's *Gulliver's Travels* (1726), George Orwell's *Animal Farm* (1946), the episodes satirizing the abuses of the antebellum American South in Mark Twain's *Adventures of Huckleberry Finn* (1885), and the passages satirizing conservative complacency and leftist self-delusion in Ralph Ellison's *Invisible Man* (1952).

While romance occurs within an ideal world, and irony/satire occurs within the real world, the remaining two mythoi involve a movement from one of these worlds to the other. *Tragedy* involves a movement from the ideal world to the real world, from innocence to experience, from the mythos of summer to the mythos of winter, and therefore Frye calls tragedy the *mythos of autumn*. In tragedy, a hero with the potential to be superior, like a romantic hero, falls from his romantic height into the real world, the world of loss and defeat, from which he can never rise. Well-known examples of tragedy include Sophocles's *Oedipus the King* (5th century B.C.), Shakespeare's *Hamlet* (1601) and *Othello* (1604), and Mary Shelley's *Frankenstein* (1818).

In contrast, *comedy* involves a movement from the real world to the ideal, from experience to innocence, from the mythos of winter to the mythos of summer, and therefore Frye calls comedy the *mythos of spring*. In comedy, a protagonist caught in a web of threatening, real-world difficulties manages, through various twists in the plot, to overcome the circumstances that have thwarted him and attain happiness. Unlike the villains who obstruct romantic heroes, those who obstruct the protagonists of comedy are absurd and humorous. And in the end, the protagonist moves, usually with his or her beloved, from the cold, troublesome real world to a happier, kinder, gentler fictional space. Examples of comedy you may be familiar with include Shakespeare's *Comedy of Errors* (1590) and *A Midsummer Night's Dream* (1595), William Wycherley's *Country Wife* (1675), and Jane Austen's *Pride and Prejudice* (1813).

This description of Frye's framework is merely a skeletal map of his detailed analysis of each mythos and the genre to which it is related. He argues that each genre identifies itself with a particular repertoire of themes, character types, moods, kinds of action, and versions of the plot formulas summarized above. Taken together, the four genres form a kind of master plot, or key to understanding narrative as a whole. And for Frye, that master plot is the structure of the quest, of which each mythos represents one leg.

Frye notes that the traditional quest has four structural components: conflict, catastrophe, disorder and confusion, and triumph. Conflict, he observes, is the basis of romance, which consists of a series of fantastic adventures in which superheroes encounter obstacles. Catastrophe is the basis of tragedy, which consists of the hero's downfall. Disorder and confusion are the basis of irony and satire, which require that confusion and anarchy reign supreme and that effective action be impossible. And triumph is the basis of comedy, in which the protagonist and his or her beloved become the centerpiece of some sort of improved social order. Taken together, then, the genres of romance, tragedy, irony/satire, and comedy—in that order—spell out the structure of what Frye calls a "total quest-myth." Thus, for Frye, all narrative is structurally related because it's all some version of some part of the quest formula.

Frye calls this method of classification *archetypal criticism* because it deals with the recurrence of certain narrative patterns throughout the history of Western literature. The word *archetype* refers to any recurring image, character type, plot formula, or pattern of action. An archetype, then, is a kind of super-type, or model, different versions of which recur throughout the history of human production: in our myths, literature, dreams, religions, and rituals of social behavior. Frye's method thus seeks the structural principles that underlie the Western literary tradition. Indeed, archetypes are themselves structural in nature: in order to be an archetype, an image, character type, or other narrative element must serve as a structural model that generates numerous different versions of itself, that is, numerous different surface phenomena with the same underlying structure. So while the specific content of particular romances, tragedies, ironic/satiric narratives, and comedies is different—that is, their surface phenomena are different—the structure of each genre remains the same.[2]

Another method with which Frye seeks the structural principles that govern genres in the Western literary tradition he calls his *theory of modes*. His classification of fiction into modes is based on the protagonist's power to take action as it compares to the power of other men and to the power of their environment (nature and/or society). Frye's modes are also determined according to whether the protagonist is superior in kind to others (of a type beyond the reach of ordinary people, like gods or demigods) or merely superior in degree (having the same positive attributes that all humans are capable of but having them to a greater degree). Perhaps a chart will help clarify Frye's system.

Protagonist's Power	Fictional Mode	Character Type
1. Superior in kind to both men and their environment	Myth	Divine beings
2. Superior in degree to both	Romance	Heroes
3. Superior in degree to men but not to their environment	High mimesis (imitation of life, like that found in epic and tragedy)	Leaders
4. Superior in no way	Low mimesis (imitation of life, like that found in comedy and realism)	Common people
5. Inferior	Irony	Antiheroes

Frye notes that, for the most part, myths, though an early form of narrative, fall outside the usual literary categories. For this reason, and because it seems somewhat odd to include comedy and realism under the same heading, Robert Scholes offers a different version of Frye's modes, one he believes will provide a more clear and useful basis of differentiation among genres by eliminating the non-literary mode of myth and inserting a new category in order to account for the difference between comedy and realism. Here's a chart outlining Scholes's system of classification.

Protagonist's Power	Fictional Mode	Character Type
1. Superior in degree to both men and their environment	Romance	Heroes
2. Superior in degree to men but not to their environment	High mimesis (Imitation of life, like that found in epic and tragedy)	Leaders
3. Equal in degree to men and their environment	Middle mimesis (Imitation of life, like that found in realism)	Ordinary people like ourselves
4. Inferior in degree to men and their environment	Low mimesis (Imitation of life, like that found in comedy)	Comic and pathetic figures
5. Inferior in kind	Irony	Antiheroes

As these two charts indicate, different structuralists can have different ways of categorizing even the same material. And there are many more structuralist theories of genre than those outlined here. This kind of structural analysis is an ongoing attempt to classify and thereby understand the relationships among literary texts by finding the most useful way to represent the structural system governing literature as a whole.

The Structure of Narrative (Narratology)

Structuralist analyses of narrative examine in minute detail the inner "workings" of literary texts in order to discover the fundamental structural units (such as units of narrative progression) or functions (such as character functions) that govern texts' narrative operations. A good deal of literary criticism that today goes under the name *narratology* belongs to this kind of structuralist approach. We'll limit ourselves to three examples that are representative of the field in general and that I think you'll find most useful at this stage in your understanding of structuralism: the work of A. J. Greimas, Tzvetan Todorov, and Gérard Genette.

Greimas observes that human beings make meaning by structuring the world in terms of two kinds of opposed pairs: "A is the opposite of B" and "–A (the negation of A) is the opposite of –B (the negation of B)." In other words, we perceive every entity as having two aspects: its opposite (the opposite of love is hate) and its negation (the negation of love is the absence of love). He believes that this fundamental structure of binary oppositions, consisting of four components arranged in two pairs, shapes our language, our experience, and the narratives through which we articulate our experience.

In our narratives, this structure is embodied in the form of plot formulas, such as conflict and resolution, struggle and reconciliation, and separation and union. These plot formulas are carried out by means of *actants*, or character functions, which are slots filled by the actual characters (surface phenomena) in a given story. A single character may perform the work of two or more separate actants. For example, in *The Great Gatsby*, Nick supplies the role of at least two actants: the hero's helper (he sympathizes with Gatsby and helps reunite him with Daisy) and a quester in his own right (Nick has come to Long Island seeking himself, seeking a purpose for his life). Analogously, two or more characters may perform the function of a single actant. For example, Tom, Wolfshiem, and Gatsby's parasitical party guests all function as a single actant: the embodiment of a corrupt world that finally destroys Gatsby.

For Greimas, the forwarding of the plot—the movement from conflict to resolution, struggle to reconciliation, separation to union, and so forth—involves the transfer of some entity (a quality or an object) from one actant to another. For example, Daisy is transferred from Tom to Gatsby (or, more precisely, from Gatsby to Tom to Gatsby then back to Tom), and Gatsby's disillusionment at the end of the story is transferred to Nick. Thus, the fundamental structure of narrative is the same as the fundamental structure of language: subject-verb-object. This basic narrative grammar generates the following three patterns of plots by aligning what Greimas sees as the six fundamental actants into three pairs of oppositions:

Actants	*Plot Type*
Subject—Object	Stories of Quest/Desire (a subject, or hero, searches for an object: a person, thing, or state of being)
Sender—Receiver	Stories of Communication (a sender—a person, god, or institution—sends the subject in search of the object, which the receiver ultimately receives)
Helper—Opponent	Sub-Plots of Stories of Quest/Desire or Communication (a helper aids the subject in the quest; an opponent tries to hinder the subject)

Of course, a given narrative can combine a story of quest/desire with a story of communication. For example, in a simple love story, the hero can be both the subject and the receiver, and his beloved can be both the object and sender. Or in stories like those about the quest for the Holy Grail, each actant can be performed by a separate character: God is the sender; the hero is the subject; the Holy Grail is the object; and humanity is the receiver.

Finally, in order to account for various possible narrative sequences, Greimas suggests the following structures, which he derived from his study of folk tales.

1. *Contractual structures* involve the making/breaking of agreements or the establishment/violation of prohibitions and the alienation or reconciliation that follows.
2. *Performative structures* involve the performance of tasks, trials, struggles, and the like.
3. *Disjunctive structures* involve travel, movement, arrivals, and departures.

Greimas uses his system to analyze the works of twentieth-century

French author Georges Bernanos, concluding that the novelist creates a world in which all conflicts reduce to the fundamental symbolic conflict between life and death. Furthermore, this key conflict expresses itself, Greimas suggests, in the following structure (which I have simplified) that governs the author's fictional universe.

Available Experiences	Possible Transformations	Ideological Choices
1. Joy/Pain	Truth: Revolt + Acceptance	Life: Joy + Pain
2. Boredom/Disgust	Lie: Refusal + Resignation	Death: Boredom + Disgust

The grammar of Bernanos's novels thus structures a world in which we can avoid feeling pain only if we are willing to give up joy as well, for the two are linked: our capacity to feel joy makes us vulnerable to pain. Thus, we must either accept the truth that life is a double-edged sword of joy and pain (though we tend, initially, to revolt against that truth), or we must refuse the truth and resign ourselves to the only alternative: boredom and disgust, which are a kind of emotional death we choose in order to protect ourselves from the emotional risks of life.

In a manner similar to that of Greimas, Todorov draws an analogy between the structural units of narrative—such as elements of characterization and plot—and the structural units of language: parts of speech and their arrangement in sentences and paragraphs.

Units of Narrative		Units of Language
characters	<————————>	proper nouns
characters' actions	<————————>	verbs
characters' attributes	<————————>	adjectives
propositions	<————————>	sentences
sequences	<————————>	paragraphs

A *proposition* is formed by combining a character with an irreducible action (for example, "X kills Y" or "X arrives in town") or irreducible attribute (for example, "X is evil" or "X is queen"), that is, an action or attribute in its most basic form. A *sequence* is a string of propositions that can stand on its own as a story. The structure of the most basic sequence is (1) attribution, (2) action, (3) attribution: the protagonist starts out with an attribute (for example, he is unloved), and by means of an action (he seeks love) that attribute is transformed (he is loved or, at least, has learned something important as a result of his quest). A story must contain at least one sequence, though it may contain many sequences. Todorov further subdivides his structural system into such categories as *negation* (the absence of an action or attribute), *comparison* (the presence of an action or attribute to different degrees), and *modes* (the qualification of an action or attribute, such as occurs when an action or attribute is desired, feared, expected, done unwillingly, and the like).

This "grammar" of narrative allows Todorov to analyze texts in terms of what he sees as their fundamental narrative properties. Once a text's propositions are discovered—by combining each character (noun) with an action (verb) or attribute (adjective)—the kinds of actions and attributes that recur in a text can be categorized as can the kinds of propositions and the relations between propositions. For example, in his analysis of the stories in Boccaccio's *The Decameron* (1350), Todorov finds, among other things, that all attributes can be reduced to three categories of adjectives: *states* (unstable attributes, such as happiness and unhappiness), *qualities* (more stable attributes, such as good and evil), and *conditions* (the most stable attributes, such as one's sex, religion, or social position).

Especially significant, I think, is his claim that all actions in *The Decameron* can be reduced to three verbs: to modify, to transgress, and to punish. For this discovery led to his observation of a significant pattern of recurrence in the tales: changes are continually made, and sins continually go unpunished. This pattern, and his knowledge of history, led Todorov to speculate that there is a connection between the values operating in Boccaccio's stories and those of the culture in which he lived. Todorov suggests that, in both *The Decameron* and Boccaccio's world, a new system of values was emerging, one that appreciated the personal daring and initiative associated with the free-enterprise system of capitalism, which was beginning to replace the older, more restrictive system of commerce.

It is important to note that both Greimas and Todorov derive their frameworks from and apply them to a large body of materials—Greimas uses all the works of a single author, and Todorov uses a long work that consists of a collection of tales—because they want to produce a structural system useful for understanding narrative in general. Similarly, Genette develops his narrative theory by means of a detailed study of Marcel Proust's seven-volume work, *Remembrance of Things Past* (1927).

Genette begins by differentiating among three levels of narrative that generally have been included under the umbrella of the term *narrative*: story, narrative, and narration.

Story consists of the succession of events being narrated. The story thus provides the content of the tale in the order in which events "actually happened" to the characters, an order which does not always coincide with the order in which they are presented in the narrative.

Narrative refers to the actual words on the page, the discourse, the text itself, from which the reader constructs both story and narration. The narrative is produced by the narrator in the act of narration.

Narration refers to the act of telling the story to some audience and thereby producing the narrative. However, just as the narrator almost never corresponds exactly to the author, the audience (*narratee*) almost never corresponds exactly to the reader.

For example, in *The Great Gatsby*, Nick is describing his summer in New York to some audience (narration). In doing so, he presents a verbal discourse, which we see as the words on the page (narrative). And that discourse represents the events in which Nick appears as a character (story).

Genette's work focuses on narrative, the words on the page, but he notes that all three levels work together. That is, for the purposes of analysis, he separates aspects of a text that don't operate separately, but he does so in order to see how they interact. And he observes that story, narrative, and narration interact by means of three qualities, which he calls tense, mood, and voice.

1. *Tense* is the arrangement of events in the narrative with respect to time. That arrangement involves the notions of order, duration, and frequency.

    a. *Order* refers to the relationship between the chronology of the story (the order in which the events of the story occur in the fictional world) and the chronology of the narrative (the order in which the narrative presents those events). For example, Jay Gatsby's story consists, in part, of the following facts in the following order: he was born to poor farmers, ran away from home, worked for Dan Cody, courted Daisy, went to war, returned, and set about acquiring a fortune and reclaiming Daisy. However, the narrative presents these events in a different order. For example, we don't learn about his boyhood until Chapter VI.

b. *Duration* refers to the relationship between the length of time over which a given event occurs in the story and the number of pages of narrative devoted to describing it. A character's trip to Europe may last five years in the story, but the narrative may describe it in five lines. Conversely, a conversation between lovers may take five minutes in the story, but the narrative may describe it in five pages. Thus, duration is what produces the sense of narrative speed.

c. *Frequency* involves the relationship between the ways in which events may be repeated in the story (the same event may occur more than once) and in the narrative (a single event may be described more than once).

2. *Mood* is the atmosphere of the narrative created by distance and perspective.

a. *Distance* is created when the narrator is one of the characters in the narrative, a "go-between" through whose consciousness the story is filtered. The more intrusive the narrator, the greater the distance between narration and story. Conversely, the least distance is created when we are unaware of the narrator's presence, when a tale seems to "tell itself." Distance is also created by the absence of descriptive detail. The less detail given, the less the effect of reality is created, and the greater the sense of distance between narration and story. The more detail given, the less distance exists. Thus, the least distance, or the greatest imitation of life, is produced by maximum information and minimum presence of the narrator.

b. *Perspective* refers to point of view, or the eyes through which we see any given part of the narrative. Although the narrator may be speaking, the point of view may be that of one of the other characters, and the feelings of a point-of-view character may be different from those of the narrator telling that character's story.

3. *Voice* refers to the voice of the narrator. The voice we hear (the
   narrator's) may not be the same as the eyes we see through (the
   perspective). When we analyze voice, we analyze the relationship
   of the narrator (the act of narration) to the story being told and
   to the narrative (the way the story is being told). Voice helps us
   determine the narrator's attitude toward the story and reliability.

It is interesting to note that tense, mood, and voice are all aspects of
verbs. For in Genette's opinion, all fiction functions like an expanded
verb: all narrative reduces to action. Although his definitions may seem
"cut and dried," he generates his categories, in large part, to be able to
show when a literary text creates its effects by "violating" those categories.
In his study of *Remembrance of Things Past*, for example, Genette shows
how Proust creates an effect of intense immediacy, of great intimacy between narration and story, by combining maximum information with
maximum presence of narrator, an effect that is traditionally produced by
combining maximum information with minimum presence of narrator.
Thus, Genette underscores the notion that systems of classification
should be used to help us illuminate the complexity of literary works, not
obscure that complexity through oversimplification.

Of course, the work of Greimas, Todorov, and Genette is far more
complex than this summary implies. Our purpose here is simply to understand the kinds of analyses made possible by structural narratology. It
might be helpful to think of this approach as looking at narrative through
a microscope in order to identify its smallest units and see how they
work. Structural narratologists thus offer us a way of seeing the details of
narrative operations and a vocabulary with which to describe them.

It is important to note, however, that Greimas, Todorov, and Genette,
once they identify the formula that structures a narrative or group of narratives, use that formula to address larger questions about literary meaning and its relationship to human life. That is, once we identify the formula of a given narrative or group of narratives, we must then ask
ourselves, "How does this formula reveal a pattern in narrative in general,
and what does this pattern imply about human experience, or the structures of human consciousness?" In other words, what does a given narrative pattern contribute to our knowledge of the relatively small number
of stories human beings have been telling themselves for thousands of
years (though the stories may take hundreds of different forms, they are
still, structurally, the same stories) in order to help themselves cope with

life? For at the heart of structuralist analysis of any kind is the desire to understand what it means to be human.

The Structure of Literary Interpretation

According to Jonathan Culler, the structural system that governs both the writing and interpretation of literary texts is the system of rules and codes, which we have consciously or unconsciously internalized, that tell us how to make meaning when we read literature. Some of these rules and codes are taken for granted by the public at large (for example, that a fairy tale is a fictional story not to be taken literally), but many of them are learned in the classroom (for example, that the use of nature imagery reveals a good deal about a work's theme).

In America, this system of rules and codes is part of the Western literary tradition as it has been passed on by our universities, and our individual *literary competence* is determined by how much of the system we have internalized. The point is not that any two competent readers would necessarily agree in their interpretation of a particular work but that both interpretations would be guided by the same structural system of interpretive rules and codes. Culler thus believes that what we refer to as the structure of literature is really the structure of the system of interpretation we bring to it. His effort is to unearth this structural system and show us how it operates. Perhaps the best way to acquaint you with the structural system Culler has identified is simply to describe some of its major components, which he has named as follows: the convention of distance and impersonality, naturalization, the rule of significance, the rule of metaphorical coherence, and the rule of thematic unity.

The convention of distance and impersonality is an assumption we make as soon as we see that we are reading a literary work, even if that work is in the form of non-literary writing, such as a letter (like Barthelme's story "The Sandman," 1972) or a journal (like Doris Lessing's *Memoirs of a Survivor*, 1974). As soon as we know we're reading a piece of fiction or poetry rather than a literal letter or journal, we read it differently than we would read a real letter or journal: we know we're entering a fictional world, and this creates a fictional distance, so to speak, that carries with it a kind of impersonality that would not be present if we knew we were reading a factual account of a human being's personal experience. The convention of distance and impersonality is the code that enables all the following codes to come into play.

Naturalization is the process by which we transform the text so that the strangeness of its literary form, which we don't see in everyday writing—for example, rhyme; meter; divisions into stanzas, acts, or chapters; and interior monologues—makes sense in terms of the world we live in. When we read, for example, "My darling is a ripening pear," we don't think the narrator is in love with a piece of fruit; we assume he is speaking metaphorically. And we appreciate the beauty and strangeness of the literary language even as we translate it into an idea we understand. Furthermore, we generally assume we are hearing the voice of a narrator, rather than that of the author, and it is to the narrator's point of view that we ascribe any inconsistencies or biases in the narration. Other ways in which we naturalize the text include recognizing the codes that tell us how to interpret such literary elements as characters and symbols. For example, in real life we don't believe that a person with fine, clear skin necessarily has a fine, clear soul, but we would accept this correlation in certain kinds of fiction.

The rule of significance is the assumption that the literary work expresses a significant attitude about some important problem, and so we pay attention to what it says in ways that we wouldn't do with other kinds of writing. If our spouse left us a note saying "I've gone to the antique store in search of a lamp," we'd probably take the message at face value: our spouse wants to buy an antique lamp. If this same sentence were broken into a four-line poem, however, the words "I've gone," "in search," "antique," and "lamp" would suddenly take on greater resonance. We might conclude, for example, that the poem represents the desire to escape some unsatisfactory situation in the present in order to return to the past and find some kind of enlightenment that can't be found in the here and now.

The rule of metaphorical coherence is the requirement that the two components of a metaphor (the vehicle, or metaphorical term, and the tenor, or subject to which the metaphor is applied) have a consistent relationship within the context of the work. Imagine, for example, a story about the plight of a penniless, aging, Native American drifter who, at the close of the tale, falls asleep forever under a freezing sky. In this context, the description of a pale, winter sunset could be a metaphor for the death of the character and perhaps for the end of an era, but it couldn't very well be a metaphor for the restful sleep that precedes the hopeful beginning of a bright new life.

The rule of thematic unity is the chief reason why there is a rule of metaphorical coherence, for the rule of thematic unity is our expectation that the literary work has a unified, coherent theme, or main point. In fact, it is because we expect a literary work to have thematic unity that we almost always manage to find it or, more precisely, construct it when we interpret the text. We tend to create thematic unity, Culler observes, by means of certain procedures, which include, among others, (1) theme as a binary opposition (good versus evil), (2) theme as the resolution of a binary opposition (good conquers evil), and (3) theme as the displacement of a binary opposition by a third term (good-versus-evil is absorbed by an all-encompassing Nature, as we see in Whitman's "Song of Myself," 1855).

It's not difficult to see why Culler's structuralist approach is of interest to reader-response theorists. Like the social reader-response theory of Stanley Fish discussed in Chapter Six, Culler's approach asserts that our understanding of literature is based on the interpretive strategies we bring to the text. As we noted earlier, structuralists believe that we "create" the world we see by projecting onto it our structures of consciousness. Apply this belief to literature, and the result is the same as the reader-response notion that we "create" the literary text as we read it. But the structuralist move Culler makes is his question, "What is the structure that underlies the surface phenomena of our interpretations?" And to find the answer, he examines interpretation as a structural system. Unlike reader-response theorists, Culler examines the *langue*, the structural system of rules and codes, that operate (consciously or unconsciously) when authors write and readers interpret within the Western literary tradition.

Even the small sampling of approaches offered here illustrates the wide range of structuralist methodologies, both in terms of the kinds of theoretical frameworks structuralists use and the kinds of texts, literary and otherwise, they analyze.

Some Questions Structuralist Critics Ask about Literary Texts

The following questions are offered to summarize structuralist approaches to literature. Keep in mind that structuralists don't try to determine whether or not a literary text constitutes great literature. Their focus is the structural systems that underlie and generate literary meaning.

1. Using a specific structuralist framework (such as the ones we examined by Frye and Scholes), how should the text be classified in terms of its genre?

2. Using a specific structuralist framework (such as that of Greimas, Todorov, or Genette), analyze the text's narrative operations. Can you speculate about the relationship between the text's "grammar" and that of similar texts? Can you speculate about the relationship between the text's grammar and the culture from which the text emerged?

3. Using Culler's theory of literary competence, what rules or codes of interpretation must be internalized in order to "make sense" of the text? Depending on the text in question, it might be necessary to identify codes in addition to those specified by Culler. (In other words, what does a given text contribute to our knowledge of literary competence?)

4. What are the semiotics of a given category of cultural phenomena, or "texts," such as high-school football games, television and/ or magazine ads for a particular brand of perfume (or any other consumer product), or even media coverage of an historical event, such as "Operation Desert Storm," an important legal case, or a presidential election campaign? In other words, analyze the non-verbal messages sent by the "texts" in question, as well as the semiotic implications of such verbal "tags" as "Desert Storm" or "White Diamonds" (a brand of perfume). What is being communicated, and how, exactly, is it being communicated?

Depending upon the literary text or texts in question, we might ask one or any combination of these questions. Or we might come up with a useful question not listed here. These are just starting points to get us thinking about productive ways to approach literature from a structuralist perspective. Remember that not all structuralists will interpret the same texts in the same way, even if they use the same approach. As in every field, even expert practitioners disagree. Our goal is to use structuralism to help us see some fundamental connections among the structures of literary texts, between the structure of literature and that of language, and among the structures of cultural phenomena of every sort, including, for example, literature, mythology, art, social rituals, sports, forms of entertainment, and advertising. The construction of a systematic, universal terminology to describe the fundamental structures of literature offers us the opportunity to make clearer and more rigorous comparisons as we try to increase our understanding of the processes at work in literary production and literary history.

The following structuralist reading of F. Scott Fitzgerald's *The Great Gatsby* is offered as an example of what a structuralist analysis of that novel might yield. Drawing on Todorov's notion of narrative "grammar," I will argue that all of the action in the novel can be reduced to three verbs: to seek, to find, and to lose. Furthermore, I will suggest that this grammar can be seen as the modern novel's rejection of the traditional seek-and-find quest formula. Finally, I will argue that *The Great Gatsby*'s seek-find-lose grammar offers us an interesting way to use Frye's theory of mythoi. For in Fitzgerald's novel, this grammar produces a narrative that embeds the mythos of summer (Gatsby's story, the genre of romance) within the mythos of winter (Nick's story, the genre of irony). And although the mythos of summer is eventually overridden by the mythos of winter, the latter structure remains "haunted" by the former.

"Seek and Ye Shall Find" . . . and Then Lose: A Structuralist Reading of *The Great Gatsby*

In many ways, F. Scott Fitzgerald's *The Great Gatsby* (1925) is so carefully organized that the novel's structure seems to draw attention to itself. A brief description of the text's structural symmetry should illustrate this point. The narrative revolves around Jay Gatsby's pursuit, attainment, and loss of Daisy Fay Buchanan. As we learn in flashback, this failed quest is a replay of the same pursuit, attainment, and loss of the same beloved that occurred in Gatsby's youth, before the novel opens. Both failed quests occur during the compressed period of a few months, and in both instances Gatsby disguises his true origins, so there is a kind of narrative symmetry between the structure of fictional past and fictional present. Another kind of structural symmetry is produced when Gatsby is reunited with Daisy in Chapter Five, at the physical center of the novel's nine chapters and at the temporal center of the narrative action: it is late July, the mid-point between Nick's first visit to the Buchanans' new home in early June, when "the history of the summer really begins" (10; ch. 1), and Gatsby's death in early September.

In addition, the narrative unfolds in a pattern of similarly structured triads, bounded at the beginning and end of the novel by narrator Nick Carraway's meditative reflections on the events he recounts:

Opening: Narrator's opening meditation (Ch. I)

    I: The world of wealth described (Ch. I)
   II: The world of poverty described (Ch. II)
  III: Intersection of I and II—rich and poor mingle at Gatsby's party
         (Ch. III)

    I: Nick hears story of Gatsby's past (Ch. IV)
   II: Nick hears story of Daisy's past (Ch. IV)
  III: Intersection of I and II—Gatsby and Daisy reunite at Nick's
         house (Ch. V)

    I: The eternal triangle appears—Tom, Daisy, and Gatsby at Gatsby's
        party (Ch. VI)
   II: The eternal triangle explodes—the confrontation scene in the
        New York hotel room (Ch. VII)
  III: Intersection of I and II—three disasters result
        A. Myrtle Wilson's death (Ch. VII)
        B. Gatsby's death (Ch. VIII)
        C. George Wilson's death (CH. VIII)

Closing: Narrator's closing meditation (Ch. IX)

Of course, any of these narrative patterns could serve as a starting point for a structural analysis of *The Great Gatsby*. The particular structure I want to focus on, however, is the one I believe is at the foundation of all the others: the novel's narrative "grammar," which is illuminated, I think, by the use of Tzvetan Todorov's schema of propositions. As you'll recall, according to this framework we try to discover how the text is structured by the pattern of relations among recurring actions (which are analogous to verbs) and attributes (which are analogous to adjectives) associated with particular characters (which are analogous to nouns). In other words, we try to discover how the text is structured by the repetition of the same grammar, the same formula, the same "sentence," so to speak.

In the case of *The Great Gatsby*, I think all the action can be reduced to three verbs: "to seek," "to find," and "to lose." These three verbs produce, in turn, the repetition of two related "sentences," or narrative patterns: (1) "X seeks, finds, and then loses Y," or simply (2) "X seeks but doesn't find Y." (X = the character in question; Y = a desired person, object, state, or condition.) In both cases, of course, the overall narrative formula is the same:

(1) attribute: X lacks Y

(2) action: X seeks Y

(3) attribute: X lacks Y (either because X doesn't find Y or
because X finds but then loses Y)

I'd like to begin my analysis of the novel by revealing how this formula structures the text as a whole by structuring the narratives of the
main characters. Then I will suggest that the seek-find-lose grammar can
be seen as the modern novel's rejection of the traditional seek-and-find
quest formula. Finally, I will try to show how this narrative grammar offers us an interesting application of Northrop Frye's theory of mythoi.
For in *The Great Gatsby*, this grammar produces a narrative that embeds
the mythos of summer (Gatsby's story, the genre of romance) within the
mythos of winter (Nick's story, the genre of irony). And although the
mythos of summer is eventually overridden by the mythos of winter, the
latter structure remains "haunted" by the former.

Of course, the "master plot" of the novel's seek-find-lose formula is
the story of its title character, Jay Gatsby. As we noted above, he seeks,
finds, and loses Daisy twice: once in his youth, before the novel begins,
and again during the summer that Nick lives next door to him on West
Egg. In addition, the narrative of Gatsby's pursuit, attainment, and loss of
Daisy is accompanied by the narrative of his pursuit, attainment, and loss
of the new life he sought when he changed his name from James Gatz to
Jay Gatsby. His seek-find-lose story is thus repeated not merely in two
different time periods but in terms of two different goals: love and social
status. Both are lost to him, of course, when he dies. Furthermore,
Gatsby's narrative provides the framework upon which the narratives of
the other characters are "strung," so to speak: it is in the unfolding of
Gatsby's story by Nick that the other stories are told.

Daisy's story mirrors not only the seek-find-lose pattern of Gatsby's
narrative but its repetitive quality as well. As we learn in flashback, the
young Daisy Fay sought excitement, found it in the form of her love for
Lieutenant Jay Gatsby, then lost him to the war. Next she sought emotional security, found it in the form of marriage to Tom Buchanan, then
lost it when she soon discovered that he was chronically unfaithful to her.
Finally, she craves the attention that she isn't getting from Tom, finds it in
Gatsby, and loses it when he dies (or, perhaps more precisely, when Tom
reveals that Gatsby isn't the man Daisy thought he was).

Similar seek-find-lose grammars structure the narratives of Tom

Buchanan, Myrtle Wilson, and her husband George. As a young man, Tom sought ego gratification, found it in his career as a college football hero, then lost it when he graduated from college. As a married man, Tom seeks a similar kind of ego gratification—the adoration of "inferiors"— by seducing a series of working-class women, the latest incarnation of which is Myrtle Wilson. In each case, however, the ego gratification lasts only as long as the affair, so Tom continually returns to the position of the unfulfilled seeker.

Analogously, Myrtle Wilson seeks escape from the boredom and economic poverty of her marriage, finds it in Tom Buchanan, then loses it when she is killed in the hit-and-run accident. Of course, even if she had lived she would not have succeeded in marrying Tom. His intention to avoid a permanent commitment to Myrtle is evident in his lie to her that Daisy's Catholicism would never permit her to divorce him. Operating as a shadow behind Myrtle's seek-find-lose narrative is that of George Wilson, who sought love, found it in his marriage to Myrtle, and lost it when she became unfaithful to him with Tom (or, perhaps more precisely, when she learned that George didn't own the suit in which he was married).

As a backdrop to these seek-find-lose grammars is a sub-set of seek-find-lose: seek-but-don't-find. We see this pattern operating in George's pursuit of financial security, which is an impossible dream, and in Jordan's pursuit of social and financial security, which seem ever to elude her grasp just as the winning putt remains, of late, just beyond her reach. The grammar of seek-but-don't-find also structures the setting in the form of the numerous minor characters who populate it. Mr. McKee seeks but doesn't find success as a photographer. Myrtle's sister Catherine seems a permanently dissatisfied seeker: her trip to Monte Carlo was a financial disaster; her "solid sticky bob of red hair," "complexion powdered milky white," and "rakish" painted eyebrows "blurred" by the plucked hairs growing back (34; ch. 2) are a fashion disaster; and her search for a good time seems merely to take her from one scene of drunken chaos to another. Even Gatsby's innumerable party guests have the air of dissatisfied wanderers, coming to his mansion from parts unknown, seeking something new in the latest dances, and seeking excitement, or perhaps just escape from their dissatisfaction, at the bottom of a bottle.

Certainly the most well-developed seek-but-don't-find narrative in the novel is that of Nick Carraway. Nick's summer in New York is just the latest in a series of unsuccessful pursuits. His experience in World War I apparently involved the pursuit of excitement from which he returned more empty-handed than when he left: "I enjoyed [World War I] so thoroughly that I came back restless. Instead of being the warm center of the world the middle-west now seemed like the ragged edge of the universe—so I decided to go east and learn the bond business" (7; ch. 1). As his narrative reveals, of course, his venture in the bond business, and in the east in general, also follows the seek-but-don't-find pattern: he abandons both within a few months of his arrival in New York. Neither is his search for the right woman successful. He leaves his home town, in part, to escape a woman he was feeling pressured to marry. He apparently cares so little about the woman at work with whom he has an affair that he allows her brother's "mean looks in [his] direction" (61; ch. 3) to drive him off. And his relationship with Jordan Baker is rather clearly an infatuation with no staying power: he tires of her as soon as he tires of the Buchanans.

Nick's most important seek-but-don't-find pattern, however, seems to be his unfulfilled search for a purpose in life. Throughout his narrative, Nick seems "at loose ends." At the age of thirty he is still without a stable career, without a serious love interest, and without a home of his own. And he feels their lack acutely: "Thirty—the promise of a decade of loneliness, a thinning list of single men to know, a thinning briefcase of enthusiasm, thinning hair" (143; ch. 7). In fact, he's still being supported by his wealthy father, who "agreed to finance [him] for a year" (7; ch. 1) while he learned the bond business. It's no wonder he seems so fascinated by Gatsby, for Gatsby has, to an extreme degree, the quality Nick lacks most, the quality he is unable to acquire despite his best efforts: purpose.

It might be interesting to think of the seek-find-lose grammar of *The Great Gatsby* as the modern novel's rejection of the traditional quest formula. The traditional quest is structured by a seek-and-find grammar. Even if the hero dies achieving the goal of his quest, or attempting to achieve it, the world is transformed in some way by his effort: something important is found. Thus, the basic plot formula Todorov isolated consists of an attribute transformed by an action: (1) attribute (for example, the protagonist is unsuccessful), (2) action (he seeks success), (3) attribute (he is successful or, at least, has learned something important as a result of his quest). The traditional quest is thus redemptive in some way.

As we have seen, in Fitzgerald's novel, the characters' attributes are not transformed by the hero's action nor by their own actions. At the novel's end the characters have the same attribute—the same lack—with which they began, and apparently nothing is learned in the process. Gatsby is dead, presumably without having admitted to himself that

Daisy has abandoned him and without living long enough to benefit from that insight had it occurred. Myrtle and George are dead, without having learned anything from their experience. The last time we see Jordan, she's putting up her usual false front, lying to Nick that she is unmoved by his withdrawal from their relationship and is engaged to someone else. Finally, Tom and Daisy, true to form, flee the chaos they helped create, "retreat[ing] back into their money or their vast carelessness or whatever it was that kept them together" (188; ch. 9).

The only exception to this rule is Nick, who is transformed by his experience in New York. As the narrative opens, he is very optimistic, feeling that "life was beginning over again with the summer" (8; ch. 1). He's excited by his new job and his new life in New York. By the end of the summer he is utterly disillusioned, abandoning his plans for a new career and a new life in the east: "When I came back from the East last autumn I felt that I wanted the world to be in uniform and at a sort of moral attention forever: I wanted no more riotous excursions with privileged glimpses into the human heart" (6; ch. 1). However, Nick's transformation is not redemptive. Although he certainly learns something important about human nature over the course of that summer, the lesson produces in him a dark vision of human life. His attitude, as the novel closes, is hopeless and despairing: "So we beat on, boats against the current, borne back ceaselessly into the past" (189; ch. 9).

If the traditional quest formula, seek-and-find (or seek-and-be-transformed), can be associated with a world view that includes the possibility of redemption, then perhaps the seek-find-lose (or seek-but-don't-find) grammar can be associated with a world view in which redemption is impossible or highly unlikely. This more pessimistic, or some would say realistic, vision of human experience is the vision associated with the modernist world view, which dominated Anglo-European literature from the beginning of World War I (1914) to the end of World War II (1945) and which *The Great Gatsby* epitomizes. We can certainly find numerous examples of this grammar in modern novels, for example, D. H. Lawrence's *Sons and Lovers* (1913) and *Women in Love* (1920), Virginia Woolf's *To the Lighthouse* (1927), and Richard Wright's *Native Son* (1940). Presumably, the readers of these works, rather than the characters that populate them, are supposed to undergo whatever transformation is possible, but the texts do not offer a world view that could be called redemptive. (Analogously, we might characterize the grammar of the postmodern novel as don't-bother-to-seek. Certainly, it might be argued that novels such as Thomas Pynchon's *The Crying of Lot 49* (1966), Joan

Didion's *Play It as It Lays* (1970), Joseph Heller's *Something Happened* (1974), and Don DeLillo's *White Noise* (1985) are structured by such a grammar.)

My speculation that *The Great Gatsby*'s seek-find-lose grammar reflect's the modern novel's rejection of the traditional quest formula is compatible with the way in which I think Fitzgerald's novel requires us to apply Northrop Frye's theory of mythoi. For according to Frye's framework, *The Great Gatsby* embeds the structure of romance (Gatsby's narrative, the mythos of summer, the quest) within the structure of irony (Nick's narrative, the mythos of winter, realism), and the second structure offers a kind of running commentary on the first, which by the novel's close, forces Nick to realize that, in the modern world, the structure of romance (Gatsby's narrative) is no longer possible. That is, in Fitzgerald's novel, the structure of irony contains and eventually overrides the structure of romance.

Gatsby is, of course, the hero of the romantic quest. Although all the other characters have "quests" of their own, only Gatsby's occurs within the mode of romance. In *Anatomy of Criticism* Frye notes, "[t]he romance is nearest of all literary forms to the wish-fulfillment dream, and for that reason . . . [i]n every age the ruling social or intellectual class tends to project its ideals in some form of romance" (186). For the get-rich-quick, Jazz Age of the American 1920s, the kind of meteoric financial rise Jay Gatsby achieved was emblematic of the American dream, which clearly was, and still is, a romantic dream of wish fulfillment. Typical of romance, too, is Gatsby's persistent search for a past Golden Age, which, for him, was his courtship of Daisy Fay in Louisville before he was sent to war. Upon his return to America after the war, he devoted himself to amassing a fortune and following her social activities in the newspapers. When he was able, finally, to buy a mansion across the bay from hers, he arranged to meet her again so that he could "fix everything just the way it was before" (17; ch. 1), so that he could return to the Golden Age.

In fact, all of Gatsby's activities between the time he met Dan Cody to the moment at which he is reunited with Daisy at Nick's cottage constitute the series of minor adventures the romantic hero must undertake before the major adventure—reclaiming Daisy for his own—occurs. His adventures with Cody taught him the skills he needed to succeed in life, including the perseverance and temperance that mark the romantic hero. His military achievements resulted in his rapid ascendancy through the ranks from lieutenant to major and covered him with medals for his valor on the battlefield. Then with similar rapidity, he ascended the ranks of Wolfshiem's organization, gaining a fortune to rival that of Tom Buchanan.

Gatsby's major adventure, his quest to regain Daisy, is also typical of the romantic quest to obtain a bride. Like the hero of the traditional quest, who is often separated from his love by a barrier of water, Gatsby is separated from Daisy by the bay between his mansion on West Egg and her home on East Egg. And, again typically, he can see the "promised land"—the green light at the end of the Buchanans' dock—from his side of the gulf that separates them. Furthermore, his quest for Daisy pits Gatsby against an antagonist with whom the reader can have little sympathy. Indeed, Tom fills the role of the usurper, from whose selfish machinations Daisy must be rescued.

The climactic struggle of the romantic conflict between hero and antagonist occurs, for Gatsby, during the confrontation scene with Tom in the New York hotel room. Although the hero sometimes dies as a result of this battle, his willingness to sacrifice himself for his quest proves him a hero. And indeed, Gatsby does die, both symbolically—"'Jay Gatsby' had broken up like glass against Tom's hard malice" (155; ch. 8)—and literally, when Tom sends George Wilson, armed and crazed, to Gatsby's house. In fact, Gatsby's willingness to sacrifice himself for Daisy becomes the dominant motif as the narrative moves toward his death.

In a subtler fashion, Gatsby's quest also resembles that of another incarnation of the romantic hero: the quester-hero who saves the kingdom from the ravages of a monster. As Frye puts it, "the quest-romance is the victory of fertility over the waste land" (193): the monster to be defeated is the sterile, fallen world that waits to be redeemed by some sort of messiah. For the modern wasteland embodied in the novel's setting—including both the valley of ashes and the empty pleasures of the idle rich—Gatsby represents the renewal of life and vitality. In Nick's words, Gatsby has a "heightened sensitivity to the promises of life," an "extraordinary gift for hope, a romantic readiness such as I have never found in any other person and which it is not likely I shall ever find again" (6; ch. 1). Gatsby has, in short, what the modern world desperately needs to save it from the hopelessness of its own sterility. Like a messiah-figure, he represents renewed hope.

Although Gatsby may seem, on one level, part of the sterile modern world—he engages in criminal activities and throws parties that inevitably turn into drunken revels—he is symbolically separate from it. Like the quester-hero who saves the imperilled kingdom, he is isolated from the world he inhabits. He lives alone and is close to no one but Daisy. He

knows none of the people at his parties, which he throws only in the hope
that Daisy will "wander i[n] . . . some night" (84; ch. 4). And he is pictured, most frequently, alone in a tableau that bespeaks his romantic isolation. For example, one evening, Nick observes, Gatsby "emerged from
the shadow of [his] mansion" and "stretched out his arms toward the
dark water" (25; ch. 1), "trembling" toward the "single green light, minute
and far away" (26; ch. 1) at the end of Daisy's dock. The night Myrtle Wilson is killed, he stands guard alone, in a "sacre[d] . . . vigil" (153; ch. 7)
outside Daisy's house, in case Tom "tries to bother her" (151; ch. 7) about
their affair. Even at his riotous parties, Gatsby is pictured in romantic isolation: "A sudden emptiness seemed to flow now from the windows and
the great doors, endowing with complete isolation the figure of the host
who stood on the porch, his hand up in a formal gesture of farewell" (60;
ch. 3). In a world of corruption, Gatsby is incorruptible because he has an
"incorruptible dream" (162; ch. 8).

Gatsby's early life, too, fits that of the quester-hero who saves the
fallen world. His origins are mysterious, and even when he reveals who
his parents are, we learn that "his imagination had never really accepted
them as his parents at all. The truth was that Jay Gatsby . . . sprang from
his Platonic conception of himself. He was a son of God. . . . [A]nd to this
conception he was faithful to the end" (104; ch. 6). Gatsby even goes
through a kind of baptism by water, typical of the messiah-figure. "It was
James Gatz who had been loafing along the beach that afternoon" (104;
ch. 6), but by the time he rowed out to Cody's yacht anchored off the
shore of Lake Superior, "it was . . . Jay Gatsby" (104; ch. 6) who emerged
from the water to accept a job as Cody's steward. And like the sun god
who, Frye tells us, "is represented as sailing in a boat on the surface of our
world" (192), Gatsby sailed with Cody for five years. Indeed, just as the
quester-hero is often "a third son, or the third to undertake the quest, or
successful on his third attempt" (Frye 187), Gatsby's travels by boat took
him "three times around the continent" (106; ch. 6) before he "landed" in
the modern world.

The narrative of Gatsby's romantic quest is embedded within a very
different kind of narrative: that of Nick's summer in New York. We learn
about Gatsby because Nick's relationship with him forms a large part of
the narrator's own experience. However, Nick's narrative is structured by
a genre that is the polar opposite of romance: the genre of irony, which,
Frye says, "is consistent . . . with complete realism of content" (224).
Irony, Frye argues, derives from the mythos of winter. In contrast to the
idealized world of romance, Frye observes, the mythos of winter "at-

tempts to give form to the shifting ambiguities and complexities of unidealized existence" (223). This "unidealized existence" is not a world of heroes but of everyday, flawed human beings. It's a world in which human misery is the result not of fate or of some kind of cosmic intervention but of sociological and psychological causes. In other words, this is the real world, warts and all.

In the real world, in which Nick and all the other non-heroic characters live, it isn't easy to amass a fortune or find your one true love. Sometimes it isn't even easy to find a satisfying career, as Nick knows, or survive financially, as George Wilson knows. In this world, people don't look "gorgeous" in their "pink rag of a suit" (162; ch. 8) or throw lavish parties in the hope that their lost love will appear, as Gatsby does. Instead, like Gatsby's guests, they go to parties to sponge off a host they've never met and get obnoxiously drunk on his liquor. Their clothing "stretch[es] tight over . . . rather wide hips" (31; ch. 2), like Myrtle's, and they have "sticky bob[s] of red hair" (34; ch. 2), as Myrtle's sister Catherine has. In the real world, "grey, scrawny Italian child[ren]" (30; ch. 2) live in places like the valley of ashes, and people enjoy standing around the scene of an accident to watch human misery.

In the real world, furthermore, a woman doesn't always wait for her knight in shining armor, even when she knows who he is. Sometimes she marries Tom Buchanan instead. Even when she has a second chance at happiness, because her knight is faithful to her to the end, a small bend in the road to true love might send her scurrying home, as Daisy scurries back to her selfish, brutish, unfaithful husband. And when her knight dies protecting her from a charge of hit-and-run homicide, she might leave town before the minister arrives for the funeral.

In the real world, a man doesn't always remain faithful to his woman, even when he's married to her. Sometimes he has frequent extramarital affairs and parades them in public places, as Tom does with Myrtle, and sometimes he breaks his mistress's nose. Here, "bad guys" like Tom Buchanan and Meyer Wolfshiem call the shots. A simple, honest man like George Wilson is deceived by his wife and manipulated by her lover into killing an innocent man. And a "great sportswom[an]" like Jordan Baker, whom Gatsby believes would "never do anything that wasn't all right" (76; ch. 4), cheats at golf, lies about damaging a borrowed car, and "deal[s] in subterfuges . . . in order to keep her cool insolent smile turned to the world and yet satisfy the demands of her hard jaunty body" (63; ch. 3).

Perhaps most important, in the real world, the death of a romantic hero is not a martyrdom that saves humanity. It's a sign that humanity is beyond saving, beyond hope. And once that sign is given, Nick knows there is nothing to do but go back home: forget his plans for the future, give up his optimism, cut his losses, and get out. In this way, Nick's narrative, grounded in the structure of irony, closes the door, so to speak, on the romantic tale it tells, that is, on the structure of romance. In other words, in *The Great Gatsby*, the ironic structure associated with the modern novel overrides the structure of romance as if to say that romance is no longer possible.

This process finds its symbolic expression in the confrontation scene between Gatsby and Tom in the New York hotel. According to the romantic formula, it is here that the hero wins his bride and reveals his true origins, which are royal or associated with some kind of important parentage. Instead, Gatsby reveals, with Tom's help, that his true origins are far beneath those of his beloved, and the result is that she abandons him. Thus, from the perspective of Frye's theory of mythoi, the romantic formula "jumps the track," ceases to function, and the void is filled by the only structure left in the narrative: that of irony.

The structure of irony does not succeed, however, in eradicating the structure of romance. Instead, the structure of irony is "haunted" by the very structure it overrides. Perhaps because he knows that romance is no longer possible, Nick's narrative is marked by an intense nostalgia for a lost past, for the lost world of romance that Gatsby represents. We see this longing in his lyric descriptions of a virginal, idyllic past: descriptions of Daisy and Jordan's "beautiful white . . . girlhood" (24; ch. 1) in Louisville and of Christmas in the midwest of his youth, with its "street lamps and sleigh bells in the frosty dark and the shadows of holly wreaths thrown by lighted windows on the snow" (184; ch. 9).

This nostalgia for a lost innocence, a lost paradise, for the mythos of summer, the genre of romance, reaches its climax in Nick's closing description of a literal paradise forever gone. As Nick sits on the beach the evening before his return to Wisconsin, he muses on

> the old island here that flowered once for Dutch sailors' eyes—a fresh green breast of the new world. Its vanished trees, the trees that had made way for Gatsby's house, had once pandered in whispers to the last and greatest of all human dreams; for a transitory enchanted moment man must have held his breath in the presence of this continent, compelled into an aesthetic contemplation he neither understood nor desired, face to face for the last time in history with something commensurate to his capacity for wonder. (189; ch. 9)

This passage is emblematic of the structural process that occurs over the course of the novel: the mythos of summer (romance, the successful quest) is overridden by the mythos of winter (irony, the complexities of reality), which remains haunted by the loss of the structure it has overcome.

In *The Great Gatsby*, then, we see the operations of quite a complex structure. We see a narrative grammar consisting of seek-find-lose and, its sub-set, seek-but-don't-find. This grammar, I have suggested, reflects a world view associated with the modernist period and with the modern novel's rejection of the traditional seek-and-find quest. Analogously, the text is structured by a struggle for dominance between two very different literary genres: romance—the mythos of summer, the genre to which Gatsby's narrative belongs—and irony, the mythos of winter, the genre to which Nick's narrative belongs. I have argued that the genre of romance is overcome by that of irony in the novel, although, throughout the text, the former "haunts" the latter in the form of the narrator's lyric descriptions of a lost past, a romantic, paradisal youth.

This analysis has thus attempted to illustrate two aspects of structuralism that sometimes seem in conflict: its reliance on formulaic description, which derives from its commitment to the kind of objectivity associated with mathematics, and its philosophical grounding as a science of humanity, which requires us to speculate on the relationship between the structural formulas we describe and the world in which we live. Although this second aspect is often forgotten in the practice of structuralist criticism, it is the dual nature of structuralism that, for many of us, makes it exciting.

Questions for Further Practice: Structuralist Approaches to Other Literary Works

The following questions are intended as models. They can help you use structuralist criticism to interpret the literary works to which they refer or other texts of your choice.

1. How might you use Frye's theory of mythoi to analyze Joseph Conrad's *Heart of Darkness* (1902)? What kind of hero is Kurtz? How would you classify Marlow? In what sense might the novel be called a tragedy? In what sense does it belong to the genre of irony? What might our difficulties (or disagreements) in classify-

ing this text suggest about Conrad's novel or about our system of classification?

2. Toni Morrison's *Beloved* (1987) is structured by the interweaving of several narratives, each the story of a particular character. There are, among others, narratives associated with Sethe, Denver, Beloved, Baby Suggs, Paul D, and Stamp Paid. Identify all the narratives present in the novel and analyze them structurally, as if they were a collection of stories (which, in a sense, they are). Is there a narrative grammar that informs all the "stories," or does a structural analysis reveal that they belong to different structural groups? What does your analysis suggest about the way in which Morrison's novel, and similar texts, make meaning?

3. William Faulkner's story "A Rose for Emily" (1931) has a complex structure that lends itself well to Genette's theoretical framework. Using Genette's categories, analyze the text in terms of the relationship among story, narrative, and narration. Be sure to discuss the functions of tense (order, duration, and frequency), mood (distance and perspective) and voice. How does your analysis help you understand the narrative effects Faulkner achieves in this story? Do your findings apply to other of Faulkner's works?

4. Although their content is quite different, Katherine Anne Porter's "The Jilting of Granny Weatherall" (1930) and Tillie Olsen's "I Stand Here Ironing" (1956) are short stories with a number of structural similarities. For example, both consist largely of interior monologues; both are narrated by a character within the story who has a very limited, subjective point of view; and both are structured by a series of flashbacks. What other structural similarities can you find? Draw on the structural narratologist(s) whose work you find most helpful in illuminating these two pieces. Are structural similarities (or dissimilarities) related to similarities (or dissimilarities) in theme?

5. John Steinbeck's political novel *The Grapes of Wrath* (1939) was produced as a Hollywood film. For the most part, the film is very faithful to the novel's structure, characterization, and theme (the capitalist exploitation of tenant farmers who fled the Dust Bowl to become migrant laborers in California). However, the film's ending is triumphantly optimistic, in direct contrast to the ending of the novel. Analyze the novel's genre using Frye's theory of myths, Frye's theory of modes, and Scholes' theory of modes.

Then analyze the ways in which the film's ending calls for a modification of your classification of the novel. What do your findings suggest about the conflict between political novels (to which category the genre of naturalism belongs) and the Hollywood tradition of "the happy ending"?

For Further Reading

All of the following works will help you develop your skills as structuralist critics. Texts listed under "Category I" are written in language accessible to most beginners. Texts listed under "Category II" employ more technical language but are well worth the extra effort that may be required of some students new to the field.

Category I

Barthes, Roland. *Mythologies*. 1957. Trans. Annette Lavers. New York: Hill and Wang, 1972.

Culler, Jonathan. "Literary Competence." *Structuralist Poetics: Structuralism, Linguistics and the Study of Literature*. Ithaca: Cornell UP, 1975. 113–130.

Frye, Northrop. *Anatomy of Criticism: Four Essays*. Princeton: Princeton UP, 1957.

Hawkes, Terence. *Structuralism and Semiotics*. Berkeley: U of California P, 1977.

Lévi-Strauss, Claude. *Tristes Tropiques*. Trans. John and Doreen Weighman. New York: Atheneum, 1974.

Pratt, Annis, et al. *Archetypal Patterns in Women's Fiction*. Ann Arbor: Books on Demand, 1981.

Rowe, John Carlos. "Structure." *Critical Terms for Literary Study*. 2nd ed. Eds. Frank Lentricchia and Thomas McLaughlin. Chicago: U of Chicago P, 1995. 23–38.

Scholes, Robert. *Structuralism in Literature: An Introduction*. New Haven: Yale UP, 1974.

Category II

Barthes, Roland. *Critical Essays*. 1964. Trans. Richard Howard. Evanston, Illinois: Northwestern UP, 1972.

Genette, Gérard. *Narrative Discourse*. Trans. Jane Lewin. Ithaca: Cornell UP, 1980.

Greimas, A. J. *On Meaning: Selected Writings in Semiotic Theory*. 1970. Trans. Paul Perron and Frank Collins. Minneapolis: U of Minnesota P, 1987.

Jakobson, Roman. "Linguistics and Poetics." *Style in Language*. Ed. T. Sebeok. Cambridge, Massachusetts: MIT P, 1960. 350–77.

Lévi-Strauss, Claude. *The Raw and the Cooked*. 1964. Trans. John and Doreen Weighman. New York: Harper, 1975.

Propp, Vladimir. *The Morphology of the Folktale*. 1928. Trans. Laurence Scott. Austin: U of Texas P, 1968.

Saussure, Ferdinand de. *Course in General Linguistics*. 1916. Trans. Wade Baskin. New York: McGraw-Hill, 1966.
Todorov, Tzvetan. *The Poetics of Prose*. Trans. Richard Howard. Ithaca: Cornell UP, 1977.

Notes

1. Frye's *Anatomy of Criticism: Four Essays* attempts to systematize literature in four different ways. He calls these approaches his (1) theory of modes, or historical criticism (tragic, comic, and thematic); (2) theory of symbols, or ethical criticism (literal/descriptive, formal, mythical, and anagogic); (3) theory of myths, or archetypal criticism (comedy, romance, tragedy, irony/satire); and (4) theory of genres, or rhetorical criticism (epos, prose, drama, lyric). Although there has been some debate concerning whether or not Frye's work falls within the category of structuralism, it seems rather clear that all four of the approaches offered in *Anatomy of Criticism* are structuralist theories of genre because all seek the structural principles—such as plot formulas and character functions—that underlie genres in the Western literary tradition.
2. Not all archetypal criticism relates the mythic motifs found in literature to literary genres. Many archetypal critics, or myth critics—most of whom have been influenced by the work of Carl Jung—analyze literary works in order to identify the specific myths upon which they draw. See, for example, Maud Bodkin, Joseph Campbell, and Carl Jung.

Works Cited

Barthes, Roland. "The World of Wrestling." *Mythologies*. 1957. Trans. Annette Lavers. New York: Hill and Wang, 1972. 15–25.
Bodkin, Maud. *Archetypal Patterns in Poetry: Psychological Studies of Imagination*. 1934. New York: Random House, 1958.
Campbell, Joseph. *The Hero with a Thousand Faces*. Rev. ed. Princeton: Princeton UP, 1968.
Culler, Jonathan. *Structuralist Poetics: Structuralism, Linguistics and the Study of Literature*. Ithaca: Cornell UP, 1975.
Frye, Northrop. *Anatomy of Criticism: Four Essays*. Princeton: Princeton UP, 1957.
Genette, Gérard. *Narrative Discourse*. Trans. Jane Lewin. Ithaca: Cornell UP, 1980.
Greimas, A. J. *Structural Semantics*. 1966. Trans. Daniele McDowell, Ronald Schleifer, and Alan Velie. Lincoln: U of Nebraska P, 1983.
Jung, Carl. *The Archetypes and the Collective Unconscious*. Vol. 9, Part I of *Collected Works*. 2nd ed. Trans. R. F. C. Hull. Princeton: Princeton UP, 1968.
———, ed. *Man and His Symbols*. Garden City, New York: Doubleday, 1964.
Lévi-Strauss, Claude. "The Structural Study of Myth." *Structural Anthropology*. 1958. Trans. Claire Jacobson and Brooke Schoepf. New York: Basic, 1963. 206–32.
Saussure, Ferdinand de. *Course in General Linguistics*. 1916. Trans. Wade Baskin. New York: McGraw-Hill, 1966.
Scholes, Robert. *Structuralism in Literature: An Introduction*. New Haven: Yale UP, 1974.
Todorov, Tzvetan. *Grammaire du Décaméron*. The Hague: Mouton, 1969.

CHAPTER 8

Deconstructive Criticism

For many of us who consider ourselves lovers of literature, phrases such as "the random play of signifiers" and "the transcendental signified" evoke the kind of fear and loathing the Crusaders must have felt when they learned that the infidels had taken the Holy City. Although deconstruction is no longer a new phenomenon on the academic scene—the theory was inaugurated by Jacques Derrida in the late 1960s and became a major influence on literary studies during the late 1970s—many students and faculty alike continue to misperceive deconstruction as a superficial analysis of wordplay that destroys our appreciation of literature and our ability to interpret it meaningfully. Perhaps one reason deconstruction is frequently misunderstood is that the writing by some of the biggest names in the field—Jacques Derrida, Luce Irigaray, Geoffrey Hartman—as well as the explanations offered by those who attempt to summarize the work of these thinkers, frequently employ such unusual language and organizational principles that they seem to defy our understanding and acceptance.

Nevertheless, deconstruction has a good deal to offer us: it can improve our ability to think critically and to see more readily the ways in which our experience is determined by ideologies of which we are unaware because they are "built into" our language. And because deconstruction offers these advantages, it can be a very useful tool for Marxism, feminism, and other theories that attempt to make us aware of the oppressive role ideology can play in our lives. In order to understand how deconstruction reveals the hidden work of ideology in our daily experience of ourselves and our world, we must first understand deconstruction's view of language because, according to Derrida, language is not the reliable tool of communication we believe it to be, but rather a fluid, ambiguous domain of complex experience in which ideologies program us without our being aware of them.

Deconstructing Language

In our daily lives, most of us take language for granted, assuming that it communicates what we want it to, and if it doesn't, we assume that the fault is in ourselves, not in language. A phrase such as "Mary, please hand John the book" usually results in the desired action, and even when it doesn't, we assume that the fault lies not in language, but in Mary's or John's failure to understand the request or refusal to act upon it. Because we are so used to the everyday patterns and rituals in which language seems to work the way we want it to, we assume that it is by nature a stable and reliable means of communicating our thoughts, feelings, and wishes. Deconstruction's theory of language, in contrast, is based on the belief that language is much more slippery and ambiguous than we realize.

Consider, for example, the following sentence: *Time flies like an arrow*. Most of us are familiar with this old saying, and we know it means that time passes quickly:

| *Time* | *flies* | *like an arrow* | = | Time passes quickly. |
| (noun) | (verb) | (adv. clause) | | |

If I asked you to suggest additional meanings, you might say that the sentence could also mean that time moves in one direction, or straight ahead, because that's how arrows fly. But what would happen if we thought of the first word of the sentence as a verb in the imperative mode—telling us to do something—and the second word as if it represented a kind of insect? Then the sentence would be giving us an order:

Time	*flies*	*like an arrow*	=	Get out your stopwatch
(verb)	(obj.)	(adv. clause)		and time the speed of
				flies as you'd time an
				arrow's flight.

And what would happen if we thought of the first two words of the sentence as if they represented a kind of insect—time flies (think of fruit flies)—and the third word as if it were a form of the verb *to like*? Then the sentence would tell us something about the emotional life of a certain kind of insect:

Time flies	*like*	*an arrow*	=	Time flies are fond of
(noun)	(verb)	(obj.)		arrows (or at least of
				one particular arrow).

This exercise shows how, without changing a word, a single sentence can have several meanings.

Changes in tone of voice and emphasis can further reveal the slippery quality of language. Imagine, for example, that a newscaster was given the following line to read: *President Reagan says the marines do not have to go to El Salvador.* Now note how the meaning of the sentence changes dramatically, depending on which word is emphasized:

1. President Reagan *says* the marines do not have to go to El Salvador (implying that he's lying).
2. President Reagan says the marines do *not* have to go to El Salvador (implying that he's correcting a false rumor).
3. President Reagan says the *marines* do not have to go to El Salvador (implying that some other group has to go).
4. *President Reagan* says the marines do not have to go to El Salvador (implying that another important person had said that the marines have to go to El Salvador).
5. President Reagan says the marines do not *have* to go to El salvador (implying that they can go if they want to).
6. President Reagan says the marines do not have to go to *El Salvador* (implying that they have to go somewhere else).

These two exercises should help you begin to see that language isn't as stable and reliable as we generally assume it is. As we saw in Chapter Seven, structuralists and semioticians use the word *sign* to denote a basic element of communication, and they define *sign* by the following formula.

sign	=	*signifier*	+	*signified*
		(sound, image,		(concept to which
		gesture, etc.)		the signifier refers)

A word is a linguistic sign. For example, if the sign is the word *rose*, then the signifier is the group of letters written or pronounced as a unit ("rose"), and the signified is the rose you picture in your mind. If the signifier (or, in this case, pair of signifiers) is "red rose," then the signified is the red rose you picture in your mind. Of course, in response to the signifier "rose," different people will probably picture different kinds of roses. And for some people, both of the above signifiers—"rose" and "red rose"—will produce the same signified because these people always picture roses as red roses unless prompted to do otherwise.

To avoid this kind of vagueness and ambiguity, let's look at a very simple, concrete phrase uttered in a context so specific that the signifiers should produce a very clear and unambiguous signified. Picture a person standing in an open field pointing to the only tree in sight. In this context, a phrase consisting of the signifiers "This tree is big" seems to imply a single, clear signified: there is only one tree in question, and we know that a claim is being made about its size. Deconstruction, however, asks us to look at the sentence's ambiguities, even when the sentence seems, at first glance, as clear and specific as this one does. When the speaker says "This tree is big," is she comparing the tree to herself? To another tree? What other tree? Is she surprised by the size of the tree? Or is she merely informing us that the tree is big? Is she informing us so that we will know something about the tree or so that we will understand something about the word *big*? What must she think of us if she believes we need such information? Does she think we are just learning to speak English? Or is she being sarcastic? If so, why? This string of questions may seem to push the point a bit far, but it does illustrate that human utterances are rarely, if ever, as clear and simple as the semiotic formula *signifier + signified* seems to imply. As we have seen, any given signifier can refer to any number of signifieds at any given moment. And although context often helps us to limit the range of possible signifieds for some signifiers, it simultaneously increases the range of possible signifieds for others. This is why communication is such a complicated and uncertain thing.

If we stopped at this point, we could rewrite the semiotic formula as *sign = signifier + signified . . . + signified*. That is, we could try to explain communication as a sliding accumulation of signifieds. But what does the term *signified* mean? If the signifier is "tree," then the signified must be the tree in our imagination that we can picture. But what do we understand by this imagined tree? Of what does our concept consist? Our concept of the tree consists of all the chains of signifiers we have come to associate with it over the course of our lives, in my own case, for example, *shade, picnics, climbing, broken collar bone, hiking, Hocking Hills, Ohio, vertigo, autumn leaves, raking, planting Douglas firs, pine needle scale, lime sulfur,* and so on. That is, what structuralism and semiotics call the signified is really always a chain of signifiers.

According to deconstruction, then, the word *tree* never reaches the point when it refers to a concept, a signified. The signifier I utter refers to chains of signifiers in my mind and evokes chains of signifiers in the mind of the person who hears my utterance. And each signifier in those chains is itself constituted by another chain of signifiers, and so on. So for deconstruction, language does not consist of the union of signifiers and signifieds; it consists only of chains of signifiers. As we saw in Chapter Seven, structuralism says that language is *non-referential* because it doesn't refer to things in the world but only to our concepts of things in the world. Deconstruction takes that idea a big step further by claiming that language is non-referential because it refers neither to things in the world nor to our concepts of things but only to the play of signifiers of which language itself consists.

Deconstruction thus offers us a radical vision of the activity of thinking. Our mental life consists not of concepts—not of solid, stable meanings—but of a fleeting, continually changing play of signifiers. These signifiers may seem to be stable concepts—they look stable enough when we hear them spoken or see them written down!—but they don't operate in a stable manner in our mind. As we saw earlier, every signifier consists of and produces more signifiers in a never-ending *deferral*, or postponement, of meaning: we seek meaning that is solid and stable, but we can never really find it because we can never get beyond the play of signifiers that is language. In Derrida's words, what we take to be meaning is really only the mental *trace* left behind by the play of signifiers. And that trace consists of the differences by which we define a word. Let me explain.

Meaning seems to reside in words (or in things) only when we distinguish their *difference* from other words (or things). For example, if we believed that all objects were the same color, we wouldn't need the word *red* (or *blue* or *green*) at all. Red is red only because we believe it to be different from blue and green (and because we believe color to be different from shape). So the word *red* carries with it the trace of all the signifiers it is not (for it is in contrast to other signifiers that we define it).

To sum up, Derrida argues that language has two important characteristics: (1) its play of signifiers continually defers, or postpones, meaning, and (2) the meaning it seems to have is the result of the differences by which we distinguish one signifier from another. He combines the French words for "to defer" and "to differ" to coin the word *différance*, which is his name for the only "meaning" language can have. At this point, you may wonder, Why use language at all if it seems to refer to a kind of stable meaning that doesn't really exist? We must use language, Derrida explains, because we must use the tool at our disposal if we don't have another. But even while we use this tool, we can be aware that it doesn't have the solidity and stability we have assumed it has, and we can therefore improvise with it, stretch it to fit new modes of thinking (an activity he calls *bricolage*). Derrida does this stretching activity, himself, when he puts words *under erasure*, as he calls it, by writing them and then crossing them out (for example, ~~meaning~~) to indicate that he's using an old word in a new way.

It seems rather important that we stretch language in new ways, given deconstruction's belief that language is what forms us and there is no way to get beyond it. There is no getting beyond language, beyond the play of signifiers, because we exist—we think, we see, we feel—within the language into which we were born. How we see and understand ourselves and the world is thus governed by the language with which we are taught to see them. That is, language *mediates* our experience of ourselves and the world. And for deconstruction, language is wholly ideological: it consists entirely of the numerous conflicting, dynamic *ideologies*—or systems of beliefs and values—operating at any given point in time in any given culture. For example, our use of the word *slut* for a woman who sleeps with many men and the word *stud* for a man who sleeps with many women reveals and perpetuates the cultural belief that sexual relations with multiple partners should be a source of shame for women and a source of pride for men.

To cite an extended example of the ideological quality of language, let me pass on a story my high-school biology teacher told us about the attempt to introduce the rhythm method of birth control in a technologically underdeveloped country many years ago. Each woman in the program was given an abacus-like device, consisting of red and white beads arranged to represent her fertility cycle. Each bead represented one day and, if a given day's bead was red, she was not to have sexual intercourse; a white bead meant that sex on that day was safe. After several months passed, statistics showed that the pregnancy rate among women in the program had not changed at all, and social workers were at a loss to understand the problem. They finally discovered that women who wanted to have sex on red-bead days would simply push the beads over until a white one appeared: they assumed the beads were a kind of magic. Thus, the program initially failed because both clients and social workers were able to view the project only in terms of their own cultural, or ideological, perspectives. Clients and social workers thought they understood each other's language, but they didn't because they didn't understand the ideologies of which each other's language was composed.

To explore the specific ways in which our language determines our experience, Derrida borrowed and transformed structuralism's idea that we tend to conceptualize our experience in terms of polar opposites, called *binary oppositions*. For example, according to structuralism, we understand the word *good* by contrasting it with the word *evil*. Similarly, we understand *reason* as the opposite of *emotion*, *masculine* as the opposite of *feminine*, *civilized* as the opposite of *primitive*, and so on. However, Derrida noted that these binary oppositions are also little hierarchies. That is, one term in the pair is always *privileged*, or considered superior to the other. (In the binary oppositions listed above, the first term in each pair is, in western culture, the privileged term.) Therefore, by finding the binary oppositions at work in a cultural production (such as a novel, a film, a conversation, a classroom, or a courtroom trial), and by identifying which member of the opposition is privileged, one can discover something about the ideology promoted by that production.

In order to discover the limitations of the ideology one thus has uncovered, Derrida observed, one must examine the ways in which the two members of the opposition are not completely opposite, the ways in which they overlap or share some things in common. For example, consider the binary opposition, in American culture, between the words *objective* and *subjective*. We tend to identify the objective with the impersonal, the rational (which implies the intelligent), and the scientific dimensions of human experience and therefore consider objectivity a necessary criterion of reliability. In sharp contrast, we tend to identify the subjective with the personal, the emotional (which implies the unintelligent), and even the irrational dimensions of human experience and therefore consider it unreliable. We can see this privileging of the objective over the subjective in our culture's praise of "objective" news reporting, in its acceptance of "objective" historical data, and in its reliance on "objective" scientific experimentation. For us, the objective is the source of knowledge; the subjective is merely the source of opinion.

To deconstruct this binary opposition and learn something about the limitations of the ideology it supports, let's consider the ways in which the objective and the subjective are not really opposites. For example, when reporters, historians, and scientists gather "objective" data, on what basis do they decide which data to use and which to discard? Even if they are following specific guidelines for data collection, how can we be sure those guidelines are "objective," and, in any case, how can we be sure that the guidelines are "objectively" interpreted and applied to each piece of data collected or discarded? That is, aren't reporters, historians, and scientists human beings with subjective needs, fears, and desires (including career motivations) that might be influencing them with or without their knowledge? Can one totally escape one's own viewpoints, feelings and biases? Surely, to claim that one has done so is to claim the impossible. Isn't objectivity, then, really a lie we tell ourselves and others about our subjectivity? Isn't objectivity, therefore, subjectivity in disguise?

Looked at from a different perspective, isn't the privileging of the objective over the subjective a product of the privileging of reason over emotion? After all, subjectivity is discredited because it is "contaminated" by emotion, which we believe clouds our thinking and undermines our ability to be objective, that is, to be rational. However, is it really rational to lump all emotions in the category of the irrational? Aren't some emotions sometimes the most "rational" response one can have to a given situation, that is, the response that produces the most accurate, useful, and reliable insights? And isn't the insistence on the rational sometimes an emotional response produced by fear of one's own feelings? The point here is that language—the meanings of words, the linguistic categories by which we organize our experience—doesn't operate in the tidy fashion we like to think it does. Language is constantly overflowing with implications, associations, and contradictions that reflect the implications, associations, and contradictions of the ideologies of which it is formed.

Deconstructing Our World

Because it is through language that a culture's ideologies are passed on, it is not unreasonable to say that it is through language that we come to conceive and perceive our world and ourselves. To put the matter in philosophical terms, for deconstruction, language is our "ground of being," or the foundation from which our experience and knowledge of the world are generated. But as we shall see, language, from a deconstructive perspective, is a very different ground of being from those generally associated with traditional western philosophies.

In the history of western thought since Plato, every philosophical system has had its ground of being. That is, all systems of western philosophy derive from and are organized around one grounding principle from which we believe we can figure out the meaning of existence. For some thinkers, the ground of being is some cosmic principle of order or harmony, as illustrated, for example, by Plato's idea of perfect Forms that exist in an abstract, timeless dimension of thought. For others, that grounding principle is rational thought engaged in the act of self-reflection, as illustrated by Descartes' famous statement, "I think; therefore I am" (*Cogito ergo sum*). For others still, the grounding principle is some innate (inborn and permanent) quality in human beings as illustrated by structuralism's belief that human language and experience are generated by innate structures of human consciousness.

While these grounding concepts produce our understanding of the dynamic, evolving world around us—and of our dynamic, evolving selves as well—the concepts, themselves, remain stable. Unlike everything they explain, they are not dynamic and evolving. They are "out of play," as Derrida would put it. This type of philosophy—in short, all western philosophy—Derrida calls *logocentric* because it places at the center (*centric*) of its understanding of the world a concept (*logos*) that organizes and explains the world for us while remaining outside of the world it organizes and explains. But for Derrida, this is western philosophy's greatest illusion. Given that each grounding concept—Plato's Forms, Descartes' *cogito*, structuralism's innate structures of human consciousness, and so on—is, itself, a human concept and therefore a product of human language, how can it be outside the ambiguities of language? That is, how can any concept be outside the dynamic, evolving, ideologically saturated operations of the language that produced it?

For Derrida, the answer is that no concept is beyond the dynamic instability of language, which *disseminates* (as a flower scatters its seeds on the wind) an infinite number of possible meanings with each written or spoken utterance. For deconstruction, then, language is the ground of being, but that ground is *not* out of play: it is, itself, as dynamic, evolving, problematical, and ideologically saturated as the world-views it produces. For this reason, there is no center to our understanding of existence. There are, instead, an infinite number of vantage points from which to view it, and each of these vantage points has a language of its own, which deconstruction calls its *discourse*. For example, there is the discourse of modern physics, the discourse of Christian fundamentalism, the discourse of liberal arts education in the 1990s, the discourse of nineteenth-century American medicine, and so on. In other words, Derrida *decentered* western

philosophy just as Copernicus decentered the earth in the 1600s by asserting that the universe does not revolve around it.

The theory that our view of the world is constructed by language
performs a key role in the decentering of western philosophy because
language is no longer seen as a product of our experience (first we see
an enormous hole in the ground; then we call it the Grand Canyon) but
rather as the conceptual framework that creates our experience. For example, when the early Spanish explorers first saw what non-Native
Americans now call the Grand Canyon, there was nothing in their conceptual repertoire—in their language—to enable them to perceive its
dimensions accurately. For example, they thought the Colorado River,
which lies about twenty-five miles down at the bottom of the Canyon,
was only a few hundred yards away. As a result, foot-soldiers in full armor were ordered to reconnoiter the area—to run down and have a
look around—and to the surprise of their countrymen, they never returned. This example illustrates how conception (what we think) precedes perception (what we experience through our senses), how our expectations, our beliefs, and our values—all of which are carried by
language—determine the way we experience our world. While structuralists were among the first to argue that our view of the world is constructed by the language we speak, they believe that language is generated by stable, innate structures of human consciousness. Thus,
deconstruction is called a *poststructuralist* theory, not only because it
emerged in the wake of structuralism's popularity but also because it
constitutes a reaction against structuralism's orderly vision of language
and human experience.

Deconstructing Human Identity

For deconstruction, if language is the ground of being, then the world is
infinite *text*, that is, an infinite chain of signifiers always in play. Because
human beings are constituted by language, they, too, are texts. In other
words, deconstruction's theory of language has implications for *subjectivity*, for what it means to be a human being.

As we have seen, deconstruction asserts that our experience of ourselves and our world is produced by the language we speak, and because
all language is an unstable, ambiguous force-field of competing ideologies, we are, ourselves, unstable and ambiguous force-fields of competing
ideologies. The self-image of a stable identity that many of us have is re-

ally just a comforting self-delusion, which we produce in collusion with our culture, for culture, too, wants to see itself as stable and coherent when in reality it is highly unstable and fragmented. We don't really have an identity because the word *identity* implies that we consist of one, singular self, when in fact we are multiple and fragmented, consisting at any moment of any number of conflicting beliefs, desires, fears, anxieties, and intentions. However, as we grow up, we internalize, through language, the ideological conflicts and contradictions of our culture, each finding our own way to "fit in" by finding our own way to deny, both to ourselves and others, the fragmented experience of ourselves produced by the fragmented, ambiguous language within which we live.

Does all this sound rather grim, if not completely confusing? Well, don't jump ship yet. Let's consider first some of the interesting vantage points on human experience deconstruction opens up for us. First of all, doesn't the idea of a fragmented self explain a good deal of our day-to-day experience? Aren't most of us very different people on the job, at the store, on a date, or alone in front of the television set? And even if we confine our investigation to our experience of ourselves on the job, for example, doesn't that experience change from day to day, sometimes from hour to hour or minute to minute, as we encounter different people or as various thoughts, memories, and emotions occur? In other words, isn't each of us really a kaleidoscope of selves? In fact, don't we sometimes have the feeling that we don't know who we really are, especially when we compare ourselves to other people who (because we view them from the outside) seem so consistent in their self-image? Similarly, if we've invented our "identity," then we can re-invent it. Isn't that exactly what many people do when they join Alcoholics Anonymous or have a "change of heart" as a result of psychological counselling or religious conversion? Finally, doesn't the ambiguous, ideological nature of language explain many of the difficulties we encounter in communicating with others, especially with others from backgrounds different from our own? Perhaps, an understanding of deconstruction's theory of language can help us see when and how such ideological differences are operating.

Deconstructing Literature

Now let's take a moment to summarize the three main points we've discussed so far in this chapter. For deconstruction, (1) language is dynamic, ambiguous, and unstable, continually disseminating possible meanings;

(2) existence has no center, no stable meaning, no fixed ground; and (3) human beings are fragmented battlefields for competing ideologies whose only "identity" is the one we invent and choose to believe. As you may have noticed, the key word here is *unstable*. It should come as no surprise, then, to learn that, for deconstruction, literature is as dynamic, ambiguous, and unstable as the language of which it is composed.

Meaning is not a stable element residing in the text for us to uncover or passively consume. Meaning is created by the reader in the act of reading. Or more precisely, meaning is produced by the play of language through the vehicle of the reader, though we generally refer to this process as "the reader." Furthermore, the meaning that is created is not a stable element capable of producing closure; that is, no interpretation has the final word. Rather, literary texts, like all texts, consist of a multiplicity of overlapping, conflicting meanings in dynamic, fluid relation to one another and to us. What have been considered the "obvious" or "commonsense" interpretations of a given text are really ideological readings—interpretations produced by a culture's values and beliefs—with which we are so familiar that we consider them "natural." In short, we create the meaning and value we "find" in the text. Just as authors can't help but draw upon the assumptions of their cultural milieux when they construct their texts, readers can't help but draw upon the assumptions of theirs when they construct their readings. Therefore, both literary and critical texts can be deconstructed.

There are generally two main purposes in deconstructing a literary text, and we may see either or both at work in any given deconstructive reading: (1) to reveal the text's "undecidability" and/or (2) to reveal the complex operations of the ideologies of which the text is constructed. At this stage in your relationship to deconstruction, I think you'll find the second procedure more meaningful and useful, so I'll provide only a brief summary of the first approach and then describe the second more fully.

To reveal a text's *undecidability* is to show that the "meaning" of the text is really an indefinite, undecidable, plural, conflicting array of possible meanings and that the text, therefore, has no meaning, in the traditional sense of the word, at all. This goal can be accomplished, in brief, by the following procedure: (1) note all the various interpretations—of characters, events, images, and so on—the text seems to offer; (2) show the ways in which these interpretations conflict with one another; (3) show how these conflicts produce still more interpretations, which produce still more conflicts, which produce still more interpretations; and (4) use steps #1, #2, and #3 to argue for the text's undecidability.

Undecidability does not mean that the reader is unable to choose among possible interpretations. And it does not mean that the text cannot "make up its mind" as to what it wants to say. Rather, undecidability means that reader and text, alike, are inextricably bound within language's dissemination of meanings. That is, reader and text are interwoven threads in the perpetually working loom of language. Specific meanings are just "moments" of meaning that give way, inevitably, to more meanings. Thus, the literary text is used to illustrate the indefinite, plural, conflicting array of possible meanings that constitutes all texts, literary and otherwise, because all texts are made of language. This is a useful and interesting endeavor because such readings serve as helpful reminders that language and all of its products, including ourselves, are rich, exciting, sometimes alarming but always interesting proliferations of meanings.

The other purpose in deconstructing a literary text, which we'll discuss at greater length, is to see what the text can show us about the ideologies of which it is constructed. This endeavor usually shows us something about the ways in which ideologies operate in our own view of the world as well. For these reasons, I think it is an extremely useful exercise whatever your theoretical preferences are. To understand how this kind of deconstruction works, let's contrast it with the New Critical approach discussed in Chapter Five because enough New Critical principles are still taught in the classroom to make that approach fairly familiar to most of us and because a New Critical reading often can serve as the first step in the deconstruction of a text.

As you may recall, New Criticism seeks to reveal how the text works as a unified whole by showing how its main theme is established by the text's formal, or stylistic, elements: imagery, symbolism, tone, rhyme, meter, plot, characterization, setting, point of view, and so forth. First, the New Critic identifies the central tension operating in the text, for example, the struggle between good and evil, the protagonist's evolution from innocence to experience, the conflict between science and religion, or some other tension that is emotionally or morally compelling. Then the New Critic shows how that tension is resolved in the text's advancement of its main theme—for example, that good and evil exist in all of us; that the evolution from innocence to experience, though necessary, can be costly as well as rewarding; that science becomes dangerous when it becomes a religion; or some other theme that has human significance—to which all the formal elements in the text contribute. While New Critics especially appreciate tension, irony, ambiguity, and paradox in a literary text, all of these qualities must serve the unifying purpose of supporting the text's main theme. Any conflicting meanings that seem to appear in the text must be shown to serve some function for the main theme so that the whole text can be seen to achieve its artistic purpose smoothly and completely.

For deconstruction, this means that the New Critic is in collusion with the text to hide the self-contradictions that reveal the limitations of its ideological framework. To find that ideological framework and understand its limitations, a deconstructive critic looks for meanings in the text that conflict with its main theme, focusing on self-contradictions of which the text seems unaware. The best way to grasp this procedure is to try it. Let's do so with Robert Frost's wonderful poem, "Mending Wall" (1914).

A Deconstructive Reading of Robert Frost's "Mending Wall"

Mending Wall

Something there is that doesn't love a wall,
That sends the frozen-ground-swell under it,
And spills the upper boulders in the sun,
And makes gaps even two can pass abreast.
The work of hunters is another thing: 5
I have come after them and made repair
Where they have left not one stone on a stone,
But they would have the rabbit out of hiding,
To please the yelping dogs. The gaps I mean,
No one has seen them made or heard them made,   10
But at spring mending-time we find them there.
I let my neighbor know beyond the hill;
And on a day we meet to walk the line
And set the wall between us once again.
We keep the wall between us as we go.   15
To each the boulders that have fallen to each.
And some are loaves and some so nearly balls
We have to use a spell to make them balance:
"Stay where you are until our backs are turned!"
We wear our fingers rough with handling them.   20
Oh, just another kind of outdoor game,
One on a side. It comes to little more:
There where it is we do not need the wall:
He is all pine and I am apple orchard.
My apple trees will never get across   25

And eat the cones under his pines, I tell him.
He only says, "Good fences make good neighbors."
Spring is the mischief in me, and I wonder
If I could put a notion in his head:
"*Why* do they make good neighbors? Isn't it   30
Where there are cows? But here there are no cows.
Before I built a wall I'd ask to know
What I was walling in or walling out,
And to whom I was like to give offense.
Something there is that doesn't love a wall,   35
That wants it down." I could say "Elves" to him,
But it's not elves exactly, and I'd rather
He said it for himself. I see him there,
Bringing a stone grasped firmly by the top
In each hand, like an old-stone savage armed.   40
He moves in darkness as it seems to me,
Not of woods only and the shade of trees.
He will not go behind his father's saying,
And he likes having thought of it so well
He says again, "Good fences make good neighbors."

A New Critical reading of the text—What is the central tension at work in this poem, and how is it resolved in the poem's unified advancement of its main theme?—is often a useful first step in deconstructing a literary work because such readings can almost always be found to rest on a binary opposition in which one member of the pair is privileged over the other. This binary opposition is usually the key to the text's ideological framework (or at least one of the text's ideological frameworks). Once a New Critical reading is formulated, the binary opposition upon which it rests can be deconstructed: that is, it can be examined to find the ways in which the opposing elements in the text overlap or aren't really opposed. And this is how we can learn something about the limitations of the ideology the text (consciously or unconsciously) promotes.

In the case of "Mending Wall," it seems rather clear that the binary opposition structuring the text can be found in the disagreement between the speaker and his neighbor. The speaker advocates nonconformity when the tradition one has followed no longer fits the circumstances in which one finds oneself. The neighbor, without even thinking about what he is doing, advocates conformity to the way things have always been done in the past. Thus the binary opposition structuring the poem is that between nonconformity and conformity. Since we see the situation from the speaker's point of view and our sympathies therefore lie with him, it is safe to say that non-conformity is the privileged term. The main theme, from a New Critical perspective—or, in deconstructive terms, the poem's overt ideological project—might be stated as follows: the poem criticizes mindless conformity to obsolete traditions for which the wall is a metaphor.

To be sure that we have identified the poem's ideological project and not just set up an easy target that we can then proceed to shoot down, we must find, in New Critical fashion, all the evidence the poem offers in support of the theme we've identified. For example, we accept the speaker's negative view of his neighbor and of obsolete traditions because he clearly shows that the wall has outlived its purpose—"My apple trees will never get across / And eat the cones under his pines" (ll. 25–26)—and because the speaker associates himself with nature ("Spring [a natural event] is the mischief in me": l. 28), which is generally presumed good. Indeed, our faith in nature's wisdom promotes our initial acceptance of the speaker's viewpoint in the poem's opening four lines, which put nature in opposition to the wall: it is nature that "sends the frozen-ground-swell" to spill "the upper boulders in the sun" (ll. 2–3).

This theme is reinforced when the men "have to use a spell" to make the unwilling boulders, natural objects, stay in place (ll. 18–19) and when it is implied that the boulders will fall as soon as the men turn their backs (l. 19). Nature's "children"—the hunters in lines 5–7 and the elves in line 36—also support the speaker's attitude toward the wall. In addition, we often associate the word *wall* with barriers to communication or emotional exchange, and this function is insisted upon in lines 13–15, thereby reinforcing our rejection of the wall and of the obsolete tradition that keeps it in place: "And on a day we meet . . . / And set the wall *between us* once again. / We keep the wall *between us* as we go" (my italics). Finally, the neighbor is compared to an "old-stone savage" who "moves in darkness . . . / Not of woods only and the shade of trees" (ll. 40–42), that is, who is unenlightened. Thus the neighbor is contrasted sharply with the enlightened speaker, who knows that obsolete traditions should be abandoned.

So far we've located the binary opposition that thematically structures the poem: nonconformity/conformity, which, given the nature of the textual evidence we found to support it, could also be expressed as progressivism/conservatism or nature/tradition. And we've determined which members of the oppositions are privileged in the poem: nonconformity, progressivism, and nature. The next step is to deconstruct this opposition by finding everything in the poem that conflicts with or un-

dermines this hierarchy. That is, we must find textual evidence that con-
tradicts the evidence we have just gathered in support of our New Critical
reading of the poem's main theme. This contradictory evidence is the
kind that tends to be overlooked when one is searching for a unified
meaning in a literary text, as the New Critics did. Our goal now is to show
that, once we begin to focus on the poem's internal contradictions instead
of its unity, the poem reveals that neither side of the binary opposition(s)
supporting the main theme can be privileged over the other. In other
words, though most readers have not been trained to see it, we will show
how the poem deconstructs itself.

In the first place, a number of conflicts revolve around the poem's
privileging of the speaker's nonconformity over the unthinking conformity of his neighbor, a difference represented by their attitudes toward
the wall that separates their property. Siding with the speaker, nature—
against tradition—wants the wall down, but so do the hunters, who function not only as emblems of nature but of tradition as well. Because they
hunt for sport (they want "the rabbit out of hiding," not necessarily for
food, but to "please the yelping dogs": ll. 8–9), the hunters evoke a sporting tradition that has its roots in the traditional hunt of the British
landed gentry. Analogously, while magic, in the form of elves, wants the
wall down (l. 36), magic, in the form of the magic "spell" in lines 18–19, is
invoked to keep the wall up. Furthermore, because elves are mischievous
creatures who, according to legend, delight in making trouble for human
beings, their desire to have the wall down can just as easily undermine
our trust in the project rather than promote it. In fact, the speaker's use of
such an ambiguous term as *elves*, and his difficulty in finding the right
word ("it's not elves exactly": l. 37), imply his own unconscious ambivalence toward the wall and toward the tradition it represents. This ambivalence is reinforced by the speaker's having repaired the wall on his own in
the past and by his having called on his neighbor to do so now. These behaviors certainly seem to contradict his nonconformist attitude toward
the wall.

A similar problem occurs in the poem's association of primitiveness,
in the form of the "old-stone savage" to which the neighbor is compared
in line 40, with tradition, which the neighbor also represents. By associating these two elements, the poem creates an uncomfortable and unstable
link between the primitive and the traditional. Since the nineteenth century, western culture has cherished the Romantic view that the primitive
is in harmony with nature, not aligned with tradition against it.

Finally, the main idea the poem criticizes—good fences make good neighbors—is actually valid within the action of the poem: it is the activity of mending the wall that brings the men together, presumably inspiring the poem's creation, and lets them *be* neighbors through the bonding activity of shared work. Evidently, this is the only time the two men meet at all. Even the poem's title suggests this idea if we read *mending* as an adjective rather than a verb: "Mending Wall" then becomes a wall that mends (for example, that mends relationships) rather than a wall that is mended.

Now that we've shown how the poem quietly collapses the binary opposition(s) supporting its own main theme, the final step of our deconstruction is to consider the implications of this collapse. It would seem, for example, that the meaning, importance, and power of conformity and the meaning, importance, and power of nonconformity are not as easily placed in opposition as "Mending Wall" initially appears to suggest. The poem calls for a rational abandonment of a seemingly empty tradition, an attitude easily associated with the scientific and technological progress that occurred during the five decades preceding the poem's publication in 1914. Yet the value of that tradition, and the dubious nature of the attempt to abandon it, form a powerful counterweight against that call. Perhaps this conflict in the text suggests that much of the power of tradition lies in its ability to influence our attitudes without our being aware of its presence.

One reason the unresolvable conflict between progressivism and conservatism occurs in the poem is that some of the terms used to evoke their difference—especially *nature* and *primitive*—themselves evoke mixed feelings in our culture. For example, we associate nature with goodness—innocence, purity, simplicity, health, intuitive wisdom—yet nature usually stands in the way of the scientific and technological progress we value so highly. Mountains are blown up to build our roads; forests are destroyed to foster our business enterprises; and air, soil, and water are polluted to promote our industries. Similarly, western culture associates the primitive with the goodness of nature, yet it also associates the primitive with ignorance, the unknown, and the sinister, and this association evokes fear and contempt. And as we have seen, conflicting associations are also evoked by the words *magic, elves,* and *hunters.* Perhaps, then, our deconstruction of "Mending Wall" should make us reconsider other binary oppositions that inform our culture, such as masculine/feminine, individual/group, and objective/subjective.

As this reading of "Mending Wall" illustrates, deconstruction does not try to resolve the thematic tensions in literary texts into some stable, unified interpretation but rather tries to sustain those tensions in order to learn from them. That a literary work has conflicting ideological projects that are not absorbed in some overarching purpose or theme is not considered a flaw, as it was for New Criticism, but a necessary product of the instability and ideological conflict inherent in language, and they are a product that can enrich our experience of the text. This is a vision of art as a seething cauldron of meanings in flux. As a dynamic entity tied to both the culture that produced it and the culture that interprets it, art becomes a vehicle for understanding our culture, our history, our language, and ourselves.

It is important to remember that all writing (or, more broadly, all communication), including our deconstruction of a literary text, continually deconstructs itself, continually disseminates meanings. In other words, strictly speaking, we do not deconstruct a text; we show how the text deconstructs itself. The process just outlined, then, helps us observe how "Mending Wall" deconstructs itself and use our observations to learn about the ideological operations of language. But we must remember that the meanings we derived from our analysis of the poem constitute only a "moment" in the text's dissemination of meanings, which it will continue to disseminate as long as the poem is read.

Some Questions Deconstructive Critics Ask about Literary Texts

The following two questions summarize the two deconstructive approaches discussed above.

1. How can we use the various conflicting interpretations a text produces (the "play of meanings"), or find the various ways in which the text doesn't answer the questions it seems to answer, to demonstrate the instability of language and the undecidability of meaning? (Remember that deconstruction uses the word *undecidability* in a special way. See pp. 252–53.)

2. What ideology does the text seem to promote—what is its main theme—and how does conflicting evidence in the text show the limitations of that ideology? We can usually discover a text's overt ideological project by finding the binary opposition(s) that structure the text's main theme(s).

Depending upon the literary text in question, we might ask one or both of these questions. Or we might come up with a useful way of deconstructing the text not listed here. These are just two starting points to get us thinking about literary texts in productive deconstructive ways. Keep in mind that not all deconstructive critics will interpret the same work in the same way, even if they focus on the same ideological projects in the text. As in every field, even expert practitioners disagree. Our goal is to use deconstruction to help enrich our reading of literary texts, to help us see some important ideas they illustrate that we might not have seen so clearly or so deeply without deconstruction, and to help us see the ways in which language blinds us to the ideologies it embodies.

The following deconstructive reading of F. Scott Fitzgerald's *The Great Gatsby* is offered as an example of what a deconstruction of that novel might yield. It is important to note that a brief deconstructive reading of the novel has already been presented in the chapter on Marxist criticism. The Marxist reading of *The Great Gatsby*, you may recall, had two components. First it showed the ways in which the text offers a powerful critique of capitalist ideology; then it showed the ways in which that critique is undermined by the text's own fascination with the capitalist world it condemns. The second component of this reading is a deconstruction of the first because it draws on elements in the novel to show the limitations of the text's own anti-capitalist ideology. Thus, as we noted earlier, because deconstruction helps us understand the hidden operations of ideology, it can be a useful tool for any critic interested in examining the oppressive role ideology can play in our lives. In fact, Marxist and feminist critics had often used deconstructive principles in their analyses of literature and culture before those principles were developed as part of a theory of language and called *deconstruction*, and they still use them today.

In the deconstruction of *The Great Gatsby* that follows, I will argue that the novel's overt ideological project—the condemnation of American decadence in the 1920s, which replaced forever the wholesome innocence of a simpler time—is undermined by the text's own ambivalence toward the binary oppositions upon which that ideological project rests: past/present, innocence/decadence, and West/East. This ambivalence finds its most conflicted expression in the characterization of Jay Gatsby, the romantic embodiment of the novel's covert fascination with the modern world it condemns. Although this deconstructive reading of the novel is much broader than the Marxist deconstruction described above, their shared focus on American decadence gives them, as we shall see, some elements in common.

"... the thrilling, returning trains of my youth ...": A Deconstructive Reading of *The Great Gatsby*

Toward the end of F. Scott Fitzgerald's *The Great Gatsby* (1925), narrator Nick Carraway, thoroughly disillusioned by his experience in the East, reminisces about his youth in Wisconsin:

> One of my most vivid memories is of coming back west from prep school and later from college at Christmas time. Those who went farther than Chicago would gather in the old dim Union Station at six o'clock of a December evening. . . .
>
> When we pulled out into the winter night and the real snow, our snow, began to stretch out beside us and twinkle against the windows, and the dim lights of small Wisconsin stations moved by, a sharp wild brace came suddenly into the air. We drew in deep breaths of it . . . unutterably aware of our identity with this country. . . .
>
> That's my middle-west . . . the thrilling, returning trains of my youth and the street lamps and sleigh bells in the frosty dark and the shadows of holly wreaths thrown by lighted windows on the snow. I am part of that, a little solemn with the feel of those long winters, a little complacent from growing up in the Carraway house in a city where dwellings are still called through decades by a family's name. (184; ch. 9)

Such nostalgia for the past emerges in various ways throughout the novel and lends emotional force to what I will argue is the text's most pervasive and overt ideological project: the condemnation of American decadence in the 1920s, which replaced forever the wholesome innocence of a simpler time. The grotesque portrayal of the modern world, the painful disillusionment of two hopeful young men—Nick Carraway and Jay Gatsby—as they are initiated into the harsh realities of that world, and the nostalgic representations of an idealized past create a novel that deeply mourns the passing of America's innocence during the decade following the end of World War I. As we shall see, however, this belief in an idealized past corrupted by the decadence of the present is, in *The Great Gatsby*, an unstable ideological project. For it is deconstructed by the text's own ambivalence toward the binary oppositions upon which that project rests—past/present, innocence/decadence, and West/East—an ambivalence that finds its most conflicted expression in the characterization of Jay Gatsby, the romantic embodiment of the novel's covert fascination with the modern world it condemns.

There is little to redeem the modern world portrayed in *The Great Gatsby*. It's a world run by men like Tom Buchanan and Meyer Wolfshiem, and despite their positions on opposite sides of the law, both characters are predators consumed by self-interest, capable of rationalizing their way around any ethical obstacle to get what they want. It's an empty world where selfishness, drunkenness, and vulgarity abound, where the graceful social art of dancing has become "old men pushing young girls backward in eternal graceless circles" and "superior couples holding each other tortuously, fashionably and keeping in the corners" (51; ch. 3). Unlike life in the Wisconsin of Nick's youth, there is no sense of permanence or stability. The Buchanans are forever "drift[ing] here and there unrestfully wherever people played polo and were rich together" (10; ch. 1). Jordan is always on the move among hotels, clubs, and other people's homes. And even George Wilson, with the scant means he has at his disposal, thinks he can solve his problems by pulling up stakes and moving west. Anonymity and isolation are the rule rather than the exception. None of the characters has close, lasting friendships, and the alienation of humanity seems to be summed up in the "poor young clerks" Nick sees on the streets of New York City, "who loitered in front of windows waiting until it was time for a solitary restaurant dinner— young clerks in the dusk, wasting the most poignant moments of night and life" (62; ch. 3).

Furthermore, the superficial values that put the pursuit of social status and good times above every other consideration are found among every group portrayed in the novel, regardless of the class, gender, or race of its members. The middle-class and working-class characters—such as the McKees, Myrtle Wilson, Myrtle's sister Catherine, and Gatsby's menagerie of party guests—are as concerned with social status and as hungry for amusement as the wealthy Buchanans. The female characters who attend Gatsby's soirées are as shallow, selfish, and drunken as the male partygoers, if not more so. And the black characters Nick sees one day on his way to New York, the only black characters in the novel, are as superficial and status-conscious as the white characters: from the back seat of their chauffeured limousine, they roll their eyes "in haughty rivalry" (73; ch. 4) toward the luxury car carrying Gatsby and Nick. The only characters who don't seem to exhibit these behaviors, George Wilson and Michaelis, the man who owns the restaurant next to Wilson's garage, are apparently too busy or too poor for such concerns: their energy is devoted to surviving the hopeless poverty of the valley of ashes, which locale is, itself, an indictment of the culture that produced it. Indeed, one could say that the valley of ashes is a metaphor for the spiritual poverty of the modern world:

> a fantastic farm where ashes grow like wheat into ridges and hills and grotesque gardens, where ashes take the forms of houses and chimneys and rising smoke and finally . . . of men who move dimly and already crumbling through the powdery air. (27; ch. 2)

Nick Carraway, the narrator and apparent moral center of the novel, enters this corrupt world with all the innocent blindness that youthful vitality and optimism can create, oblivious, at first, to the "foul dust" (6; ch. 1) and "abortive sorrows" (7; ch. 1) that are the inevitable products of such a world. In the world in which Nick grew up, fathers gave sons advice about "the fundamental decencies" (6; ch. 1); sons graduated from Yale just as their fathers had before them; young men were considered engaged to be married if they had been seen in the company of the same young women too often; and no one could have imagined that "one man" could fix the World Series, as Meyer Wolfshiem did, "with the single-mindedness of a burglar blowing a safe" (78; ch. 4). It is early summer in 1922 as Nick arrives at his rented cottage in West Egg to begin a new career and a new life, and we see his enthusiasm in his description of his new neighborhood, with its "great bursts of leaves growing on the trees. . . . and so much fine health to be pulled down out of the young breath-giving air" (8; ch. 1). Even New York City, where Nick works as a bond salesman, seems young and virginal to his eager eyes: "The city seen from the Queensboro Bridge is always the city seen for the *first* time, in its *first* wild *promise* of all the *mystery* and *beauty* in the world" (73; ch. 4, my italics).

By the end of the summer, however, Nick has turned thirty and feels he has nothing to look forward to but "a decade of loneliness, a thinning list of single men to know, a thinning brief-case of enthusiasm, thinning hair" (143; ch. 7). He has discovered that the Buchanans and their lot are "a rotten crowd" (162), and he has "had enough of all of them" (150; ch. 7). Thus, after spending a single summer in the East, Nick prepares, as the novel closes, to return once again to the Midwest, longing for the order and predictability of the life he knew there, sick of the spiritual bankruptcy of life in the modern world. As he tells us at the beginning of the novel, in a retrospective prologue to his narrative, "When I came back from the East last autumn I felt that I wanted the world to be in uniform and at a sort of moral attention forever; I wanted no more riotous excursions with privileged glimpses into the human heart" (6; ch. 1). And to complete the progression from Nick's youthful optimism to disillusion-ment, the novel ends in the autumn of that same year, "when the blue smoke of brittle leaves was in the air and the wind blew the wet laundry stiff on the line" (185; ch. 9), the time of year when nature's decay under-scores the spiritual exhaustion that results from Nick's sojourn in the East.

Of course, Gatsby is part of the corrupt world Nick enters when he moves East, but "Gatsby . . . was exempt from [Nick's] reaction" because, as the narrator observes, "Gatsby turned out all right at the end; it is what preyed on Gatsby, what foul dust floated in the wake of his dreams" that elicits Nick's "unaffected scorn" (6; ch. 1). It is Gatsby's quality as a ro-mantic dreamer—his "heightened sensitivity to the promises of life" and his "romantic readiness" (6; ch. 1)—that insulates him from the corrupt world in which he lives and, therefore, from Nick's censure. Indeed, Gatsby has all the makings of a romantic hero, American style. His rags-to-riches success evokes the American romantic ideal of the self-made man, and even his boyhood "schedule" at the back of his Hopalong Cassidy book recalls the self-improvement maxims of Benjamin Franklin, an icon of America's romantic past. Gatsby's status as a war hero increases his value as a romantic symbol as does the fact that his meteoric financial rise was accomplished to win the woman of his dreams. His boyish good looks, his quiet, gentlemanly manners, and his flawless grooming accen-tuate his youth and innocence. Finally, his absolute devotion to Daisy, epitomized in the idealized image of the young lover "stretch[ing] out his arms" (25; ch. 1) toward the green light at the end of Daisy's dock, "trem-bling" (26; ch. 1), completes the romantic incarnation.

Unfortunately, Gatsby's unique romantic qualities, which echo the chivalry of ages past, ill suit him to survive the shallow vulgarity of the time in which he lives. Indeed, it is the empty values of the modern world, embodied in Tom and Daisy Buchanan, that crush Gatsby: when Daisy abandons him during his confrontation with Tom at the hotel in New York, "drawing further and further into herself" (142; ch. 7), Gatsby "br[eaks] like glass against Tom's hard malice" (155; ch. 8). With his death, which is the direct result of his chivalrously taking the blame for Daisy's hit-and-run killing of Myrtle, the modern world loses forever the gift that Gatsby had brought to it: "an extraordinary gift for hope . . . such as [Nick] ha[s] never found in any other person and which it is not likely [he] shall find again" (6; ch. 1). Indeed, that Gatsby's "romantic readiness" and "gift for hope" can't survive in the modern world depicted in the novel is one of the text's severest indictments of that world.

Juxtaposed against the fast-paced, shallow decadence of the American 1920s are passages that evoke an idyllic past, passages that serve to remind us of what it is America has lost. One of the most effective is the passage quoted at the opening of this essay, the passage in which Nick reminisces about his youth in Wisconsin. Phrases such as "the real snow, our snow, began to stretch out beside us and twinkle" and "a sharp wild brace came suddenly into the air" (184; ch. 9) evoke open spaces—clean, white, and shining—that invigorate not just the body but the spirit as well. "[T]he real snow" refers, of course, to the enormous quantity of clean, white snow that falls in Wisconsin and lasts all winter, as contrasted with the sooty snow that becomes slush under the wheels of New York traffic. But the phrase also reinforces the notion that life in the Midwest of Nick's youth is more real, more genuine, than the artificial atmosphere he associates with his adult life in the East. Certainly, life in the Wisconsin of Nick's youth was more stable and secure as well. For as this same passage indicates, "dwellings are still called through decades by a family's name" (184; ch. 9), which suggests a sense of permanence and personal connection among residents of the community that Nick doesn't find in the East.

This contrast between past and present, between innocence and decadence, between West and East, is heightened by the narrator's description of his dreams about the East, which immediately follows his recollection of Wisconsin winters:

> Even when the East excited me most . . . it had always for me a quality of distortion. West Egg especially still figures in my more fantastic dreams. I see it as a night scene by El Greco: a hundred houses, at once conventional and grotesque, crouching under a sullen, overhanging sky and a lustreless moon. In the foreground four solemn men in dress suits are walking along the sidewalk with a stretcher on which lies a drunken woman in a white evening dress. Her hand, which dangles over the side, sparkles cold with jewels. Gravely the men turn in at a house—the wrong house. But no one knows the woman's name, and no one cares. (184–85; ch. 9)

The images of human alienation here—the hundred grotesque houses, the drunken woman, the men who deliver her to the wrong house because they don't know her name and don't care to know it—are reinforced by images of an alienated, exhausted nature that contrast sharply with Nick's description of the Midwest of his youth: unlike the clean, bracing, Wisconsin sky, the Eastern sky is "sullen" and "overhanging," and

even the woman's cold jewels have more "sparkle" than the "lustreless"
Eastern moon.

Other references to an idyllic past revolve around Daisy and Jordan's
beautiful "white girlhood" (24; ch. 1) in Louisville, where, Nick imagines,
Jordan "first learned to walk upon golf courses on clean, crisp mornings"
(55; ch. 3). This is a romantic past where, Jordan recalls, she walked on
"soft ground" in her "new plaid skirt . . . that blew a little in the wind"
(79; ch. 4) and where Daisy was

> by far the most popular of all the young girls. . . . She dressed in white
> and had a little white roadster and all day long the telephone rang in
> her house and excited young officers from Camp Taylor demanded
> the privilege of monopolizing her that night, "anyways for an hour!"
> (79; ch. 4)

This is a world in which young girls made bandages for the Red Cross and
a handsome young officer named Jay Gatsby "looked at Daisy . . . in a way
that every young girl wants to be looked at sometime" (80; ch. 4). This is a
world of virginal romance: clean, crisp mornings, soft ground, new skirts,
white dresses, white roadsters, ringing telephones, and handsome young
officers. And the young Jay Gatsby was not immune to its charms:

> There was a ripe mystery about [Daisy's house], a hint of bedrooms
> upstairs more beautiful and cool than other bedrooms, of gay and
> radiant activities taking place through its corridors and of romances
> that were not musty and laid away already in lavender but fresh and
> breathing and redolent of this year's shining motor cars and of dances
> whose flowers were scarcely withered. (156; ch. 8)

Only such an idyllic past could produce the deed worthy of its romantic
ambience: Gatsby's committing himself to Daisy as "to the following of a
grail" (156; ch. 8).

Perhaps the most powerful passage that evokes an idyllic past forever
vanished is the one that closes the novel. As Nick sits on the beach the
evening before his return to Wisconsin, he muses on

> the old island here that flowered once for Dutch sailor's eyes—a fresh
> green breast of the new world. Its vanished trees, the trees that had
> made way for Gatsby's house, had once pandered in whispers to the
> last and greatest of all human dreams; for a transitory enchanted
> moment man must have held his breath in the presence of this conti-

nent, compelled into an aesthetic contemplation he neither understood nor desired, face to face for the last time in history with something commensurate to his capacity for wonder. (189; ch. 9)

In this passage, all the losses represented in the novel—the loss of values in
modern America, the loss of a nation's innocence and vitality, the loss of
Gatsby's dream—are associated with a loss of global historical magnitude:
the original loss of a pristine American continent that was exploited, polluted, destroyed by Europe's lust for more colonies and greater wealth.

Clearly, *The Great Gatsby* paints a grim picture of America in the
1920s. However, the novel's representation of this culture's decadence is
undermined by the text's own ambivalence toward the binary oppositions
upon which this representation rests. As we have seen, the novel associates America's innocence, now vanished, with the youthful vitality of the
past, especially as it is invoked by the text's descriptions of the West. In
contrast, America's decadence is associated with the present-day setting
of the novel—the modern world of the 1920s—and with the East, where
Nick gets his first taste of the selfishness and superficiality that mark the
decline in national values. If we examine the instability of these oppositions—past/present, innocence/decadence, and West/East—we will be
able to see how the novel deconstructs its own ideological project.

The novel's evocation of an idyllic past in order to underscore, by
contrast, the spiritual emptiness of modern America creates an unstable
opposition between past and present because it undermines the text's
own awareness that the past was not idyllic for everyone. Certainly, Jay
Gatsby's past was not so. "His parents were shiftless and unsuccessful
farm people" (104; ch. 6), and his father tells Nick, "He told me I et like a
hog once and I beat him for it" (182; ch. 9). In fact, Gatsby found his past
so unacceptable that he reinvented it: he left home, changed his name
from Jimmy Gatz, and "invented just the sort of Jay Gatsby that a seven-
teen year old boy would be likely to invent, and to this conception he was
faithful to the end" (104; ch. 6). As a penniless young lieutenant "he let
[Daisy] believe that he was a person from much the same strata as herself" (156; ch. 8), and he tells Nick, "My family all died and I came into a
good deal of money. . . . After that I lived like a young rajah in all the capitals of Europe . . . collecting jewels . . . hunting big game, painting a little"
(70; ch. 4). In this context, even Gatsby's singular determination to "repeat the past" (116; ch. 6) is really a determination to escape the past. For
the past he wants to repeat is his initial liaison with Daisy, which was built
upon an invented past, a past that never existed. Thus, for the character

who embodies the novel's notion of the romantic past, the romantic past is, in reality, a tissue of lies.

Another problem with the opposition between past and present in *The Great Gatsby* is its link to the novel's opposition of innocence and decadence, which is, itself, an unstable opposition. For example, although Nick is the novel's chief spokesperson against the decadence of the age, he is very much attracted by it. Nick says,

> I began to like New York, the racy adventurous feel of it at night and the satisfaction that the constant flicker of men and women and machines gives to the restless eye. I liked to walk up Fifth Avenue and pick out romantic women from the crowd and imagine that *in a few minutes I was going to enter into their lives, and no one would ever know or disapprove.* Sometimes, in my mind, I followed them to their apartments on the corners of hidden streets, and they turned and smiled back at me before they faded through a door into warm darkness. (61; ch. 3, my italics).

Although Nick doesn't complete the thought, the italicized portion of the passage makes it clear that he imagines himself following these women into the "warm darkness"; their smile is a smile of invitation. In other words, the "racy adventurous feel" of the city is produced, for him, by the infinity of illicit sexual possibilities it offers. This is not the Wisconsin of Nick's youth, with its "interminable inquisitions which spared only the children and the very old" (185; ch. 9), and he's very glad it isn't.

A similar attraction to the decadence the novel condemns is revealed in the narrator's attraction to Jordan Baker. For she is not the "great sportswoman" who would "never do anything that wasn't all right" (76; ch. 4), as Gatsby believes. She's a cheat and a liar, and Nick knows it. Although he dismisses her dishonest behavior as if it were not a serious flaw—"Dishonesty in a woman is a thing you never blame deeply" (63; ch. 3)—it's her dishonesty that, in fact, attracts him because he believes it serves to mask a secret, illicit sexuality that he wants to experience: "I suppose she had begun dealing in subterfuges when she was very young in order to keep that cool insolent smile turned to the world and yet satisfy the demands of her hard jaunty body" (63; ch. 3).

It's interesting to note, in this context, that Nick seems to have great difficulty leaving the scenes that epitomize the superficial values he condemns. For example, he's among the very last to leave both of the parties he attends at Gatsby's house. Even more puzzling, he doesn't seem to be able to extract himself from the drunken revel at Tom and Myrtle's apartment:

I wanted to get out and walk eastward toward the park through the soft twilight but each time I tried to go I became entangled in some wild strident argument which pulled me back, as if with ropes, into my chair. (40; ch. 2)

Nick says that it's the "inexhaustible variety of life" that "simultaneously enchant[s] and repel[s]" him (40; ch. 2), but it seems to be the inexhaustible vulgarity of the modern world that, beneath his overt revulsion, fascinates him. And so we see him at the novel's close, once again the last to leave, lingering on the beach at West Egg long after Tom, Daisy, Jordan, and Gatsby are gone.

Another problem with *The Great Gatsby*'s opposition of innocence and decadence is the concept of innocence, itself. As the above discussion of Nick implies, he is fascinated by decadence because he is innocent—that is, inexperienced—and therefore hungry for knowledge of the world. Analogously, Nick falls prey, at least for a time, to the decadence he condemns because he is innocent—that is, ignorant—and therefore doesn't understand the kind of moral danger that is confronting him. In other words, the concept of innocence, because it includes the concepts of inexperience and ignorance, has built into it, so to speak, a vulnerability to decadence that is almost sure to result in a fall. Thus, it is not unreasonable to say that innocence leads to decadence; in fact, it creates decadence where before there was none.

A particularly revealing problem with the novel's opposition of innocence and decadence is seen in the characterization of George Wilson. In many ways, he is the only truly innocent character in the story. He harms no one, he trusts everyone, and he is rather childlike in his simplicity. Unlike Nick, who is fascinated by his first encounter with decadence, George's first experience of it—in the form of his wife's infidelity—literally makes him ill: "He had discovered that Myrtle had some sort of life apart from him in another world and the shock had made him physically sick" (130; ch. 7). Yet George's innocence is portrayed not as a positive quality in its own right but as an absence of qualities of any kind. Wilson has almost no personality at all. As Michaelis notices, "when [George] wasn't working he sat on a chair in the doorway and stared at the people and the cars that passed along the road. When anyone spoke to him he invariably laughed in an agreeable colorless way" (144; ch. 7). He didn't even have a friend, Michaelis learns without surprise: there wasn't even "enough of him for his wife" (167; ch. 8). Thus, in a novel that mourns the loss of innocence, innocence is portrayed as ignorance, as the absence of qualities, as a kind of

nothingness. And although decadence is overtly condemned by the narrator and by the novel's unsympathetic portrayals of decadent characters, the text seems to find decadence infinitely more interesting than
innocence. Innocence is boring; decadence is not.

The thematic structure supported by the binary oppositions past/
present and innocence/decadence is tied to a geographic structure that
opposes West and East. As we have seen, the innocence of the past is associated with Nick's Wisconsin and the Louisville in which Daisy and Jordan grew up. And though Gatsby's youth in North Dakota and Minnesota
was an unhappy time in his life, the novel nevertheless associates the West
with the innocent dreams of seventeen-year-old Jimmy Gatz, who
"loaf[ed] along the beach [of Lake Superior] . . . in a torn green jersey
and a pair of canvas pants" (104; ch. 6) before he ever met Dan Cody or
heard of Meyer Wolfshiem. In contrast, the decadence of the present is
associated with the East, specifically with New York in the 1920s. However, the opposition between West and East in *The Great Gatsby* isn't entirely a matter of geography. For example, Chicago and Detroit are in the
Midwest, yet the novel indicates that they share the decadence of New
York. Neither is the opposition between West and East entirely that between countryside and city, for Nick's innocent youth, as well as those of
Daisy and Jordan, were passed in Midwestern cities.

The real distinction between West and East in the novel is the distinction between pristine nature—the "real snow" of Nick's Wisconsin and
the "old island that flowered once for Dutch sailors"—and the corrupting
effects of civilization. That is, regardless of the geography involved, the
word *West* invokes, for Americans, untouched, uncorrupted nature. The
word *East*, in contrast, is associated with old, corrupt societies. Therefore,
the "old island" Nick refers to, though it is New York's Long Island, is associated with the word *West* not only because it is west of the European
civilization that colonized it, but because when the Dutch sailors first arrived there, it was pristine.

In *The Great Gatsby*, however, nature, even at its most youthful, energetic, and magical, is inextricably bound to the corrupt civilization of
modern America, and this tie between the two further deconstructs the
opposition between West and East. Nick associates nature with civilization, for example, in his opening description of early summer in West
Egg. He compares the "great bursts of leaves growing on the trees" to the
way "things grow in fast movies" (8; ch. 1). And in the very next sentence
after he describes the "fine health to be pulled down out of the young
breath-giving air," he speaks, in the same exalted tone, of the "shining se-

crets" he will learn about making his fortune from the "dozen volumes on banking and credit and investment securities" he bought, which "stood on [his] shelf in red and gold like new money from the mint" (8; ch. 1). Similarly, the text can't separate the beauty and vitality of nature from the corrupt power of the wealthy who "own" it, as we see in the following description of the Buchanans' home:

> The lawn started at the beach and ran toward the front door for a quarter of a mile, jumping over sun-dials and brick walks and burning gardens—finally when it reached the house drifting up the side in bright vines as though from the momentum of its run. (11; ch. 1)

Although the estate is on the edge of the sea, one of the most powerful natural forces on earth, nature, in this passage, is utterly domesticated. The wild grasses that normally border the ocean have been replaced by a "lawn," which "jump[s] over" objects like a trained dog, while vines adorn the house like jewelry. Yet the sensuous beauty of the lengthy description of the Buchanans' home, of which this passage is but a small part, suggests that the text is unaware of how images such as "the fresh grass outside . . . seemed to grow a little way into the house" (12; ch. 1) use the purity of nature to validate the decadent civilization it decorates. Indeed, the beauties of nature are often referred to as if they were manufactured by civilization, as when Nick, attending one of Gatsby's parties, says that "the premature moon [was] produced like the supper, no doubt, out of a caterer's basket" (47; ch. 3). And the blending of nature and civilization is complete when the products of civilization are described as if they were products of nature, as when we're told that "two windows" on the second floor of the Buchanans' house "*bloomed* with light among the vines" (149; ch. 7, my italics).

We see the instability of all three oppositions—past/present, innocence/decadence, and West/East—in the person of Dan Cody, "a product of the Nevada silver fields, of the Yukon, of every rush for metal since Seventy-five" (105; ch. 6), a "florid man with a hard empty face—the pioneer debauchee who during one phase of American life brought back to the eastern seaboard the savage violence of the frontier brothel and saloon" (106; ch. 6). In the person of Dan Cody, and the historical period he represents, we see the past, not the present, associated with decadence, and we see the West corrupting the East.

The most pervasive source of the novel's ambivalence toward its own ideological project, however, is its characterization of Jay Gatsby. As we have seen, Gatsby is portrayed as a romantic hero: a rebellious boy, an ambitious young roughneck, an idealistic dreamer, a devoted lover, a brave soldier, a lavish host. The physical descriptions of his person also generate an ambience of innocence, vitality, and beauty: "[T]here was something gorgeous about him" (6; ch. 1), with his "gorgeous pink rag of a suit" (162; ch. 8), "his tanned skin . . . drawn attractively tight on his face" (54; ch. 3), and his "rare smil[e] . . . with a quality of eternal reassurance in it" (52; ch. 3). He is like a romantic knight of ages past somehow displaced in history, lost, with his "incorruptible dream" (162; ch. 8), in a time too superficial to appreciate him. Yet he is also the romantic embodiment of the modern world the novel condemns. That is, by romanticizing Gatsby, the novel also romanticizes the corruption that produced him, the corruption in which he willingly and successfully participates.

"I raised him up out of nothing, right out of the gutter" (179; ch. 9), says Meyer Wolfshiem, the man who fixed the 1919 World Series and the most sinister representative of the criminal world the novel offers. And through bootlegged liquor and fraudulent bonds, Gatsby made his extraordinary fortune in record time. Like the characters the novel condemns, Gatsby succeeds in a world of predators and prey. His illegal, and thus often imperfect, liquor is sold over the counter to anyone with the money to pay for it, and his false bonds are passed in small towns to unsuspecting investors. Some of the people who buy the liquor may become ill from it; some may die. All of the small investors who buy the fraudulent bonds will lose money that they probably can't afford to lose. And when the inevitable mistakes are made and the law steps in, someone will have to be sacrificed, as Gatsby sacrifices Walter Chase.

Even the protagonist's desire for Daisy—which creates, for many readers, the most romantic image of him—is not free from the taint of his underworld view of life: when Gatsby first courted Daisy at her parents' home in Louisville, "[h]e took what he could get, ravenously and unscrupulously—eventually he took Daisy" (156; ch. 8). Gatsby did not just make love to Daisy; he "took" her "ravenously and unscrupulously." This language resonates strongly with his dubious association with Dan Cody before meeting Daisy and with his criminal activities subsequent to their initial affair. Gatsby's "incorruptible dream" (162; ch. 8) is thus mired in the corruption he participated in to fulfill it.

The novel's confusion of the opposing worlds Gatsby represents is largely responsible for the problematic nature of the closing passage we discussed earlier. Let's look at it again. As Nick stands on the beach at West Egg for the last time, he tells us that he

became aware of the old island here that flowered once for Dutch sailors' eyes—a fresh, green breast of the new world. Its vanished trees, the
trees that had made way for Gatsby's house, had once pandered in
whispers to the last and greatest of all human dreams; for a transitory
enchanted moment man must have held his breath in the presence of
this continent, compelled into an aesthetic contemplation he neither
understood nor desired, face to face for the last time in history with
something commensurate to his capacity for wonder. (189; ch. 9)

Although Nick reminds us that the "fresh, green breast of the new world,"
that setting "commensurate to [our] capacity for wonder," "vanished" to
make "way for Gatsby's house"—that is, was obliterated by civilization—
Nick also associates this "enchanted" dream of the Dutch sailors with
Gatsby's dream, which Gatsby attempted to fulfill through the criminal
means of the corrupt civilization of which he was a part. For Nick says,
"[A]s I sat there brooding on the old, unknown world, I thought of
Gatsby's wonder when he first picked out the green light at the end of
Daisy's dock" (189; ch. 9). In other words, the text associates the "fresh,
green breast of the new world" with the "green light at the end of Daisy's
dock," thus tying the romantic sublime of pristine nature to the corrupt
civilization that replaced it—in the form of Gatsby—in a way that makes
the two, emotionally if not logically, almost impossible to untangle. Furthermore, the "vanished trees," the pristine past, "*pandered* in whispers"
(my italics). To pander means to pimp, to sell one's services to help satisfy
another's vices. Thus, pristine nature, the innocent past, cannot be separated, in this passage, from the civilization that exploits it, just as Jay
Gatsby cannot be separated from the corrupt world that exploits and is
exploited by him.

The Great Gatsby condemns the modern decadence that, the novel
suggests, replaced the innocent America of the past, an America associated with the unspoiled West. But this ideological project is undermined
by the inseparability, in the text itself, of past and present, innocence and
decadence, and West and East. Nevertheless, the novel's nostalgia for a
lost past, an innocent past, a happier past, is a nostalgia shared, at least
according to western literature of the last several hundred years, by
people from every age. Although our deconstructive reading of *The Great
Gatsby* surely will not eliminate an emotional investment of such long
standing, it can help us understand the ideological limitations of that investment. In addition, our analysis of Fitzgerald's novel illustrates the validity of deconstruction's view of fiction. According to deconstruction,
because fiction is made of language, it embodies the ideologies of the cul-

ture that produces it. Fiction can therefore show us the various ways in which our ideologies operate to create our perceptions of the world. In other words, as our deconstructive reading of *The Great Gatsby* demonstrates, fiction doesn't represent the world as it really is; it represents the world as we perceive it to be. And for deconstruction, the world as we perceive it to be is the only world we know.

Questions for Further Practice: Deconstructive Approaches to Other Literary Works

The following questions are intended as models. They can help you use deconstructive criticism to interpret the literary works to which they refer or other texts of your choice.

1. The overt ideological project of Luis Valdez's "Los Vendidos" (1967) seems to be to ridicule the ethnic stereotypes that have been imposed on Mexican Americans. First, show how this one-act play accomplishes this ideological project. Then, show how the text deconstructs its own project by inadvertently re-asserting, at the end of the play, some of the same stereotypes it has worked to undermine. What does this ideological conflict suggest about the difficulties involved in the attempt to avoid stereotypes or about the difficulty any oppressed group might have asserting its own identity in the face of prejudice?

2. How does Kate Chopin's "The Storm" (1898) forward its theme of the importance of sexual fulfillment for women, which seems to be the story's overt ideological project? How does the text's use of nature imagery and the standard fairy-tale happy ending both promote and undermine this project? What does this ideological conflict imply about the story's attempt to transcend the nineteenth-century social values of the culture it represents?

3. Robert Frost's "The Road Not Taken" (1916) has become an American icon of the value of nonconformity: "I took the one less traveled by, / And that has made all the difference." Deconstruct this overt ideological project by finding all the evidence in the poem that seems to undermine the value of nonconformity, for example, the ways in which the two roads are the same and the

speaker's own apparent conformity at various points in the poem. You may find that there is, in fact, not as much support in the poem as you expected for the ideology of nonconformity. How might we account for the apparent failure of the American public to recognize this aspect of the poem? How does this poem illustrate deconstruction's notion of undecidability?

4. Mary Shelley's *Frankenstein* (1818), which was produced during England's Romantic period by an author who associated with some of the leading Romantic poets of her day, frequently represents nature as Romantic sublime: the contemplation of nature's awesome grandeur—great mountains, storms at sea, huge trees blasted by lightning, and the like—can produce in human beings lofty, noble thoughts and feelings that take them beyond the finite boundaries of mundane experience. Find textual evidence to support this claim. Then show how the novel deconstructs this ideological project by finding, in the text, the ways in which nature does not live up to this definition. Speculate on the reasons why this ideological conflict is present in this text.

5. How does William Blake's "The Little Black Boy" forward its theme of racial equality, which seems to be the poem's overt ideological project? How is this project undermined by the use of the color white as the standard of excellence and by the attitude of the black child toward the white child in the final stanza? What are the implications of this ideological conflict?

For Further Reading

All of the following works will help you develop your skills as deconstructive critics. Texts listed under "Category I" are written in language accessible to most beginners. Texts listed under "Category II" employ more technical language but are well worth the extra effort that may be required of some students new to the field.

Category I

Atkins, G. Douglas. *Reading Deconstruction: Deconstructive Reading.* Lexington: U of Kentucky P, 1983.

Belsey, Catherine. *Critical Practice.* New York: Routledge, 1980. (See, especially, "Deconstructing the Text," 103–24.)

Crowley, Sharon. *A Teacher's Introduction to Deconstruction*. Urbana, Illinois: NCTE, 1989.

Fink, Thomas. "Reading Deconstructively in the Two-Year College Introductory Literature Classroom." *Practicing Theory in Introductory College Literature Courses*. Eds. James M. Cahalan and David B. Downing. Urbana, Illinois: NCTE, 1991. 239–47.

Leitch, Vincent B. *Deconstructive Criticism: An Advanced Introduction*. New York: Columbia UP, 1983.

Sarup, Mandan. *An Introductory Guide to Post-Structuralism and Postmodernism*. Athens: U of Georgia P, 1989.

Category II

Abel, Elizabeth. *Writing and Sexual Difference*. Chicago: U of Chicago P, 1982.

Barthes, Roland. *S/Z*. 1970. Trans. Richard Miller. New York: Hill and Wang, 1975.

Bloom, Harold, et al. *Deconstruction and Criticism*. New York: Seabury, 1979.

de Man, Paul. *Allegories of Reading: Figural Language in Rousseau, Nietzsche, Rilke, and Proust*. New Haven: Yale UP, 1979.

———. *Blindness and Insight*. 2nd ed. Minneapolis: U of Minnesota P, 1983.

Derrida, Jacques. *Of Grammatology*. 1967. Trans. Gayatri Chakravorty Spivak. Baltimore: Johns Hopkins UP, 1976.

———. "Structure, Sign, and Play in the Discourse of the Human Sciences." 1966. *The Languages of Criticism and the Sciences of Man*. Eds. Richard Macksey and Eugenio Donato. Baltimore: Johns Hopkins UP, 1970. 247–65.

Esch, Deborah. "Deconstruction." *Redrawing the Boundaries: The Transformation of English and American Literary Studies*. Eds. Stephen Greenblatt and Giles Gunn. New York: Modern Language Association, 1992. 374–91.

Gasché, Rodolphe. *The Tain of the Mirror: Derrida and the Philosophy of Reflection*. Cambridge, Massachusetts: Harvard UP, 1976.

CHAPTER 9

New Historical and Cultural Criticism

As we've seen in previous chapters, critical theories can overlap with one another in a number of ways. Marxists can draw on psychoanalytic concepts to help them analyze the debilitating psychological effects of capitalism. Feminists can draw on Marxist concepts to examine the socioeconomic oppression of women. Essays analyzing the conventions of American literary interpretation can be included both in structuralist anthologies and in reader-response anthologies. And so forth.

Despite such overlap, however, most critical theories remain distinct from one another in terms of their purpose. Let's look, for example, at the very different goals of the critical theories just mentioned. Marxism attempts to reveal the ways in which our socioeconomic system is the ultimate source of our experience. Feminism attempts to reveal the ways in which patriarchal gender roles are the ultimate source of our experience. Psychoanalysis attempts to reveal the ways in which repressed psychological conflicts are the ultimate source of our experience. Structuralism attempts to reveal the simple structural systems that make possible our understanding of an otherwise chaotic world. And reader-response theory attempts to reveal the operations whereby readers create the texts they read.

Sometimes critical theories overlap so much, however, that it is difficult to determine the ways in which they are different, especially when practitioners disagree about what those differences are. Such is the case with new historicism and cultural criticism. As we'll see, these two fields share so much common theoretical ground that their approaches to literary interpretation are often quite similar. For the sake of clarity, however,

and in order to fully appreciate the differences that do exist between new
historicism and cultural criticism, we will begin by discussing the two
fields separately. And because new historicists have articulated their theoretical premises more thoroughly than have cultural critics, we'll start
with new historicism. Once you have a fairly clear idea of the new historical enterprise, it will be easier to see the ways in which cultural criticism
compares and contrasts with it.

New Historicism

Most of us raised to think about history in the traditional way would read
an account of a Revolutionary War battle written by an American historian in 1944 and ask, if we asked anything at all, "Is this account accurate?" or "What does this battle tell us about the 'spirit of the age' in which
it was fought?" In contrast, a new historicist would read the same account
of that battle and ask, "What does this account tell us about the political
agendas and ideological conflicts of the culture that produced and read
the account in 1944?" New historical interest in the battle itself would
produce such questions as, "At the time in which it was fought, how was
this battle represented (in newspapers, magazines, tracts, government
documents, stories, speeches, drawings, and photographs) by the American colonies or by Britain (or by European countries), and what do these
representations tell us about how the American Revolution shaped and
was shaped by the cultures that represented it?"

As you can see, the questions asked by traditional historians and by
new historicists are quite different, and that's because these two approaches to history are based on very different views of what history is
and how we can know it. Traditional historians ask, "What happened?"
and "What does the event tell us about history?" In contrast, new historicists ask, "How has the event been interpreted?" and "What do the interpretations tell us about the interpreters?"

For most traditional historians, history is a series of events that have
a *linear, causal* relationship: event A caused event B; event B caused event
C; and so on. Furthermore, they believe we are perfectly capable, through
objective analysis, of uncovering the facts about historical events, and
those facts can sometimes reveal the spirit of the age, that is, the world
view held by the culture to which those facts refer. Indeed, some of the
most popular traditional historical accounts have offered a key concept
that would explain the world view of a given historical population, such

as the Renaissance notion of the Great Chain of Being—the cosmic hierarchy of creation, with God at the top of the ladder, human beings at the middle, and the lowliest creatures at the bottom—which has been used to argue that the guiding spirit of Elizabethan culture was a belief in the importance of order in all domains of human life.[1] You can see this aspect of the traditional approach in history classes that study past events in terms of the spirit of an age, such as the Age of Reason or the Age of Enlightenment, and you can see it in literature classes that study literary works in terms of historical periods, such as the Neoclassical, Romantic, or Modernist periods. Finally, traditional historians generally believe that history is *progressive*, that the human species is improving over the course of time, advancing in its moral, cultural, and technological accomplishments.

New historicists, in contrast, don't believe we have clear access to any but the most basic facts of history. We can know, for example, that George Washington was the first American president and that Napoleon was defeated at Waterloo. But our understanding of what such facts mean, of how they fit within the complex web of competing ideologies and conflicting social, political, and cultural agendas of the time and place in which they occurred is, for new historicists, strictly a matter of interpretation, not fact. Even when traditional historians believe they are sticking to the facts, the way they contextualize those facts (including which facts are deemed important enough to report and which are left out) determines what story those facts will tell. From this perspective, there is no such thing as a presentation of facts; there is only interpretation. Furthermore, new historicists argue that reliable interpretations are, for a number of reasons, difficult to produce.

The first and most important reason for this difficulty, new historicists believe, is the *impossibility of objective analysis*. Like all human beings, historians live in a particular time and place, and their views of both current and past events are influenced in innumerable conscious and unconscious ways by their own experience within their own culture. Historians may believe they're being objective, but their own views of what is right and wrong, what is civilized and uncivilized, what is important and unimportant, and the like, will strongly influence the ways in which they interpret events. For example, the traditional view that history is progressive is based on the belief, held in the past by many Anglo-European historians, that the so-called "primitive" cultures of native peoples are less evolved than, and therefore inferior to, the so-called "civilized" Anglo-European cultures. As a result, ancient cultures with highly developed art forms, ethical codes, and spiritual philosophies, such as the tribal cultures of Native Americans and Africans, were often misrepresented as lawless, superstitious, and savage.

Another reason for the difficulty in producing reliable interpretations of history is its complexity. For new historicists, history cannot be understood simply as a linear progression of events. At any given point in history, any given culture may be progressing in some areas and regressing in others. And any two historians may disagree about what constitutes progress and what doesn't, for these terms are matters of definition. That is, history isn't an orderly parade into a continually improving future, as many traditional historians have believed. It's more like an improvised dance consisting of an infinite variety of steps, following any new route at any given moment, and having no particular goal or destination. Individuals and groups of people may have goals, but human history does not.

Similarly, while events certainly have causes, new historicists argue that those causes are usually multiple, complex, and difficult to analyze. One cannot make simple causal statements with any certainty. In addition, causality is not a one-way street from cause to effect. Any given event—whether it be a political election or a children's cartoon show—is a product of its culture, but it also affects that culture in return. In other words, all events—including everything from the creation of an art work, to a televised murder trial, to the persistence of or change in the condition of the poor—*are shaped by and shape* the culture in which they emerge.

In a similar manner, our *subjectivity*, or selfhood, is shaped by and shapes the culture into which we were born. For most new historicists, our individual identity is not merely a product of society. Neither is it merely a product of our own individual will and desire. Instead, individual identity and its cultural milieu inhabit, reflect, and define each other. Their relationship is mutually constitutive (they create each other) and dynamically unstable. Thus, the old argument between determinism and free will can't be settled because it rests on the wrong question: "Is human identity socially determined or are human beings free agents?" For new historicism, this question cannot be answered because it involves a choice between two entities that are not wholly separate. Rather, the proper question is, "What are the processes by which individual identity and social formations—such as political, educational, legal, and religious institutions and ideologies—create, promote, or change each other?" For every society constrains individual thought and action within a network of cultural limitations while it simultaneously enables individuals to think and act. Our subjectivity, then, is a lifelong *process* of negotiating our way, consciously and unconsciously, among the constraints and freedoms offered, at any given moment in time, by the society in which we live.

Thus, according to new historicists, *power* does not emanate only from the top of the political and socioeconomic structure. According to French philosopher Michel Foucault, whose ideas have strongly influenced the development of new historicism, power *circulates* in all directions, to and from all social levels, at all times. And the vehicle by which power circulates is a never-ending proliferation of *exchange*: (1) the exchange of material goods through such practices as buying and selling, bartering, gambling, taxation, charity, and various forms of theft; (2) the exchange of people through such institutions as marriage, adoption, kidnapping, and slavery; and (3) the exchange of ideas through the various discourses a culture produces.

A *discourse* is a social language created by particular cultural conditions at a particular time and place, and it expresses a particular way of understanding human experience. For example, you may be familiar with the discourse of modern science, the discourse of liberal humanism, the discourse of white supremacy, the discourse of ecological awareness, the discourse of Christian fundamentalism, and the like. And as you read the chapters of this textbook, you will become familiar with the discourses of psychoanalytic criticism, Marxist criticism, feminist criticism, and so on. Although the word *discourse* has roughly the same meaning as the word *ideology*, and the two terms are often used interchangeably, the word *discourse* draws attention to the role of language as the vehicle of ideology.

From a new historical perspective, no discourse, by itself, can adequately explain the complex cultural dynamics of social power. For there is no *monolithic* (single, unified, universal) spirit of an age, and there is no adequate *totalizing* explanation of history (an explanation that provides a single key to all aspects of a given culture). There is, instead, a dynamic, unstable interplay among discourses: they are always in a state of flux, overlapping and competing with one another (or, to use new historical terminology, *negotiating* exchanges of power) in any number of ways at any given point in time. Furthermore, no discourse is permanent. Discourses wield power for those in charge, but they also stimulate opposition to that power. This is one reason why new historicists believe that the relationship between individual identity and society is mutually constitutive: on the whole, human beings are never merely victims of an oppressive society, for they can find various ways to oppose authority in their personal and public lives.

For new historicism, even the dictator of a small country doesn't wield absolute power on his own. To maintain dominance, his power must circulate in numerous discourses, for example, in the discourse of religion (which can promote belief in the "divine right" of kings or in God's love of hierarchical society), in the discourse of science (which can support the reigning elite in terms of a theory of Darwinian "survival of the fittest"), in the discourse of fashion (which can promote the popularity of leaders by promoting copycat attire, as we saw when Nehru jackets were popular and when the fashion world copied the style of First Lady Jacqueline Kennedy), in the discourse of the law (which can make it a treasonous offense to disagree with a ruler's decisions), and so on.

As these examples suggest, what is "right," "natural," and "normal" are matters of definition. Thus, in different cultures at different points in history, homosexuality has been deemed abnormal, normal, criminal, or admirable. The same can be said of incest, cannibalism, and women's desire for political equality. In fact, Michel Foucault has suggested that all definitions of "insanity," "crime," and sexual "perversion" are social constructs by means of which ruling powers maintain their control. We accept these definitions as "natural" only because they are so ingrained in our culture.

Just as definitions of social and anti-social behavior promote the power of certain individuals and groups, so do particular versions of historical events. Certainly, the whitewashing of General Custer's now-infamous military campaigns against Native Americans served the desire of the white American power structure of his day to obliterate Native American peoples so that the government could seize their lands. And that same whitewashing continued to serve the white American power structure for many a decade beyond Custer's time, for even those who had knowledge of Custer's misdeeds deemed it unwise to air America's dirty historical laundry, even in front of Americans. Analogously, had the Nazis won World War II, we would all be reading a very different account of the war, and of the genocide of millions of Jews, than the accounts we read in American history books today. Thus, new historicism views historical accounts as narratives, as stories, that are inevitably biased according to the point of view, conscious or unconscious, of those who write them. The more unaware historians are of their biases—that is, the more "objective" they think they are—the more those biases are able to control their narratives.

So far, we've seen new historicism's claims about what historical analysis *cannot* do. Historical analysis (1) cannot be objective, (2) cannot adequately demonstrate that a particular spirit of the times or world view accounts for the complexities of any given culture, and (3) cannot adequately demonstrate that history is linear, causal, or progressive. We can't understand a historical event, object, or person in isolation from the web of discourses in which it was represented because we can't understand it in isolation from the meanings it carried at that time. The more we isolate it, the more we will tend to view it through the meanings of our own time and place and, perhaps, our own desire to believe that the human race is improving with the passage of time.

Given these limitations, what *can* historical analysis accomplish? What approaches to historical understanding can be developed, and, most important for our purposes, what kinds of analysis can new historical literary critics attempt? If you've read Chapter Eight, "Deconstructive Criticism," you're in a good position to understand the answer to these questions because a good deal of new historical practice incorporates deconstructive insights about human language and experience. For example, we might say that new historicism deconstructs the traditional opposition between history (traditionally thought of as factual) and literature (traditionally thought of as fictional). For new historicism considers history a text that can be interpreted the same way literary critics interpret literary texts, and conversely, it considers literary texts cultural artifacts that can tell us something about the interplay of discourses, the web of social meanings, operating in the time and place in which those texts were written. Let's take a closer look at each of these claims by discussing, first, the key elements of new historical practice and, then, the implications of new historicism for literary criticism.

By and large, we know history only in its textual form, that is, in the form of the documents, written statistics, legal codes, diaries, letters, speeches, tracts, news articles, and the like in which are recorded the attitudes, policies, procedures, and events that occurred in a given time and place. That is, even when historians base their findings on the kinds of "primary sources" listed above, rather than on the interpretations of other historians (secondary sources), those primary sources are almost always in the form of some sort of writing. As such, they require the same kinds of analysis literary critics perform on literary texts. For example, historical documents can be studied in terms of their rhetorical strategies (the stylistic devices by which texts try to achieve their purposes); they can be deconstructed to reveal the limitations of their own ideological assumptions; and they can be examined for the purpose of revealing their explicit and implicit patriarchal, racist, and homophobic agendas. In addition, historical accounts—secondary sources, written during the period in question or at a later date—can be analyzed in the same manner.

In other words, new historicists consider both primary and secondary sources of historical information forms of narrative. Both tell some kind of story, and therefore those stories can be analyzed using the tools of literary criticism. Indeed, we might say that in bringing to the foreground the suppressed historical narratives of marginalized groups—such as women, people of color, the poor, the working class, gay men and lesbians, prisoners, the inhabitants of mental institutions, and so on—new historicism has deconstructed the white, male, Anglo-European historical narrative to reveal its disturbing, hidden sub-text: the experiences of those peoples it has oppressed in order to maintain the dominance that allowed it to control what most Americans know about history.

In fact, a focus on the historical narratives of marginalized peoples has been such an important feature of new historicism that some theorists have asked how new historicists can accept narratives from oppressed peoples any more readily than they have accepted narratives from the patriarchal Anglo-European power structure. One answer to this question is that a plurality of voices, including an equal representation of historical narratives from all groups, helps insure that a *master narrative*—a narrative told from a single cultural point of view that, nevertheless, presumes to offer the only accurate version of history—will no longer control our historical understanding. At this point in time, we still do not have an equal representation of historical narratives from all groups. And even as the historical narratives of some groups are becoming more and more numerous, such as those of women and people of color, those narratives generally do not receive the same kind of attention as patriarchal Anglo-European narratives do in the classroom, where most of us learn about history. Therefore, new historicism tries to promote the development of and gain attention for the histories of marginalized peoples.

A plurality of historical voices also tends to raise issues that new historicism considers important, such as how ideology operates in the formation of personal and group identity, how a culture's perception of itself (for example, Americans' belief that they are rugged individualists) influences its political, legal, and social policies and customs, and how power circulates in a given culture. We can see how a plurality of historical voices tends to raise these kinds of issues if we imagine the differences among the following hypothetical college courses on the American Revolution: (1) a course that studies traditional American accounts of the war; (2) a course that contrasts traditional American accounts of the war with traditional British, French, Dutch, and Spanish accounts of the war, countries for whom the American Revolution was but a moment in their struggle for colonial power, primarily in the Caribbean; (3) and a course that contrasts the above accounts with Native American accounts of the war recorded from the oral histories of tribes that were affected by it.

As we move, in our imagination, from the first course to the second and then to the third, our focus moves farther away from the "factual" content of historical accounts and foregrounds, instead, the ways in which history is a text that is interpreted by different cultures to fit the ideological needs of their own power structures, which is a new historical concern. In this context, new historicism might be defined as the history of stories cultures tell themselves about themselves. Or, as a corrective to some traditional historical accounts, new historicism might be defined as the history of lies cultures tell themselves. Thus, there is no history, in the traditional sense of the term. There are only representations of history.

In addition to its focus on marginalized historical narratives, new historical analysis involves what is called *thick description*, a term borrowed from anthropology. Thick description attempts, through close, detailed examination of a given cultural production—such as birthing practices, ritual ceremonies, games, penal codes, works of art, copyright laws, and the like—to discover the meanings that particular cultural production had for the people in whose community it occurred and to reveal the social conventions, cultural codes, and ways of seeing the world that gave that production those meanings. Thus, thick description is not a search for facts but a search for meanings, and as the examples of cultural productions listed above illustrate, thick description focuses on the personal side of history—the history of family dynamics, of leisure activities, of sexual practices, of childrearing customs—as much as or more than on such traditional historical topics as military campaigns and the passage of laws. Indeed, because traditional historicism tended to ignore or marginalize private life as subjective and irrelevant, new historicism tries to compensate for this omission by bringing issues concerned with private life into the foreground of historical enquiry.

Let me summarize an example of thick description offered by anthropologist Clifford Geertz in *The Interpretation of Cultures*. Imagine a young man winking at someone across a crowded room. A "thin description" of the event would describe it as a rapid contraction of the right eyelid—period. A thick description would attempt to find out what the wink *meant* in the context in which it occurred. First, was it a wink—that is, a public gesture intended to communicate a message—or just an involuntary twitch? If it was a wink, was it a wink performing its usual activity of imparting a conspiratorial signal? Or was it a fake wink, intended to make others believe a conspiracy was underway when, in fact, it was not? In this case, the wink would not mean conspiracy but deception. Or was it a parody of the fake wink just described, intended to satirize the person who winked in order to deceive? In this case, the wink would mean neither conspiracy nor deception, but ridicule. Now suppose that, in this last example, the would-be satirist is unsure of his ability: he doesn't want to be mistaken for someone merely twitching or winking; he wants his friends to know that he's mocking someone. So to be sure he can do it properly, he practices his satirical wink in front of a mirror. In this case, the wink would have a complicated meaning: it would be the rehearsal of a parody of a friend faking a wink to deceive others that a conspiracy is underway. Although this example of thick description may push the point a bit far, it illustrates the new historical notion that history is a matter of interpretations, not facts, and that interpretations always occur within a framework of social conventions.

Finally, new historicism's claim that historical analysis is unavoidably subjective is not an attempt to legitimize a self-indulgent, "anything goes" attitude toward the writing of history. Rather, the inevitability of personal bias makes it imperative that new historicists be as aware of and as forthright as possible about their own psychological and ideological positions relative to the material they analyze so that their readers can have some idea of the human "lens" through which they are viewing the historical issues at hand. This practice is called *self positioning*.

For example, near the end of Louis Montrose's new historical essay, "Professing the Renaissance: The Poetics and Politics of Culture," he announces his own biases, which include those produced by his role as a Renaissance scholar and professor. He tells us that he has a personal investment in those representations of the Renaissance in texts for which he feels a particular affinity, such as those of Shakespeare and Spenser. Furthermore, he acknowledges that, in analyzing these texts, he writes about issues that are socially relevant today because he wants to participate not only in the current re-thinking of Elizabethan culture but in the current re-thinking of our own. Finally, Montrose admits that although his writing works to undermine traditional historical approaches to literary scholarship—such as the traditional demarcation of a finite period called the Renaissance to which specific cultural qualities are attributed—he has, as a professor and Renaissance scholar, "a complex and substantial stake in sustaining and reproducing the very institutions whose operations [he] wish[es] to call into question" (30).

Before we discuss the implications of new historicism for literary criticism, let's pause for a moment to review its key concepts.

1. The writing of history is a matter of interpretations, not facts. Thus, all historical accounts are narratives and can be analyzed using many of the tools used by literary critics to analyze narrative.

2. History is neither linear (it does not proceed neatly from cause A to effect B and from cause B to effect C) nor progressive (the human species is not steadily improving over the course of time).

3. Power is never wholly confined to a single person or a single level of society. Rather, power circulates in a culture through exchanges of material goods, exchanges of human beings, and most important for literary critics, as we'll see below, exchanges of ideas through the various discourses a culture produces.

4. There is no monolithic (single, unified, universal) spirit of an age, and there is no adequate totalizing explanation of history (an explanation that provides a single key to all aspects of a given culture). There is only a dynamic, unstable interplay among discourses, the meanings of which the historian can try to analyze, though that analysis will always be incomplete, accounting for only a part of the historical picture.

5. Personal identity—like historical events, texts, and artifacts—is shaped by and shapes the culture in which it emerges. Thus, cultural categories such as normal and abnormal, sane and insane, are matters of definition. Put another way, our individual identity consists of the narratives we tell ourselves about ourselves, and we draw the material for our narratives from the circulation of discourses that constitutes our culture.

6. All historical analysis is unavoidably subjective. Historians must therefore reveal the ways in which they know they have been positioned, by their own cultural experience, to interpret history.

New Historicism and Literature

How, specifically, do new historical concepts operate in the domain of literary criticism? Although new historical literary criticism embeds our study of literary texts in the study of history, the study of history, as we've just seen, isn't what it used to be. Therefore, new historical criticism has little in common with traditional historical criticism. The latter, which dominated literary studies in the nineteenth century and the early decades of the twentieth, confined itself largely to studies of the author's life, in order to discover his or her intentions in writing the work, or to studies of the historical period in which the work was written, in order to reveal the spirit of the age, which the text was then shown to embody. For traditional literary historians, literature existed in a purely subjective realm, unlike history, which consisted of objectively discernable facts. Therefore, literature could never be interpreted to mean anything that history didn't authorize it to mean.

As you may recall from Chapter Five, the New Criticism, which dethroned traditional historical criticism and controlled literary studies from the 1940s to the 1960s, rejected traditional historicism's approach to literature. For the New Critics, the only thing literary historians could offer was interesting background material about literary works. The understanding of a text's meaning, however, has nothing whatsoever to do with history, the New Critics argued, because great literary works are timeless, autonomous (self-sufficient) art objects that exist in a realm beyond history. As a result of New Critical dominance, the historical study of literature faded into the background and tried to content itself with the tasks New Criticism deemed its proper work: for example, providing background material on authors' lives and times—which would not, however, be used to interpret their works—and preserving, through the provision of accurate editions of revered works, the canon of great literature.

New historicism, which emerged in the late 1970s, rejects both traditional historicism's marginalization of literature and New Criticism's enshrinement of the literary text in a timeless dimension beyond history. For new historical critics, a literary text doesn't embody the author's intention or illustrate the spirit of the age that produced it, as traditional literary historians asserted. Nor are literary texts self-sufficient art objects that transcend the time and place in which they were written, as New Critics believed. Rather, literary texts are cultural artifacts that can tell us something about the interplay of discourses, the web of social meanings, operating in the time and place in which the text was written. And they can do so because the literary text is, itself, part of the interplay of discourses, a thread in the dynamic web of social meaning. For new historicism, the literary text and the historical situation from which it emerged are equally important because text (the literary work) and context (the historical conditions that produced it) are mutually constitutive: they create each other. Like the dynamic interplay between individual identity and society, literary texts shape and are shaped by their historical contexts.

Perhaps we can best see how new historical critics differ from their traditional counterparts by noting some of the ways in which new historical readings of specific literary works might contrast with traditional historical readings of those same works. We'll look at two well-known texts, Joseph Conrad's *Heart of Darkness* (1902) and Toni Morrison's *Beloved* (1987). It's interesting to note that, in our first example, the author wrote about a situation—Europe's commercial exploitation of Africa—produced by his own society and one that he'd experienced first-hand. In our second example, the author wrote about a population—former slaves struggling to survive both their own memories of the past and the harsh realities of daily life in antebellum Ohio—that had lived over one hundred years before the publication of her novel. However, neither Conrad's first-hand experience with his subject matter nor Morrison's temporal distance from hers means that either narrative is necessarily more "accurate" than the other. For traditional historical criticism, the historical accuracy of both texts must be judged by comparisons with historical accounts of the populations represented. And for new historicism, historical "accuracy" is never a certainty: *Heart of Darkness* and *Beloved* offer us interpretations of the populations they depict, which we can use, in turn, to help us interpret both those populations and the circulation of discourses within which Conrad and Morrison wrote these novels.

A traditional historical reading of *Heart of Darkness* might analyze, based on historical accounts of European activities in the Congo during the nineteenth century, how faithful the novel is to the historical realities of European exploitation of human and natural resources in its quest for ivory. Was the waste of human life as flagrant as Conrad portrays it? What were the politics involved in the division of African territories among various European powers and in the administration of those territories? Or a traditional literary historian might examine biographical materials in order to determine what parts of the novel are drawn from Conrad's actual experience during his own trip up the Congo River as a steamship captain for a Belgian company. To what extent are Marlow's experiences actually those of Conrad? To what extent does the novel depict events that Conrad saw or heard about himself? Finally, a traditional historical critic might analyze biographical materials in order to learn about Conrad's creative imagination. What was the influence on Conrad's writing of his early interest in the great explorers of the nineteenth century? Did he keep extensive journals of his experiences as a sailor, or did he write largely from memory? How did his experience in the Congo, including the permanent impairment of his health that resulted therefrom, affect his artistic production?

Similarly, a traditional historical reading of *Beloved* might analyze— based on historical accounts of nineteenth-century American slaves, slave holders, and former slaves—whether or not Morrison's depiction of this aspect of American experience is faithful to historical reality. Do her portraits of the Garners, their neighbors, Schoolteacher, and the Bodwins accurately represent the range of values held by slave owners and abolitionists at that time? Did Morrison capture the conflicting viewpoints that delineate the spirit of that troubled age? Or a traditional historical reading might investigate the circumstances of the novel's composition in order to find the historical sources of her characters, setting, and plot. For example, to what extent was Sethe's story modeled on that of runaway-slave Margaret Garner, who, like Sethe, killed her baby daughter to save her from being returned to her master's plantation? What other characters and events in the novel are based on actual historical figures and events? What specific historical sources—newspaper accounts, slave narratives, legal documents, records of the middle passage, history books, and the like—did Morrison draw upon? Finally, a traditional historical critic might analyze the author's reading habits in order to find evidence of the influence of other literary works on her own artistic technique. What African-American literature, historical fiction, or southern fiction did she read, and can their influence be perceived in the novel's plot, characterization, or style?

In contrast to these traditional historical concerns, a new historical analysis of *Heart of Darkness* might examine the ways in which Conrad's narrative embodies two conflicting discourses present in his own culture: anti-colonialism and Eurocentrism. The novel's anti-colonialist theme, which seems to be a primary focus of the text, can be seen in its representation of the evils of Europe's subordination and exploitation of African peoples. However, as Chinua Achebe observes, the novel nevertheless speaks from an (apparently unconscious) Eurocentric perspective: Marlow's harrowing insight into the European character consists of his realization that Europeans are, beneath their veneer of civilization, as "savage" as the African peoples they intend to subdue, which means that African tribal culture is held to epitomize "savagery." Or, despite the novel's Eurocentric bias, a new historical critic might analyze the text as a kind of prototype, or early embodiment, of new historical analysis. As Brook Thomas points out, Conrad's novel debunks the traditional historicist belief that history is progressive, that the human species improves over time; and its narrative structure, which obscures plot events behind a hazy veil of subjective description, implies that we do not have access to a clear, unbiased view of the past. Finally, a new historical analysis of *Heart of Darkness* might examine the history of the novel's reception by critics and the reading public to discover how the novel shaped and was shaped by discourses circulating at its point of origin (the time and place in which the book was written and published) and over the passage of time, including speculations about its relationship to possible future audiences. For example, how might the novel's reception over time reveal the ways in which interpretations of the text shaped and have been shaped by the discourses of historical progressivism, social Darwinism, white supremacy, Afrocentrism, multiculturalism, new historicism, and so on?

Similarly, a new historical analysis of *Beloved* might examine how the novel's departures from the historical accounts on which it is based constitute a revision of those accounts, that is, an interpretation of the history it represents. For example, to what extent do the transformations of Denver and Paul D, as they come to understand Sethe's experience, function as a guide for our own understanding of Sethe's historical situation? Or a new historical critic might examine how *Beloved* was shaped by and has shaped the modern debate between two conflicting views of slavery: (1) that slaves were, for the most part, reduced to a childlike dependency upon their masters and (2) that slaves managed, much more thoroughly and consistently than has been reported by traditional white historians, to build a coherent system of resistance through the creation of their own coded forms of communication, the establishment of their own communal ties, and the strategic use of personae (such as the "happy slave" or the "dim-witted slave") as camouflage for their opinions, intentions, and subversive activities. Finally, a new historical reading might investigate the circulation of mid-nineteenth-century discourses with which specific elements of the plot interact. For example, how do the various views of Sethe depicted in the novel—such as those of Schoolteacher, Mrs. Garner, Amy Denver, Mr. Bodwin, Stamp Paid, Ella, Beloved, and Paul D—reinforce or undermine the mid-nineteenth-century discourses of white supremacy, abolitionism, male supremacy, and motherly love?

As you may have noticed, in all of the above examples of traditional historical criticism, history—the historical situation represented in the text, the population portrayed, the author's life and times—is an objective reality that can be known and against which the subjective literary work is interpreted or measured. In contrast, in the new historical examples, the focus is on how the literary text functions, itself, as a historical discourse interacting with other historical discourses: those circulating at the time and place in which the text is set, at the time the text was published, or at later points in the history of the text's reception. For new historicism is concerned not with historical events as events, but with the ways in which events are interpreted, with historical discourses, with ways of seeing the world and modes of meaning. Indeed, as we saw earlier, historical events are viewed by new historicists not as facts to be documented but as "texts" to be "read" in order to help us speculate about how human cultures, at various historical "moments," have made sense of themselves and their world. We can't really know exactly what happened at any given point in history, but we can know what the people involved believed happened—we can know from their own accounts the various ways in which they interpreted their experience—and we can interpret those interpretations.

For new historical literary critics, then, the literary text, through its representation of human experience at a given time and place, is an interpretation of history. As such, the literary text maps the discourses circulating at the time it was written and is, itself, one of those discourses. That is, the literary text shaped and was shaped by the discourses circulating in the culture in which it was produced. Likewise, our interpretations of literature shape and are shaped by the culture in which we live.

Cultural Criticism

If you've just read the sections on new historicism, you're already acquainted with many of the theoretical premises of cultural criticism, for the two fields share a good deal of the same theoretical ground. In fact, there are more similarities between them than there are differences. For example, cultural criticism shares with new historicism the view that human history and culture constitute a complex arena of dynamic forces of which we can construct only a partial, subjective picture. Both fields share the belief that individual human subjectivity (selfhood) develops in a give-and-take relationship with its cultural milieu: while we are constrained within the limits set for us by our culture, we may struggle against those limits or transform them. And both fields are interdisciplinary or, perhaps more accurately, anti-disciplinary, for both argue that human experience, which is the stuff of human history and culture, cannot be adequately understood by means of academic disciplines that carve it up into such artificially separated categories as sociology, psychology, literature, and so forth. Indeed, both cultural criticism and new historicism draw heavily on the same philosophical sources, in particular the work of French philosopher Michel Foucault, and in practice, cultural criticism is not always readily distinguishable from new historicism.

In addition to its similarity to new historicism, cultural criticism can pose an initial problem for beginners in the way the term is often used, in its broadest sense, to refer to any kind of analysis of any aspect of culture. For example, the readings of *The Great Gatsby* offered in this textbook in the chapters on Marxist criticism, feminist criticism, lesbian/gay/queer criticism, and postcolonial/African-American criticism could all be considered examples of cultural criticism, in its broadest sense, because all of these interpretations use the novel to explore some aspect of American culture. Even my psychoanalytic reading of Fitzgerald's novel—which suggests that the story illustrates the psychology of dysfunctional love— could be revised to function as a cultural critique if I were to argue that the kind of dysfunctional love illustrated in *The Great Gatsby* is a form of cultural malaise produced by the cultural values that came to the fore during the American 1920s. And herein lies one important difference between cultural criticism and new historicism. Cultural criticism often draws upon such political theories as those listed above because it tends to be much more politically oriented than new historicism.

Originally an outgrowth of Marxist criticism, then organized as an analytical approach in its own right during the mid-1960s, cultural criticism, in the narrower definition of the term, argues that working-class culture has been misunderstood and undervalued. The dominant class dictates what forms of art are to be considered "high" (superior) culture, such as the ballet, the opera, and the other "fine" arts. Forms of popular culture, on the other hand—such as television situation comedies, popular music, and "pulp" fiction—have been relegated to the status of "low" (inferior) culture. For cultural critics, however, there is no meaningful distinction between so-called "high" and "low" forms of culture. For all cultural productions can be analyzed to reveal the *cultural work* they perform—that is, the ways in which they shape our experience by transmitting or transforming ideologies—which means, of course, the role of cultural productions in the circulation of power.

Indeed, cultural critics believe that the dominant class defines "high" and "low" culture in order to reinforce its own image of superiority and thus its own power. Nevertheless, cultural critics argue, subordinate populations produce forms of art that not only transform their own experience but affect the whole culture, as well. The AIDS quilt might be considered an example of such a cultural production. Clearly, many cultural critics draw upon Marxist, feminist, or other political theories in performing their analyses because those analyses often have political agendas, such as analyzing (and valorizing) the cultural productions of an oppressed group or exploring the power relations at work in the categorization of specific art forms as examples of "high" or "low" culture. As we saw earlier, many new historians, in contrast, believe that any single critical theory, political or otherwise, is too narrowly focused to adequately examine the complex operations of human culture.

So far, we've been using the word *culture* without actually defining what cultural criticism means by the term. For cultural critics, *culture* is a process, not a product; it is a lived experience, not a fixed definition. More precisely, a culture is a collection of interactive cultures, each of which is growing and changing, each of which is constituted at any given moment in time by the intersection of gender, race, ethnicity, sexual orientation, socioeconomic class, occupation, and similar factors that contribute to the experience of its members.

To sum up, then, cultural criticism shares new historicism's theoretical premises except in the following three instances.

1. Cultural criticism tends to be more overtly political in its support of oppressed groups.

2. Because of its political orientation, cultural criticism often draws upon Marxist, feminist, and other political theories in performing its analyses.

3. Cultural criticism, in the narrower sense of the term, is especially interested in popular culture.

It is important to remember, however, that even when cultural criticism analyzes the operations of oppression, it does not view oppressed peoples, as political theories sometimes do, as helpless victims. Rather, like new historicism, cultural criticism views oppressed peoples as both victimized by the dominant power structure and capable of resisting or transforming that power structure.

Cultural Criticism and Literature

For cultural critics, a literary text, or any other kind of cultural production, performs cultural work to the extent to which it shapes the cultural experience of those who encounter it, that is, to the extent to which it shapes our experience as members of a cultural group. According to Stephen Greenblatt, the following questions can help us begin to examine the kinds of cultural work performed by a literary text.

1. What kinds of behavior, what models of practice, does this work seem to enforce?
2. Why might readers at a particular time and place find this work compelling?
3. Are there differences between my values and the values implicit in the work I am reading?
4. Upon what social understandings does the work depend?
5. Whose freedom of thought or movement might be constrained implicitly or explicitly by this work?
6. What are the larger social structures with which these particular acts of praise or blame [that is, the text's apparent ethical orientation] might be connected? (226)

In Greenblatt's words, it might "appear that the analysis of culture is the servant of literary study, but in a liberal education broadly conceived it is literary study that is the servant of cultural understanding" (227). Thus, all of the above questions ask us to make connections between the literary text, the culture in which it emerged, and the cultures in which it is interpreted.

Perhaps it would help, at this point, to consider some specific applications of cultural criticism to literary works. Let's start by describing what a cultural critic might do with Joseph Conrad's *Heart of Darkness* and Toni Morrison's *Beloved*, the two texts we used earlier to illustrate the differences between traditional and new historical approaches to literature. As I mentioned before, many new historical readings could be considered forms of cultural criticism, broadly conceived. So all of the examples of new historical interpretations of Conrad's and Morrison's novels discussed earlier could be considered examples of cultural criticism to the extent that these interpretations examine the kind of cultural work performed by the literary text.

Let's look, however, at what kinds of readings might distinguish cul

tural critiques of *Heart of Darkness* and *Beloved* from new historical interpretations of these works. Given that both novels have been canonized as
works of "high" culture, a cultural critic, in the narrower sense of the
term, might choose to analyze popular representations of these novels,
rather than just the novels themselves. For example, a cultural critic
might study Francis Ford Coppola's *Apocalypse Now* (1978), which as
most film fans know is based on Conrad's novel, or the made-for-television version of *Heart of Darkness* starring John Malkovich (1993). Similarly, a cultural critic might examine the film version of *Beloved* starring
Oprah Winfrey (1998) or a television mini-series that might someday be
produced based on Morrison's novel.

In analyzing these popular forms of canonized works, a cultural critic
might try to determine the ways in which the popular versions transform
the ideological content of the novels. For example, does the film version
seem to have a darker vision of human nature than the novel? Or, in contrast, does the film provide a more optimistic view of the human condition that the novel does not offer? How does the film version handle narrative ambiguities, such as Marlow's reliability in *Heart of Darkness* or the
meaning of the baby ghost in *Beloved*? Most important, what do these
transformations suggest about the popular imagination—that is, about
the psychological and ideological needs of the viewing public—or about
the entertainment industry's conception of the viewing public?

A cultural critic would also be inclined to take into account the ways in
which a media production might not be viewed the way the entertainment
industry intends it to be viewed. For example, as John Fiske observes,

> [h]omeless Native Americans . . . chose to watch old westerns on the
> VCR in their shelter, but they selected only the first half of them, and
> switched off the movie at the point when the wagon train had been
> successfully attacked, the fort captured—they chose not to watch the
> reassertion of white empire. Aboriginal people watching the Rambo
> movies in Australia chose to ignore the conflict between the free west
> and the communist east and focused instead on the conflict between
> Rambo, whom they saw, by a selection of physical and behavioral char-
> acteristics, as a member of the third world like them, and the white
> officer class that systematically and mistakenly underestimated his abili-
> ties. (327)

So whether examining popular culture, "high" culture, or both, cultural
critics try to map the changing ideological functions that a given cultural
production performs at the hands of those who respond to it.

Some Questions New Historical and Cultural Critics Ask about Literary Texts

The following questions are intended to summarize approaches to literary analysis employed by new historicists and cultural critics. In the terminology of cultural criticism, these questions all offer us ways to examine the cultural work performed by literary texts. As you read these questions and imagine the ways in which a new historical or cultural critic might address them, keep in mind that, for such critics, no historical event, artifact, or ideology can be completely understood in isolation from the innumerable historical events, artifacts, and ideologies among which it circulates, and our own cultural experience inevitably influences our perceptions, making true objectivity impossible. For we can use new historical and cultural criticism properly only if we keep clearly in mind that our analysis is always incomplete, partial, and our perspective is always subjective. We can't stand outside our own culture and analyze texts from an objective vantage point. We can write only from within our own historical moment.

1. How does the literary text function as part of a continuum with other historical/cultural texts from the same period, for example, penal codes, birthing practices, educational priorities, the treatment of children under the law, other art forms (including popular art forms), attitudes toward sexuality, and the like? That is, taken as part of a "thick description" of a given culture at a given point in history, what does this literary work add to our tentative understanding of human experience in that particular time and place, including the ways in which individual identity shapes and is shaped by cultural institutions?

2. How can we use a literary work to "map" the interplay of both traditional and subversive discourses circulating in the culture in which that work emerged and/or the cultures in which the work has been interpreted? Put another way, how does the text promote ideologies that support and/or undermine the prevailing power structures of the time and place in which it was written and/or interpreted?

3. Using rhetorical analysis (analysis of a text's purpose and the stylistic means by which it tries to achieve that purpose), what does the literary text add to our understanding of the ways in

which literary and non-literary discourses (such as political, scientific, economic, and educational theories) have influenced, overlapped with, and competed with one another at specific historical moments?

4. What does the literary work suggest about the experience of groups of people who have been ignored, under-represented, or misrepresented by traditional history (for example, laborers, prisoners, women, people of color, lesbians and gay men, children, the insane, and so on)? Keep in mind that new historical and cultural criticism usually include attention to the intersection of the literary work with non-literary discourses prevalent in the culture in which the work emerged and/or in the cultures in which it has been interpreted and often focus on such issues as the circulation of power and the dynamics of personal and group identity.

5. How has the work's reception by literary critics and the reading public—including the reception at its point of origin, changing responses to the work over time, and its possible future relationship with its audience—been shaped by and shaped the culture in which that reception occurred?

Depending upon the literary text in question, we might ask one or any combination of these questions. Or we might come up with a useful question not listed here. These are just some starting points to get us thinking about literary texts as new historical and cultural critics do. Keep in mind that not all new historical or cultural critics will interpret the same work in the same way even if they focus on the same theoretical concepts and have the same purpose. As in every field, even expert practitioners disagree. Our goal is to use new historicism and cultural criticism to help enrich our reading of literature by helping us see how literary texts participate in the circulation of discourses, shaping and shaped by the culture in which they emerge and by the cultures in which they are interpreted; by helping us see the ways in which the circulation of discourses *is* the circulation of political/social/intellectual/economic power; and by helping us see the ways in which our own cultural positioning influences our interpretations of literary and non-literary texts.

The following reading of F. Scott Fitzgerald's *The Great Gatsby* is offered as an example of what a new historical interpretation of that novel might yield. In the terminology of the cultural critics, it analyzes the cultural work performed by the novel. I call my interpretation of Fitzgerald's novel a new historical reading because it doesn't have the kind of overt political agenda often associated with cultural criticism and because I rely rather heavily on terminology associated with new historicism. However, the overlap between the two fields is such that my interpretation could also be called, quite legitimately, a cultural critique, especially because my argument makes no distinction between Fitzgerald's canonized "classic" and various forms of popular culture informed by the same ideology.

Specifically, I argue that the novel circulates one of the dominant discourses of the period in which it was written: the discourse of the self-made man, which held that any poor boy in America, if he had the right personal qualities, could rise to the top of the financial world. In addition, I examine the ways in which *The Great Gatsby* embodies one of the central contradictions of the discourse of the self-made man: although this discourse claims to open the annals of American history to all those who have the ambition and perseverance required to "make their mark," the discourse is permeated by the desire to "escape" history, to transcend the historical realities of time, place, and human limitation.

The Discourse of the Self-Made Man: A New Historical Reading of *The Great Gatsby*

F. Scott Fitzgerald's *The Great Gatsby* (1925) was published during one of America's greatest periods of economic growth. As the nation expanded its borders and developed its industries between the end of the Civil War in 1865 and the stock-market crash in 1929, many private fortunes were made. Everyone in America knew the success stories of millionaires like John D. Rockefeller, Jay Gould, Jim Fisk, Andrew Carnegie, J. P. Morgan, Philip Armour, and James J. Hill. Even Gatsby's father, an uneducated and unsuccessful farmer, is aware of these stories. He says of his son, "If he'd of lived he'd of been a great man. A man like James J. Hill. He'd of helped build up the country" (176; ch. 9). With the exception of J. P. Morgan, the son of a wealthy banker, all of these millionaires were self-made men: from very humble beginnings they rose to their position at the top of the financial world. And popular belief held that any poor boy in America, with the right personal qualities, could do the same.

Thus, a dominant discourse of the period was the discourse of the self-made man, which circulated in the so-called "success manuals" of the period; in the self-improvement speeches and essays composed by the self-made millionaires of that era; in the Horatio Alger novels; in the McGuffey Readers, which were used throughout the nation to teach young children to read; and in the biographies of famous self-made men. Fitzgerald's novel participates in the circulation of this discourse, I think, in at least two significant ways. It reflects the major tenets of the discourse and, I would argue, it embodies one of its central contradictions: the discourse of the self-made man, while it claims to open the annals of American history to all those who have the ambition and perseverance required to "make their mark," is permeated by the desire to "escape" history, to transcend the historical realities of time, place, and human limitation.

Let's begin by examining the ways in which *The Great Gatsby* reflects the major tenets of the discourse of the self-made man. Of course, readers frequently notice the similarities between Gatsby's boyhood "schedule"—in which the young man divided his day among physical exercise, the study of electricity, work, sports, the practice of elocution and poise, and the study of needed inventions—and the self-improvement ideology found in the autobiography of Benjamin Franklin, America's original self-made man. Obviously, Gatsby hoped, indeed planned, to live the "rags-to-riches" life associated with the self-made millionaires of his day. However, the characterization of Gatsby draws on the self-improvement tradition more thoroughly than some readers today may realize.

During the period in which Gatsby lived, 1890–1922—roughly the same historical period from which the novel emerged, for Fitzgerald was born in 1896 and *The Great Gatsby* was published in 1925—books that explained how poor boys could rise to heights of great wealth, called "success manuals," flourished. In Austin Bierbower's *How to Succeed* (1900), a representative example of the genre, the following advice is given to the prospective self-made man: work hard, have a clear purpose, be prepared for opportunity, don't procrastinate, persevere, keep in good physical condition, and avoid drink. Poor boys have an advantage over rich boys, Bierbower notes, because they are introduced to hard work at a young age and motivated by financial need to apply themselves. In contrast, many wealthy youth, the author points out, avoid hard work and focus instead on insubstantial goals like fashion and etiquette, thereby sometimes failing to increase or even maintain the fortunes they inherited. The virtues extolled in similar publications include, in addition, the importance of saving money and of avoiding such slothful behaviors as smoking, using slang, and keeping bad company. In short, rising young men were advised to avoid any behavior that wasted time, cost money, or was injurious to health or reputation.

Making himself useful to his parents was also considered a good way for a young boy to develop the traits of industry and initiative, which would serve him well later in life. And for similar reasons, it was generally accepted that a rural upbringing, preferably on a farm, was superior to a boyhood spent in the city.[2]

Jay Gatsby fits this profile in a number of ways. He was born to poor "farm people" (104; ch. 6) and spent his youth in rural Minnesota. His boyhood list of "General Resolves," found in his copy of *Hopalong Cassidy* just below his Franklinesque daily schedule of activities, reads like a mini-success manual:

> No wasting time at Shafters or [a name, indecipherable]
> No more smokeing or chewing
> Bath every other day
> Read one improving book or magazine per week
> Save $5.00 [crossed out] $3.00 per week
> Be better to parents (181–82; ch. 9)

Gatsby's physical fitness, a frequently mentioned self-improvement virtue, is evident in Nick's description of his "balancing himself on the dashboard of his car with that resourcefulness of movement that is so peculiarly American—that comes . . . with the formless grace of our nervous, sporadic games" (68; ch. 4). Gatsby's "elaborate formality of speech," which gives Nick the impression that he is "picking his words with care" (53; ch. 3), illustrates the self-improvement virtue of avoiding slang, and we see another behavior recommended by success manuals in Gatsby's strict avoidance of alcohol, even at his own parties.

Unlike Tom Buchanan and Nick Carraway, Gatsby was motivated by financial need to apply himself: he made his fortune during his first three years with Wolfshiem. Even Gatsby's outstanding war record marked him as a young man certain to get ahead in the world, while Nick's military experience seems singularly undistinguished, and we hear no mention of Tom's at all. Indeed, the characterization of Tom and Nick exemplify the dictum of the self-improvement tradition that inherited wealth is a handicap to self-improvement: Tom does nothing with his life but find more and more extravagant ways to spend his inherited fortune, while Nick, thirty years old and still being supported by his father while he learns the bond business, feels he has no clear direction in life. Finally, George Wilson's rather pathetic failure to adequately support himself and his wife serves as an implicit warning about the fate of poor men who, unlike Gatsby, lack the fortitude and drive to "pull themselves up by their bootstraps."

We see the same kind of success ideology at work in the speeches and essays in which many self-made millionaires, themselves, revealed the secrets of their success, as Andrew Carnegie often did. In "The Road to Business Success" (1885), for example, Carnegie tells the would-be self-made man to aim high, save his money, and avoid liquor. To rise in the business world, Carnegie notes, a young man must be able to think for himself: "There never was a great character who did not sometimes smash the routine regulations and make new ones for himself" (8). In "How to Win Fortune" (1890), Carnegie argues that, given the competitive nature of the business world, it is unwise for the prospective self-made man to waste precious time acquiring a college education, even if he were able to somehow work his way through, because the time he spends in college will put him behind the young man who apprentices himself to a captain of industry at an early age. A "college education," Carnegie says, "seems almost fatal to [the] success" (91) of the self-made man.

As we saw above, Gatsby believed, even as a teenager, in the importance of saving money, and "he formed the habit of letting liquor alone" (107; ch. 6) early in life as well. In contrast to Tom and Nick, who both graduated from Yale, Gatsby refused to waste time attending college: led by an "instinct toward his future glory," he quit after two weeks at "the small Lutheran college of Saint Olaf" (105; ch. 6). Perhaps the most interesting similarity between Carnegie's advice and Gatsby's behavior, however, is seen in Gatsby's consistent tendency to aim high and "smash the routine regulations" in order to "make new ones for himself" (Carnegie, "The Road" 8). Gatsby rose quickly in the esteem of Dan Cody, who "repos[ed] more and more trust in [him]" (106; ch. 6), just as he rose quickly to the rank of army major during World War I, just as he rose quickly in the organization of Meyer Wolfshiem. By the time we meet him, Gatsby clearly occupies an executive position, either in Wolfshiem's organization or in one of his own: he receives phone calls, at all hours and from various parts of the country, during which he makes decisions and gives orders to his underlings. And though Carnegie certainly didn't intend his advice to be taken in quite this way, Gatsby's disregard for routine regulations is obvious, of course, in his choice of a criminal career: he made his fortune in the management of bootlegging operations and the sale of fraudulent bonds.

Another kind of text that circulated the discourse of the self-made man were the novels of Horatio Alger, which were immensely popular during the late nineteenth and early twentieth centuries. In these tales, the hero is always a poor young boy who is hardworking, honest, neat, self-reliant, persevering, modest, kind, generous, and lucky. Luck, for Alger, included being ready to seize an opportunity when it occurs, which requires both imagination and nerve. In all of Alger's novels, the hero has obstacles to overcome, including a villain who cheats him in some way; there is a lesser hero in the story who helps him in some way; and there are one or more father figures in the form of successful, benevolent businessmen. The hero's outstanding qualities always end up bringing him some sort of financial success, and the stories thus extol the same virtues of the self-made man we see in the success manuals.

The Great Gatsby shares many important features with the Horatio Alger formula novel. Jay Gatsby's well-groomed appearance and quiet amiability, which is noted several times by Nick, give him much of the same appeal as the Alger hero, even if he doesn't share the latter's ethics. More striking, however, is the similarity in structure between Fitzgerald's novel and those of Alger. Like the Alger hero, Gatsby is of humble origins, willing to work hard to make his way in the world, and had more than enough imagination and nerve at his disposal when opportunity unexpectedly knocked in the form of Dan Cody:

> It was James Gatz who had been loafing along the beach that afternoon . . . but it was already Jay Gatsby who borrowed a row-boat, pulled out to the *Tuolomee* and informed Cody that a wind might catch him and break him up in half an hour. (104; ch. 6)

After working for Cody for five years and learning the ways of the world, Gatsby is cheated, again like the Alger hero, of his rightful reward: "a legacy of twenty-five thousand dollars" (107; ch. 6), promised to the twenty-three-year-old Gatsby in Cody's will, went instead, through some "legal device that was used against him" (107; ch. 6), to Cody's companion, Ella Kaye. Gatsby is also, in a sense, cheated out of Daisy Fay when Tom marries her while Gatsby is still overseas after World War I. Fitzgerald's hero perseveres, however, in his pursuit both of fortune and of Daisy, and before the novel closes he attains both goals. Finally, the role of the lesser hero who helps the Alger hero in some way is played by Nick Carraway, and the role of the businessman-father figure is played by Dan Cody, as we saw above, and by Meyer Wolfshiem, who "raised him up out of nothing" (179; ch. 9) when Gatsby returned penniless from the war.

Perhaps the most pervasive vehicles for the ideology of the self-made man were the McGuffey Readers, a series of elementary-school books used to teach reading, which were a dominant force in American education from the mid-nineteenth century to the early 1920s. The stories and poems contained in the Readers extol the same virtues promoted by the success manuals of the period: honesty, hard work, kindness, and the avoidance of alcohol and bad company. In addition, like the success manuals, Horatio Alger novels, and other texts that circulated the discourse of the self-made man, the Readers illustrated the belief that success is a product of good character. For example, a poor boy receives a job because the old man he has kindly helped cross the street turns out to own his own business. Or an orphan boy is adopted by a wealthy man because he has resisted the temptation to steal the man's gold watch.

As we have seen, Gatsby has many traits in common with the self-made hero, of which McGuffey's protagonists are just another version. And the job Gatsby receives from Dan Cody, which serves as his introduction to the world of financial success to which he has always aspired, is the product of the good deed he performed in rowing out to Cody's yacht to warn him of an impending storm, just as the success of McGuffey's boys is a product of their good character.

Finally, there is a startling resemblance between Gatsby's early life and the formative years of America's most famous self-made millionaires, the oft-told stories of which were another way in which the discourse of the self-made man circulated. In *The Robber Barons* (1934), Matthew Josephson details many of the common experiences shared by such self-made millionaires of the late nineteenth century as Jay Gould, Jim Fisk, Philip Armour, Andrew Carnegie, James Hill, John Rockefeller, and Jay Cooke. Although Josephson is not interested in literary analysis and makes no comparisons with *The Great Gatsby*, the similarities between the life stories Josephson narrates and the biography of Jay Gatsby are too striking to be ignored.

Born into poverty, "most of these young men," Josephson notes, "left the paternal shelter early in youth, to wander alone and make their own way. . . . [T]hey showed promising signs of shiftiness and self-reliance in boyhood" (33). Although their companions often drank and gambled, these young men did not. Cool under pressure, "violence [did] not shake [them]" (35). Indeed, they often made their fortunes in the rush for gold or for the monopoly of natural resources, railroad lines, or stocks, all of which pursuits were not merely financially dangerous but physically dangerous as well: as fortunes were quickly made and lost, one's companions on the frontier, or even a group of stockholders one had defrauded on Wall Street, could turn into an angry, vengeful mob. And "[a]t the center of the stirring, shifting drama of material progress toward new railroads or gold fields," Josephson observes, "was the notion of individual fortune and change of station" (37).

In other words, much like Jay Gatsby, the self-made men of whom Josephson writes were driven by a desire to become rich and rise up out of the class into which they were born. And much like these self-made men, Gatsby left his parents' home as a teenager, wandered alone, and made his own way. Like them, he did not adopt the debilitating personal habits of his companions, and he made his fortune according to the dangerous rules of a violent sub-culture.

Clearly, *The Great Gatsby* reflects the discourse of the self-made man circulating in so many of the texts that both shaped and were shaped by American culture during the final decades of the nineteenth century and the early decades of the twentieth. For ideology does not observe boundaries between "high" and "popular" culture: a discourse circulating in such practical and mundane texts as success manuals, children's readers, and didactic formula-novels can also saturate the pages of one of the era's most sophisticated artistic productions.

However, the novel also serves as a comment upon the discourse of the self-made man to the extent that it reveals one of its central contradictions, which concerns the relationship of that discourse to history. Although the discourse of the self-made man claims to open the annals of American history to all those who have the ambition and perseverance required to "make their mark" on its pages, the discourse is permeated by the desire to escape history, to transcend the historical realities of time, place, and human limitation.

This contradiction appears in many of the autobiographical stories of the self-made millionaires mentioned above. Although self-made men often spoke of the harsh historical realities they experienced as children, particularly of their poverty, they did so only to celebrate how far they had come. And the form that celebration took, I would argue, constitutes a denial of historical reality because it was a way of reinventing the suffering self-made men saw in their youth as nothing but a prelude to their success. Looking back on their lives, they saw their boyhood selves as "future millionaires in training," so to speak, being honed in the workshop of "hard knocks" and fired in the kiln of poverty. Such an ideology didn't permit them to see the debilitating effects of the poverty they escaped on those who didn't manage to do the same.

Among the general population of America's impoverished, relatively few, in any generation, have become millionaires. According to the discourse of the self-made man, those who didn't rise to the top had only themselves to blame, which implies, of course, that poverty and the degrading influence of tenement life (not to mention the almost insurmountable obstacles raised against business opportunities for women and people of color) are no excuse for the failure to rise in the business world. Such failure was defined as a failure of one's character, pure and simple. This is why many self-made millionaires refused to give money to charity, confining their philanthropy to endowing libraries, museums, and universities, which could, they reasoned, help only those who were willing to help themselves and not encourage the slothful behavior that charity would, they believed, encourage.[3]

For example, in his autobiography, Andrew Carnegie describes the happy family life he enjoyed as a child of poor immigrant parents. He notes, in addition to his family's economic hardship, how politically active his relatives were, how education was valued by his parents, and how he was trained by his home environment to engage in rigorous debate on the issues of the day. Indeed, Carnegie observes that the economic poverty he suffered in childhood was richly compensated by the training and support he received in the bosom of a strong family. Yet he was apparently unable to realize that many other poor youngsters in his own neighborhood—for example, the sons of parents who did not understand the value of education or the sons of drunken, abusive parents—did not have the same advantages he had and therefore could not be expected to raise themselves up as readily as he did. That is, in Carnegie's desire to focus on his own transcendence of historical reality, he ignores those aspects of history that cannot be overcome so readily.

The Great Gatsby reflects this same desire to transcend history in Gatsby's efforts to deny his true origins. Gatsby's "parents were shiftless and unsuccessful farm people," but "his imagination had never really accepted them as his parents at all" (104; ch. 6). Instead, Gatsby invented a family, an Oxford education, and an inheritance in order to convince himself and others that he was born to wealth and social position. That is, Gatsby wants to deny the historical realities of socioeconomic class to which he had been subjected all his life. As Nick puts it, "Jay Gatsby . . . sprang from his Platonic conception of himself" (104; ch. 6). A Platonic conception is one that, by definition, is outside history: it exists in a timeless dimension untouched by daily occurrences in the material world. And this is the dimension in which Gatsby wants to live.

Gatsby's claim that Daisy's love for Tom "was just personal" (160; ch. 8), a statement that confuses Nick as well as many readers, makes sense in this context. In Gatsby's eyes, Daisy's love for Tom exists within history, within the domain of the personal, and is thus no competition for the love she and Gatsby share, which exists in a timeless dimension beyond history. Similarly, Gatsby's belief in our power over the past makes sense only if he conceives of his own life outside the bounds of historical reality. His conviction that the three years Daisy has spent married to Tom can be "obliterated" by her telling Tom that she never loved him, and that they can "repeat the past" by "go[ing] back to Louisville and be[ing] married from her house—just as if it were five years ago" (116; ch. 6) is a conviction one can hold only from a place outside history, a place where the past is repeatable because it is timelessly preserved, forever accessible.

The discourse of the self-made man also "erases history" in choosing to ignore or marginalize the enormous character flaws of many famous self-made men while simultaneously defining self-made success as a product of one's character rather than of one's environment. The success manuals from this period offered very little, if any, practical advice about business matters. All of their advice focused, instead, on attributes of character—from honesty and integrity in the workplace to frugality and sobriety in the home—because it was believed that success comes from within the man. Therefore, character, rather than education or business acumen, was considered the foundation of the self-made man. Yet some of the moral failings of self-made millionaires were the very factors that enabled them to rise to the top by enabling them to ruthlessly, and often unethically, destroy their business rivals. Of course, this aspect of historical reality was absent from the proliferation of texts that extolled the virtues of the self-made man, or it was recast, in the popular imagination, as a capitalist virtue: competitiveness, aggressiveness, toughness.

It is interesting to note, in this context, that since the publication of The Great Gatsby, the majority of critical response to the novel's title character has romanticized him much as American culture has romanticized the self-made man, by idealizing his desire to succeed and ignoring or marginalizing the means by which he fulfilled that desire. What an early reviewer said of Gatsby in 1925 has continued to represent the feeling of a good many readers over the course of the novel's reception: Gatsby's "is a vitality . . . the inner fire [of] which comes from living with an incorruptible dream, even if extraordinary material corruption has been practised in its realization" (E. K. 426). William Troy describes Gatsby, in 1945, as the "projected wish fulfillment" of the "consciousness of a race" (21). And Tom Burnam argues in 1952 that Gatsby "survives sound and whole in character, uncorrupted by the corruption which surrounded him" (105). In 1954 Marius Bewley writes that Gatsby is "all aspiration and goodness" (25): "an heroic personification of the American romantic hero" (14), who represents "the energy of the spirit's resistance" and "immunity to the final contamination" of "cheapness and vulgarity" (13). And Barry Edward Gross suggests in 1963 that "Gatsby's dream is essentially 'incorruptible'" because it "is essentially immaterial," which is why "he turns 'out all right at the end'" (57). Similarly, in 1978 Rose Adrienne Gallo argues that Gatsby "maintained his innocence" to the end (43), or as André Le Vot puts it in 1983, Gatsby never loses his "fundamental integrity, his spiritual intactness" (144). Even when the protagonist's darker side is acknowledged, it is excused. As Kent Cartwright argues in 1984, "Gatsby can be both criminal and romantic hero because the book creates for him a visionary moral standard that transcends the conventional and that his life affirms" (232). Or as Andrew Dillon sums up, in 1988, what he sees as the protagonist's merger of worldliness and spirituality, Gatsby is "a sensual saint" (50).[4]

Finally, the connection between the discourse of the self-made man and the desire to transcend history can be seen in the McGuffey Readers. In the self-improvement discourse that informs the bulk of the material in the Readers there is a striking absence of reference to historical reality. Even during the period directly after the Civil War, when poems and songs about the War abounded, the only "historical" piece included isn't historical at all: it's a sentimental poem called "The Blue and the Gray" (1867) in which soldiers from both sides are glorified in terms such that they could be soldiers from almost any war fought during almost any historical period. In other words, the poem creates a timeless world that remains untouched by historical events. As Henry Steele Commager puts it,

> [t]hough the original volumes of the Readers appeared when men could still remember the Revolutionary War and the War of 1812—McGuffey himself lived through that war, and on the Ohio frontier, too—there is no ardent hostility to Britain, no execration of George III, no atrocity story about the Indians. And though new Readers, and revisions of old Readers, poured from the presses all through the era of the Mexican War, of Manifest Destiny, and of Young America, the Readers reflect none of this: even the Oregon Trail and the gold rush to California were not allowed to ruffle the serenity of their pages. Even more startling is the fact that those who later revised the

> Readers . . . managed to avoid the Civil War! Aside from Francis Finch's
> "The Blue and the Gray"—a masterpiece of impartiality—the war
> might never have happened, as far as the Readers are concerned. (xiii)

History is also transcended in the McGuffey Readers through the
sentimentalization of experience. The Readers are full of sentimental descriptions of injured animals, of virtuous children rewarded for their un-
selfishness by some monetary windfall, of the peaceful deaths of angelic
children, and of heroic deeds. When experience is depicted in sentimental
terms, that experience becomes general rather than specific, "larger than
life" in the same way that fairy tales are larger than life: they exist in some
timeless dimension beyond the daily course of human events, beyond
history. As Stanley W. Lindberg observes about one of McGuffey's war
poems, it is "safely sentimental" (320), by which he means, of course, outside the fray of the political and social issues of the day, that is, outside
history.

There is a striking similarity between the overblown sentimentality
of the McGuffey Readers and the "appalling sentimentality" (118; ch. 6)
of the autobiographical narrative Gatsby offers Nick, a sentimentality
that removes Gatsby's life, just as it removed the McGuffey Readers, from
the realities of history. Gatsby tells Nick,

> My family all died and I came into a good deal of money. . . . After
> that I lived like a young rajah in all the capitals of Europe . . . collecting
> jewels, chiefly rubies, hunting big game, painting a little . . . and try-
> ing to forget something very sad that had happened to me long ago.
> (70; ch. 4)

Gatsby's autobiographical sketch sounds more like an outline for a staged
Victorian melodrama than a narrative about an actual life. As Nick puts
it, "The very phrases were worn so threadbare that they evoked no image
except that of a turbaned "character" leaking sawdust at every pore" (70;
ch. 4). But it is this sentimental "translation" of his life—which he offers,
Nick says, in a "solemn" voice, "as if the memory . . . still haunted him"
(70; ch. 4)—that allows Gatsby to escape historical reality into a "larger
than life" fairy tale.

Of course, the discourse of the self-made man retains much of its
vitality today. On an episode of the television series *Matlock*, for example, a son attempts to recuperate his murdered father's reputation as
a ruthless, unethical business executive by saying that his father was a
self-made man. Thus, the phrase still has the power to suggest that men

capable of achieving such an important and respected goal should not be judged too harshly for their ruthless, unethical behavior because it requires "toughness" to make it as a self-made man. Similarly, the television series *America's Castles*, which offers guided tours of America's great mansions and of the lives of the men who built them, relies heavily on the discourse of the self-made man, even quoting uncritically the self-serving statements of nineteenth- and early-twentieth-century self-made millionaires concerning their own hard work and integrity.

Furthermore, Jay Gatsby remains the icon of America's romanticization of the self-made man. That actor Robert Redford, who is generally typecast as a romantic hero, was chosen to play Gatsby in the movie version of Fitzgerald's novel released in 1974 reveals the persistence of a romantic view of Gatsby in the American popular imagination. Indeed, during a discussion of self-made, Oklahoma oil millionaire E. W. Marland on a recently aired episode of *America's Castles*, the narrator notes Fitzgerald's belief that the story of a hero is always a tragic story while it superimposes the cover of *The Great Gatsby* over a photo of Marland's mansion. In other words, the television show attempts to romanticize Marland by associating him with Jay Gatsby.

Clearly, *The Great Gatsby*'s embodiment of the complexities and contradictions of the discourse of the self-made man reveals the complexities and contradictions that informed the attitude of Fitzgerald's America toward the achievement of financial success. Without the discourse of the self-made man, Fitzgerald's best-known novel would not be possible. For the character of Jay Gatsby would simply be the "cheap sharper" (159; ch. 8)—just another criminal—he fears people will see in him. It is this discourse, as much as his devotion to Daisy and his boyish optimism, that makes it possible for Gatsby to remain the romantic figure he is today.

Fitzgerald's novel also shows us how the circulation of discourses has very personal implications for all of us. For it illustrates the ways in which cultural discourses are the raw materials from which we fashion our individual identity. Nick Carraway may think that Gatsby "sprang from his Platonic," ahistorical "conception of himself" (104; ch. 6), a belief Gatsby clearly shares, but Gatsby's personal identity did not so originate. As we have seen, James Gatz's creation of Jay Gatsby drew heavily upon the discourse of the self-made man, one of the dominant discourses circulating in the culture in which he lived. And like Jay Gatsby, all of us do the same. We each may draw upon different discourses, and we each may draw upon them in different ways, but it is through the discourses circulating in our culture that our individual identities are formed, are linked to one another, and are linked to the culture that both shapes and is shaped by each of us.

Questions for Further Practice: New Historical and Cultural Criticism of Other Literary Works

The following questions are intended as models. They can help you use new historical and cultural criticism to interpret the literary works to which they refer or other texts of your choice. Your purpose in addressing these questions, the way in which you focus your essay, and your own self-identified critical orientation will determine whether your essay is considered an example of new historical or cultural criticism.

1. What is the relationship between Hawthorne's depiction of Hester Prynne's transgression, in thought and deed, of repressive Puritan values in *The Scarlet Letter* (1850) and such revolutionary nineteenth-century activities as the abolitionist movement and the women's movement? In other words, how does the story of Hester Prynne (a colonial Puritan) embody and/or criticize these nineteenth-century ideologies as they were circulated in pamphlets, popular stories, political activities, and other cultural texts?

2. Toni Morrison's *The Bluest Eye* (1970) was published at a time when conservative American ideologies concerning race, class, gender, and social justice were being called into question in almost every domain of American life. What does the history of this novel's reception suggest about the circulation of conservative and liberal discourses addressing these pressing social issues since the time of the novel's publication to the present?

3. How was John Steinbeck's *The Grapes of Wrath* (1939) shaped by, and how did it shape, debates about the rights and responsibilities of workers circulating at the time the novel was published, for example, debates concerning the appropriate relationship among American business, government agencies, and the individual

citizen? In other words, what kinds of cultural work did the novel perform at the time of its publication?

4. In what ways does Kate Chopin's *The Awakening* (1899) interact with (reproduce, comment upon, question) debates about women's rights and responsibilities circulating at the time the novel was written, for example, debates concerning women's suffrage, economic independence, marriage, and motherhood?

5. What is the relationship between William Blake's "The Little Black Boy" (1789) and discourses concerning Africa and Africans circulating in England during the second half of the eighteenth century?

For Further Reading

All of the following works will help you develop your skills as new historical and cultural critics. Texts listed under "Category I" are written in language accessible to most beginners. Texts listed under "Category II" employ more technical language but are well worth the extra effort that may be required of some students new to the field.

Category I

Cox, Jeffrey N., and Larry J. Reynolds, eds. *New Historical Literary Study: Essays on Reproducing Texts, Representing History*. Princeton: Princeton UP, 1993.

Fiske, John. "Popular Culture." *Critical Terms for Literary Study*. 2nd ed. Eds. Frank Lentricchia and Thomas McLaughlin. Chicago: U of Chicago P, 1995. 321–335.

Foucault, Michel. *The Foucault Reader*. Ed. Paul Rabinow. New York: Pantheon, 1984.

Greenblatt, Stephen. "Culture." *Critical Terms for Literary Study*. 2nd ed. Eds. Frank Lentricchia and Thomas McLaughlin. Chicago: U of Chicago P, 1995. 225–232.

———. "The Circulation of Social Energy." *Shakespearean Negotiations: The Circulation of Social Energy in Renaissance England*. Berkeley: U of California P, 1988. 1–20.

Patterson, Lee. "Literary History." *Critical Terms for Literary Study*. 2nd ed. Eds. Frank Lentricchia and Thomas McLaughlin. Chicago: U of Chicago P, 1995. 250–262.

Veeser, H. Aram, ed. *The New Historicism*. New York: Routledge, 1989. (See, especially, Aram H. Veeser, "Introduction," ix–xvi; Stephen Greenblatt, "Towards a Poetics of Culture," 1–14; Louis Montrose, "Professing the Renaissance: The Poetics and Politics of Culture," 15–36; and Catherine Gallagher, "Marxism and the New Historicism," 37–48.)

Williams, Raymond. *Culture and Society 1780–1950*. New York: Harper, 1958.

Category II

Foucault, Michel. *Discipline and Punish: The Birth of the Prison.* Trans. Alan Sheridan. New York: Vintage, 1979.

———. *The Order of Things.* New York: Pantheon, 1972.

Geertz, Clifford. *The Interpretation of Cultures: Selected Essays.* New York: Basic Books, 1973.

———. *Local Knowledge: Further Essays in Interpretive Anthropology.* New York: Basic Books, 1983.

Greenblatt, Stephen. *Learning to Curse: Essays in Early Modern Culture.* New York: Routledge, 1991.

———. *Renaissance Self-Fashioning: From More to Shakespeare.* Chicago: U of Chicago P, 1980.

———. *Shakespearean Negotiations: The Circulation of Social Energy in Renaissance England.* Berkeley: U of California P, 1988.

Grossberg, Lawrence, Cary Nelson, and Paula Treichler, eds. *Cultural Studies.* New York: Routledge, 1992.

Hunt, Lynn, ed. *The New Cultural History.* Berkeley: U of California P, 1989. 97–128.

McGann, Jerome. *The Beauty of Inflections: Literary Investigations in Historical Method and Theory.* Oxford: Clarendon-Oxford UP, 1985.

Montrose, Louis. "New Historicisms." *Redrawing the Boundaries: The Transformation of English and American Literary Studies.* Eds. Stephen Greenblatt and Giles Gunn. New York: Modern Language Association, 1992. 392–418.

Notes

1. Tillyard's *Elizabethan World Picture* makes this argument and is a frequently cited example of traditional literary history. Another oft cited example of the traditional historical approach is Taine's *History of English Literature.*
2. Very much the same advice is offered in all the success manuals of the period. See, for example, those by Fowler and Marden.
3. Andrew Carnegie makes this argument in "The Gospel of Wealth."
4. For similar views of Gatsby, see Chase, Hart, Moore, Nash, Stern, and Trilling.

Works Cited

Achebe, Chinua. "An Image of Africa: Racism in Conrad's *Heart of Darkness.*" *Massachusetts Review* 18 (1977): 782–94. Rpt. in *Hopes and Impediments, Selected Essays.* New York: Anchor, 1989. 1–20.

Bewley, Marius. "Scott Fitzgerald's Criticism of America." *Sewanee Review* 62 (1954): 223–46. Rpt. in *Modern Critical Interpretations: F. Scott Fitzgerald's* The Great Gatsby. Ed. Harold Bloom. New York: Chelsea House, 1986. 11–27.

Burnam, Tom. "The Eyes of Dr. Eckleburg: A Re-Examination of *The Great Gatsby.*" *College English* 13 (1952). Rpt. in *F. Scott Fitzgerald: A Collection of Critical Essays.* Ed. Arthur Mizener. Englewood Cliffs: Prentice-Hall, 1963. 104–11.

Bierbower, Austin. *How to Succeed.* New York: R. F. Fenno, 1900.

Carnegie, Andrew. *The Autobiography of Andrew Carnegie*. New York, 1920.

———. "The Gospel of Wealth." *North American Review* CXLVIII (June 1889): 653–64 and CXLIX (December 1889): 682–98. Rpt. in *The Gospel of Wealth, and Other Timely Essays*. Ed. Edward C. Kirkland. Cambridge: Belknap Press of Harvard UP, 1962. 14–49.

———. "How to Win Fortune." 1890. *The Empire of Business*. Garden City, New York: Doubleday, Doran, 1933. 85–101.

———. "The Road to Business Success: A Talk to Young Men." 1885. *The Empire of Business*. Garden City, New York: Doubleday, Doran, 1933. 1–13.

Cartwright, Kent. "Nick Carraway as Unreliable Narrator." *Papers on Language and Literature* 20.2 (1984): 218–32.

Chase, Richard. *"The Great Gatsby." The American Novel and Its Traditions*. New York: Doubleday, 1957. 162–67. Rpt. in The Great Gatsby: *A Study*. Ed. Frederick J. Hoffman. New York: Scribner's, 1962. 297–302.

Commager, Henry Steele. Foreword. *McGuffey's Sixth Eclectic Reader* (1879 Edition). New York: Signet, 1963. vii–xvi.

Dillon, Andrew. "*The Great Gatsby*: The Vitality of Illusion." *Arizona Quarterly* 44.1 (1988): 49–61.

E. K. "Review of *The Great Gatsby*." *Literary Digest International Book Review*. May 1925: 426–27. Excerpted in *Gatsby*. Ed. Harold Bloom. New York: Chelsea House, 1991, 7.

Fiske, John. "Popular Culture." *Critical Terms for Literary Study*. 2nd ed. Eds. Frank Lentricchia and Thomas McLaughlin. Chicago: U of Chicago P, 1995. 321–35.

Fowler, Jr., Nathaniel C. *Beginning Right: How to Succeed*. New York: George Sully, 1916.

Gallo, Rose Adrienne. *F. Scott Fitzgerald*. New York: Ungar, 1978.

Geertz, Clifford. "Thick Description: Toward an Interpretive Theory of Culture." *The Interpretation of Cultures: Selected Essays by Clifford Geertz*. New York: Basic Books, 1973. 3–30.

Greenblatt, Stephen. "Culture." *Critical Terms for Literary Study*. 2nd ed. Eds. Frank Lentricchia and Thomas McLaughlin. Chicago: U of Chicago P, 1995. 225–32.

Gross, Barry Edward. "Jay Gatsby and Myrtle Wilson: A Kinship." *Tennessee Studies in Literature* 8 (1963): 57–60. Excerpted in *Gatsby*. Ed. Harold Bloom. New York: Chelsea House, 1991. 23–25.

Hart, Jeffrey. "'Out of it ere night': The WASP Gentleman as Cultural Ideal." *New Criterion* 7.5 (1989): 27–34.

Josephson, Matthew. *The Robber Barons: The Great American Capitalists, 1861–1901*. 1934. New York: Harvest, 1962.

Le Vot, André. *F. Scott Fitzgerald: A Biography*. Trans. William Byron. Garden City, New York: Doubleday, 1983.

Lindberg, Stanley W. *The Annotated McGuffey: Selections from the McGuffey Eclectic Readers 1836–1920*. New York: Van Nostrand Reinhold, 1976.

Marden, Orison Swett. *How to Succeed; Or, Stepping-Stones to Fame and Fortune*. New York: The Christian Herald, 1896.

Montrose, Louis. "Professing the Renaissance: The Poetics and Politics of Culture." *The New Historicism*. Ed. H. Aram Veeser. New York: Routledge, 1989. 15–36.

Moore, Benita A. *Escape into a Labyrinth: F. Scott Fitzgerald, Catholic Sensibility, and the American Way*. New York: Garland, 1988.

Nash, Charles C. "From West Egg to Short Hills: The Decline of the Pastoral Ideal from *The Great Gatsby* to Philip Roth's *Goodbye, Columbus.*" *Philological Association* 13 (1988): 22–27.

Stern, Milton R. *The Golden Moment: The Novels of F. Scott Fitzgerald*. Urbana: U of Illinois P, 1970.

Taine, Hippolyte. *History of English Literature*. 1864. Trans. H. Van Laun. London: Chatto and Windus, 1897.

Thomas, Brook. "Preserving and Keeping Order by Killing Time in *Heart of Darkness.*" Heart of Darkness: *A Case Study in Contemporary Criticism*. Ed. Ross C. Murfin. New York: Bedford, 1989. 237–55.

Tillyard, E. M. W. *Elizabethan World Picture*. New York: Macmillan, 1944.

Trilling, Lionel. "F. Scott Fitzgerald." *The Liberal Imagination*. New York: Viking, 1950. 243–54. Rpt. in The Great Gatsby: *A Study*. Ed. Frederick J. Hoffman. New York: Scribner's, 1962. 232–43.

Troy, William. "Scott Fitzgerald—The Authority of Failure." *Accent* 6 (1945). Rpt. in *F. Scott Fitzgerald: A Collection of Critical Essays*. Ed. Arthur Mizener. Englewood Cliffs: Prentice-Hall, 1963. 20–24.

CHAPTER 10

Lesbian, Gay, and Queer Criticism

In the critical-theory survey course I teach, I sometimes open the unit on lesbian, gay, and queer criticism by reading the class a list of frequently an-thologized British and American writers: for example, Oscar Wilde, Ten-nessee Williams, Willa Cather, James Baldwin, Adrienne Rich, Walt Whitman, Virginia Woolf, Elizabeth Bishop, Langston Hughes, Edward Albee, Gertrude Stein, Allen Ginsberg, W. H. Auden, William Shakespeare, Carson McCullers, Somerset Maugham, T. S. Eliot, James Merrill, H.D., Sa-rah Orne Jewett, Hart Crane, William S. Burroughs, and Amy Lowell. Then I ask my students if they are aware that these writers are gay, lesbian, or bi-sexual. Sometimes that question is met by an initial reticence to respond, a difficulty not encountered in our opening discussions of other theories.

Of course, I know that, unfortunately, the stigma attached to being thought gay or lesbian is still quite strong in America today, and some students may be unwilling to express anything on the subject until they see how the rest of the group responds. As one student told me, after sign-ing out a number of books on lesbian and gay theory from the university library for a paper she was writing for my class, she wondered if the stu-dent who waited on her at the circulation desk thought she were gay, and to her embarrassment she found herself wanting to shout, "Hey, wait a minute; I'm not a lesbian!"

Another reason for my students' difficulty, however, is their lack of knowledge. The work of gay and lesbian writers forms a major part of the literary canon and is therefore included in most literature courses, but many undergraduate students, if not most, assume that these writers are heterosexual. And their assumptions are rarely corrected. Of course, our anthologies of English and American literature usually include biographical introductions to the writers whose works they contain, and professors frequently offer additional information about authors' personal lives. We may be told, for example, that Charlotte Perkins Gilman suffered a deep depression after the birth of her only child; that, as a young man, Langston Hughes's difficult relationship with his father almost drove him to suicide; or that Robert Frost's dying wife refused to admit him to her room. But usually we are given very little, if any, biographical information about a writer's lesbian or gay sexual orientation, let alone information concerning how that orientation affected her or his life and literary production.

If personal information about writers' heterosexual lives is relevant to our appreciation of their work, why is personal information about writers' homosexual lives so often excluded from the realm of pertinent historical data? If the experience of gender and/or racial discrimination is an important factor in writers' lives, then why isn't it important to know about the oppression suffered by gay and lesbian writers? Clearly, in many of our college classrooms today, homosexuality is still considered an uncomfortable, if not inappropriate, topic of discussion. Many literature professors simply avoid addressing lesbian and gay issues in undergraduate courses not specifically devoted to lesbian and gay writers. And at many colleges, although courses on gay and lesbian writers can be offered occasionally as "special topics" courses, they do not always occur as regular course offerings in undergraduate English Departments, despite the progress made by gay studies programs since the 1970s and the emergence of lesbian, gay, and queer theory as an important force in academia in the early 1990s.

In other words, my students' uncertainty concerning the sexual orientation of the writers they read reflects the silence of many of their professors on that subject, including the silence of those professors who compile our anthologies. Furthermore, I would argue that the silence of many English faculty on the subject of gay and lesbian writers reflects, in turn, the long-standing silence of many literary critics who have minimized or ignored the sexual identities of lesbian and gay writers and distorted or overlooked the representations of gay and lesbian characters in literary works.

The Marginalization of Lesbians and Gay Men

Consider, for example, the critical response, analyzed by Lillian Faderman, to Henry James' *The Bostonians* (1885). As Faderman explains,

James's novel, by his own testimony, describes a "Boston marriage," a term used in late nineteenth-century New England to refer to a monogamous relationship of long standing between two single women, who were usually financially independent and often shared interests in culture, feminist issues, the betterment of society, and professional careers. Such relationships were not that uncommon, and although it's impossible to know how many of them included sex, it is clear that the women involved shared a strong emotional tie and focused their time, attention, and energy on each other and on their women friends.

In James's novel, such a relationship exists between Olive and Verena, who are active in the women's movement of their day. Their relationship is broken up by Basil, whose overpowering determination finally convinces Verena, almost by the sheer force of his will, to abandon Olive and marry him. Although, as Faderman points out, James does not portray Olive heroically, and indeed satirizes her and her women companions, it is obvious the author has no sympathy for Basil either, whom he depicts as a selfish, brutish, competitive manipulator who is infuriated by the women's movement and sure to give Verena an unhappy life. In contrast, Verena's life with Olive is happy and productive. Yet, Faderman observes, critics have argued that Basil rescues Verena from what they see as her unnatural relationship with Olive and restores her to what they assume is the true love a woman can find only in the arms of a "real" man.

How can these critics ignore the very positive aspects of Verena's relationship with Olive and completely distort James's portrayal of Basil? Clearly, their interpretation rests on, and imposes on the novel, a view of heterosexual love as the only kind of normal, healthy love there is. Any other kind of love is presumed abnormal, unhealthy, and to be avoided. As a result, these critics are unable to recognize Basil's obvious and serious character flaws. Because he is heterosexual and takes Verena away from Olive, he is often viewed in a very positive, even heroic, light.

This kind of interpretation is an example of a *homophobic* reading, that is, a reading informed by the fear and loathing of homosexuality. Thus, it is part of a larger cultural context in which homophobia has long played a major role. Although gay people are no longer placed in mental institutions for "treatment"—which sometimes included aversion therapy, electric shock treatment, and even lobotomies—it wasn't until 1974 that such practices officially ended, when the category of homosexuality was removed from the American Psychiatric Association's list of psychological disorders. Moreover, it wasn't until 1990 that the 1952 immigration policy restricting homosexual immigration into the United

States was lifted. And homophobia is evident in many forms of discrimination against gay men and lesbians still practiced today, despite the enormous social and political gains achieved by gay and lesbian activist groups since the Gay Liberation Movement began in 1969, after the gay and lesbian patrons of Greenwich Village's Stonewall Inn bar finally responded to police brutality by fighting back, two thousand strong, during two nights of rioting. This momentous event, referred to as *Stonewall*, has great symbolic significance because it marks the turning point when gay men and women renounced their victim status and stood up, collectively, for their rights as American citizens.

In the 1990s, gay men and lesbians in America still face discrimination in the military; in obtaining jobs and housing; in using public facilities, such as hotels and taverns; in areas of family law such as the right to marry, retain custody of their children, adopt children, or provide foster care; as victims of police harassment and violent hate crimes; and in AIDS-related discrimination.[1] Gay men and lesbians who are members of racial minorities in America face a complex system of discrimination. For in addition to the oppression they suffer in white heterosexist culture, gay and lesbian African Americans, Asian Americans, Chicanos, and Latinos are sometimes heavily stigmatized in their own communities.

Part and parcel of the discrimination practiced against lesbians and gay men are the negative myths that used to be generally accepted as truth and that still exert some influence today. These include the myth that gay people are sick, evil, or both and that it is therefore in their "nature" to be insatiable sexual predators, to molest children, and to corrupt youths by "recruiting" them to become homosexual. Another myth portrays gay men and lesbians as a very small population of deviants, when, in fact, it is estimated that gay people comprise at least 10% of the population of the United States. Other common misconceptions include the belief that children raised by gay men or lesbians will grow up to be gay, that unchecked homosexuality will result in the extinction of the human race, and that gay people are responsible for declines in U.S. foreign power.

This might be a good place to pause and define some terms, many of which are related to discrimination against lesbians and gay men. These are terms that you may encounter when you read lesbian and gay criticism. While the word *homophobia* is generally used to refer to an individual's pathological dread of same-sex love, I used the term above to refer to institutionalized discrimination (discrimination that is built into a culture's laws and customs) against gay people because I think we would be hard pressed to argue that such discrimination is based on anything

other than a collective, if sometimes unconscious, homophobia promoted by traditional American culture, or what feminism calls patriarchy. *Internalized homophobia* refers to the self-hatred some gay people experience because, in their growth through adolescence to adulthood,
they've internalized the homophobia pressed upon them by heterosexual
America.

The word more commonly used to refer to institutionalized discrimination against homosexuality, and the privileging of heterosexuality
that accompanies it, is *heterosexism.* For example, a heterosexist culture
enforces *compulsory heterosexuality*, a term used by Adrienne Rich,
among others, to describe the enormous pressure to be heterosexual
placed on young people by the family, the school, the church, the medical
professions, and all forms of the media. *Heterocentrism*, a more subtle
form of prejudice against gay men and lesbians, is the assumption, often
unconscious, that heterosexuality is the universal norm by which
everyone's experience can be understood. Heterocentrism renders lesbian
and gay experience invisible, making it possible in decades past, for example, for fans of Walt Whitman to be blind to the homoerotic dimension of his poetry. It is interesting to note that the words *homophobia,*
heterosexism, and *heterocentrism* are sometimes used interchangeably, the
difference among them apparently being one of degree: *homophobia* suggests the most virulent anti-gay sentiment, *heterocentrism* the least virulent.

By focusing our attention on gay men and lesbians as an oppressed
group, the words *homophobia, heterosexism,* and *heterocentrism* tend to
spotlight the ways in which gay people constitute a political minority. As
a minority they deserve, of course, the same protection under the law afforded to racial, ethnic, and religious minorities in America. Another
concept that emphasizes the minority status of lesbians and gay men is
biological essentialism, the idea that a fixed segment of the population is
naturally gay, just as the rest of the population is naturally heterosexual.
Conversely, some lesbian and gay theorists argue that, although gay
people constitute an oppressed political minority in America, all human
beings have the potential for same-sex desire or sexual activity. According
to this view, which is called *social constructionism,* homosexuality and
heterosexuality are products of social, not biological, forces. Ways of understanding gay and lesbian experience that focus on their minority status are called *minoritizing* views. Ways of understanding gay and lesbian
experience that focus on the homosexual potential in all people are called
universalizing views.[2]

Interestingly, both essentialist (minoritizing) and constructionist (universalizing) views have been used to attack homosexuality: for example, (1) gay people are born sick (or evil); (2) gay people are sick (or evil) products of a sick (or evil) environment. By the same token, both essentialist and constructionist views have been used to defend or celebrate homosexuality: for example, (1) it is biologically natural for some people to be gay, no matter what environment they're born into, and therefore they should be accepted as natural; (2) homosexuality is a normal response to particular environmental factors, and therefore gay people should be accepted as normal.

Finally, two oft-used words that refer to same-sex relationships are *homoerotic*, which I used earlier to describe Whitman's poetry, and *homosocial*. *Homoerotic* denotes erotic (though not necessarily overtly sexual) depictions that imply same-sex attraction or that might appeal sexually to a same-sex reader, for example, a sensually evocative description of women in the process of helping each other undress or of nude men bathing in a pond. Such depictions can occur in any medium, such as film, painting, sculpture, photography, and, of course, literature. The word *homosocial* denotes same-sex friendship of the kind seen in female- or male-bonding activities. For example, the relationship among the three prostitutes—China, Poland, and Miss Marie—in Toni Morrison's *The Bluest Eye* (1970) is homosocial, as is the relationship between Huck and Jim in Mark Twain's *Adventures of Huckleberry Finn* (1885) and between Edna Pontellier and Adèle Ratignolle in Kate Chopin's *The Awakening* (1899). Furthermore, in the descriptions of Edna's sensual response to Adèle's voluptuous beauty, the relationship between these two characters is homoerotic as well.

So far, I have discussed gay men and lesbians as a group. Indeed, even the inclusion of gay and lesbian criticism in the same chapter implies that they constitute some sort of homogenous collectivity. Certainly, they share in common the political, economic, social, and psychological oppression they suffer as members of a sexual minority. And for many thinkers, the enormity of this shared experience, and the potential for political power generated when gay men and lesbians act as a group, is sufficient to support the claim that they should be considered in this light.

Many lesbians and gay men, however, argue that oppression is one of the few experiences, if not the only one, they have in common and that, in most other ways, gay men and lesbians are polar opposites. For example, many gay men and lesbians have their most significant social, political, and personal experiences, if not all of their experiences, in same-sex groups. In addition, many lesbians identify exclusively with women, while many gay men identify exclusively with men. Furthermore, lesbians, even if "closeted" (posing as heterosexual), have experienced the gender oppression that all women, straight or gay, have experienced, while closeted gay men have had the opportunity to enjoy the patriarchal privileges extended to straight men. And whether closeted or not, gay male writers have enjoyed an incomparably greater representation in literary history than lesbians (or heterosexual women) because, until recently, works by male authors were much more readily canonized than works by female authors.

In order to appreciate the distinctive features of lesbian and gay criticism, we'll discuss them under separate headings. Then, in order to consider the most recent developments in lesbian and gay criticism, we'll discuss a relatively new field of inquiry called queer theory, which is based upon the insights of deconstruction and is relevant to issues of heterosexual identity as well as to issues of gay and lesbian sexual identity.

Lesbian Criticism

Perhaps because lesbian criticism and feminist criticism grew from the same soil—as responses to patriarchal oppression—and because so many lesbian critics are feminists, lesbian criticism is concerned with issues of personal identity and politics analogous to those analyzed by feminists (see Chapter Four). However, while feminism addresses issues related to sexism and the difficulties involved in carving out a space for personal identity and political action beyond the influence of sexist ideologies, lesbian critics address issues related to both sexism and heterosexism. In other words, lesbian critics must deal with the psychological, social, economic, and political oppression fostered not only by patriarchal male privilege, but by heterosexual privilege as well. And this second form of privilege has often put heterosexual and lesbian feminists at odds.

Indeed, feminism has been, at various times, vulnerable to charges of heterocentrism, in its tendency to focus on the oppression of heterosexual women rather than on the oppression of all women, including lesbians; of heterosexism, in the heterosexual orientation of its most visible leadership; and of homophobia, in its legitimate fear of being "branded" a lesbian movement by the patriarchal power structure in America (legitimate because homophobia is such a pervasive and disarming force). Analogously, lesbians of color and working-class lesbians have suffered a history of marginalization, if not exclusion, within the lesbian-feminist movement, which, like the feminist movement, emerged largely from the white middle class and, therefore, has been limited—until relatively recently—by white middle-class perspectives and goals.

I mention these problems up front because, especially since the mid–1980s, lesbians have refused to be marginalized by heterosexual feminists; and lesbians of color and working-class lesbians have refused to be marginalized by white middle-class lesbians. As a result, lesbian criticism has become one of the richest and most exciting domains of theoretical inquiry and political activity. Questions that have long been central to lesbian critical inquiry—such as, "What is a lesbian?" and "What constitutes a lesbian literary text?"—are problematized in very productive ways when lesbian critics take into account both the limitations imposed on their viewpoints by their class origins and race, and the beauty and importance of the complex heritage bestowed upon us all by the ultimate inseparability of race, class, gender, and sexual orientation in the experience of our daily lives.

In addition to generating fundamental issues of lesbian inquiry, the questions "What is a lesbian?" and "What constitutes a lesbian literary text?" belong to a self-questioning form of theoretical activity not generally performed by gay criticism. So let's take a closer look at these two questions.

Can a lesbian be defined as a woman who has sex with another woman? What activity constitutes sex? (Must there be genital contact?) How would such a definition work if we applied it to heterosexuality? Presumably, it would mean that virgins who thought of themselves as heterosexuals would have no right to call themselves heterosexuals unless and until they had genital sex with men. So one's sexuality must be defined, it seems, in terms of one's sexual desire.

Perhaps a better way to define a lesbian, then, is to say that she is a woman whose sexual desire is directed toward women. The advantage of a definition of this sort is that it allows us to recognize lesbian existence even within the confines of heterosexual marriage. For throughout history, women often have had to marry, whether they wanted to or not, in order to survive economically or because the rigid social system in which they lived offered them no other social or psychological option. And some of these women, though they may have loved and respected their husbands, were passionately attracted to women rather than to men. Virginia Woolf, who was married but who had a passionate, long-standing affair with Vita Sackville-West, is a case in point.

What if, however, there is evidence of a passionate attachment between two women—such as a long exchange of letters in which passionate love is expressed—but because the relationship occurred in a different historical period from our own, we can't be certain exactly what it was that was being expressed? For example, how do we interpret the "romantic friendships," as they are called, between women in nineteenth-century Britain and America—one embodiment of which was the "Boston marriage" discussed earlier—in which the most passionate attachment and the tenderest love are expressed, but for which there is no concrete evidence of sexual activity or sexual desire?

The period is known for its overblown sentimentality and excesses of verbal expression, and effusions of physical affection between women were accepted, even encouraged, by patriarchy as charming displays of women's "overemotional nature." So we can't assume with any certainty that women's exchanges of letters filled with exuberant expressions of passion—such as "I love you my darling, more than I can express, more than I am conscious of myself"[3]—are indicative of sexual desire, let alone sexual activity. On the other hand, many such relationships might have involved a sexual dimension to which nineteenth-century heterocentric patriarchy would have been utterly blind. Indeed, given the nineteenth century's restriction of women's sexuality and sexual awareness, many women might have had enormous sexual desire for other women without ever recognizing it as such.

Thus, a strict focus on what we would define today as sexual activity or sexual desire runs the risk of erasing an important dimension of women's lives that very well might be understood fully only through a lesbian lens. In order to avoid this kind of erasure, and to promote solidarity among all women, some lesbian theorists have suggested that lesbian identity is not restricted to the sexual domain but consists of directing the bulk of one's attention and emotional energy to other women and having other women as one's primary source of emotional sustenance and psychological support. That is, a lesbian is a *woman-identified woman*.

Adrienne Rich makes use of this idea when she argues for the existence of what she calls a *lesbian continuum*. A lesbian continuum, Rich explains, "include[s] a range—through each woman's life and throughout history—of woman-identified experience, not simply the fact that a woman has had or consciously desired genital sexual experience with another woman" (239). Woman-identified experience includes, for example, emotional bonding through shared work or play, the giving or receiving of psychological support, and the shared experience of joy in any form. Woman-identification does not preclude sexual desire or sexual activity, but neither does it require them. A woman can thus move in and out of the lesbian continuum throughout her life or remain within it entirely. From this perspective, women's romantic friendships during the nineteenth century, whether or not they involved sexual activity or desire, are indeed an appropriate subject for lesbian analysis.

Of course, to underplay the sexual dimension of lesbian experience is to underplay, some theorists argue, that which is most unique and liberating in lesbian life. In bonding with one another sexually and denying men access to their bodies, lesbians deny patriarchy one of its most powerful tools: heterosexuality. For heterosexuality is not a "natural" sexual orientation for "normal" women but a political institution that subordinates women to patriarchy in that women's subservience to men is built into heterosexual definitions of feminine sexuality. In other words, from this point of view, patriarchy and heterosexuality are inseparable. To resist the former, one must resist the latter.

For this reason, some lesbians are *separatists*. They dissociate themselves as much as possible from all men, including gay men, and from heterosexual women as well. They may also dissociate themselves from lesbians who don't share their views. Recalling the sexism of the male-dominated Gay Liberation Movement of the 1970s and, as we noted above, the heterosexist tendencies of feminism, lesbian separatists believe that only lesbian organizations will give priority to lesbian issues. For separatists, just as for the majority of lesbian feminists who are not separatists, lesbianism is a political stance, not merely an issue of personal sexuality.

Nevertheless, as Marilyn Frye argues, while separatism is a deliberate, systematic political policy, it is not the only form in which women's separation from patriarchal domination occurs. In fact, separation is enacted to varying degrees across a range of institutional practices that increase women's power, including, for example, the provision of shelters for battered women, divorce, the increased availability of daycare, women's studies programs, women's bars, and the legalization of abortion. Even such apparently personal behaviors as breaking up a close relationship, excluding someone from one's house or one's company, withholding one's support, withdrawing one's loyalty, refusing to watch sexist television programs or listen to sexist music, and rejecting obnoxious individuals are all forms of separation from males or from male-dominated institutions that can increase women's power. As Frye puts it, "Access is one of the faces of Power. . . . It is always the privilege of the master to enter the slave's hut. The slave who decides to exclude the master from her hut is declaring herself not a slave" (95–96). Thus, although most women do not choose separatist politics, neither should they find them completely alien to their own experience or be unsympathetic to women who do choose them.

Clearly, attempts to define the word *lesbian*, or even to articulate the full political implications of various forms of women's separation, are as problematic as they are exciting. Equally difficult, and equally rewarding, are efforts to answer the question "What constitutes a lesbian literary text?" As we can't always be sure whether or not a particular writer was a lesbian, especially given the difficulties we've just discussed concerning the definition of that term, we can't depend on an author's sexual orientation, even if we know it, to tell us whether or not we are reading a lesbian text. Of course, how the critic defines *lesbian* will determine her definition of both lesbian writers and lesbian texts.

For example, a lesbian critic might argue that a writer known to have been a sexually active lesbian, such as Willa Cather, *coded* lesbian meaning in an apparently heterosexual narrative because she knew that she couldn't write about lesbian desire openly, at least not if she hoped to have her work published and to avoid public censure if not criminal prosecution. Judith Fetterly makes this argument in her interpretation of Cather's *My Ántonia* (1918). Among other codings, Fetterly argues that narrator Jim Burden, whose characterization is frequently contradictory and whom many critics have difficulty interpreting, can be understood if we see him as the embodiment of Cather's own lesbian desire. Fetterly notes, among other evidence, that despite Jim's frequent admissions of love for Ántonia and of his desire to have her as his sweetheart or his wife, for some unexplained reason he can't have her. Furthermore, he behaves in ways that are traditionally female. He spends most of his time in the kitchen, in women's space. We never see him participating in the boys' world of hunting and fishing. He doesn't identify with the men of his town and is hostile to the patriarchal privilege they abuse. And when Jim takes Ántonia's place in the home of Wick Cutter, her sexually predatory employer whose strange behavior is frightening her, Jim doesn't defend the woman he loves by beating up Wick. Instead, he is apparently raped in her place, for he runs home to his grandmother, repulsed and shamed by what he calls Cutter's disgusting behavior, and he begs his grandmother to tell no one, not even the doctor. Finally, Jim reveals a loathing of male sexuality, for example in his description of Wick Cutter, which is filled with snakelike, phallic imagery: "His abominable masculinity, his loathsome, fluid motion somehow made me sick. He was as thick as my leg, and looked as if millstones couldn't crush the disgusting vitality out of him. . . . He seemed like the ancient, eldest Evil" (Cather 45–47; quoted in Fetterly 152). These narrative problems are resolved, Fetterly argues, when we realize that Jim is a stand-in for Cather, which makes even more sense when we learn that the tale is autobiographical.

Another task a lesbian critic might perform is to argue that a writer's literary output establishes her lesbian status even when available biographical material posits only a passionate emotional bond, a "romantic friendship," with another woman. For example, Paula Bennett argues persuasively that Emily Dickinson's poetic strategies reveal a homoerotic dimension of the author's poetry that is related, Bennett points out, to the "enormous amount of comfort, both emotional and sexual," she drew from her "relationships with women throughout her life" (109). For example, among other poetic strategies, Dickinson associates phallic imagery with fear and revulsion. As we see in "I started Early—Took my Dog" (#520), the speaker, pursued by the sea (whose "overflow" of "Pearl" is obviously male and obviously sexual), flees in terror because she fears it will consume her. Similarly, in "In Winter in my Room" (#1670), the speaker is disturbed by the presence of a "Worm—/ Pink, lank and warm" that terrifies and repels her when it transforms itself into "A snake . . . ringed with power."

Conversely, Bennett observes, Dickinson links female sexual imagery—specifically, images associated with the clitoris and vaginal lips—with "Edenic pleasures" (111) that are "typically oral" and described in a manner that is "open, eager, and lush" (110). For example, "All the letters I can write" (#334) calls upon a lover (who is represented by the diminutive form of a hummingbird and whose gender is referred to, ambiguously, as "it") to "Play it . . . / . . . just sipped" her "Depths of Ruby, undrained, / Hid, Lip, for Thee." Similarly, "I tend my flowers for thee" (#339) includes such female sexual images as "My Fuchsia's Coral Seams / Rip—while the Sower—dreams" and "My Cactus—splits her Beard / To show her throat." Whether or not the speaker in such poems adopts a male point of view, Dickinson's "focus is obviously on female sexuality itself" (111) and "bespeaks the poet's overwhelming physical attraction to her own sex" (110). Significantly, Dickinson's letters to Susan Gilbert, her lifelong friend, were published only after they were edited by the poet's niece, who scrupulously eliminated Dickinson's exuberant expressions of passionate love for Gilbert.

Another task a lesbian critic might perform is to show the ways in which a text that is clearly heterosexual in its intention nevertheless has an important lesbian dimension. Using a definition of *lesbian* that does not require same-sex desire—for example, the woman-identified woman—Barbara Smith makes this case for Toni Morrison's *Sula* (1973), in which two young black girls bond together to survive the racism and sexism that constrict their lives. In addition to what Smith notes as Morrison's "consistently critical stance toward the heterosexual institutions of male/female relationships, marriage, and the family" (165), this critic argues forcefully that the only deep and sustained love experienced in the novel is between two women: the main characters Nel and Sula. Their primary identification is with each other, their primary emotional sustenance comes from each other, and no man, including Nel's husband, is more influential or important in their lives than each other. In fact, both women's relationships with men are unsatisfactory. Finally, Sula's unconventional behavior—her refusal to marry and have children, her dismissive attitude toward the married men with whom she has one-night stands, and the like—represents a transgressive sexuality, a violation of patriarchal norms, that resonates strongly with lesbian violations of patriarchy. Indeed, Sula goes to bed with men, not in order to experience communion with them, which doesn't occur, but in order to learn about her own internal power and experience her own inner harmony.

Of course lesbian literary critics perform a number of other tasks. Among other things, they try to decide what constitutes a lesbian literary tradition and what writers and works belong to it. They attempt to determine what might constitute a lesbian poetics, that is, a uniquely lesbian way of writing. They analyze how the sexual/emotional orientation of lesbian writers has affected their literary expression; how the intersection of race and sexual/emotional orientation has affected the literary expression of lesbians of color; and how the intersection of class, race, and sexual/emotional orientation has affected the literary expression of lesbians of working-class origins. Lesbian critics also analyze the sexual politics of specific texts by examining, for example, how lesbian characters or "masculine" women are portrayed in literature by and about lesbians. They study canonized heterosexual texts, too, in order to learn what attitudes toward lesbians they embody explicitly or implicitly. And they identify and correct heterosexist interpretations of literature that fail to recognize or appreciate the lesbian dimensions of specific literary works.

Clearly, these tasks do not exhaust the field. They are intended merely
as a representative sample. Only your own reading of the work done by
lesbian critics will acquaint you with the breadth and depth of their enterprise, which continues to expand and evolve with each passing year.

In addition, you might want to acquaint yourself, if you haven't al-
ready done so, with literary works by contemporary lesbian writers, who
are receiving much critical acclaim. These writers include, among others,
Jeanette Winterson, Gloria Anzaldúa, Leslie Feinberg, Minnie Bruce Pratt,
Rita Mae Brown, Paula Gunn Allen, Dorothy Allison, Ann Allen Shockley,
Monique Wittig, Jewelle Gomez, June Arnold, Valerie Miner, Jane Rule,
Bertha Harris, Sarah Shulman, Nicole Brossard, and, of course, Audre
Lorde and Adrienne Rich.

Gay Criticism

As we noted above, unlike lesbian criticism, gay criticism doesn't tend to
focus on efforts to define homosexuality. Sexual relations between men,
or even just the sexual desire of one man for another, is the generally accepted criterion of gayness in white middle-class America today. Nevertheless, not all cultures share this definition. For example, in Mexican and
South American cultures, the mere fact of sexual activity with or desire
for another male does not indicate that a man is homosexual. As long as
he behaves in a traditionally masculine manner—strong, dominant, decisive—and consistently assumes the male sexual role as penetrator (never
allowing himself to be penetrated, orally or anally), a man remains a *macho*, a "real" man. As a *macho*, a man can have sex with both men and
women and not be considered what North Americans call homosexual.
The same definition of homosexuality was used in white American working-class culture around the turn of the twentieth century: only men who
allowed themselves to be penetrated by a man during sex and behaved in
a traditionally feminine manner—submissive, coy, flirtatious, "soft"—
were considered homosexual.

A similar problem for contemporary white middle-class assumptions about homosexuality is offered by ancient Athens, where there
was no polar opposition between homosexual and heterosexual behavior. Sexual partners were chosen along caste lines, not according to their
biological sex. In Athens, a member of the elite male ruling class could
have legitimate sexual relations only with his social inferiors: women of
any age and from any class, free-born boys past the age of puberty but

not old enough for citizenship, slaves, and foreigners.

In fact, it wasn't until the nineteenth century that the notion of homosexual identity, or even the word *homosexual*, was adopted in Anglo-European and American culture. Before that time, certain sexual acts—generally speaking, all forms of nonprocreative sex—were forbidden by church or state, but they weren't viewed as evidence of a specific sexual identity. The idea that one could *be* a homosexual came along with the idea, promoted by the medical professions, that such an identity was a form of pathology. This is why many gay men today prefer to refer to themselves as gay: the word *homosexual* is associated, for many, with the belief that homosexuality is a medical or psychological disorder.

Similarly, "the masturbator" also became a pathological sexual identity in the nineteenth century. An act that the medical professions today consider a normal, healthy outlet was considered so dangerous in the nineteenth century that children "suffering" from the "affliction" were tied to their beds at night to prevent their touching themselves, and there are several case histories of doctors' burning the genitals of little girls in order to "cure" them.

The point here is that attitudes toward homosexuality, like attitudes toward sexuality in general, differ widely from one place to another and from one historical period to another. The intense anti-gay sentiment that emerged in an especially concentrated and virulent form in America during the early 1950s and that lingers today does not represent some kind of universally held attitude toward, or even definition of, homosexuality.

The kinds of analysis that tend to engage the attention of gay critics often fall under the heading of *gay sensibility*. How does being gay influence the way one sees the world, sees oneself and others, creates and responds to art and music, creates and interprets literature, experiences and expresses emotion? In a heterosexist culture such as the one we inhabit at the turn of the twenty-first century in America, gay sensibility includes an awareness of being different, at least in certain ways, from the members of the mainstream, dominant culture, and the complex feelings that result from an implicit, ongoing social oppression. In other words, part of seeing the world as a gay man includes the ways in which one deals with being oppressed as a gay man. Among others, three important domains of gay sensibility, all of which involve responses to heterosexist oppression, are drag, camp, and dealing with the issue of AIDS.

Drag is the practice of dressing in women's clothing. *Drag queens* are gay men who dress in drag on a regular basis or who do it professionally.

However, not all gay people cross dress, not all cross-dressers are gay, and not all gay people approve of drag. But for some, it's a source of self-expression and entertainment that can also be a political statement against traditional gender roles. Drag doesn't necessarily involve (and perhaps never involves) the fantasy that one is a woman. Rather it is a way for a man to express his feminine side or his sense of the outrageous or his nonconformity. For other gay men, drag is a form of political activism used to draw attention to gay issues, criticize homophobic government and religious policies, and raise funds to fight AIDS. Whatever the purpose, drag is a way of refusing to be intimidated by heterosexist gender boundaries and a way of getting all of us to think about our own sexuality by challenging gender roles.

Lesbians sometimes cross dress, too. In fact, there are some *drag kings*, such as Elvis Herselvis, who satirizes Elvis impersonators and includes in her act a discussion of Elvis's drug problem and sexual proclivities. However, drag doesn't seem to be for lesbians the major issue it is for gay men. One reason may be that, at least since the late 1960s, women's adoption of masculine attire and grooming is not considered outrageous or even unfashionable. Also, in general, the lesbian community's adoption of male clothing and grooming (for example butch attire) or of androgenous clothing and grooming (for example, lesbian-feminist attire of the 1970s) has tended to be a matter of personal self-expression and/or quiet political statement that hasn't had the theatrical quality of gay drag. Therefore, although butch lesbians frequently have been beaten and raped, especially during such repressive periods as the 1950s, their cross dressing never drew the national attention focused on gay drag.

Camp, of which flamboyant gay drag is an example, is a form of expression characterized by irreverence, artifice, exaggeration, and theatricality. It's ironic, witty, and humorous and often involves a blurring or crossing of gender lines. It's subversive in that it mocks authority and traditional standards of behavior by imitating them in outrageous ways, often through the use of exaggerated gestures, postures, and voice. Imagine, as an example of camp, a humorous drag representation of the royal wedding of Queen Elizabeth and Prince Philip or a drag spoof of anti-gay activist Anita Bryant addressing Congress on the topic of "family values." One doesn't have to be gay to produce camp. Camp is as much, or more, in the eye of the beholder as in the intention of the person who produces it. Thus, the flamboyant theatricality of Judy Garland and the flamboyant irreverence of Bette Midler are appreciated for their camp qualities by many gay fans. Not unlike drag (which, if outrageous or humorous, can

be viewed as a sub-set of camp), camp is a way of affirming one's difference from heterosexual culture. It's a way of disarming heterosexism and
healing oneself through laughter. And thus it's a way of transforming
victimhood into power.

Of course, living with the reality of AIDS, which includes AIDS-related discrimination, has become part of gay sensibility in the late 1980s
and 1990s. It can't help but affect the way gay men see the world to know
that the federal government was reticent to fund AIDS research until the
disease became a threat for heterosexual citizens as well, to be aware of
the lingering reluctance of some medical professionals to treat AIDS patients or to treat them with respect, to encounter discrimination in the
workplace against people who have AIDS or who are HIV positive (who
do not have AIDS but who will presumably develop the disease at some
future point), and to put forth the daily physical and emotional labor of
caring for friends and loved ones dying of AIDS.

AIDS was first identified in 1981, and by the end of the decade a generation of men had died from it, six times the number of American soldiers killed in Viet Nam. The gay community's response to this national
health emergency has been extremely active and positive. They have
formed political organizations, such as the AIDS Coalition to Unleash
Power (ACT UP), to publicize and gain support for their cause through
public demonstrations and protests in an effort to get drug companies,
insurance companies, government agencies, and the medical bureaucracy
to respond appropriately to this epidemic. And as lesbians rallied to the
support of gay men, joining their protests and playing a significant role in
caring for the sick and dying, a new spirit of solidarity emerged between
these two communities. As Margaret Cruikshank puts it, "those who had
been labeled misfits and unAmerican perverts launched a typically
American self-help movement which was probably one of the largest volunteer efforts in the nation's history" (182–83).

Despite their focus on different theoretical issues, there is a good deal
of similarity in the way gay and lesbian critics approach literary texts. For
example, like lesbian critics, gay critics attempt to determine what might
constitute a gay poetics, or a way of writing that is uniquely gay; to establish a gay literary tradition; and to decide what writers and works belong
to that tradition. Gay critics also examine how gay sensibility affects literary expression and study the ways in which heterosexual texts can have a
homoerotic dimension. They try to rediscover gay writers from the past
whose work was underappreciated, distorted, or suppressed, including
gay writers who have been presumed heterosexual. They try to determine

the sexual politics of specific texts, analyzing, for example, how gay characters or "feminine" men are portrayed in both gay and heterosexual
texts. Finally, gay critics identify and correct heterosexist interpretations
of literature that fail to recognize or appreciate the gay sensibility informing specific literary works. To get an idea of the kinds of insights into literature these approaches can produce, let's take a brief look at three specific examples: an analysis of Walt Whitman's poetic voice, a study of the
representation of gay identity in the work of contemporary novelist
Edmund White, and a defense of the gay sensibility in Tennessee
Williams's plays.

In "Walt Whitman Camping," Karl Keller extends our understanding
of Whitman's poetic project through his interesting analysis of the ways
in which Whitman's poetic self-presentation is a form of camp. "We see
this," Keller argues, "in the flamboyant gestures, the exaggerated tone, the
operatic voice, the inflated role-playing, the dilation of language" (115)
that frequently characterize Whitman's speaker, for example the speaker
in "Song of Myself" (1855). Keller says, "Those who have bemoaned the
contradiction between Whitman's claim that his poetry . . . revealed his
personality well and the paucity of autobiographical detail in the poems
have only failed to look . . . at the workings of Whitman's voice" (115).
"The poet is *performing*" (115), Keller asserts, and the camp quality of his
performance reveals the seductive "come-on" (116), in his voice and in
his pose, that humorously sexualizes his transcendentalist ideals of bonding with nature and with other human beings. Whitman "is not making
fun of the things he talks about but making fun out of them," Keller observes, in order to "intensif[y] his enjoyment of the world around him"
(118). Referring to the poet as "the Mae West of American literature,"
Keller argues that Whitman reveals himself to the reader, not by "flashing
his entire person at us," but by "showing the range of *possibilities* of his
personality" (115).

Another representative example of gay literary criticism is Nicholas F.
Radel's thoughtful essay "Self as Other: The Politics of Identity in the
Works of Edmund White." "Gay identity," Radel observes, "is the explicit
subject of many of White's works," and many of his gay characters "fail to
achieve a coherent sense of self," a failure that "can be attributed to the
politics of sexual and gender difference" (175). In other words, White examines the damaging effects of homophobic American culture upon the
gay men and boys who grow up within it, and its most damaging effect is
the internalized homophobia, the learned self-hatred, of his gay characters. Indeed, Radel points out that White's gay characters experience a

distinct split within themselves between what they consider their "essential selves" and "a homosexual self as Other that they themselves conceive as being separate" (176) from them. This experience of being alienated from oneself undermines both gay identity and gay community. How can a man feel he belongs to a gay community if he is alienated from his own gayness? Furthermore, Radel argues, self-alienation in White's work is not due to individual psychological problems but is the direct result of the politics of heterosexist oppression. Therefore, "we might view White's novels as part of the historical apparatus for revealing a gay subject [selfhood] as it responds to political pressure from the culture at large" (176).

Finally, in "Camp and the Gay Sensibility," Jack Babuscio argues that gay sensibility has something to offer everyone: the relevance of its insights is not limited, as some critics believe, to the gay community. As a case in point, Babuscio observes that critics have failed to fully appreciate the insights into human life offered by Tennessee Williams's heroines—the most famous of whom is probably Blanche Dubois in A Streetcar Named Desire (1947)—because these characters represent Williams's own emotions as a gay man. In other words, Williams's heroines are Williams himself, in drag, so to speak, expressing his own anxieties about being gay: for example, his battle between the demands of the flesh and those of the spirit, his desire to be promiscuous and yet still keep his pride, and his fear of aging in a youth-oriented, homosexual sub-culture. Critics have concluded therefore, Babuscio notes, that Williams's work is not relevant to mainstream heterosexual culture. In short, they believe that gay sensibility speaks only to gay men.

In contrast, Babuscio asserts that Williams's experience on the margins of mainstream America, as an object of "fear, suspicion, and, even, hatred" (34), gave him a privileged position from which to understand the conflicts of human life—the same privileged position occupied, for example, by members of racial minorities—because he had to deal with those conflicts in a particularly intense form. Furthermore, Babuscio notes, the act of literary creation involves, for all good writers, the transformation of their own experience into literary form. So when Maxine Faulk, in The Night of the Iguana (1961), says that we all reach a point in our lives, sooner or later, where we must settle for something that works for us, she is speaking not just to the gay community but to the entire human community.

Of course, just as in the case of our discussion of lesbian literary criticism, the examples of gay criticism provided here do not exhaust the field but are intended only as a representative sample of the kind of work done by gay critics. Your own reading of gay criticism will expand your understanding of this growing body of work.

In addition, you might want to acquaint yourself, if you haven't already done so, with literary works by contemporary gay writers, who are receiving much critical acclaim. These writers include, among others, David Feinberg, Tony Kushner, David Leavitt, Edmund White, Armistead Maupin, Paul Monette, Mark Doty, Randy Shilts, Dennis Cooper, Neil Bartlett, Allen Gurganus, Andrew Holleran, Samuel R. Delany, Dale Peck, John Rechy, Paul Russell, Matthew Stadler, and Peter Weltner.

Queer Criticism

One of the first questions asked by students new to the study of gay and lesbian criticism is why gay men and women have chosen the homophobic word *queer* to designate an approach within their own discipline. I think there are several answers to that question, and they will serve as an introduction to some of the basic premises of queer theory.

First, the use of the term *queer* can be seen as an attempt to reappropriate the word from what has been its homophobic usage in order to demonstrate that heterosexists shouldn't be allowed to define gay and lesbian experience. The act of defining the terms of one's own self-reference is a powerful move that says, among other things, "We're not afraid to be seen!"; "You don't tell us who we are—*we* tell us who we are!"; and "We're proud to be different!" Or, as the popular queer slogan sums it up, "We're here, we're queer—get used to it!" As gay men and lesbians have learned, language is a tool for repression, but it's also a tool for change.

Furthermore, some lesbians and gay men have adopted the word *queer* as an inclusive category for referring to a common political or cultural ground shared by gay men, lesbians, bisexuals, and all people who consider themselves, for whatever reasons, nonstraight. Used in this way, the term tries to reunite the heretofore divided camps that resulted, in part, from the white middle-class roots of the gay liberation and lesbian feminist movements of the early 1970s. As products of the white middle class, these movements were blind to their own white middle-class privilege. As a result, through the 1970s and into the 1980s, the experience of gay people of color and of working-class gay men and lesbians was generally ignored, for these groups had little or no opportunity to assume visible leadership positions within the gay power-structure. In addition, certain forms of gay sexual expression were excluded or marginalized, such as the butch-femme lesbian couples who played such an important role in lesbian culture during the 1950s and 1960s. Butch-femme couples resemble heterosexual couples in terms of clothing, grooming, and personal style. Although they did not necessarily resemble heterosexual couples in terms of emotional or sexual relatedness, it was usually assumed that they did, and they were therefore criticized for reproducing the same power imbalance generally found in heterosexual relationships. The word *queer*, then, as an inclusive term, seeks to heal these divisions by offering a collective identity to which all nonstraight people can belong.

For the most part, however, the word *queer* is used to indicate a specific theoretical perspective. From a theoretical point of view, the words *gay* and *lesbian* imply a definable category—homosexuality—that is clearly opposite to another definable category: heterosexuality. However, for queer theory, categories of sexuality cannot be defined by such simple oppositions as homosexual/heterosexual. Building on deconstruction's insights into human subjectivity (selfhood) as a fluid, fragmented, dynamic collectivity of possible "selves," queer theory defines individual sexuality as a fluid, fragmented, dynamic collectivity of possible sexualities. Our sexuality may be different at different times over the course of our lives or even at different times over the course of a week because sexuality is a dynamic range of desire. Gay sexuality, lesbian sexuality, bisexuality, and heterosexuality are, for all of us, possibilities along a continuum of sexual possibilities. And what these categories mean to different individuals will be influenced by how they conceive their own racial and class identities, as well. Thus, sexuality is controlled neither by our biological sex (male or female) nor by the way our culture translates biological sex into gender roles (masculine or feminine). Sexuality exceeds these definitions and has a will, a creativity, an expressive need of its own.

Moreover, heterosexuality is not a norm against which homosexuality can be defined because the range of human sexuality cannot be completely understood in terms of such limited concepts as homosexual and heterosexual. For one thing, these concepts reduce sexuality to the biological sex of one's partner, or, in psychological terms, one's *object choice*. There are a host of other factors that make up human sexual desire. As Eve Kosofsky Sedgwick argues, the intricacies of human sexuality could be understood just as well, or better, in terms of any number of paired opposites other than same-sex or different-sex object choice. For example, the definition of one's sexuality might be based on one's preference for someone older or younger, for a human or an animal, for a single partner or a group activity, for oneself alone (as in masturbation) or for a variety of different partners. Other dimensions of sexuality don't even involve object choice. For example, Sedgwick notes, the definition of one's sexuality might be based on such oppositions as "orgasmic/nonorgasmic, noncommercial/commercial, using bodies only/using manufactured objects, in private/in public, spontaneous/scripted" (57). Or the definition of one's sexuality might be based on one's preference for particular acts, sensations, or physical types.

For queer theory, then, our sexuality is socially constructed (rather than inborn) because it is based on the way in which sexuality is defined by the culture in which we live. We saw examples of the social construction of sexuality earlier, when we discussed ancient Athens, where sexual categories were based on a caste system that didn't differentiate between male and female, and the very different definitions of homosexuality operating in Mexico and South America, early-twentieth-century working-class America, and white middle-class America today. The belief that sexuality is socially constructed is behind efforts to read literature from the past not just in terms of our own definitions of sexuality, but in terms of those definitions operating in the culture from which that literature emerged.

Clearly, the word *queer* has a range of meanings in literary studies today. As an inclusive term, it can refer to any piece of literary criticism that interprets a text from a nonstraight perspective. Therefore, any of the examples of gay and lesbian criticism discussed earlier could be included in a collection of queer essays. However, if we restrict ourselves to its narrower theoretical meaning—its deconstructive dimension—queer criticism reads texts to reveal the problematic quality of their representations of sexual categories, in other words, to show the various ways in which the categories homosexual and heterosexual break down, overlap, or do not adequately represent the dynamic range of human sexuality. These kinds of readings can be rather complex. So let me offer you a few simplified examples.

A queer reading of William Faulkner's "A Rose for Emily" (1931) might examine how traditional definitions of gender identity (masculine vs. feminine) and sexuality (homosexual vs. heterosexual) fail to explain or contain the character of Emily Greirson. Her gender categorization is not fixed but crosses back and forth between the masculine and the feminine. She's both the slender virgin in white dominated by her father and the defiant individualist who violates class norms and moral law to take what she wants from Homer Barron, including his life. She's both the childlike recluse who teaches the feminine art of china painting and the dominant presence with iron-gray hair, like that of a vigorous man, who imposes her will on the male power structure, including the post office, the tax collectors, the church, and, in the person of the pharmacist, the medical profession.

More tellingly, the characterization of Emily exceeds the opposition between homosexual and heterosexual. In terms of their biological sex, Homer and Emily are a heterosexual couple: he's a man; she's a woman. However, as we've just seen, the text constructs Emily's gender as a vacillation between the feminine and the masculine. Indeed, much of the powerfully defiant behavior traditionally associated with men is ascribed to Emily during her relationship with Homer. In terms of gender, then, one might argue that Homer and Emily are a homosexual couple: they are both men. Thus, "A Rose for Emily," ostensibly a text about heterosexual passion and transgression, is also (or more so) a queer text that reveals the limits of traditional definitions of gender and sexuality.

Similarly, a queer reading of Walt Whitman's "Song of Myself" might examine how the poem's erotic dimension requires us to expand our understanding of the sexual. One of the hallmarks of Whitman's remarkable poem is its exuberant response to life: the speaker, who identifies himself as Whitman, revels in the beauty of nature, experiences spiritual union with fellow Americans from all walks of life, and celebrates the pure joy of just being alive. As we saw earlier, critic Karl Keller examines how Whitman's camp style reveals, among other things, a seductive tone of voice and pose that humorously sexualize the poet's transcendentalist ideals of bonding with nature and with other human beings. Reading the poem through a queer lens, however, we might focus, in ways that Keller does not, on Whitman's eroticization of experience as it exceeds the contemporary white middle-class definition of homosexuality. For one might argue that the sexuality represented in "Song of Myself" is too fluid to be contained within the boundaries of male same-sex desire.

Indeed, the poem's implicit definition of sexuality includes many of those dimensions of erotic experience that, as we saw earlier, Eve Kosofsky Sedgwick argues have been neglected in sexual definitions structured by the homosexual/heterosexual opposition. Under Whitman's gaze, almost all experience has an intensely erotic quality: he offers erotic descriptions not just of young men bathing in a river (a traditional homoerotic image), but of the young woman watching them from a distance, and of the natural setting itself, which is simultaneously private (isolated) and public (out in the open). Similarly, Whitman's gaze eroticizes not only the healthy bodies of men and women at their various modes of employment, but the modes of employment as well, and the places in which they perform them: the magnificent mountains, the fertile plains, the busy harbors, and the thriving cities. In addition, the poet eroticizes—among other persons, places, things, and activities—venerable old men and women, the strength and serenity of animals, the sea, and every conceivable zone of his own body. A queer reading of "Song of Myself" might argue, therefore, that Whitman's poem is not homoerotic but cosmically erotic, or perhaps more accurately, that Whitman's homoeroticism can be fully comprehended only by transcending definitions of human sexuality that rest upon the biological sex of one's object choice or upon object choice at all.

Finally, a queer reading of Toni Morrison's *Beloved* (1987) might explore the ways in which the novel's evocative richness, its multi-layered meanings, depend in part upon its crossing or transforming or abandoning traditional demarcations between same-sex and opposite-sex love and between the "natural" and the "unnatural." For example, imitating the mating turtles she sees in the woods (that is, imitating the natural), Beloved has sex with Paul D and presumably becomes pregnant as a result (witness her swollen belly near the novel's close and the reference to her pregnancy by the women who come to rescue Sethe). In a more meaningful sense, however, Beloved is "pregnant" with herself: she's trying to give birth to herself, to a new self able to take its place in the natural world inhabited by Sethe and Denver, and thereby emerge permanently from the ghostly, supernatural darkness that continually threatens to swallow her up. And this "pregnancy" has no father. Rather, it has two mothers: Beloved and Sethe. For Beloved, like a predatory lover, consumes Sethe's life in order to give birth to her own, which we see quite literally as Sethe grows thinner while Beloved grows larger. And this strand of the narrative occurs against a backdrop of same-sex love—a blend of familial and romantic devotion among Denver, Beloved, and Sethe—that is much more powerful than Beloved's zombie-like sex with Paul D and that triumphs, at least temporarily, over the heterosexual coupling of Paul D and Sethe. Indeed, Beloved's passionate attachment to Sethe, like Denver's to Beloved, is described in romantic, even sexual, language that carries some of the most intense emotional charge of the novel. *Beloved* is thus infused with a queerness—with a refusal to limit itself to traditional notions of sexuality and of the natural—that is responsible for a good deal of the novel's narrative progression, thematic content, and emotional force.

If these examples of queer criticism seem more slippery, more indefinite, and more complicated than the examples of lesbian and gay criti-cism cited earlier, keep in mind that it is the slippery, indefinite, and com-plicated quality of human sexuality that queer criticism's deconstructive project tries to underscore. As the most recent and most philosophical trend in lesbian and gay literary studies, queer criticism promises us an exciting future of theoretical exploration and experimentation.

Some Shared Features of Lesbian, Gay, and Queer Criticism

Regardless of the differences we've just seen among lesbian, gay, and queer criticism, there is a good deal of overlap in the ways all three domains ap-proach literary interpretation. Note, for example, the similarities in the tasks performed by lesbian and gay critics discussed earlier. In addition, many gay and lesbian critics combine some of the deconstructive insights offered by queer theory with the social and political concerns associated with more traditional forms of lesbian and gay criticism. Indeed, many devotees of queer theory still refer to themselves as gay or lesbian critics.

Furthermore, critics from all three domains have taken an interest in recurring themes that appear throughout gay and lesbian literature and that constitute part of an evolving literary tradition. These themes include the following: initiation, including discovering one's queer sexual orienta-tion, experiencing one's first sexual encounters as a gay person, and "learn-ing the ropes" in the gay or lesbian subculture; "coming out" to family and friends; "coming out" at the workplace; dealing with homophobia and with heterosexist discrimination; the psychology of gay self-hatred; overcoming gay self-hatred; the role of camp and drag in gay life; dealing with loneliness and alienation; finding love; building a life with a gay or lesbian partner; the quest to build a lesbian utopia; life before and after Stonewall; life before and after AIDS (in terms of both one's personal life and the collective life of the gay and lesbian communities); caring for loved ones with AIDS; mourning the death of AIDS victims; and the importance of gay and les-bian community. Of course, the themes in gay and lesbian writing change over time as the social and political situation of gay and lesbian writers changes. And themes that occur openly in contemporary works may ap-pear, in literature from earlier periods, only in disguised forms (as we saw in our discussion of the work of Willa Cather) or in playful forms (con-sider, for example, the double meanings of the word play in Oscar Wilde's *The Importance of Being Earnest*, 1894).

Finally, lesbian, gay, and queer criticism often rely on similar kinds of textual evidence. For example, in addition to the more obvious forms of textual cues—such as homoerotic imagery and erotic encounters between same-sex characters—there are rather subtle textual cues that can create a homoerotic atmosphere even in an otherwise heterosexual text, as we saw in the examples of lesbian, gay, and queer criticism provided earlier. No single textual cue can stand on its own as evidence of a homoerotic atmosphere in a text. Nor can a small number of such cues support a lesbian, gay, or queer reading. But a preponderance of these cues, especially if coupled with other kinds of textual or biographical evidence, can strengthen a lesbian, gay, or queer interpretation even of an apparently heterosexual text. Let's take a closer look at a few of the most common examples of these subtle cues.

1. *Homosocial bonding*—The depiction of strong emotional ties between same-sex characters can create a homosocial atmosphere that may be subtly or overtly homoerotic. Whether homoerotic or not, however, the depiction of homosocial bonding foregrounds the profound importance of same-sex emotional ties in the development of human identity and community, which is a human potential often devalued, marginalized, or trivialized by the homophobic anxiety of heterosexist culture.

2. *Gay or lesbian "signs"*—Gay or lesbian signs are of two types. The first type consists of characteristics that heterosexist culture stereotypically associates with gay men or lesbians, such as might be evident, for example, in the appearance and behavior of "feminine" male characters or "masculine" female characters. The second type are coded signs created by the gay or lesbian subculture itself. For example, the word *gay*, as used in the writing of Gertrude Stein in the early decades of the twentieth century, may well have been an "in-group" coded sign that heterosexual culture of the period would not have recognized. And certainly the lesbian images in Emily Dickinson's poetry, discussed earlier, operate as coded signs generally not recognized by heterosexual readers. Interpreting both kinds of signs can be tricky because both the signs created by gay subcultures and the stereotypes created by heterosexual culture change over time. So we must use this kind of evidence cautiously and in conjunction with other forms of evidence.

Some authors may have deliberately included gay or lesbian signs in their literary works because they felt it was the only safe way, in heterosexist culture, to express their own gay or lesbian experience or to speak to a queer readership. Other authors may have included these signs for any number of conscious or unconscious reasons and may not have intended them as gay or lesbian signs. Whether or not we take into account an author's intention, our goal is to analyze how these signs function in the text to create the potential for a queer interpretation.

3. *Same-sex "doubles"*—A more subtle, somewhat abstract form of gay and lesbian signs consists of same-sex characters who look alike, act alike, or have parallel experiences. Because gay and lesbian sexuality foregrounds sexual similarity, same-sex characters who function as some sort of "mirror image" of each other can also function as gay or lesbian signs. Same-sex doubles may share a homoerotic bond, a homosocial bond, or they may not know each other at all.

4. *Transgressive sexuality*—A text's focus on transgressive sexuality, including transgressive heterosexuality (such as extramarital romance), throws into question the rules of traditional heterosexuality and thus opens the door of imagination to transgressive sexualities of all kinds. Of course, a great deal of literature deals with heterosexual transgression without necessarily having a queer sub-text. But some representations of heterosexual transgression—for example, those that involve several characters, the leading of double lives, the relaxing of inhibitions associated with alcohol and riotous parties—create an atmosphere of sexual experimentation that sets the stage, so to speak, for a queer interpretation. While a set stage is not sufficient, by itself, for a queer reading, it can provide an evocative backdrop to complement more concrete textual evidence.

Clearly, the boundaries among lesbian, gay, and queer criticism remain somewhat fluid. Your purpose in using the kinds of textual evidence just described, as well as your own self-indentified critical orientation, will determine whether your interpretation of a literary work is a lesbian, gay, or queer reading.

Some Questions Lesbian, Gay, and Queer Critics Ask about Literary Texts

The following questions are offered to summarize lesbian, gay, or queer approaches to literature. Question #7—because it rests on a deconstructive view of sexuality—is the only question that falls within the narrower theoretical definition of queer criticism. The remaining questions can be answered from any one of the three perspectives.

1. What are the politics (ideological agendas) of specific gay, lesbian, or queer works, and how are those politics revealed in, for example, the work's thematic content or portrayals of its characters?

2. What are the poetics (literary devices and strategies) of specific lesbian, gay, or queer works? What does the work contribute to the ongoing attempt to define a uniquely lesbian, gay, or queer poetics, literary tradition, or canon?

3. What does the work contribute to our knowledge of queer, gay, or lesbian experience and history, including literary history?

4. How is queer, gay, or lesbian experience coded in texts that are apparently heterosexual? (This analysis is usually done for works by writers who lived at a time when openly queer, gay, or lesbian texts would have been considered unacceptable, or it is done in order to help reformulate the sexual orientation of a writer formerly presumed heterosexual.)

5. How might the works of heterosexual writers be re-read to reveal an unspoken or unconscious lesbian, gay, or queer presence? That is, does the work have an unconscious lesbian, gay, or queer desire or conflict that it submerges (or that heterosexual readers have submerged)?

6. What does the work reveal about the operations (socially, politically, psychologically) of heterosexism? Is the work (consciously or unconsciously) homophobic? Does the work critique, celebrate, or blindly accept heterosexist values?

7. How does the literary text illustrate the problematics of sexuality and sexual "identity," that is, the ways in which human sexuality does not fall neatly into the separate categories defined by the words *homosexual* and *heterosexual*?

Depending upon the literary text in question, we might ask one or any combination of these questions. Or we might come up with a useful question not listed here. These are just some starting points to get us to look at literature through a lesbian, gay, or queer lens. Remember, not all these critics will interpret the same work in the same way, even if they use the same theoretical concepts. As in every field, even expert practitioners disagree. Our goal is to use lesbian, gay, and queer criticism to help enrich our reading of literary works, to help us see some important ideas they illustrate that we might not have seen so clearly or so deeply without these forms of criticism, and to help us appreciate the history and literary production of nonstraight people.

The following reading of *The Great Gatsby* is offered as an example of what a queer interpretation of Fitzgerald's novel might yield. I call my reading queer in both the inclusive sense of the term—my discussion will not be limited to characters of a single sex or a single sexuality—and in its deconstructive sense: my reading explores the vagaries and instabilities of the novel's representation of sexuality. Specifically, I will argue that *The Great Gatsby* is a sexually ambiguous novel: it raises a number of questions about the sexuality of its characters, but it does not answer them. And I will argue that this ambiguity results from the delivery of a heterosexual plot through the medium of a closeted gay sensibility, that of narrator Nick Carraway. Finally, I will suggest that the novel's sexual ambiguity is a reflection of Fitzgerald's apparent conflicts concerning his own sexuality.

Will the Real Nick Carraway Please Come Out? A Queer Reading of *The Great Gatsby*

Certainly, we couldn't ask for a more overtly heterosexual plot than that of F. Scott Fitzgerald's *The Great Gatsby* (1925). The novel's narrative progression is driven by Jay Gatsby's tragic love for Daisy Fay Buchanan and by three overlapping heterosexual romantic triangles: Gatsby-Daisy-Tom, Tom-Myrtle-George, and Myrtle-Tom-Daisy. This heterosexual narrative is shadowed, however, by a homoerotic sub-text, which though it remains closeted, so to speak, by the spectacular twists and turns of the heterosexual plot, is a pervasive presence in the novel.

Specifically, I will argue that the novel's treatment of sexual transgression and its proliferation of gay and lesbian signs work together to create a homoerotic sub-text that disrupts and de-stabilizes the heterosexual narrative, creating, in the process, a sexually ambiguous novel. And as we shall see, this homoerotic sub-text finds its most complete embodiment in the characterization of narrator Nick Carraway, who is, I believe, unaware of his gay orientation. Put another way, *The Great Gatsby*'s sexual ambiguity results from the delivery of a heterosexual plot through the medium of a closeted gay sensibility. In addition, I will suggest that the novel's sexual ambiguity mirrors the conflicts Fitzgerald apparently experienced concerning his own sexuality.

Although the depiction of transgressive heterosexuality cannot, by itself, create a queer sub-text in a heterosexual novel, *The Great Gatsby*'s apparent obsession with sexual transgression, which as we shall see includes intimations of gay and lesbian sexuality, sets the stage for a queer interpretation. For one thing, the three romantic triangles that generate most of the novel's action are all adulterous: Daisy, Tom, and Myrtle are all breaking their marital vows. And Daisy's illicit reunion with Gatsby is arranged by Nick, a male relative who, traditionally, should protect her virtue but, instead, facilitates her losing it. Furthermore, Gatsby had premarital sex with Daisy during their initial courtship, when "he took [her] one still October night, took her . . . ravenously and unscrupulously . . . because he had no real right to touch her hand" (156; ch. 8). And Nick and Jordan, too, are apparently engaged in a premarital affair, neither of them for the first time. Indeed, Nick believes that Jordan is sexually promiscuous: he speculates that she is "incurably dishonest" because she wants to "keep that cool insolent smile turned to the world and yet satisfy the demands of her hard jaunty body" (63; ch. 3).

Of course, the riotous parties depicted, both in Tom and Myrtle's apartment and on Gatsby's lawn, also contribute an ambience of sexual transgression. For example, Tom and Myrtle's party is an outgrowth of their illicit affair, about which they and their guests talk openly. And the descriptions of Gatsby's parties are peppered with sexually transgressive images, such as Tom's attempting to pick up a "common but pretty" young woman (112; ch. 6); Gatsby and Daisy's sneaking away from the party to be alone at Nick's cottage while Nick stands guard lest they be intruded upon; the unidentified man "talking with curious intensity to a young actress" while his wife "hisse[s] 'You promised!' into his ear" (56; ch. 3); "Beluga's girls" (66; ch. 4), with the implication that phrase carries of their being his sexual objects; and such implicitly transgressive couples as "Hubert Auerbach and Mr. Chrystie's wife" (66; ch. 4) and "Miss Claudia Hip with a man reputed to be her chauffeur" (67; ch. 4). What Nick says of New York City is thus true of the sexual atmosphere that pervades the novel: this is a place where "[a]nything can happen . . . anything at all" (73; ch. 4).

Indeed, it is at these parties where we see the striking examples of gay and lesbian "signs" that initiate the development of the novel's homo-erotic sub-text. For example, at the party where Nick first meets Gatsby, he sees "two girls in twin yellow dresses who stopped at the foot of the steps. 'Hello!' they cried together" (47; ch. 3). These two young women are a striking example of same-sex "doubles" that function as lesbian signs: they look alike, talk alike, are dressed alike, are apparently insepa-rable, and turn out to be a "pair of stage 'twins'" who do "a baby act in costume" (51; ch. 3) at the party. In fact, the depiction of these two char-acters in the 1974 film version of the novel are that film's only concession to the possibility of a queer dimension in the story: in the film, the women are portrayed dancing a tango together in a manner the sexual meaning of which cannot be missed.

At the party in Tom and Myrtle's apartment, we see a series of gay signs during the encounter between Nick and Mr. McKee, "a pale, femi-nine man" (34; ch. 2) who lives with his wife in a neighboring apartment. The encounter begins when McKee falls asleep in his chair. Nick tells us, "Taking out my handkerchief I wiped from his cheek the remains of the spot of dried lather that had worried me all the afternoon" (41; ch. 2). When McKee wakes up and leaves the party, he leaves his wife—whom Nick describes as "shrill, languid, handsome and horrible" (34; ch. 2)—behind. Nick "follow[s]" (42; ch. 2) McKee out, and the latter invites him to lunch one day. Nick agrees.

> "All right," I agreed, "I'll be glad to."
>   . . . I was standing beside his bed and he was sitting up between the sheets, clad in his underwear, with a great portfolio in his hands.
>   "Beauty and the Beast . . . Loneliness . . . Old Grocery Horse . . . Brook'n Bridge. . . ."
>   Then I was lying half asleep in the cold lower level of the Penn-sylvania Station, staring at the morning "Tribune" and waiting for the four o'clock train. (Fitzgerald's ellipses, 42; ch. 2)

Obviously, both men are very drunk, and the scene easily can be in-terpreted as nothing more than a representation of their drunkenness. From this perspective, the ellipses refer to the memory lapses that com-monly occur in such a state of inebriation. Nick is saying, in effect, "That's how drunk I was," and that's all he's saying.

Through a queer lens, however, the scene suggests another reading.

The gay signs here are numerous, and the order in which they appear implies the progression of a homoerotic attraction between the two men, if not the equally likely possibility of a sexual encounter in McKee's bedroom. These signs include McKee's feminine appearance, the masculine (aggressive, overbearing, "handsome") quality of his wife, Nick's attention to the spot of lather on McKee's face (in other words, Nick's fastidious attention to McKee's grooming), Nick's "following" him out of the room, the lunch invitation, Nick's following McKee into his bedroom, McKee's sitting in bed attired only in his underwear, and Nick's remembering nothing else until he wakes up at four o'clock in the morning on the floor of the train station (so whatever occurred in the interim has the status of a repressed memory). None of these signs would, by itself, carry much weight. But when clustered in this fashion they suggest a homoerotic sub-text that no queer critic would miss.

Perhaps the most numerous gay and lesbian signs are associated, however, with Jay Gatsby and Jordan Baker. Gatsby's fastidious grooming and flamboyant clothing and other possessions function effectively as gay signs. "[H]is short hair looked as though it were trimmed every day" (54; ch. 3), and his impeccable wardrobe features various shades of lavender and pink, two colors that have been long associated with gayness. We are told that Gatsby owns dozens of "shirts with stripes and scrolls and plaids in coral and apple green and lavender and faint orange with monograms of Indian blue" (97–98; ch. 5), and his pink suit is mentioned at least three times.

In fact, the manner in which Gatsby's pink suit is mentioned underscores its function as a gay sign. Nick's two references to the pink suit are phrased quite romantically, as if the clothing of a desirable woman were being described: "I could think of nothing but the luminosity of his pink suit under the moon" (150; ch. 7) and "[H]is gorgeous pink rag of a suit made a bright spot of color against the white steps" (162; ch. 8). And Tom's reference to the suit foregrounds its function as a gay sign because that seems to be precisely how Tom, who is clearly homophobic, sees it. Let's consider this last point a bit further.

Tom's numerous extramarital affairs with working-class women, whom he parades in public (28; ch. 2) and whose socioeconomic vulnerability gives him a great deal of power over them, suggests a need to reassure himself of his heterosexuality, as does his constant, aggressive assertion of his manhood, which we see throughout the novel. As Nick puts it,

> There was a touch of paternal contempt in [his voice], even toward people he liked. . . .

"Now, don't think my opinion on these matters is final," he seemed to say, "just because I'm stronger and more of a man than you are." (11; ch. 1)

This kind of macho overcompensation is directly related to homophobia: Tom's need to prove his own manhood leads him to attack anything he perceives as an indication of homosexuality in others. So when Tom's contempt for Gatsby expresses itself in a derogatory reference to the latter's pink suit, it underscores the suit's function as a gay sign: "An Oxford man! . . . Like hell he is! He wears a pink suit" (129; ch. 7).

Gatsby's other possessions also function as gay signs. Much of the decor of his house is extravagantly feminine: "Marie Antoinette music rooms and Restoration salons . . . [and] period bedrooms swathed in rose and lavender silk and vivid with new flowers" (96; ch. 5). And Gatsby's car has the flamboyance, as Tom puts it, of a "circus wagon" (128; ch. 7): "It was a rich cream color," Nick says, "bright with nickel, swollen here and there in its monstrous length with triumphant hatboxes and supper-boxes and tool-boxes, and terraced with a labyrinth of windshields that mirrored a dozen suns" (68; ch. 4). In fact, the artifice and theatricality of the life Gatsby has created for himself has a camp quality about it, a quality evident even in the fictional "autobiography" in which Gatsby describes himself as a "young rajah . . . collecting jewels, chiefly rubies, hunting big game, [and] painting" (70; ch. 4).

Analogously, Jordan Baker, whose name could belong to a man or a woman, is associated with numerous lesbian signs. She makes her living in the, then, male domain of professional golf. And just as Gatsby is frequently described in feminine terms, Jordan is frequently described in masculine terms. Upon first meeting her, Nick says, "I enjoyed looking at her. She was a slender, small-breasted girl with an erect carriage which she accentuated by throwing her body backward at the shoulders like a young cadet" (15; ch. 1), that is, like a young boy at military school. Even when dressed in her most feminine attire, she is described in rather masculine terms: "she wore her evening dress, all her dresses, like sports clothes—there was a jauntiness about her movements as if she had first learned to walk upon golf courses on clean, crisp mornings" (55; ch 3). Indeed, Nick's frequent descriptions of Jordan's appearance and behavior almost always evoke rather masculine images: she has a "hard jaunty body" (63; ch. 3); "[h]er body asserted itself with a restless movement" (22; ch. 1); "her brown hand waved a jaunty salute" (57; ch. 3); she has a "wan scornful mouth" (85; ch. 4); "her face [had] the same brown tint as the fingerless glove on her knee" (185; ch. 9); she "seemed to have mastered a certain hardy skepticism" (20; ch. 1); she's a "clean, hard, limited person" (84; ch. 4); and the like.

The possibility of a lesbian sub-text in Jordan's characterization is re-inforced by her relationships with men. As Nick observes, Jordan "in-stinctively avoided clever shrewd men . . . because she felt safer on a plane where any divergence from a code would be thought impossible" (63; ch. 3). In other words, Jordan doesn't want to be seen through. She doesn't want to be thought to have a private life that "diverges" from the code, so she dates men she can manipulate, like the obviously immature escort who accompanies her to one of Gatsby's parties, "a persistent under-graduate given to violent innuendo" (49; ch. 3), or like Nick, who is "flat-tered" to be seen with "a golf champion" (62; ch. 3) and whom she can wrap around her little finger simply by saying "I like you" (63; ch. 3). In this context, and despite her sexual relationship with Nick, the "demands of her hard jaunty body" that Jordan "satisf[ies]" by "dealing in subter-fuges" (63; ch. 3) imply lesbian desire.

Given their function as repositories of gay signs, it is meaningful, from a queer perspective, that Gatsby and Jordan are the two characters in whom Nick takes the most personal interest. That Nick's attraction to Gatsby is homoerotic is suggested by his focus on Gatsby's feminine qualities, which mirrors his focus on McKee; his intense appreciation of Gatsby's "gor-geous" appearance and "romantic readiness" (6; ch. 1); his frequent, pas-sionate, and often blind defense of Gatsby as the victim of others' selfish-ness and corruption; and the deep bond he feels with Gatsby after the latter's death, when it is "safe" to feel love for him. Similarly, Nick's attach-ment to Jordan seems as much the product of homoerotic as heterosexual attraction because he sees her primarily as a young boy.

In this context, Nick's successful effort to help Gatsby rekindle his af-fair with the unsuspecting Daisy also has a homoerotic sub-text. Because of Nick's homoerotic attraction to Gatsby, he is likely to be curious about Gatsby's sexuality and to want to be involved in his personal life in any way he can. "Pimping" for Gatsby (which is what Nick's "procurement" of Daisy amounts to, as Gatsby's offer to pay him for the service suggests) may let Nick feel sexually close to him. (An analogous argument can be made, of course, that Jordan's interest in promoting Daisy's affair with Gatsby springs from Jordan's sexual attraction to and curiosity about Daisy.) In addition, by helping Daisy and Gatsby reunite in his own home, Nick may also experience a vicarious sexual thrill by identifying with Daisy during this episode. This is just what he seems to do as he

chastises Gatsby for being insensitive to Daisy's feelings: "'Daisy's embar-
rassed too. . . . You're acting like a little boy,' I broke out impatiently. 'Not
only that but you're rude. Daisy's sitting in there all alone.'" (93; ch. 5).
And during the subsequent tour of Gatsby's mansion, Nick's position is
parallel to that of Daisy, as he, too, is getting a glimpse of Gatsby's private
domain for the first time.

Indeed, Nick is, himself, a repository of gay signs, a fact that underscores the homoerotic dimension of his characterization. He is just turning thirty, has never married or been engaged, and his heterosexual affairs
notwithstanding, he doesn't let his romantic relationships with women
get serious. In fact, Nick fits the profile of thousands of young men who
discovered their gay orientation during World War I. As George
Chauncey observes in his gay history of New York City,

> [M]ilitary mobilization [during World War I], by removing men from
> the supervision of their families and small-town neighborhoods and
> placing them in a single-sex environment, increased the chances that
> they would encounter self-identified gay men and explore their homo-
> sexual interests. An extensive investigation of homosexuality among
> the men stationed at the Naval Training Station in Newport, Rhode
> Island, conducted by naval officials immediately following the war re-
> vealed that numerous sailors there had begun to forge identities as fair-
> ies and queers after meeting other gay-identified sailors during the war,
> and that a much larger number of men who did not consider them-
> selves homosexual had nonetheless become familiar with the gay world
> and had homosexual experiences. Many of these men believed they
> could continue their homosexual lives only with great difficulty and
> circumspection if they returned to their hometowns, both because of
> the need to hide their homosexuality from their parents and because
> of the limited gay life available in most small towns.
>
> Military mobilization also gave many recruits the chance to see
> the sort of gay life that large cities, especially New York [the major port
> from which American troops embarked for Europe], had to offer. . . . It
> is impossible to determine how many gay soldiers stayed in New York
> after the war, but the growing visibility of gay institutions in the city in
> the 1920s . . . suggests that many of them did so—that it was, indeed,
> hard to keep them down on the farm after they'd seen gay New York.
> (145)

Nick is a Midwesterner, and like the soldiers described above, he returned from the war unable to readjust to life in his home town. Nick
says,

> I participated in that delayed Teutonic migration known as the Great
> War. I enjoyed the counter-raid so thoroughly that I came back rest-
> less. Instead of being the warm center of the world the middle-west
> now seemed like the ragged edge of the universe—so I decided to go
> east. . . . (7; ch. 1)

And where in the East does he go? He goes to New York City, which both
he and Jordan associate with transgressive sexuality. Nick says of New
York, "I began to like . . . the racy, adventurous feel of it at night" (61; ch.
3), and Jordan observes, "There's something very sensuous about it—
overripe, as if all sort of funny fruits were going to fall into your hands"
(132; ch. 7).

More precisely, Nick works in New York City, where he also spends
most of his evenings, and lives at West Egg, "this unprecedented 'place,'"
as he puts it, "that Broadway had begotten upon a Long Island fishing village" (113–14; ch. 6), "a world complete in itself, with its own standards
and its own great figures" (110; ch. 6), a world with a "raw vigor that
chafed under the old euphemisms" (114; ch. 6). In other words, Nick is
implying that he inhabits a transgressive sub-culture. And Nick's observation that Broadway is responsible for this sub-culture is noteworthy both
because Broadway was a gay cruising area in New York City at this time
(Chauncey 146) and because the theatrical profession has always been associated, whether accurately so or not, with sexual tolerance and experimentation. Of course, when we analyze Nick, we're analyzing the novel's
narrator. So it is Nick's point of view that produces the novel's sexual ambiguities. Let's take a moment to sum up those ambiguities. As we have
seen, *The Great Gatsby* is a novel that seems obsessed with sexual transgression, but the nature of that transgression is not always clear. Nick
sleeps with women but seems to be sexually attracted to McKee and,
more profoundly, to Gatsby. Nick's attraction to Jordan seems, itself, to
have a homoerotic dimension because of his fixation on her boyish appearance. Jordan, who is having an affair with Nick and could have married "several" men "at a nod of her head" (186; ch. 9), is a repository of
lesbian signs. Gatsby, the novel's most important heterosexual romantic
figure, is a repository of gay signs. Finally, Gatsby and Daisy, the heterosexual icon of the romantic couple, are brought together by Nick and Jordan, the novel's embodiment of closeted gay and lesbian desire.

The novel thus raises a number of questions about the sexuality of its
characters, but it does not answer them. Is Nick heterosexual, gay, or bi-
sexual? If there is a gay dimension to his sexuality, does he know it, and
has he acted on it? What is Jordan's sexual orientation? Is she aware of it?

What should we make of Gatsby's feminine, even camp, characteristics, given his romantic devotion to Daisy? Is the atmosphere of sexual freedom, even sexual license, that pervades the novel limited to the heterosexual domain, or does it include the gay world, and if so, in what ways?

The explanation that, I think, best accounts for most of the novel's sexual ambiguity is that Nick's sexual orientation is gay, and his gay sensibility influences his perception of the events he narrates. Thus, Gatsby and Jordan are repositories of gay and lesbian signs because we see them through Nick's eyes, and this is how *he* sees them. His perceptions may result from his own projection (he has gay desire, so he sees signs of it in others), or he may be sensitive to the queer aspects of Gatsby's and Jordan's sexuality because he shares them, or both. But Nick has closeted the queer dimension of his narrative, made it a sub-text of the heterosexual love story, because, I would argue, he has closeted his own gay desire. In other words, the novel's sexual ambiguity is the result of a heterosexual plot delivered by means of a gay sensibility that is hidden not only from others, but from itself as well.

That Nick is denying his gay orientation is suggested not merely by his sexual affairs with women, which gay men in denial often have, but by his self-presentation, which seems to try too hard to convince us, and himself, of his conventionality. For example, concerning romantic matters, Nick represents himself as the conservative, almost puritanical, consciousness of the novel. When he learns that Tom is having an affair with "some woman in New York" (19; ch. 1), he says, "[M]y own instinct was to telephone immediately for the police" (20; ch. 1) and "It seemed to me that the thing for Daisy to do was to rush out of the house, child in arms—but apparently there were no such intentions in her head" (25; ch. 1). Similarly, before he allows himself to become romantically involved with Jordan, Nick feels that he must officially end his relationship with a young woman he'd been seeing back home because, as he puts it, "I am . . . full of interior rules that act as brakes on my desires" (63–64; ch. 3). In fact, so repelled is Nick by the moral laxity of New York that when he returns to the Midwest after Gatsby's death, he tells us, "I wanted the world to be in uniform and at a sort of moral attention forever" (6; ch. 1).

At the same time, however, Nick seems to go out of his way to be sure we see him as an active heterosexual. For example, he tells us he "had a short affair with a girl who . . . worked in the accounting department" (61; ch. 3) at his place of employment. Why does he give us this apparently irrelevant bit of information except to make sure we know he's heterosexual? Having told us that the young woman he'd been seeing back home, whom everyone expected him to marry, was just "an old friend" (24; ch. 1), he wants to reassure us that he's capable of being more than just friends with a woman. Similarly, when he describes his evenings in New York City, "loiter[ing] in front of windows" (62; ch. 3) with other young men like himself, Nick deflates the homoerotic potential of the scene by relating in detail his fantasies about following "romantic women . . . to their apartments on the corners of hidden streets" (61; ch. 3).

Finally, when Nick talks about dating Jordan Baker he implies, as we saw earlier, that she is sexually promiscuous. And to make sure we know that Nick is a recipient of her sexual favors, he ends Chapter Four with a description of his kissing Jordan during a romantic carriage ride through Central Park—"I drew up [Jordan] beside me, tightening my arms. . . . [She] smiled and so I drew her up again, closer, this time to my face" (85; ch. 4)—and opens Chapter Five by telling us how late he got home: "When I came home to West Egg that night . . . [it was] [t]wo o'clock" (86; ch. 5) in the morning. In other words, Nick wants us to know that the kiss was just the beginning of his romantic encounter with Jordan.

Indeed, it seems that Nick insists on his "normality" and honesty rather too much. On the very first page of the novel Nick contrasts himself to the "wild, unknown men" at his college who wanted to reveal their "secret griefs" to him because they knew he was "inclined to reserve all judgments" (5; ch. 1). He says, "The abnormal mind is quick to detect and attach itself to this quality when it appears in a normal person" (5; ch. 1). That is, Nick may be surrounded by "abnormal" men who press themselves upon him, but he, himself, is "normal." Later, he tells us, "I am one of the few honest people that I have ever known" (64; ch. 3). And lest we forget, he reminds us in the very last chapter, "I'm thirty. . . . I'm five years too old to lie to myself and call it honor" (186; ch. 9).

Jordan, however, finally sees through Nick's self-deception. She tells him,

"You said a bad driver was only safe until she met another bad driver? Well I met another bad driver, didn't I? I mean it was careless of me to make such a wrong guess. I thought you were rather an honest, straightforward person. I thought it was your secret pride." (186; ch. 9)

In other words, Jordan has come to believe that Nick is (as is she) transgressive and dishonest about his transgression. Through a queer lens, by this point in the narrative Jordan's observation carries some weight: Nick's insistence on his "normality" and honesty has worn rather thin.

It's interesting to note that Nick, apparently without intending it, is especially ambiguous about his sexuality in the passage in which he first realizes he wants to become involved with Jordan. He says,

> I knew that first I had to get myself definitely out of that tangle back home. I'd been writing letters once a week and signing them "Love, Nick," and all I could think of was how, when that certain girl played tennis, a faint mustache of perspiration appeared on her upper lip. Nevertheless there was a vague understanding that had to be tactfully broken off before I was free. (64; ch. 3)

In this passage Nick is, characteristically, emphasizing both his honesty and his heterosexuality. But his response to that "faint mustache of perspiration"—an emblem of masculinity—is unclear. Is he attracted or repelled by this queer sign? We don't know because it is unclear whether "that certain girl" who gets the "mustache of perspiration" refers to the girl back home, with whom he wants to end his relationship, or to Jordan. If it's the girl back home, then presumably the mustache is a turn-off. If he's referring to Jordan, then presumably the mustache is a turn-on. We know it's one or the other, but we can't be certain which it is.

Of course, we can't be sure whether or not Nick is aware of the gay dimension of his sexuality. But I think if he were aware of it, he wouldn't insist so repeatedly on his heterosexuality, on his "normality," on his honesty. That is, his denial seems to go beyond the strategic need to hide his gay orientation from other characters or from heterosexist readers. His protestations of his own conventionality constitute a rhetoric of psychological denial that suggests he is hiding his gay orientation from himself, as well. In keeping with the psychology of denial, I think Nick's blindness to his sexual orientation is precisely what gives his gay sensibility the power it has to project itself into his narrative so thoroughly, layering the novel with multiple meanings, infusing it with interpretive possibilities that, from a queer perspective, greatly enrich the reading experience it offers.

Interestingly, the sexual ambiguity Nick's gay sensibility creates in the novel, as well as his apparent denial of his gay orientation, mirror the conflicts Fitzgerald seemed to have experienced concerning his own sexuality. While we are not required to explain authors' representations of sexuality in terms of their own sexual orientations, in Fitzgerald's case, the correlations between his life and his work are too striking to be overlooked.

Much like *The Great Gatsby*, Fitzgerald, himself, seemed obsessed with transgressive sexuality. "For years Fitzgerald would annoy friends and new acquaintances by asking whether they had slept with their wives before they were married" (Bruccoli 114). And he sometimes seemed drawn to people who liked to talk of little else. According to his wife Zelda, "all [Fitzgerald and his friends] talk[ed] about [wa]s sex—sex plain, striped, mixed, and fancy" (Mayfield 138). Fitzgerald seemed especially fascinated, however, by gay sexuality, toward which his attitude ranged, at different times during his life, from playful to homophobic.

As a Princeton undergraduate, Fitzgerald posed for a publicity photo, dressed as a showgirl, to advertise one of the University's all-male theatrical productions. The photo

> appeared in several newspapers, including *The New York Times*, and brought him fan letters from men who wanted to meet him and from an agent who offered to book him for a vaudeville tour as a female impersonator. (Bruccoli 62)

Although all the female roles at Princeton were played by male college students, Fitzgerald's experimentation with drag didn't stop there. He dressed as a woman and attended a fraternity dance at the University of Minnesota, where he "shocked his [male] dancing partners [who thought he was a young woman] with a racy line" (Bruccoli 65). And he kept the photos of himself dressed as a showgirl and liked to show them to friends (Mayfield 134).

Fitzgerald also liked to banter about himself as if he were gay. "While he was in the army, he sent Edmund Wilson [his friend and literary critic] two photographs of himself in a letter, saying that he enclosed the two pictures for Wilson to give to some poor, motherless . . . fairy who had no dream" (Mayfield 134). Later, he told Wilson that one of his longings was "to go with a young man *affectueux* [affectionate] for a paid amorous weekend on the coast. It was, he added, deep calling to deep" (Mayfield 134). Certainly, Fitzgerald intended these remarks as "off-color jokes about himself" (Mayfield 134), but they reveal his curiosity about gay life as well as the gay dimension of his sexual imagination.

At other times, Fitzgerald's interest in homosexuality was clearly homophobic: "He had always been outspokenly contemptuous of 'fairies'" (Bruccoli 278), and he and Ernest Hemingway liked to joke "about pederasty, anal eroticism, and other forms of perversion" (Mayfield 133). Indeed, it was "the fairies" whom Fitzgerald blamed for "spoil[ing]" his close friendship with Hemingway (Mayfield 142). Presumably, Fitzgerald was referring to the rumors that he and Hemingway were gay, which upset him greatly (Bruccoli 278). Yet Fitzgerald was "not averse" to implying, himself, that Hemingway was gay, "referring to him as 'Hemophile, the Bleeding Boy'" (Mayfield 136).

Gay sexuality was also an issue of concern in Fitzgerald's marriage. Zelda believed that her husband "was involved in a homosexual liaison with Hemingway" (Bruccoli 278), and "to verify his masculinity, Fitzgerald decided to try sleeping with a whore and purchased condoms; Zelda found them, and a bitter argument ensued" (Bruccoli 279). Zelda also believed that she, herself, "was a latent lesbian," and "Fitzgerald was furious when Dolly Wilde, a notorious Paris 'amazon,' made a pass at Zelda" (Bruccoli 279).

Although it's impossible to draw any reliable conclusions about Fitzgerald's sexual orientation—there is no concrete data about his sexual activity, and evidence of his sexual desire is often marred by contradictory hearsay—we can very safely say that sexuality, especially gay sexuality, was an important issue for him. It is clear that he was intensely curious about gay life and intensely conflicted about it as well, for he was both drawn to and repulsed by the sexual possibilities it offered. And his homophobic response to the gay world reveals, if it reveals nothing else, that Fitzgerald did not want to admit the conflicts he experienced concerning his sexuality.

Given Fitzgerald's consistent reliance on his own personal experience for the material he used in his novels, it should not be surprising that *The Great Gatsby*'s focus on transgressive sexuality should include a queer dimension, whether the author intended it so or not. For as we have seen, Fitzgerald's fascination with transgressive sexuality was in no way limited to the heterosexual domain. And if, as the author's own life suggests, Jay Gatsby embodies Fitzgerald's capacity to devote himself to the pursuit of a heterosexual ideal, then surely Nick Carraway embodies his capacity to deny the gay dimension of his conflicted sexuality. Through a queer lens, then, the real Nick Carraway does come out—or at least comes into focus—as we see the ways in which his closeted gay sensibility opens one of America's best-known heterosexual love stories to queer interpretations.

Questions for Further Practice:
Lesbian, Gay, and Queer Approaches to Other Literary Works

The following questions are intended as models. They can help you use lesbian, gay, and queer criticism to interpret the literary works to which they refer or other texts of your choice. Your purpose in addressing these questions, the way in which you focus your essay, and your own self-identified critical orientation will determine whether your essay is considered an example of lesbian, gay, or queer criticism.

1. How does Willa Cather's "Paul's Case" (1905) represent, among other things, the social and psychological conflicts of gay identity coming of age in a heterosexist world? In what ways might the story be said to illustrate the operations of compulsory heterosexuality?

2. How do representations of sexuality in Toni Morrison's *The Bluest Eye* (1970) exceed traditional definitions of homosexuality and heterosexuality? Consider, for example the prostitutes' relationship to men, to sex, and to one another; Geraldine's relationship to her husband and to the cat; Cholly's relationship to the hunters, Darlene, Pauline, and Pecola; Pecola's relationship to the Mary Jane candies; Soaphead Church's relationship to Velma and to little girls; Mr. Henry's relationship to the prostitutes and to the MacTeer girls; and so forth. In other words, how does the novel reveal the inadequacy of the categories "heterosexual" and "homosexual" for our understanding of human sexuality?

3. Although Henry James apparently led a celibate life, many scholars claim his work for the gay canon because of its gay sensibility and because of the author's long-term relationships with the younger men whom he mentored and to whom he wrote letters expressing his love and devotion. The master-pupil relationship is also a recurring theme in James's fiction. Explore the author's representation of the master-pupil relationship in *The Turn of the Screw* (1898). Might Quint's relationship to Miles represent the dark potential of the master-pupil bond, while the governess (a stand-in for James?) illustrates its self-sacrificing devotion? From this perspective, what do we make of Miles's death? (It is interesting to note that the sudden, mysterious death of an exceptional male pupil is a recurring theme in James's fiction.)

4. Analyze the sexual politics of Jeanette Winterson's *Oranges Are Not the Only Fruit* (1985). What does the text want its readers to understand about the relationship among lesbian sexuality and such social/psychological/political forces as the heterosexual family and the church? How might the attitude of the repressive

religious sect represented in the novel illustrate the oppression of lesbianism by society in general?

5. Examine the (apparently unconscious) homoerotic subtext of Mary Shelley's *Frankenstein* (1848). How might we argue that Victor's true love is Clerval (whose self-sacrificing care nurses the protagonist through a long illness) rather than Elizabeth? How is this same-sex bond paralleled in Walton's romantic admiration of Victor? What similarities might we find between Elizabeth's relationship to Victor and Clerval, and Mary Shelley's relationship to her husband Percy and their mutual friend and companion Lord Byron?

For Further Reading

All of the following works will help you develop your skills as lesbian, gay, and queer critics. Texts listed under "Category I" are written in language accessible to most beginners. Texts listed under "Category II" employ more technical language but are well worth the extra effort that may be required of some students new to the field.

Category I

Abelove, Henry, Michèle Aina Barale, and David M. Halperin, eds. *The Lesbian and Gay Studies Reader*. New York: Routledge, 1993.

Cruikshank, Margaret. *The Gay and Lesbian Liberation Movement*. New York: Routledge, 1992.

———. *Lesbian Studies, Present and Future*. New York: The Feminist Press, 1982.

Faderman, Lillian. *Surpassing the Love of Men: Romantic Friendship and Love Between Women from the Renaissance to the Present*. New York: William Morrow, 1981.

Freud, Sigmund. *Three Essays on the Theory of Sexuality*. 1905. *The Standard Edition of the Complete Psychological Works of Sigmund Freud*. J. Strachey et al., trans. and eds. 24 vols. London: Hogarth, 1966–74. Vol. 7.

Frye, Marilyn. *Willful Virgin: Essays in Feminism*. Freedom, CA: Crossing, 1992.

Jay, Karla, and Joanne Glasgow. *Lesbian Texts and Contexts: Radical Revisions*. New York: New York UP, 1990.

Lorde, Audre. *Sister Outsider: Essays and Speeches*. Trumansburg: Crossing, 1984.

Moraga, Cherríe, and Gloria Anzaldúa, eds. *This Bridge Called My Back: Writings by Radical Women of Color*. 2nd ed. New York: Kitchen Table: Women of Color Press, 1983.

Rich, Adrienne. *On Lies, Secrets, and Silence: Selected Prose*. New York: W. W. Norton, 1979.

Sedgwick, Eve Kosofsky. "Gender Criticism." *Redrawing the Boundaries: The Transformation of English and American Literary Studies.* Eds. Stephen Greenblatt and Giles Gunn. New York: Modern Language Association, 1992. 271–302.

Summers, Claude J., ed. *The Gay and Lesbian Literary Heritage: A Reader's Companion to the Writers and Their Works, from Antiquity to the Present.* New York: Henry Holt, 1995.

Zimmerman, Bonnie. *The Safe Sea of Women: Lesbian Fiction 1969–1989.* Boston: Beacon, 1990.

Category II

Anzaldúa, Gloria. *Borderlands/La Frontera: The New Mestiza.* San Francisco: Aunt Lute Books, 1987.

Butler, Judith. *Gender Trouble: Feminism and the Subversion of Identity.* New York: Routledge, 1990.

Butters, Ronald R., John M. Clum, and Michael Moon, eds. *Displacing Homophobia: Gay Male Perspectives in Literature and Culture.* Durham: Duke UP, 1989.

Foucault, Michel. *The History of Sexuality.* Vol. 1, *An Introduction.* Trans. Robert Hurley. New York: Pantheon, 1978.

Haggerty, George E., and Bonnie Zimmerman, eds. *Professions of Desire: Lesbian and Gay Studies in Literature.* New York: Modern Language Association, 1995.

Nelson, Emmanuel S., ed. *Critical Essays: Gay and Lesbian Writers of Color.* New York: Haworth, 1993.

Sedgwick, Eve Kosofsky. *Epistemology of the Closet.* Berkeley: U of California P, 1990.

Notes

1. For a complete discussion of discrimination against lesbians and gay men, see Cruikshank.
2. The functions of "minoritizing" and "universalizing" views of homosexuality were developed by Eve Kosofsky Sedgwick in *Epistemology of the Closet.*
3. See *Selections from the Letters of Geraldine Endsor Jewsbury to Jane Welsh Carlyle,* edited by Mrs. Alexander Ireland (London: Longmans, Green and Co., 1892), p. 38. This quotation is taken from a letter dated October 29, 1841 (cited in Faderman, p. 164).

Works Cited

Babuscio, Jack. "Camp and the Gay Sensibility." *Gays and Films.* British Film Institute, 1977. Rpt. in *Campgrounds: Style and Homosexuality.* Ed. David Bergman. Amherst: U of Massachusetts P, 1993. 19–38.

Bennett, Paula. "The Pea That Duty Locks: Lesbian and Feminist-Heterosexual Readings of Emily Dickinson's Poetry." *Lesbian Texts and Contexts: Radical Revisions.* Eds. Karla Jay and Joanne Glasgow. New York: New York UP, 1990. 104–25.

Bruccoli, Matthew J. *Some Sort of Epic Grandeur: The Life of F. Scott Fitzgerald.* New York: Harcourt Brace Jovanovich, 1981.

Cather, Willa. *My Ántonia*. 1918. Rev. 1926. Rpt. Boston: Houghton, 1980.

Chauncey, George. *Gay New York: Gender, Urban Culture, and the Making of the Gay Male World, 1890–1940*. New York: Basic, 1994.

Cruikshank, Margaret. "Gay and Lesbian Liberation as a Political Movement." *The Gay and Lesbian Liberation Movement*. New York: Routledge, 1992. 57–89.

Dickinson, Emily. *The Poems of Emily Dickinson*. Ed. Thomas H. Johnson. 3 vols. Cambridge, MA: Belknap Press of Harvard UP, 1958.

Faderman, Lillian. "Boston Marriage." *Surpassing the Love of Men: Romantic Friendship and Love between Women from the Renaissance to the Present*. New York: William Morrow, 1981. 190–203.

Fetterly, Judith. "*My Ántonia*, Jim Burden, and the Dilemma of the Lesbian Writer." *Lesbian Texts and Contexts: Radical Revisions*. Eds. Karla Jay and Joanne Glasgow. New York: New York UP, 1990. 145–63.

Frye, Marilyn. "Some Reflections on Separatism and Power." *Sinister Wisdom* 6 (1978). Rpt. in *The Lesbian and Gay Studies Reader*. Eds. Henry Abelove, Michèle Aina Barale, and David M. Halperin. New York: Routledge, 1993. 91–98.

Keller, Karl. "Walt Whitman Camping." *Walt Whitman Review* 26 (1981). Rpt. in *Campgrounds: Style and Homosexuality*. Ed. David Bergman. Amherst: U of Massachusetts P, 1993. 113–20.

Mayfield, Sara. *Exiles from Paradise: Zelda and Scott Fitzgerald*. New York: Delacorte, 1971.

Radel, Nicholas F. "Self as Other: The Politics of Identity in the Works of Edmund White." *Queer Words, Queer Images: Communication and the Construction of Homosexuality*. Ed. R. Jeffrey Ringer. New York: New York UP, 1994. 175–92.

Rich, Adrienne. "Compulsory Heterosexuality and Lesbian Existence." *Signs* 5.4 (1980): 631–60. Rpt. in *The Lesbian and Gay Studies Reader*. Eds. Henry Abelove, Michèle Aina Barale, and David M. Halperin. New York: Routledge, 1993. 227–54.

Sedgwick, Eve Kosofsky. "Across Gender, Across Sexuality: Willa Cather and Others." *Displacing Homophobia: Gay Male Perspectives in Literature and Culture*. Eds. Ronald R. Butters, John M. Clum, and Michael Moon. Durham: Duke UP, 1989. 53–72.

———. *Epistemology of the Closet*. Berkeley: U of California P, 1990.

Smith, Barbara. "Toward a Black Feminist Criticism." 1977. *All the Women Are White, All the Blacks Are Men, But Some of Us Are Brave*. Eds. Gloria T. Hull, Patricia Bell Scott, and Barbara Smith. Old Westbury, NY: The Feminist Press, 1982. 157–75.

CHAPTER 11

Postcolonial and African American Criticism

Perhaps one of the most important abilities critical theory develops in us is the ability to see connections where we didn't know they existed: for example, connections between our personal psychological conflicts and the way we interpret a poem, between the ideologies we've internalized and the literary works we find aesthetically pleasing, between a nation's political climate and what its intellectuals consider "great" literature, and so forth. Most of the critical theories we've studied so far have encouraged us to make connections along one or all of these lines. Postcolonial and African American criticism are particularly effective at helping us see connections among all the domains of our experience—the psychological, ideological, social, political, intellectual, and aesthetic—in ways that show us just how inseparable these categories are in our lived experience of ourselves and our world.

As we'll see, postcolonial and African American criticism also share a number of theoretical assumptions and political concerns because both fields focus on the experience and literary production of peoples whose history is characterized by extreme political, social, and psychological oppression. However, much postcolonial criticism, perhaps because it attempts to understand the similarities among formerly colonized populations all over the globe, tends to be rather abstract and general in its analyses. African American criticism, in contrast, examines the experience and literary production of a single formerly "colonized" population—Americans of African descent—and much of its analysis therefore tends to be more concrete and specific. In terms both of their similarities and their differences, however, the study of postcolonial and African

American criticism is complementary: what we learn from each field helps illuminate the other.

Because postcolonial criticism defines formerly colonized peoples as any population that has been subjected to the political domination of another population, you may see postcolonial critics draw examples from the literary works of African Americans as well as from, for example, the literature of Australian aboriginal peoples or the formerly colonized population of India. However, the tendency of postcolonial criticism to focus on global issues, on comparisons and contrasts among various peoples, means that it is up to the individual members of specific populations to develop their own body of criticism on the history, traditions, and interpretation of their own literature. Of course, this is precisely what African American critics have been doing for some time, indeed long before postcolonial criticism emerged as a powerful force in literary studies in the early 1990s. To provide the broadest context for our discussion, we'll begin with an examination of postcolonial criticism as a bird's-eye view of global issues from which we'll then focus in on the more specific territory of African American criticism.

Postcolonial Criticism

As most of us can recall from our high-school history classes, European domination of the New World began in the fifteenth century. Spain, France, England, Portugal, and the Netherlands were the main contenders for the plunder of natural and human resources, and over the next few centuries European empires extended themselves around the globe. During the nineteenth century Britain emerged as the largest imperial power, and by the turn of the twentieth century the British Empire ruled one quarter of the earth's surface, including India, Australia, New Zealand, Canada, Ireland, and significant holdings in Africa, the West Indies, South America, the Middle East, and Southeast Asia. British colonial domination continued until the end of World War II, when India gained independence in 1947, and other colonies gradually followed suit. By 1980 Britain had lost all but a few of its colonial holdings.

Although postcolonial criticism didn't become a major force in literary studies until the early 1990s, the cultural analysis of colonialism upon which it draws has played an important role in anti-colonial political movements everywhere and took its place as a field of intellectual inquiry when colonial regimes began to topple after World War II. As a domain within literary studies, postcolonial criticism is both a subject matter and a theoretical framework. As a subject matter, postcolonial criticism analyzes literature produced by cultures that developed in response to colonial domination, from the first point of colonial contact to the present. (You may recall reading postcolonial literature under the heading of "Commonwealth literature," which it was called until the 1980s.) Some of this literature was written by the colonizers. Much more of it was written, and is being written, by colonized and formerly colonized peoples. As a subject matter any analysis of a postcolonial literary work, regardless of the theoretical framework used, might be called postcolonial criticism. For English majors, of course, postcolonial criticism focuses on the literature of cultures that developed in response to British colonial domination because English Departments study literatures written in English.

However, as a theoretical framework, and this is our primary concern here, postcolonial criticism seeks to understand the operations—politically, socially, culturally, and psychologically—of colonialist and anti-colonialist ideologies. For example, a good deal of postcolonial criticism analyzes the ideological forces that, on the one hand, pressed the colonized to internalize the colonizers' values and, on the other hand, promoted the resistance of colonized peoples against their oppressors, a resistance that is as old as colonialism itself. And as we'll see, because colonialist and anti-colonialist ideologies can be present in any literary text, a work doesn't have to be categorized as postcolonial for us to be able to use postcolonial criticism to analyze it.

Postcolonial Identity

That so many peoples formerly colonized by Britain, in addition to the local languages they may use at home, speak English, write in English, use English in their schools and universities, and conduct government business in English is an indication of the residual effect of colonial domination on their cultures. In fact, the dynamic psychological and social interplay between what ex-colonial populations consider their native, indigenous, pre-colonial cultures and the British culture that was imposed upon them constitutes a large portion of the field of study for postcolonial critics. For postcolonial cultures include both a merger of and antagonism between the culture of the colonized and that of the colonizer, which, at this point in time, are difficult to identify and separate into discrete entities, so complete was the British intrusion into the government, education, cultural values, and daily lives of its colonial subjects.

In short, although the colonizers retreated and left the lands they had invaded in the hands of those they had colonized, de-colonization often has been confined largely to the removal of British military forces and government officials. What has been left behind is a deeply embedded *cultural colonization*, the inculcation of a British system of government and education, British culture, and British values that denigrate the culture, morals, and even physical appearance of formerly subjugated peoples. Thus, ex-colonials often were left with a psychological "inheritance" of a negative self-image and alienation from their own indigenous cultures, which had been forbidden or devalued for so long that much pre-colonial culture has been lost.

Given that a good deal of postcolonial criticism addresses the problem of cultural identity as it is represented in postcolonial literature, let's take a closer look at the issue of postcolonial identity. In order to do so, however, we must first understand colonialist ideology, the reactions to which constitute the origin of postcolonial identity.

Colonialist ideology, often referred to as *colonialist discourse* to mark its relationship to the language in which colonialist thinking was expressed, was based on the colonizers' assumption of their own superiority, which they contrasted with the alleged inferiority of native (indigenous) peoples, the original inhabitants of the lands they invaded. The colonizers believed that only their own Anglo-European culture was civilized, sophisticated, or as postcolonial critics put it, *metropolitan*. Therefore, native peoples were defined as savage, backward, undeveloped. Because their technology was more highly advanced, the colonizers believed that their whole culture was more highly advanced, and they ignored or swept aside the religions, customs, and codes of behavior of the peoples they subjugated. So the colonizers saw themselves at the center of the world; the colonized were at the margins. The colonizers saw themselves as the embodiment of what a human being should be, the proper "self"; native peoples were "other," different, and therefore inferior. This practice of judging all who are different as inferior is called *othering*, and it divides the world between "us," the "civilized," and "them"—the "others"—the "savages." The "savage" is usually considered evil as well as inferior (the *demonic other*). But sometimes the "savage" is perceived as possessing a "primitive" beauty or nobility born of a closeness to nature (the *exotic other*). In either case, however, the "savage" remains other and, therefore, not fully human.

Today, this attitude—the use of European culture as the standard to which all other cultures are negatively contrasted—is called *Eurocentrism*.

A common example of Eurocentrism in literary studies is the long-standing philosophy of so-called *universalism*. British, European, and later, American cultural standard-bearers judged all literature in terms of its "universality": to be considered a great work, a literary text had to have "universal" characters and themes. However, whether or not a text's characters and themes were considered "universal" depended on whether or not they resembled those of European literature. Thus, the assumption was that European ideas, ideals, and experience were universal, that is, the standard for all humankind.

An example of Eurocentric language can be seen in the terms *First World*, *Second World*, *Third World*, and *Fourth World* to refer to, respectively, (1) Britain, Europe, and the United States; (2) the white populations of Canada, Australia, New Zealand, and southern Africa (and/or, for some theorists, the former Soviet bloc); (3) the developing nations, such as India and those of Africa, Central and South America, and Southeast Asia; and (4) the indigenous populations subjugated by white settlers and governed today by the majority culture that surrounds them, such as Native Americans and aboriginal Australians (and, for some theorists, non-white populations who have minority status in "First-World" countries, such as African Americans). Although these four "worlds" are commonly referred to today, we should be aware of their Eurocentric implications. Such language makes sense only if history begins with Europe and is organized in terms of European colonial conquest. It ignores the existence of earlier worlds, such as those of Greece, Egypt, and Africa, and it privileges European military conquest as the primary means of organizing world history.

Another example of Eurocentrism is a specific form of othering called *orientalism*, analyzed by Edward Said (pronounced sah-eed), which has been practiced in Europe, Britain, and America. Its purpose is to produce a positive national self-definition for Western nations by contrast with Eastern nations upon which the West projects all the negative characteristics it doesn't want to believe exist among its own people. Thus the Chinese or the Arabs, or whatever Asian or Middle Eastern population is politically convenient, are defined as cruel, sneaky, evil, cunning, dishonest, given to sexual promiscuity and perversion, and the like. (Think of the cruel, deceitful Arab merchant in Mary Shelley's *Frankenstein*, published in 1818, who is saved from prison by the young De Lacey, a European, whom the Arab subsequently betrays.) Citizens of the West then define themselves, in contrast to the imaginary "oriental" they've created, as kind, straightforward, good, upright, honest, and moral. In short, the "oriental" is an invention of the West, by contrast to whom it has been able to define itself positively and justify any acts of military or economic aggression it has found advantageous.

Thus, colonialist ideology, which is inherently Eurocentric, was a pervasive force in the British schools established in the colonies to inculcate British culture and values in the indigenous peoples and thereby forestall rebellion. It's difficult to rebel against a system or a people one has been programmed, over several generations, to consider superior. The plan was extremely successful and resulted in the creation of *colonial subjects*, colonized persons who did not resist colonial subjugation because they were taught to believe in British superiority and, therefore, in their own inferiority. Many of these individuals tried to imitate the colonizers, as much as possible, in dress, speech, behavior, and lifestyle, a phenomenon postcolonial critics refer to as *mimicry*. Postcolonial theorists often describe the colonial subject as having a *double consciousness* or *double vision*, in other words, a consciousness or a way of perceiving the world that is divided between two antagonistic cultures: that of the colonizer and that of the indigenous community.[2]

Double consciousness often produced an unstable sense of self, which was heightened by the forced migration colonialism frequently caused, for example, from the rural farm or village to the city in search of employment. (Forced migration, either as a quest for employment, including indentured servitude, or as the result of enslavement, scattered large numbers of peoples around the globe, and large populations of their descendants have remained in the *diaspora*, or separated from their original homeland.) This feeling of being caught between cultures, of belonging to neither rather than to both, of finding oneself arrested in a psychological limbo that results not merely from some individual psychological disorder but from the trauma of the cultural displacement within which one lives, is referred to by Homi Bhabha and others as *unhomeliness*. Being "unhomed" is not the same as being homeless. To be unhomed is to feel not at home even in your own home because you are not at home in yourself: your cultural identity crisis has made you a psychological refugee, so to speak.

Double consciousness and unhomeliness persist in de-colonized nations today. So among the tasks formerly colonized peoples face is the rejection of colonialist ideology, which defined them as inferior, and the reclamation of their pre-colonial past. Both tasks involve many complex problems of interest to postcolonial critics. For example, in order to reject colonialist ideology and embrace their pre-colonial culture, some native authors, such as Kenyan writer Ngugi wa Thiong'o, write in their own local languages. When they do so, however, they face the difficulty of surviving in a publishing industry, both in their own countries and internationally, that requires the use of English. The use of native languages therefore often requires native writers to put forth the double effort of writing in their indigenous languages and then translating their work into English or having it translated.

On the other hand, many indigenous writers from former British colonies prefer to write in English because that is the language in which they first learned to write. As Nigerian writer Chinua Achebe observes, "[F]or me there is no other choice. I have been given the language and I intend to use it" (*Morning Yet on Creation Day* 62). Some argue, as well, that English provides a common language for the various indigenous peoples within Third- and Fourth-World nations, who speak a number of different local languages, to communicate with one another. And they point out that English, as a world language, facilitates the emergence of those nations into global politics and economics.

Another problem that complicates the desire to reclaim a pre-colonial past is that it is not always easy to discover that past. As we noted earlier, much pre-colonial culture has been lost over many generations of colonial domination. In addition, many postcolonial theorists argue that, even had there been no colonization, the ancient culture would have changed by now: no culture stands still, frozen in time. Furthermore, most cultures are changed by cross-cultural contact, often through military invasion. For example, ancient Celtic culture was changed by the Roman legions who occupied the British Isles. And Anglo-Saxon culture was changed by the many generations of French rule that followed the Norman conquest of that same territory in the eleventh century. By the same token, the pre-colonial cultures of colonized peoples influenced European culture. For example, Picasso's art was greatly influenced by his study of African masks. Therefore, many postcolonial theorists argue that postcolonial identity is necessarily a dynamic, constantly evolving *hybrid* of native and colonial cultures. Moreover, they assert that this *hybridity*, or *syncretism*, as it's sometimes called, does not consist of a stalemate between two warring cultures but is, rather, a productive, exciting, positive force in a shrinking world that is itself becoming more and more culturally hybrid. This view encourages ex-colonials to embrace the multiple and often conflicting aspects of the blended culture that is theirs and that is an indelible fact of history.

It is important to note, however, that these arguments don't take into account the need of formerly colonized peoples to rediscover and affirm their pre-colonial civilization for the very good reason that the colonizers told them they didn't have any pre-colonial civilization. Before colonization, the colonizers claimed, native peoples lived a barbaric existence whose customs, systems of government, and religions were either non-existent or not worth sustaining in the face of the "superior" civilization offered them by the Europeans. Many ex-colonials therefore feel they must assert a native culture both to avoid being swamped by the Western culture so firmly planted on their soil and to recuperate their national image in their own eyes and in the eyes of others. This emphasis on indigenous culture, especially when accompanied by the attempt to eliminate Western influences, is called *nativism* or *nationalism*. From a nativist perspective, there is a big difference between a culture changing over time and a people being cut off from their culture.

If you've read Chapter Four, "Feminist Criticism," you've probably noted, as many postcolonial critics have, a number of similarities in the theoretical issues that concern feminist and postcolonial criticism. For example, patriarchal subjugation of women is analogous to colonial subjugation of indigenous populations. And the resultant devaluation of women and colonized peoples poses very similar problems for both groups in terms of achieving an independent personal and group identity; gaining access to political power and economic opportunities; and finding ways to think, speak, and create that are not dominated by the ideology of the oppressor.

These parallels between feminist and postcolonial concerns also underscore the double oppression suffered by postcolonial women. For they are the victims of both colonialist ideology, which devalues them because of their race, and patriarchal ideology, which devalues them because of their gender. Sadly, postcolonial women have suffered patriarchal oppression not only at the hands of colonialists, but within their own patriarchal cultures as well. As Anne McClintock observes, "In a world where women do two-thirds of the world's work, earn 10 percent of the world's income, and own less than 1 percent of the world's property, the promise of 'post-colonialism' [national independence] has been a history of hopes postponed" (298). And predictably, international aid to developing countries reinforces this pattern, giving the money, the machinery, and the training to men alone, even in Africa, where "women farmers produce 65–80 percent of all agricultural produce, yet do not own the land they work, and are consistently by-passed by aid programs and 'development' projects" (McClintock 298).

Postcolonial Debates

As you may have noticed, our focus, so far, on the political, social, cultural, and psychological colonization of indigenous peoples has limited our discussion to *invader colonies*—colonies established among non-white peoples through the force of British arms, such as those established in India, Africa, the West Indies, South America, the Middle East, and Southeast Asia—for no one debates the inclusion of literature from these cultures in postcolonial literary studies. There is also a general consensus that the United States and Ireland are not postcolonial nations, the first because it has been independent for so long and has, itself, colonized others, the second because it has long been an integral part of British culture (though some Irish people, especially in the North, would surely disagree with this assessment, and many postcolonial critics cite the work of Irish poet W. B. Yeats as emblematic of anti-colonialist nationalism). However, there is much debate among postcolonial critics concerning whether or not the literature of *white settler colonies*—specifically, those established in Canada, Australia, New Zealand, and southern Africa—should be included in the study of postcolonial literature.

Those who argue that the term *postcolonial* should be reserved for "Third-" and "Fourth-World" writers observe that white settler cultures share a tremendous common ground with Britain, including race, language, and culture. These colonies viewed Britain as the "mother country," not as an imperial invader, and they were treated very differently from the non-white colonies Britain controlled. For example, white settler colonies were permitted a good deal of self-government and were granted Dominion status (political autonomy within the British Commonwealth) without having to take up arms to achieve it. Indeed, it was white settlers who, as Britain did elsewhere, subjugated non-white indigenous peoples and took their land and natural resources. In other words, these theorists argue, the inclusion of white settler cultures under the postcolonial rubric ignores the enormous difference race has played in the history of colonization and continues to play today in the racist attitudes that keep "Third-" and "Fourth-World" peoples economically oppressed.

On the other hand, theorists who believe white settler cultures should be included in the term *postcolonial* argue that the foundational concept of postcolonial criticism is anti-colonial resistance, and the literatures of white settler cultures have a good deal to teach us about the complexities of anti-colonial resistance because their own resistance to cultural obliteration by an overwhelming British cultural presence has occurred without the help of a clear distinction between colonized and colonizer, a distinction that non-white invader colonies have been able to count on. In other words, white colonial subjects experience—in a subtler, less clearly demarcated form—the same double consciousness experienced by non-white colonial subjects. From this perspective, we can't simply ignore the anti-colonialist literature produced by the "Second World" while we uncritically assume that all the literature produced by non-white colonized peoples is necessarily a literature of resistance.

Another debate engaging the attention of postcolonial critics concerns the politics of their own critical agenda. For example, the term *postcolonial criticism* implies that colonialism is a thing of the past. In reality, it is not. Colonialism is no longer practiced as it was between the late fifteenth and mid-twentieth centuries, through the direct, overt administration of governors and educators from the colonizing country. Today, through different means, the same kind of political, economic, and cultural subjugation of vulnerable nations occurs at the hands of international corporations from such world powers as the United States, Germany, and Japan. Indeed, Japan has become so Americanized since the end of World War II that it is considered a "Western" power.

This *neo-colonialism*, as it's called, exploits the cheap labor available in developing countries, often at the expense of those countries' own struggling businesses, cultural traditions, and ecological well-being. Neo-colonialist corporate enterprise is supported, when the need arises, by puppet regimes (local rulers paid by a corporation to support its interests) and by covert military intervention (sometimes in the form of financing troops loyal to corporate political interests, sometimes in the form of enlisting military aid from the Western power most closely aligned with the corporation's concerns). In other words, just as in the case of old-style European colonialism, there is big money to be made in this game, and the major players are too powerful to be bound by any rules of fair play.

Cultural imperialism,[1] a direct result of economic domination, consists of the "takeover" of one culture by another: the food, clothing, customs, recreation, and values of the economically dominant culture increasingly replace those of the economically vulnerable culture until the latter appears to be a kind of imitation of the former. American cultural imperialism has been one of the most pervasive forms of this phenom-enon, as we see American fashions, movies, music, sports, fast food, and consumerism squeeze out indigenous cultures all over the world.

Some theorists believe that postcolonial criticism is, itself, a form of cultural imperialism. For one thing, most postcolonial critics—including those born in formerly colonized nations, many of whom were educated at European universities and live abroad—all belong to an intellectual elite, an academic ruling class that has, it would seem, little in common with *subalterns*, or people of inferior status, that is, with the majority of poor, exploited ex-colonial peoples who are the object of their concern.

Furthermore, postcolonial criticism's analysis of the problem of cultural identity—specifically, its focus on the instability and dynamic, hybrid forms of cultural identity—is largely a product of the post-structuralist, deconstructive theory of the "First World." As you may re-call from Chapter Eight, deconstruction defines the self as a fragmented pastiche of numerous "selves" within a world that has no stable mean-ing and no value beyond that which we assign it. Such a theory is ex-tremely helpful in allowing us to understand how we construct the illu-sion of our own identity out of the ideological materials provided by our culture. And deconstruction has been used effectively to reveal the Eurocentrism and cultural imperialism of the Western philosophy and literature that have been imposed upon the rest of the world. However, it is understandable that nations struggling to define their cultural identity might not find this destabilizing theory very attractive and might mistrust Western theories in general, having suffered Western domination for so long.

Finally, because postcolonial criticism can be used to interpret litera-ture in the Western literary canon, some theorists are concerned that it will become just one more way to read the same canonized authors we've been reading for years, rather than a method that brings the works of "Third-" and "Fourth-World" writers to the fore. It seems unlikely this will happen, given the international success of such postcolonial writers as Chinua Achebe (Nigeria), Salman Rushdie (India), Jamaica Kincaid (Antigua, The West Indies), and Ngugi wa Thiong'o (Kenya). Indeed, the Nobel Prize was won by Wole Soyinka (Nigeria) in 1986, by Nadine Gordimer (South Africa) in 1991, and by Derek Walcott (St. Lucia, The West Indies) in 1992. And there has been a rapid increase in the number of colleges offering postcolonial or "Third-World" literature courses. Nevertheless, it's not unreasonable to be apprehensive that postcolonial literature will be "colonized"—that is, interpreted according to European

norms and standards—by the cultural Eurocentrism that dominates literary education and literary criticism the world over.

Postcolonial Theory and Literature

Wherever postcolonial critics place themselves in terms of these debates,
however, most interpret postcolonial literature in terms of a number of
overlapping themes. These include the following: the initial encounter
with the colonizer and the disruption of indigenous culture; the journey
of the European outsider through an unfamiliar wilderness with a native
guide; othering and colonial oppression in all its forms; mimicry (the attempt of the colonized to imitate the dress, behavior, speech, and lifestyle
of the colonizer); exile (the experience of being an "outsider" in one's
own land or a foreign wanderer in Britain); post-independence exuber-
ance followed by disillusionment; the struggle for individual and collective cultural identity and the related themes of alienation, unhomeliness,
double consciousness, and hybridity; and the need for continuity with a
pre-colonial past and self-definition of the political future. These themes
illustrate postcolonial criticism's recognition of the close relationship between psychology and ideology, or more specifically, between individual
identity and cultural beliefs.

In addition, most postcolonial critics analyze the ways in which a literary text, whatever its themes, is colonialist or anti-colonialist, that is, the
ways in which the text reinforces or resists colonialism's oppressive ideology. For example, in the simplest terms, a text can reinforce colonialist ideology through positive portrayals of the colonizers, negative portrayals of
the colonized, or the uncritical representation of the benefits of colonialism
for the colonized. Analogously, texts can resist colonialist ideology by depicting the misdeeds of the colonizers, the suffering of the colonized, or the
detrimental effects of colonialism on the colonized.

Such analysis is not always as straightforward as this simple outline
might lead you to expect, however. For the ideological content of literary
texts is rarely able to confine itself to such tidy categories. Joseph
Conrad's *Heart of Darkness* (1902), for example, is extremely anti-
colonialist in its negative representation of the colonial enterprise: the
Europeans conducting the ivory trade in the Congo are portrayed as
heartless, greedy thieves who virtually enslave the indigenous population
to help collect and transport their "loot," and the negative effects of the
European presence on the native peoples are graphically depicted. However, as Chinua Achebe observes, the novel's condemnation of Europeans

is based on a definition of Africans as savages: beneath their veneer of civilization, the Europeans are, the novel tells us, as barbaric as the Africans. And indeed, Achebe notes, the novel portrays Africans as a pre-historic mass of frenzied, howling, incomprehensible barbarians: "Africa [is a] setting and backdrop which eliminates the African as human factor. Africa [is] a [symbolic] battlefield devoid of all recognizable humanity, into which the wandering European enters at his peril" ("An Image of Africa" 12). In other words, despite *Heart of Darkness*'s obvious anti-colonialist agenda, the novel points to the colonized population as the standard of savagery to which Europeans are contrasted. Thus, Achebe uncovers the novel's colonialist sub-text, of which it does not seem to be aware.

Let's look at a few more brief examples of postcolonial interpretations of literary texts. Homi Bhabha gives us a wonderful example of the global orientation of much postcolonial criticism when he offers a new way to analyze world literature, not in terms of national traditions, which is how it generally has been studied, but in terms of postcolonial themes that cut across national boundaries. For example, Bhabha suggests that world literature might be studied in terms of the different ways cultures have experienced historical trauma, perhaps such traumas as slavery, revolution, civil war, political mass murder, oppressive military regimes, the loss of cultural identity, and the like. Or world literature might be seen as the study of the ways in which cultures define themselves by "othering" groups whom they demonize or otherwise devalue for that purpose. Or we might analyze world literature by examining the representations of people and events that occur across cultural boundaries, rather than within them, such as representations of migrants, political refugees, and colonized peoples. "The centre of such a study," Bhabha says, "would neither be the 'sovereignty' of national cultures, nor the universalism of human culture, but a focus on . . . the unspoken, unrepresented pasts that haunt the historical present" (12). That is, we might study what world literature tells us about the personal experience of people whom history has ignored—the disenfranchised, the marginalized, the unhomed—such as are found in the work of South African writer Nadine Gordimer and African American writer Toni Morrison.

For example, Bhabha argues that Gordimer's *My Son's Story* (1990) and Morrison's *Beloved* (1987) are unhomely novels in which the female protagonists—Aila and Sethe, respectively—live in the hinterland between cultures. Aila is unhomed because she is imprisoned for using her house as a cover for gun-running in an effort to resist South Africa's racist government; Sethe, because she has killed her baby daughter in order to save the child from the abuses of a cruel slavemaster. Thus, Bhabha observes, these two characters are doubly marginalized: first as women of color living in racist societies, second as women whose actions have placed them outside the circle of their own communities. In representing the psychological and historical complexities of these characters' ethical choices, both novels reveal the ways in which historical reality is not something that happens just on the battlefield or in the government office. Rather, historical reality comes into our homes and affects our personal lives in the deepest possible ways. Marginalized people may be more aware of this fact because it is pressed upon them by violence and oppression, but it is true for everyone.

Another attempt to find a common denominator in postcolonial literature is made by Helen Tiffin, who claims that the "subversive [anticolonialist] manoeuvr[e] . . . characteristic of post-colonial texts" does not lie in "the construction or reconstruction" of national cultural identity, but rather in "the rereading and rewriting of the European historical and fictional record" (95). Tiffin argues that, as it is impossible to retrieve a precolonial past or construct a new cultural identity completely free of the colonial past, most postcolonial literature has attempted, instead, "to investigate the means by which Europe imposed and maintained . . . colonial domination of so much of the rest of the world" (95). One of the many ways postcolonial literature accomplishes this task, Tiffin maintains, is through the use of what she calls "canonical counter-discourse," a strategy whereby "a post-colonial writer takes up a character or characters, or the basic assumptions of a British canonical text, and unveils [its colonialist] assumptions, subverting the text for post-colonial purposes" (97).

Tiffin sees this kind of "literary revolution" (97) in, for example, *Wide Sargasso Sea* (1966) by Jamaican-born writer Jean Rhys. Rhys's novel, a postcolonial response to Charlotte Brontë's *Jane Eyre* (1847), "writes back" (98) to Brontë's novel by, among other things, reinterpreting Bertha Mason, Rochester's West Indian wife. Brontë's novel portrays Bertha, the descendent of white colonial settlers, as an insane, drunken, violent, and lascivious woman who tricked Rochester into marriage and whom her husband must keep locked in the attic for her own and everyone else's protection. In contrast, Rhys's novel depicts Bertha, in Gayatri Spivak's words, as a "critic of imperialism" (Spivak 271), a sane woman driven to violent behavior by Rochester's imperialist oppression. Rhys's narrative thereby unmasks the colonialist ideology informing Brontë's narrative.

And part of *Jane Eyre*'s colonialist ideology, we might add, is revealed when the novel associates Bertha with the non-white native population as seen through the eyes of colonialist Europe: Bertha's face is a "black and scarlet visage" (Brontë 273), and the room she inhabits is "a wild beast's den" (Brontë 272). In other words, according to the colonialist discourse in which *Jane Eyre* participates, to be insane, drunken, violent, and lascivious is the equivalent of being non-white.

Tiffin notes that similar canonical counter-discourse can be found, for example, in *Foe* (1988), by South African writer J. M. Coetzee, in the way the novel reveals the colonialist ideology of Daniel Defoe's *Robinson Crusoe* (1719), an ideology manifest in Crusoe's colonialist attitude toward the land upon which he's shipwrecked and toward the black man he "colonizes" and names Friday. And of course, canonical counter-discourse occurs in the numerous modern Caribbean and South American performances of Shakespeare's *The Tempest* (1611), which reveal the political and psychological operations of Prospero's colonialist subjugation of Caliban in the original play. As Tiffin observes, canonical counter-discourse doesn't unmask merely the literary works to which it responds, but the whole fabric of colonialist discourse in which those works participate.

Finally, Edward Said demonstrates how postcolonial criticism of a canonized literary work often involves moving the "margins" of the work (for example, minor characters and peripheral geographical locations) to the center of our attention. This is what he does in his analysis of Jane Austen's *Mansfield Park* (1814). The entire novel is set in England around the turn of the nineteenth century, most of it on the sizeable estate of the wealthy Sir Thomas Bertram, who epitomizes the positive image of the traditional English gentleman of property: well bred, rational, honorable, and highly moral—the proper patriarchal head of his home and of the overseas agricultural enterprise that financially sustains that home.

This enterprise is in Antigua, in the Caribbean British colonies, and it is maintained by slave labor. But things are not going well in Antigua, and Sir Thomas must travel there to take control personally. And take control he does, apparently with the same efficiency with which he rules his home. For having set his "colonial garden" (*Culture and Imperialism* 86) in order, as Said puts it, Sir Thomas returns home to quickly set to rights his household, which, without his paternal guidance, has gotten out of order: his grown children have fought among themselves, engaged in clandestine courtships, and generally created a domestic uproar. Thus, among other things, Said notes that the novel draws a strong parallel between "domestic [and] international authority" (*Culture and Imperialism* 97). For the financial well-being of the British estate is dependent upon the success of the colonial enterprise, and the orderly operation of both is dependent upon the guidance of the British patriarch.

Although Sir Thomas's trip to Antigua is peripheral to the narration—it is mentioned only in passing and we see nothing that goes on there—it is "absolutely crucial to the action" (*Culture and Imperialism* (89). In Said's words,

> *Mansfield Park* [is] part of the structure of [Britain's] expanding imperialist venture. . . . [And] we can sense how ideas about dependent races and territories were held [not only] by foreign-office executives, colonial bureaucrats, and military strategists [but also] by intelligent novel-readers educating themselves in the fine points of moral evaluation, literary balance, and stylistic finish" (*Culture and Imperialism* 95).

In other words, the colonialist ideology contained in literature is deposited there by writers and absorbed by readers without their necessarily realizing it.

Some Questions Postcolonial Critics Ask about Literary Texts

The questions that follow are offered to summarize postcolonial approaches to literature. Keep in mind that most postcolonial analyses, regardless of the issues on which they focus, will include some attention to whether the text is colonialist, anti-colonialist, or some combination of the two, that is, ideologically conflicted.

1. How does the literary text, explicitly or allegorically, represent various aspects of colonial oppression? Special attention is often given to those areas where political and cultural oppression overlap, as it does, for example, in the colonizers' control of language, communication, and knowledge in colonized countries.

2. What does the text reveal about the problematics of postcolonial identity, including the relationship between personal and cultural identity and such issues as double consciousness and hybridity?

3. What does the text reveal about the politics and/or psychology of anti-colonialist resistance? For example, what does the text suggest about the ideological, political, social, economic, or psychological forces that promote or inhibit resistance? How does the text suggest that resistance can be achieved and sustained by an individual or a group?

4. What does the text reveal about the operations of cultural difference—the ways in which race, religion, class, gender, sexual orientation, cultural beliefs, and customs combine to form individual identity—in shaping our perceptions of ourselves, others, and the world in which we live? "Othering" might be one area of analysis here.

5. How does the text respond to or comment upon the characters, themes, or assumptions of a canonized (colonialist) work? Following Helen Tiffin's lead, examine how the postcolonial text reshapes our previous interpretations of a canonical text.

6. Are there meaningful similarities among the literatures of different postcolonial populations? One might compare, for example, the literatures of native peoples from different countries whose land was invaded by colonizers, the literatures of white settler colonies in different countries, or the literatures of different populations in the African diaspora. Or one might compare literary works from all three of these categories in order to investigate, for example, if the experience of colonization creates some common elements of cultural identity that outweigh differences in race and nationality.

7. How does a literary text in the Western canon reinforce or undermine colonialist ideology through its representation of colonization and/or its inappropriate silence about colonized peoples? Does the text teach us anything about colonialist or anti-colonialist ideology through its illustration of any of the postcolonial concepts we've discussed? (A text does not have to treat the subject of colonization in order to do this.)

Depending on the literary work in question, we might ask one or any combination of these questions. Or we might come up with a useful question not listed here. These are just some starting points to get us thinking productively about literature from a postcolonial perspective. Keep in mind that not all postcolonial critics will interpret the same text in the same way, even if they focus on the same postcolonial concepts. As in every field, even expert practitioners disagree.

African American Criticism[3]

I'm always alarmed to learn, each semester, how many students in my critical theory course—including senior English majors of all races—are unacquainted or minimally acquainted with such milestones of African American history as the Middle Passage, the Underground Railroad, the Great Migration, the Harlem Renaissance, the Civil Rights movement, the Black Power movement, and the Black Arts movement. Despite the increased focus on multicultural education in America's high schools and the increased provision of college courses in African American experience, history, and literature, educational efforts in these areas remain inadequate to the needs of students in a multicultural society such as ours, especially in light of their future role as world citizens of a rapidly shrinking globe.

Because African Americans constitute such a large population in the United States, and because they have contributed so much to the arts—including an enormous, internationally acclaimed literary output—I should be able to assume that my senior English majors have a certain amount of knowledge about African American history and literature upon which I can build. But much of my job consists of providing background knowledge, for lack of a better term. And given the constraints of time, I often find myself outlining what I think students *should* know and, hopefully, promoting their desire to know it, so that they'll become interested enough in the field to pursue more knowledge on their own. In a sense, that's what I'll be trying to do here: acquaint you with the basic issues that have informed African American literary history, explain the primary concerns of African American literary critics today, and hope that you'll become interested enough to pursue this exciting field of literary study on your own.

Racial Issues and African American Literary History

The virtual exclusion of African American history and culture from American education, which began to be addressed only in the late 1960s, reflects the virtual exclusion of African American history and culture from official versions of American history before that time. Only over the past few decades have American history books begun to include information about black Americans that had been repressed in order to maintain the cultural *hegemony*, or dominance, of white America. For example, textbooks that were used to teach American history (which, more accurately, should have been called white American history) said little or nothing about the slave uprisings during the horrific Middle Passage (the transportation of slaves from Africa to America), the numerous slave rebellions on the plantations, and the network of communication and resistance developed by slaves right under the noses of the slave masters. And such accomplishments as the tremendous outpouring of black literature, philosophy, art, and music associated with Harlem during the 1920s, known as the Harlem Renaissance, were not given the attention they deserved.

I choose these two examples—slave resistance and the Harlem Renaissance—because I think they illustrate most clearly the political motives that lay behind the exclusion of African Americans from American history. A conscientious history of slave resistance would have blasted the racist stereotype of the contented, dim-witted slave who was grateful for the paternal guidance of the white master, without whom the slave would have been either a lost child or a dangerous savage. And a conscientious history of African American literary genius would have blasted the myth of African American inferiority upon which so many racist policies and practices rested.

Given that so much African American literature deals with racism—as a literary record of African American experience, how could it not?—let's take a moment to define some key concepts concerning that issue about which many people still have misconceptions. *Racialism*, a word we don't often hear in everyday speech, refers to the belief in racial superiority, inferiority, and purity based on the conviction that moral and intellectual characteristics, just like physical characteristics, are biological properties that differentiate the races. *Racism* refers to the unequal power relations that grow from the sociopolitical domination of one race by another and that result in systematic discriminatory practices (for example, segregation, domination, and persecution). Therefore, although anyone can be a racialist, in order to be a racist—in order to be in a position to segregate, dominate, or persecute—one has to be in a position of power as a member of the politically dominant group, which in America usually means that one has to be white. In other words, the systematic practice of racism (for example, denying qualified persons of color employment, housing, education, or anything else to which they're entitled) can occur on a regular basis only when those who do it can expect, by and large, to get away with it. And those who do it can expect to get away with it when the group to which they belong controls most of the positions of power in the political, judicial, and law-enforcement systems.

To put the matter another way, the systematic practice of racial discrimination can occur only when racism has become institutionalized. *Institutionalized racism* refers to the incorporation of racist policies and practices in the institutions by which a society operates: for example, education; federal, state, and local governments; the law, both in terms of what is written on the books and how it is implemented by the courts and by police officials; health care, which can be racially biased in everything from the allocation of research dollars, to the location of hospitals, to the treatment of individual patients; and the corporate world, which often practices racial discrimination in its hiring and promotion despite whatever equal-opportunity policies it officially claims to have.

One area in which institutionalized racism has been very effective in discriminating against African Americans is the American literary canon. As we saw in the section on postcolonial criticism, the Western (British, European, and American) literary canon has been dominated by a *Eurocentric* definition of *universalism*: literary works have been defined as great art, as "universal," and included in the canon only when they reflect European experience and conform to the style and subject matter of the European literary tradition, that is, when they resemble those European works already deemed "great." Although African Americans can boast a long and impressive literary history dating back to the eighteenth century, white American literary historians considered black writers, when they considered them at all, as a tributary or an off-shoot rather than part and parcel of American literary history. Therefore, until recently, anthologies of American literature, including those used to teach high-school and college courses, were confined largely to the work of white male writers. The literary canon has thus been used to maintain white cultural hegemony.

This situation has begun to change, of course, but that change is coming rather slowly. Although contemporary black American authors certainly hold top honors today—with Toni Morrison (who won the Nobel Prize in 1993), Alice Walker, John Edgar Wideman, Maya Angelou, Gloria Naylor, Ishmael Reed, Nikki Giovanni, Charles Johnson, Rita Dove, Sherley Anne Williams, and August Wilson, among many others, producing some of the most widely acclaimed literature in America— works by black writers, past and present, are still too often under-represented on course syllabi in American literature courses.

The promotion of racial discrimination by institutionalized racism is often mirrored in a society's racist stereotypes and in its adherence to a narrow standard of Anglo-Saxon beauty. Before "Black is beautiful!" and "Say it loud: I'm black and I'm proud!" sounded the call for a radical change in Afro-American self-definition and self-perception in the late 1960s, many African Americans suffered from internalized racism. And despite the success of black-pride advocates, many people of color continue to suffer from it today. *Internalized racism* results from the psychological programming by which a racist society indoctrinates people of color to believe in white superiority. Victims of internalized racism generally feel inferior to whites, less attractive, less worthwhile, less capable, and often wish they were white or looked more white. Toni Morrison provides us with one of the most chilling portraits of internalized racism in *The Bluest Eye* (1970), in which Pecola Breedlove, a young black girl who can't see her own beauty, believes she would be pretty, happy, and loved if only she had blue eyes.

Internalized racism often results in *intra-racial racism*, which refers to discrimination, within the black community, against those with darker skin and more African features. We see this phenomenon illustrated in *The Bluest Eye* when Pecola is picked on by other black children for having dark skin, while another black child, the light-skinned Maureen Peal, is treated by the same black youngsters as if she were superior to them. Film-maker Spike Lee also portrays intra-racial racism in *School Daze* (1988), in which students at a historically black college form two rival groups based on the relative "whiteness" or "blackness" of their physical appearance. While the economic hardship and social marginalization caused by institutionalized racism are common knowledge, internalized racism and intra-racial racism illustrate the devastating psychological experiences that also result.

Given the multiple forms of racism with which African Americans have had to contend, it should come as no surprise that, like many of the postcolonial peoples discussed earlier, many African Americans experience *double consciousness* or *double vision*, the awareness of belonging to two conflicting cultures: the black culture, which grew from African roots and was transformed by its own unique history on American soil, and the European culture imposed by white America. For many black Americans this means having one cultural self at home and another cultural self in white-dominated public space, such as the workplace and the school. And double consciousness sometimes involves speaking two languages. For the black culture lived at home sometimes includes the use of *Black Vernacular English* (*BVE*, also called *Ebonics* or

Black English), which fulfills all the grammatical criteria of a genuine language but is still dismissed by many white and some black Americans as sub-standard or incorrect English rather than recognized as a language in its own right.

For black writers, double consciousness has meant having to decide whether to write primarily for a black audience, a white audience, or both. This decision involves, in turn, the kind of language the writer uses. For example, Harlem Renaissance poet Countee Cullen chose to use highly polished, standard white English and a classically allusive style that conforms to the best of the European literary tradition. This style is evident, for example, in the Greek mythological allusions in the following lines from his sonnet "Yet Do I Marvel" (1947). The speaker, questioning why God would "make a poet black, and bid him sing," says that, if "He stoop[ed] to quibble," God could

> Make plain the reason tortured Tantalus
> Is baited by the fickle fruit, declare
> If merely brute caprice dooms Sisyphus
> To struggle up a never-ending stair.

Although most of Cullen's poetry contains political themes relating to race, he believed black authors should be as free as white authors to create according to the dictates of their own artistic inspiration without being obliged to consider the political needs of their people. Of course, this poet's use of formal English and Greek mythology raised questions about the validity of his artistic inspiration because it derived from the racist culture that had oppressed African peoples for centuries. But Cullen's classically crafted verse nevertheless demonstrated that African American writers were more than capable of writing in whatever style they preferred and thus provided a powerful argument against the racist assumption of African inferiority.

In contrast, much of the work of Langston Hughes, another writer who emerged during the Harlem Renaissance, uses vernacular English resonant with the rhythms of black speech patterns and blues music. His powerfully moving writing—which white readers, too, can appreciate and from which they can learn about the beauty of black culture—speaks of and for African Americans, celebrating their rich cultural heritage and calling for equal opportunity for black citizens. We see this style, for example, in the concrete imagery and the streetwise, vernacular quality of the voice in the following lines from "Good Morning" (1951). The speaker laments the dashed hopes of people of color, in search of a better life, who've "come dark / wondering / wide-eyed / dreaming / out of Penn Station" in New York:

> The gates open—
> but there're bars
> at each gate.
> What happens
> to a dream deferred?
> Daddy, ain't you heard?

Although our discussion of literary language and style is a discussion of poetics—that is, of literary devices and strategies—it is clearly also a discussion of politics, that is, of the realities of political, social, and economic power. For as the example of Cullen and Hughes demonstrates, the literary style black writers choose cannot be separated from their political views on the writer's role as a member of an oppressed group. Indeed, one of the oldest issues in the black literary community concerns the social role of the black writer in a racist society.

After all, African American writing began during the eighteenth century largely as the effort of African slaves to prove their humanity to whites. For slaveholders, as one of their many attempts to justify slavery, claimed that Africans weren't fully human because they couldn't write poetry! (Of course, slaveholders conveniently neglected to consider that they had made it illegal for slaves to learn even to read.) In fact, Phillis Wheatley's owners encouraged her to write poetry to prove this racist argument wrong. Slaves also wrote autobiographical narratives to alert white Northerners to their plight. Harriet Jacobs's *Incidents in the Life of a Slave Girl* (1861) is one such text. Yet so widespread was the belief, even in the North, that African slaves were incapable of writing, let alone of literary production, that many narratives were prefaced by the statements of white patrons, testifying to the identity of the writer and the authenticity of the narrative. Indeed, finding ways to pull white readers into texts they otherwise might have resisted has remained a task that many black writers still face.

The anti-racist politics of early African American writers have remained relevant to the needs of black Americans over the long history of their struggle for justice. It is not surprising, therefore, that writing as a form of purely individual expression has been viewed by many African Americans as a luxury the race could not afford while so many of its members were oppressed.

The social role of the black writer remained an important issue during the *Black Arts movement* of the 1960s, the literary and artistic off-shoot of the Black Power movement. Some of the most vocal spokespersons for the movement, such as the poet Amiri Baraka, believed that black writers have an obligation to help the race through such literary means as depicting the evils of racism, providing positive images of African Americans, and offering possible solutions to social problems confronting the black community. Similarly, the Black Arts movement affected the role of African American literary critics by emphasizing their job as cultural critics. That is, black critics were called upon to interpret literature in terms of its representation of and relationship to the political and economic situation of African Americans, a task analogous to that performed by Marxist critics but with the focus, of course, on race. For example, Afro-American critics analyzed the ways in which literary texts undermine or reinforce the racist ideologies that have kept black Americans politically oppressed and economically disadvantaged. This approach remains an important part of African American criticism today.

The Black Arts movement also called into question the appropriateness of white critical theories for the interpretation of black literature. After all, it was a Eurocentric definition of "great" literature that marginalized black authors in American literary history and virtually excluded them from the American canon. And most contemporary mainstream critical theories, including all the theories discussed in the other chapters of this textbook, have European roots. The question of the appropriateness of white theories for the interpretation of black texts remains pertinent today in light of the reservations some critics have about the widespread influence of deconstructive theory on all forms of literary criticism. As Barbara Christian observes, the abstract discourse of deconstruction, which argues that such concepts as "center" and "periphery" are illusory and which allows those few who are especially fluent in deconstruction "to control the critical scene," emerged "just when the literature of peoples of color . . . began to move to 'the centre'" (459). In addition, as we saw in the section on postcolonial criticism, deconstruction critiques the concept of a stable, inherently meaningful cultural identity. And as Henry Louis Gates, Jr. points out, it isn't fair "to deny [African Americans] the process of exploring and reclaiming our [cultural identity] before we critique it" ("The Master's Pieces" 32).

On the other hand, many African American critics believe that elements from any number of contemporary critical theories, including deconstruction, can be adapted for use by African American criticism. For despite the dangers involved in the uncritical application of European

American theories to African American literature, many critics feel that the wholesale exclusion of white critical theory from the black critical repertoire deny black critics some potentially useful critical tools and would, in addition, close off avenues of communication between African American critics and their colleagues. As Henry Louis Gates, Jr. argues, "*any* tool that enables the critic to explain the complex workings of the language of a text is an appropriate tool. For it is language, the black language of black texts, that expresses the distinctive quality of our literary tradition" (*Figures in Black* xxi). And as we have seen in other chapters, most critical theories can be used to explain the operations of language, for example by calling our attention to the various ways in which language carries ideological content that can affect us without our even being aware of it.

The idea of the distinctiveness of black literature to which Gates refers was another important issue explored during the Black Arts movement that remains with us today. In opposition to the notion of the "universality" of all literature, many writers of the Black Arts movement argued that African American literature has its own unique qualities, its own politics and poetics, that cannot be fully explained by or contained within the larger framework of European American literature. Some theorists believe that this uniqueness derives from the African American oral tradition of storytelling, folklore, and oral history, which has its roots in African culture and, according to some critics, relates to an essential "blackness," a way of thinking, feeling, and creating shared by all peoples of African descent. Others argue that there is no such thing as an essential blackness, that the qualities African American texts have in common result from the shared history and culture of their authors. For some of these critics, the distinctive quality of African American literature follows from its unique blending of both African and European American cultural traditions.

In either case, the *Afrocentricity* of African American texts—that is, the primacy of their relationship to African history and culture—must not be overlooked when we interpret them or we risk deforming African American literature in very important ways. For example, as John W. Roberts observes, the African American trickster tales that emerged during slavery, such as those about Br'er Rabbit, "exhibi[t] a close kinship to trickster tales in African oral tradition" (97). However, Eurocentric American folklorists, assuming that enslavement had abolished African Americans' cultural ties to Africa, argued that these tales derived from the European American tradition. Or they asserted that it didn't matter

where the tales originated because slaves transformed them to fit a very
specific psychological need: the need to compensate for their powerlessness under slavery by identifying with a small, disadvantaged animal who
rebels against the moral order and, through cunning and deceit, fools the
larger, more powerful animals, punishes them, takes their food, and so
forth.

Afrocentric folklorists have corrected this misinterpretation, Roberts
observes, by showing, among other things, that both African and African
American trickster tales "revolv[e] around behaviors designed to compensate for chronic shortages of material necessities and existence in a
rigid social hierarchy" (107). In short, the similarities between African
and African American trickster tales derived from the fact that both
populations, though for very different reasons, had to learn how to survive an uncertain and often inadequate food supply. And the differences
between the two groups of tales resulted from the differences between the
strict social order of African culture, in which the welfare of the community always took precedence over individual gain, and the strict social order of American plantation culture, in which the individual gain of the
slaveholder always took precedence over the welfare of the community of
slaves that worked for him. An Afrocentric reading of the trickster tales
thus accounts for both the continuity and the transformation of the tales
without severing African American culture from its African roots.

African American Criticism Today

Whether critics have sought to explain the unique quality of African
American literature by citing its African sources or its African and European American sources, much effort has been expended in delineating
the distinguishing features of what has been identified as the *African
American literary tradition*. Generally speaking, critics agree that African
American literature has focused on a number of recurring historical and
sociological themes, all of which reflect the politics—the realities of political, social, and economic power—of black American experience.
Among these themes are the following: reclaiming the African past; surviving the horrors of the Middle Passage; surviving the ordeal of slavery;
the quest for freedom from slavery and from other forms of oppression;
the quest for literacy; the experience of African Americans during the
Civil War and Reconstruction; surviving life in the South under segregation; the problems and conflicts of mulattoes in a racist society; the difficulties of economic survival; the migration North and the related themes

of urbanization, alienation, and the quest to reconcile double consciousness; the role of religion in personal and collective survival; the importance of cultural heritage; and the importance of family and community.
Of course, surviving the combined oppression of racism, classism, and
sexism is also a recurring theme, but until the mid-twentieth century,
black writers had to treat this subject carefully or encode it in their writing (indicate it through subtle references that black readers and sympathetic white readers would catch but that unsympathetic white readers
wouldn't readily notice) in order to be published by white editors and
read by white audiences.

As these themes suggest, the political content of African American
literature includes correcting stereotypes of African Americans; correcting the misrepresentation of African Americans in American history and
the omission of African Americans from American history; celebrating
African American culture, experience, and achievement; and exploring
racial issues, including institutionalized racism, internalized racism, intra-racial racism, and the combined oppression of racism, classism, and
sexism. You'll notice, too, that many of these themes involve surviving
life's negative experiences and questing for the positive. For spiritual survival and the realization of African Americans' full human potential are
values frequently celebrated in African American writing.

In terms of its poetics, the African American literary tradition is distinguished by, among other characteristics, two prominent features: orality and folk motifs. Orality, or the spoken quality of its language, gives a
literary work a sense of immediacy, of human presence, by giving readers
the feeling they are hearing a human voice. In African American literature, orality is usually achieved by using black vernacular and by copying
the rhythms of black speech, including, for example, the repetition of important phrases and alternating voices, devices associated with church
sermons and with blues, jazz, and rap music. As we saw earlier, the work
of Langston Hughes is noted for its orality, and so is the poetry of Sonia
Sanchez and Nikki Giovanni. Toni Morrison's *The Bluest Eye* (1970), too,
offers us a striking example of orality in the range of black voices it represents, the most "audible" of which include those of Mrs. MacTeer, Pauline
Breedlove, and Miss Marie.

The use of folk motifs includes a wide range of character types and
folk practices and creates a sense of continuity with the African and African American past. These character types include, for example, the local
healer, the conjurer, the matriarch, the local storyteller, the trickster, the
religious leader, and the folk hero. Folk practices include, for example,
singing worksongs, hymns, and the blues; engaging in folk and religious

rituals as a way of maintaining community and continuity with the past; storytelling as a way of relating personal and group history and passing down traditional wisdom; and emphasizing the importance of naming, including pet names, nicknames, and being called out of one's name (being called a derogatory name).

Among the best known contemporary attempts to analyze the African American literary tradition are *The Signifying Monkey*, by Henry Louis Gates, Jr., and Houston Baker's *Blues, Ideology, and Afro-American Literature*. Gates attempts to chart African American literary history as a history of relationships among literary texts. He argues that black texts "talk" about one another—for example, by copying, altering, or parodying one another's literary devices—the same way that black people talk about one another when they engage in the African American folk practice called *signifying*.

Signifyin(g), which Gates spells in this manner to emphasize the folk pronunciation of the word and to distinguish it from other definitions of the term, refers to various indirect, clever, ironic, and playful ways of giving your opinion about another person—for example, insulting someone, deflating someone's pretentiousness, or paying someone a compliment—without saying explicitly what you mean. To cite the simplest example, if you want to tell your roommate to quit hogging all the ice-cream, you can say to a third party, in your roommate's presence, "Something must be wrong with this refrigerator because every time I put a half-gallon of chocolate-chip-mint in here it turns into a pint overnight." When your roommate responds with "I don't eat all the ice-cream," you can then say, "Did I mention your name? I wasn't even talking to you! You must have a guilty conscience!" This would be called signifying on your roommate. The figure Gates chooses to embody this process of indirect communication is the Signifying Monkey, the master trickster of African American folk tales. Let's look briefly at a literary application of Gates's theory.

Richard Wright and Ralph Ellison, two great African American writers who emerged during the 1940s and 1950s, disagreed about how black experience should be rendered in literature. Wright was a naturalist: he believed that the harsh, inescapable realities of racist oppression should be represented in straightforward, stark language in order to convey as powerfully as possible the evils of racism and the depth of black suffering. This is exactly what Wright did in works like *Native Son* (1940) and *Black Boy* (1945). Ralph Ellison, in contrast, was a modernist: he believed that the complexities, ambiguities, and uncertainties of human experience could best be represented by ambiguous, metaphorical language and a complex narrative with multiple layers of meaning. In *Invisible Man* (1952), Ellison "signifies upon Wright by parodying Wright's literary structures through repetition and difference" (*Signifying Monkey* 106). That is, *Invisible Man* indirectly and cleverly reveals Ellison's disagreement with Wright's literary vision by echoing certain key elements in Wright's texts in a manner that reverses them.

For example, Gates explains, Wright's titles, *Native Son* and *Black Boy*, suggest a concrete, visible, racial presence. Ellison signifies upon these titles by calling his novel *Invisible Man*. While *man* "suggests a more mature and stronger status than either *son* or *boy*" (*Signifying Monkey* 106), Ellison's *man* is "invisible," an absence rather than a presence, which is how black people historically have been treated by white America: as if they were invisible. Ellison also signifies on Wright's protagonist, Bigger Thomas. Bigger is "voiceless": he never speaks up for himself and, indeed, rarely speaks at all. He doesn't act so much as react to the circumstances around him. Ellison responds with a protagonist who "is nothing *but* voice": we are never told his name, but "it is he who shapes, edits, and narrates his own tale" (*Signifying Monkey* 106). In short,

> Bigger's voicelessness and powerlessness to act (as opposed to react) signify an absence, despite the metaphor of presence found in the novel's title; the reverse obtains in *Invisible Man*, where the absence implied by invisibility is undermined by the presence of the narrator as the author of his own text. (*Signifying Monkey* 106)

Gates points out numerous other ways in which the works of Ellison signify upon those of Wright in Ellison's attempt to show that naturalism's unrelenting gloom does not adequately represent black experience. In fact, disagreements over the best way to represent black experience form the contested ground upon which Gates maps all the acts of literary signifyin(g) he analyzes, including, in addition to Ralph Ellison's, those of Richard Wright, Zora Neale Hurston, Jean Toomer, Paul Laurence Dunbar, Ishmael Reed, Alice Walker, and others.

Houston Baker also attempts to relate the African American literary tradition to an African American folk art: the blues. Baker argues that the blues are a form of African American cultural self-expression that both influences and is influenced by, that both affects and reflects, all other forms of African American expressive culture. The blues are a "matrix"— "a womb, a network . . . a point of ceaseless input and output" (3)—and as such, they are also a metaphor for African American culture as a whole.

In short, the blues are a language, a cultural code that gets "spoken" in many different ways by many different African American art forms, including literature. Thus, the blues offer a specifically African American approach to African American literary history. Let's take a brief look at one of Baker's many different examples of the complex relationship between the blues and African American literature.

Throughout African American literary history, Baker observes, we find texts with a thematic structure akin to that of the blues. Blues songs, he notes, generally have a double theme: a spiritual theme, usually about loss and desire, and a material theme, usually about the exigencies of economic necessity. Baker sees this same doubleness in African American literary texts, in which the material theme is the sub-text that drives the work's overt spiritual theme. For example, *The Life of Olaudah Equiano, or Gustavus Vassa, the African. Written by Himself* (1789), Frederick Douglass's *Narrative of the Life of Frederick Douglass, An American Slave* (1845), and Harriet Jacobs's *Incidents in the Life of a Slave Girl* (1861) share a common spiritual theme: the journey to spiritual awakening, to finding oneself, which is an important dimension of their journey to freedom. Their common sub-text, which lies below the spiritual theme and quietly competes with it, is the economic realities upon which the protagonists' spiritual quests depend. Equiano, Douglass, and Jacobs's Linda Brent must all find ways to get the money they need in order to achieve their freedom, which is the soil in which their spiritual goals are planted.

Of course, the economic sub-text of all African American texts does not lie in the financial requirements of escaping from or buying oneself out of slavery. But Baker nevertheless refers to the "economic grounding" (39) of African American literature as the "'economics of slavery'" (13) because the economic oppression of black Americans is slavery's legacy, and economic oppression is, itself, a form of bondage. Baker's project, then, is to chart those moments in African American literary history when the blues, in one form or another, are being played: "when personae, protagonists, autobiographical narrators, or literary critics successfully negotiate an obdurate 'economics of slavery' and achieve a resonant, improvisational expressive dignity" (13). In contemporary literature, such a moment occurs, for example, when *Beloved*'s Baby Suggs, who administers to the emotional deprivations of the former slaves, urges them, in improvisational blues fashion, to laugh and cry at the same time.

There has also been a good deal of work done to define the contours of a literary tradition specific to the writing of African American women, who were excluded from or marginalized by the African American literary canon as defined both by black male writers and by the white literary establishment. Furthermore, in literary works by white authors and black male authors alike, the representation of African American women generally was restricted to minor or stereotyped characters. As a result, black women writers have been concerned, throughout their literary history, to portray black women as real people with all the complexity and depth that black women have. As Mary Helen Washington puts it, "[O]ne of the main preoccupations of the Black woman writer has been the Black woman herself—her aspirations, her conflicts, her relationship to her men and her children, her creativity" (*Black-Eyed Susans* x).

Relationship is a key word in Washington's statement. For as we saw in Chapter Four, "Feminist Criticism," black women must negotiate the conflicting requirements of their relationship to the black community as a whole—their solidarity with black men against racist oppression—and their relationship to women of all races in an effort to resist sexist oppression. In particular, the dilemma created by the conflicting requirements of black men's demands for racial solidarity and white feminists demands for gender solidarity has forced many African American women engaged in literary criticism to address gender issues in black women's writing without mentioning feminism. (See Chapter Four for further discussion of this issue.)

The focus on black women's identity in writing by African American women is embodied in a number of recurring themes. Among them are the following: the victimization of black women as underpaid workers forced into the lowliest jobs and as victims of violence and sexual exploitation; the black woman as suppressed artist; the importance of black women's community for psychological (and sometimes physical and economic) survival, which includes relationships among grandmothers, mothers, and daughters; the initiation of young black girls into the harsh realities of racism and sexism; the role of skin color, hair texture, and white standards of beauty in the black woman's self-perception and status within the community; the importance of the relationships between black women and men; and a more sustained focus on the combined oppression of racism, sexism, and classism than we find in the work of black male writers or white writers. In earlier literary works by black women we also see the theme of passing for white. And in literature written over the past two decades the theme of lesbian relationships has emerged. In addition, "[l]argely because degraded images of black women have persisted throughout history, both in and out of literature," Deborah E. McDowell observes, "Black women novelists [and, we might add, poets and playwrights as well] have assumed throughout their tradition a revisionist mission aimed at substituting reality for stereotype" (94–95).

This revisionist mission has included the provision of realistic female character types. In "Teaching Black-Eyed Susans," Mary Helen Washington draws on the insights of Alice Walker to describe three salient types, which frequently have been used by black women writers to represent black women from different historical periods. The first is the "suspended woman," the victim of men and of society as a whole, with few or no options, "suspended" because she can't do anything about her situation. This type is often found in works set in the nineteenth and early twentieth centuries. Examples include Nannie in Zora Neale Hurston's *Their Eyes Were Watching God* (1937) and Pauline Breedlove in Toni Morrison's *The Bluest Eye* (1970). The second type is the "assimilated woman," who is not victimized by physical violence and has much more control of her life, but who is victimized by psychological violence in that she is cut off from her African American roots by her desire to be accepted by white society. This type is often found in works set in the 1940s and 1950s. Examples include Mrs. Turner in *Their Eyes Were Watching God* and Geraldine in *The Bluest Eye*. Finally, the third character type is the "emergent woman," who is coming to an awareness of her own psychological and political oppression and becoming capable of creating a new life and new choices for herself, usually through a harsh experience of initiation that makes her ready for the change. This type is often found in works set in the 1960s. Examples include Meridian in Alice Walker's *Meridian* (1976) and Janie in *Their Eyes Were Watching God*. As the example of Janie illustrates, these character types are not confined to the historical settings with which they are generally associated.

Some critics might argue, I think, that we should add a fourth character type to this useful list: that of the "liberated woman," who has discovered her abilities, knows what she needs, and goes about getting it. We might say, in short, that the "liberated woman" has already found herself and likes what she has found. Although we might expect that this character type would appear most often, or most visibly, in black women's writing set in the 1970s and later, I think she can be found in works set in earlier periods as well. Examples of the "liberated woman" include Shug Avery in Alice Walker's *The Color Purple* (1982) and Pilate in Toni Morrison's *Song of Solomon* (1977), both of which are set in the decades of the first half of the twentieth century.

Finally, African American women's poetics traditionally include a number of recurring literary strategies. For example, black women writers frequently use a black female character as the narrator in a novel or work of short fiction or as the speaker in a poem or dramatic monologue in order to give black women authority as the tellers of their own stories. When third-person narration is used, the point-of-view character (the character through whose eyes we see the story) is usually a black woman or girl. To emphasize the importance of relationships between black women, sometimes the narrative is framed as a conversation (a real conversation, one imagined by the protagonist, or one that takes place through letters) between two black women or girls.

In order to evoke a world that resonates with black women's experience, the use of imagery associated with black women's domestic space and activity is also a frequently employed literary strategy: for example, imagery associated with the kitchen and other locations within the home where such traditional skills as quilting, canning, the performance of garden and farm chores, and the passing down of family and cultural heritage to children occur. Or the world of black women may be evoked by imagery associated with black women's physical appearance, such as clothing, hair styles, skin color, cosmetics, and the like.

Generally speaking, all the literary devices we've discussed emphasize the struggle of black women to assert their own identity. That identity may take the form of sacrificing oneself for the good of the family, the community, or the race, as it does in many earlier works. Or it may take the form of exploring one's own abilities, needs, and desires, as it does in many contemporary literary texts. But whatever form it takes, the complex psychological, social, and economic dynamics of black women's self-definition occupies an important place in their writing.

Of course, the unique perspectives of African American criticism can also offer us insights into literary works by white American writers. In *Playing in the Dark: Whiteness and the Literary Imagination*, Toni Morrison offers us a very productive approach to reading white mainstream literature from an African American perspective that reveals the ways in which white texts construct, for their own purposes, what she calls the *Africanist* presence in American history. Morrison uses the word *Africanist* as "a term for the denotative and connotative blackness that African peoples have come to signify as well as the entire range of views, assumptions, readings, and misreadings that accompany Eurocentric learning about these people" (6–7). In short, *Africanism*, in Morrison's sense of the word, is a white conception (or more accurately, misconception) of African and African American people upon which white authors have projected their own fears, needs, desires, and conflicts.

In white mainstream literature, an Africanist presence can take the form of black characters, stories about black people, representations of black speech, and images associated with Africa or with blackness. In calling for investigations of how these devices function in the work of white writers, Morrison is not suggesting that we analyze racism in literature—such analyses have been and are being conducted—nor that we judge the quality of a work based on its representation of nonwhite characters. Rather, she encourages us to examine the ways in which

> the major and championed characteristics of our national [white] literature—individualism, masculinity, social engagement versus historical isolation; acute and ambiguous moral problematics; the thematics of innocence coupled with an obsession with figurations of death and hell—are . . . responses to a dark, abiding . . . Africanist presence. (5)

That is, Morrison wants to analyze the ways in which canonized white American literature has defined a positive "quintessential American identity" (44) by contrast with an invented Africanist identity, "raw and savage . . . bound and unfree, rebellious but serviceable" (45), against which whites have been able to define their own civilized virtues. "These topics," Morrison observes, "seem to me to render the nation's literature a much more complex and rewarding body of knowledge" (53).

Among the many ways in which white writers have employed the Africanist presence, Morrison notes, is the use of black characters as a sign of and "vehicle for," among other things, "illegal sexuality, fear of madness, expulsion, [and] self-loathing" (52) as well as "to define the goals and enhance the qualities of white characters" (52–53). For example, Morrison argues that Ernest Hemingway's *To Have and Have Not* (1937), among other strategic uses of Africanist characters, employs a black crewman on a fishing boat to "solicit our admiration" (80) for the boat's white captain, protagonist Harry Morgan, a deep-sea fisherman. "Harry Morgan," Morrison notes,

> seems to represent the classic American hero: a solitary man battling a government that would limit his freedom and his individuality. He is romantically . . . respectful of the nature he destroys for a living . . . competent . . . virile, free, brave, and moral. (70)

How does Hemingway show the reader that Harry has these qualities? He does so largely by contrasting the protagonist with a "'nigger' in
his crew, a man who, throughout all of part one, has no name" (70). In
part two, when Hemingway switches from Harry's first-person narration
to a third-person narrator, the black character is "named" in two different
ways: "Harry *says* 'Wesley' when speaking to the black man in direct dialogue; Hemingway *writes* 'nigger' when as narrator he refers to him" (71).
The word *man*, however, is reserved for Harry.

Furthermore, "[t]his black character either does not speak (as a
'nigger' he is silent) or speaks in very legislated and manipulated ways (as
a 'Wesley' his speech serves Harry's needs)" (71). Even when the black
man is the first to spot the flying fish for which everyone on board has
been waiting, Hemingway does not let him "cry out at the sighting" (73),
which would be the natural thing for him to do. Instead, the author gives
Harry the awkwardly constructed phrase, "I looked and saw he had seen a
patch of flying fish" (Hemingway 13) because "the logic of the narrative's
[racial] discrimination" dictates that it must be Harry, "the powerful one,
the authoritative one, who sees," even if it requires a less "graceful" syntax
to achieve this goal (73).

Finally, when the black crewman finally does begin to speak a good
deal, after their boat has been fired upon, it serves the clear purpose of
foregrounding Harry's bravery. Morrison points out that

> [w]e hear the grumbles, the groans, the weakness as Wesley's responses
> to his gunshot wounds for three pages before we learn that Harry is
> also shot, and much worse than Wesley is. By contrast, Harry has not
> only not mentioned his own pain, he has taken Wesley's whining with
> compassion and done the difficult work of steering and tossing the
> contraband [the illegal goods the boat is transporting] overboard in
> swift, stoic gestures of manliness. (74–75)

Thus, we admire Harry the more because we don't admire Wesley, who is
depicted as his opposite. Harry's narrative power, so to speak—his authority, strength, and bravery—are enhanced by the black character's silence,
weakness, and cowardice. This is just one of the many ways in which an
Africanist presence performs a major function in white mainstream literature, a function that merits further study. As Morrison puts it, "All of us,
readers and writers, are bereft when criticism remains too polite or too
fearful to notice a disrupting darkness before its eyes" (90–91).

Before we draw this section to a close, let me pause here to answer a question frequently asked by students: Why are we studying African American criticism and not the criticism of other ethnic literatures, as well? Certainly, African Americans aren't the only American racial minority to produce a body of exquisite literature. Among others, Native Americans, Asian Americans, Chicanos, and Latinos have contributed a great deal to the literary output of the United States. African American literature, however, has played a significant role in American history since the eighteenth century, and Black Studies has been an important field in American academia since the 1960s. In contrast, theoretically-oriented bodies of criticism of these other wonderful literatures are just beginning to emerge. So it seems logical, at this point in time, to focus our attention on African American criticism, both to acquaint you with the work being done in this exciting field and to encourage you to investigate the literature and criticism of other American racial minorities, an endeavor for which a thorough grounding in African American criticism can serve as both a useful model and a point of departure for comparison and contrast with other American literatures.

Some Questions African American Critics Ask About Literary Texts

The following questions are offered to summarize African American approaches to literature. Keep in mind that, like postcolonial criticism, African American criticism is both a subject matter—the study of a body of literature—and a theoretical framework. As a subject matter, any analysis of a literary work written by an African American, regardless of the theoretical framework used, might be called African American criticism, even if no attention is paid to elements in the text that are specifically African American. However, as a theoretical framework—and this is our primary concern here—African American criticism foregrounds race (racial identity, African American cultural traditions, psychology, politics, and so forth) as the object of analysis because race, in America, informs our individual and cultural psychology, and therefore our literature, in profound ways. As a theoretical framework, then, African American criticism can be used to analyze any literary text that speaks to African American issues, regardless of the race of its author, although the work of African American writers is the primary focus.

1. What can the work teach us about the specifics of African heritage, African American culture and experience, and/or

African American history (including but not limited to the history of marginalization)?

2. What are the politics (ideological agendas related to political, social, and economic power) of specific African American works? For example, does the work correct stereotypes of African Americans; correct historical misrepresentations of African Americans; celebrate Afro-American culture, experience, and achievement; or explore racial issues, including, among others, the psychological effects of racism?

3. What are the poetics (literary devices and strategies) of specific African American works? For example, does the work use black vernacular or standard white English? Does the work draw on African myths or African American folk tales or folk motifs? Does the work provide imagery that resonates with African American women's domestic space, African American cultural practices, history, or heritage? What are the effects of these literary devices and how do they relate to the theme, or meaning, of the work?

4. How does the work participate in the African American literary tradition? To what group of African American texts might we say it belongs in terms of its politics and poetics? How does it conform to those texts? How does it break with them, perhaps seeking to redefine literary aesthetics by experimenting with new forms? In short, what place does it occupy in African American literary history or in African American women's literary history?

5. How does the text compare with texts from other parts of the African diaspora (peoples of African descent who do not live in Africa), for example texts by Afro-Cuban or other black Caribbean writers, or with other (non-black) American works? Do we find a common thread of themes, character types, or literary strategies? What are the areas of greatest contrast and how might we account for them?

6. How is an Africanist presence—black characters, stories about black people, representations of black speech, images associated with Africa or with blackness—used in works by white writers to construct positive portrayals of white characters?

Depending upon the literary work in question, we might ask one or any combination of these questions. Or we might come up with a useful question of our own not listed here. These are just some starting points to get us thinking productively about literary texts from an African American perspective. Remember, not all African American critics will interpret the same work in the same way, even if they employ the same theoretical concepts. As always, even expert practitioners disagree.

Some Shared Features of Postcolonial and African American Criticism

As you can see, although postcolonial and African American criticism are two distinct critical approaches, they nevertheless share some important features. For example, both forms of criticism seek to analyze the politics and psychology of subjugation, in other words, political and psychological strategies of domination. And both seek to analyze the politics and psychology of resistance, in other words, political and psychological strategies of personal and cultural survival.

Furthermore, a postcolonial critic may draw on an African American work as an example of postcolonial literature, as we saw earlier in Homi Bhabha's comparison of Toni Morrison's *Beloved* with *My Son's Story*, by South African writer Nadine Gordimer. Analogously, an African American critic may want to compare an Afro-American literary work with one from another part of the African diaspora in terms of some theme that is common to both. Indeed, Barbadian-born writer Edward Kamau Braithwaite directly credits the Black Power movement in America for inspiring his epic trilogy *The Arrivants* (1973). And the West Indian Rasta culture, of which musician Bob Marley was a popular exponent, has inspired and shaped some areas of African American culture.

Finally, postcolonial and African American criticism share some common terminology—such as double-consciousness—and some overlapping concepts. For example, colonialist ideology is inherently racist and the indoctrination of colonial subjects of color is accomplished by forcing them to internalize white racist beliefs, that is, by promoting internalized racism, which is an important concept in African American criticism as well. Thus we might say that a nation can "colonize" its own citizens by indoctrinating them in such colonialist ideologies as white supremacy.

Whatever ways we may choose to apply postcolonial and African American criticism, our goal in using these approaches is to learn to see some important aspects of literature that we might not have seen so clearly or so deeply without these theoretical perspectives; to appreciate the opportunities and the responsibilities of living in a culturally diverse world; and to understand that culture is not just a fixed collection of artifacts and customs frozen in time but a way of relating to oneself and to the world, a psychological and social frame of reference that necessarily alters in response to cross-cultural encounters, whether those encounters occur in our community or on the pages of a literary text. And for many postcolonial and African American critics, the most painful lessons in the history of human culture are often the most valuable. As Homi Bhabha puts it, "It is from those who have suffered the sentence of history—subjugation, domination, diaspora, displacement—that we learn our most enduring lessons for living and thinking" (172).

The following reading of F. Scott Fitzgerald's *The Great Gatsby* is offered as an example of what a postcolonial interpretation of that novel might yield. You'll notice that my postcolonial reading relies a good deal on psychological analysis and is similar, in some ways, to my discussion of the novel in Chapter Three, "Marxist Criticism." This kind of theoretical "overlap" is quite common because postcolonial criticism draws on these two theories, among others, in its attempt to analyze all aspects of colonialist and anti-colonialist ideologies. Although my reading includes an analysis of the novel's black characters and of its erasure of the African American presence in Jazz-Age New York City, I call my interpretation postcolonial, rather than African American, because it focuses on what I will argue is the novel's colonialist ideology, an ideology that can subjugate minority populations within a nation's borders as well as colonized populations elsewhere on the globe.

Although I believe that one of the greatest products of postcolonial and African American criticism is their potential to bring the works of marginalized writers of color to the fore, I hope that my reading of Fitzgerald's novel serves anti-colonialist intellectual efforts by illustrating the ways in which colonialist ideology is inherently racist, classist, and sexist and is a fundamental element lurking at the core of American cultural identity. As many postcolonial critics attest, the key concern of postcolonial criticism is resistance to colonialist ideology in all its forms, and we can't resist an ideology until we know where it's hiding.

The Colony Within: A Postcolonial Reading of *The Great Gatsby*

As such critical frameworks as Marxism, feminism, lesbian/gay/queer theory, and African American criticism have taught us, no ideology is really separate from the psychology it produces. Ideology cannot exist without the psychology appropriate to it, without the psychology that sustains it. Thus, such ideologies as classism, sexism, heterosexism, and racism are not merely belief systems. They are also ways of relating to oneself and others and, as such, involve complex psychological modes of being.

Perhaps nowhere is the intimate connection between ideology and psychology demonstrated more clearly than in postcolonial criticism. For one of postcolonial theory's most definitive goals is to combat colonialist ideology by understanding the ways in which it operates to form the identity—the psychology—of both the colonizer and the colonized. And as a pervasive force in Western civilization, colonialist ideology can be found operating, sometimes invisibly but almost always effectively, even in those cultural practices and productions in which we would not expect to find it, for example in an American novel that doesn't seem concerned with colonialism at all: F. Scott Fitzgerald's *The Great Gatsby* (1925). For looked at through a postcolonial lens, Fitzgerald's famous novel about the American Jazz Age is the quintessential text about "othering," a psychological operation upon which colonialist ideology depends and that is its unmistakable hallmark.

As the history of Western civilization has shown repeatedly, in order to subjugate an "alien" people, a nation must convince itself that those people are "different," and "different" must mean inferior to the point of being less than human. In postcolonial terminology, the subjugated people must be "othered." In our own country, for example, the justification for exterminating some Native American nations and assimilating others through compulsory colonialist education was that Native Americans were "savages," literally inhuman. Similarly, the enslavement of Africans and their indoctrination in the colonialist ideology of white superiority was justified by officially defining Africans as only three-fifths human. As our own national history reveals, then, colonialism doesn't require a colonized population beyond a nation's geographical borders. Colonized populations can exist within the geographical borders of the colonizing nation.

As *The Great Gatsby* illustrates, colonialism exists "within" in another sense of the term, as well: it exists within the individual psyche, where it influences our personal identity and our perceptions of others. Specifically, I will argue that Fitzgerald's novel reveals the colonialist ideology hiding at the heart of American culture by revealing the colonialist psychology that lurks at the core of American cultural identity.

As might be expected, colonialist psychology consists of, among other things, those (often unconscious) attitudes and behaviors by which a culturally privileged group others a culturally subordinate group, that is, by which the culturally privileged distance themselves emotionally from populations over whom they want to gain or maintain control. There are many political and economic motives for othering, but the primary psychological motive seems to be the need to feel powerful, in control, superior. Thus colonialist psychology finds in the insecure individual fertile ground upon which to establish itself. And as we shall see, colonialist psychology is self-perpetuating: it encourages the personal insecurity that facilitates its operations. Because othering is the activity that both fuels and expresses it, colonialist psychology depends heavily on racism and classism, two very successful forms of othering. Of course, sexism often overlaps with racism and, as we shall see below, with classism, thus subjecting women from culturally subordinate groups to complex forms of multiple othering. Indeed, it is the practice of multiple forms of othering that distinguishes colonialist psychology.

In *The Great Gatsby*, colonialist psychology is not confined to the depiction of characters the novel itself discredits, such as Tom Buchanan. Rather, colonialist psychology is a pervasive presence in the narrative as a whole because that psychology is central to the characterization of the narrator, Nick Carraway. In addition, the novel helps us understand colonialist psychology from the viewpoint of the colonial subject, who, remaining a cultural outsider whether or not he achieves financial success, wants only to be accepted by the cultural elite, a position epitomized by the character of Jay Gatsby. Finally, in the character of Tom Buchanan, *The Great Gatsby* reveals the detrimental effects of colonialist psychology even on the culturally privileged who seem to be its beneficiaries.

Nick Carraway strikes many readers, as indeed he wants to strike them, as a very tolerant person. Because, as he says, he is "inclined to reserve all judgements," he "was privy to the secret griefs" (5; ch. 1) of his acquaintances when he was an undergraduate at Yale. And so is he still when we meet him in the novel as a man just turning thirty. Almost all the main characters confide in Nick. Daisy tells him about her marital troubles; Tom talks to him about Myrtle; Gatsby tells him the truth about his past life and his initial relationship with Daisy; and even Myrtle describes to him her excitement at meeting Tom and having an extramarital affair for the first time. And though Nick functions as the novel's moral center—he's the only character who cares about others, who takes a genuine personal interest in their happiness and their sorrows, and who expresses strong ethical reservations about their obvious selfishness—he is extremely tolerant of the personal choices they make in their private lives.

While he feels he must break off his correspondence with a young woman he knew back home before he can date Jordan, he seems perfectly comfortable with the very different lifestyle of the group he has fallen in with on Long Island. Indeed, Nick agrees to arrange Gatsby's reunion with Daisy and to stand guard while the two meet at his cottage during one of Gatsby's parties.

So it seems especially significant that there is one area in which Nick continually makes judgements about others with no apparent consciousness of doing so: in his numerous references to the plethora of minor characters who are in some way foreign, in some way alien, to the privileged cultural group of his day, of which he is a member: white, upper-class, Anglo-Saxon Protestants, born of families who had prospered in America for several generations. Whenever Nick has cause to mention people from a different culture, he emphasizes their ethnicity as if that were their primary or only feature and thus foregrounds their "alien" quality. For example, the woman he has hired to keep his house and cook his breakfast, whom he sees every day, is referred to six different times and always by such appellations as "my Finn" (88; ch. 5) and "the Finn" (89: ch. 5). Her language consists of "mutter[ing] Finnish wisdom to herself over the electric stove" (8; ch. 1), and even her walk—"the Finnish tread" (89; ch. 5)—is described in a way that foregrounds her ethnic difference.

Similarly, Wolfshiem's secretary is "a lovely Jewess" (178; ch. 9); the witness talking to the police officer at the scene of Myrtle's death is "the Negro" (148; ch. 7); the youngster playing with fireworks in the Valley of Ashes is "a grey, scrawny Italian child" (30; ch. 2); and the people in the funeral procession Nick sees one day on his way to New York City have "the tragic eyes and short upper lips of south-eastern Europe" (73; ch. 4). While Nick's choice of words is certainly effective as colorful description, its relentless focus on the ethnicity of characters outside the dominant culture of Jazz-Age America hints at a disquieting dimension of his attitude toward "foreigners," a dimension that becomes clear when he speaks of Meyer Wolfshiem.

Nick introduces Wolfshiem to us as a "small flat-nosed Jew" (75; ch. 4), and we are told very little else about his appearance except for his nose. But his nose is mentioned so frequently and in such descriptive detail that Wolfshiem is reduced to the single physical feature that, as the statement just cited indicates, Nick finds the most unattractive and associates the most strongly with Wolfshiem's ethnicity. For example, Nick says, Wolfshiem raised his "head and regarded me with two fine growths of hair which luxuriated in either nostril" (73–74; ch. 4), and "dropp[ing] my hand [he] covered Gatsby with his expressive nose" (74; ch. 4). Apparently, all of Wolfshiem's expressiveness, in Nick's opinion, resides in his nose, for when Nick wants to tell us that Wolfshiem has become angry, he says, "Mr. Wolfshiem's nose flashed at me indignantly" (75; ch. 4). When Wolfshiem is interested in something Nick has said, Nick reports, "His nostrils turned to me in an interested way" (75; ch. 4). When Wolfshiem is emotionally moved, Nick communicates this fact by saying, "[H]is tragic nose was trembling" (77; ch. 4) or "The hair in his nostrils quivered slightly" (180; ch. 9).

Nick is clearly othering Wolfshiem, as he others almost all the ethnic characters he sees. And in doing so he dehumanizes them. Othering dehumanizes because it permits one to identify oneself as "the human being" and people who are different as something "other" than human. Othering thus facilitates the demonization of people we define as different from us, as we see when Nick's description of Wolfshiem turns that character into a version of "the Jew as monster," a form of othering that served Hitler well in Nazi Germany. Nick achieves this effect, apparently with no consciousness of doing anything amiss, with the only descriptions we get of Wolfshiem that do not include his nose: in Nick's words, Wolfshiem has a "large head" (73; ch. 4), "tiny eyes" (74; ch. 4), "bulbous fingers" (179; ch. 9), and finally, "cuff buttons" made of "human molars" (77; ch. 4). Of course, Nick is demonizing Wolfshiem because this character is a criminal of rather vast proportions. But Nick foregrounds Wolfshiem's Jewishness to such a degree that even Wolfshiem's criminal status becomes associated with his ethnicity.

Another significant example of Nick's othering of ethnic characters occurs when Gatsby is driving him to New York City in his enormous luxury car. Nick sees "three modish [fashionable] Negroes" in "a limousine . . . driven by a white chauffeur" (73; ch. 4). He describes them as "two bucks and a girl" and says, "I laughed aloud as the yolks of their eyeballs rolled toward us in haughty rivalry" (73; ch. 4). Of course Nick's unself-conscious racism is obvious in his othering of these characters: the black men are "bucks"—animals rather than men—and the description of their wide-stretched, rolling eyes resonates strongly with racist stereotypes that portrayed African Americans as foolish, childish, overly dramatic, comic characters.

In addition, Nick's description of these characters fulfills the kind of narrative function Toni Morrison describes in her analysis of the Africanist presence in white American literature. These black characters—fashionably dressed, riding in a chauffeured limousine, very conscious of their social status in the eyes of others—are the mirror and shadow of Gatsby. The only obvious difference between them is that Gatsby can hide his origins, which he does, whereas they can't because they can't hide their color. From Nick's point of view, despite Gatsby's "elaborate formality of speech [that] just missed being absurd" (53; ch. 3), his ridiculous fabrication of wealthy "ancestors" (69; ch. 4), his "circus wagon" (128; ch. 7) of a car, as Tom calls it, and all his other ludicrous affectations, he is the romantic embodiment of success. The black characters, however, are its parody. In barely more than one sentence, in the single image with which Nick describes the black characters, he projects onto them everything about Gatsby that he, and perhaps the reader, hold in contempt. *They* are preposterous, not Gatsby. Thus, Nick's othering of these characters facilitates their function as scapegoats sacrificed to Nick's, and the text's, recuperation of Gatsby.

To put the matter another way, the novel erases real African Americans, who were a very visible and important presence in New York City during the 1920s, where much of the novel is set, and substitutes in their place a comic stereotype—a colonialist other—that reinforces white superiority. This is no small move, given the historical reality of New York City during the 1920s, which was home to the Harlem Renaissance as well as to such sites of black cultural production as The Cotton Club, where African American jazz greats attracted wealthy white patrons in droves. In fact, given Fitzgerald's penchant for creating a strong sense of place through the evocation of specific cultural details, it wouldn't be unreasonable to argue that the text falls short of the demands of its setting by not having one of the main characters visit the Cotton Club, or at least refer to a visit there, for that is surely what fashionable young people such as the Buchanans, Nick, and Jordan would have done. The novel's erasure of African Americans becomes even more ironic when we consider that *The Great Gatsby* is credited with representing the Jazz Age, a term coined by Fitzgerald. Yet black Americans, who invented jazz and who were its most famous musicians, are conspicuously absent from the text.

Indeed, the novel's erasure of this local, "colonized" population is a feature of colonialist ideology that often accompanies othering. The colonized other doesn't count, becomes invisible to the eyes of the colonizer, who not only takes the fruits of colonized labor but takes credit for those fruits as well. It should be no surprise, then, that the novel gives the credit for jazz, symbolically, to whites. The only musicians we see playing jazz are the white musicians at Gatsby's party. And they are "no thin five piece affair," Nick tells us, "but a whole pit full of oboes and trombones and saxophones and viols and cornets and piccolos and low and high drums" (44; ch. 3). In other words, jazz has been "elevated" to the status of high culture in the form of an orchestra, and high culture belongs to white, not black, Americans.

Significantly, the orchestra spotlights its performance of a piece that, the conductor informs us, was played at Carnegie Hall: "Vladimir Tostoff's Jazz History of the World" (54; ch. 3). Could Fitzgerald have found a more conspicuously European—that is, white—name than Vladimir Tostoff? There's no way a reader could mistake him for an African American. In the world of this novel, jazz is, symbolically at least, a European invention. Thus, Tom's warning that "[i]t's up to us who are the dominant race to watch out or these other races will have control of things" (17; ch. 1), though mocked by Nick and by the novel's unflattering characterization of Tom, is an attitude the novel seems, unconsciously, to share.

There is, however, an important exception to Nick's othering of ethnic characters. "The young Greek, Michaelis, who ran the coffee joint" (143; ch. 7) next to George Wilson's garage, is a well-developed, sympathetic character who is not reduced to his ethnicity. Michaelis takes an interest in Wilson's concerns. He spends the whole night sitting up with George, trying to help and comfort him, after Myrtle is killed. He cooks breakfast for himself, George, and "one of the watchers of the night before" (168; ch. 8) who returns the next morning to help out. And the text gives Michaelis a good deal of authority by making him "the principal witness at the inquest" (143; ch. 7) concerning Myrtle's death. This exception makes sense, however, when we recall that white Americans consider Greece the cradle of Western civilization. It can hardly be coincidental that, in a novel filled with one-dimensional, dehumanized ethnic characters, the single ethnic character given fully human status is associated with Greece, an important source of white civilization's superior image of itself.

Why does Nick engage in this kind of ethnic othering? Of course, one important reason is that, as a member of the dominant cultural group, he was programmed to do so. However, Nick also has some personal insecurity that makes him need to feel he is in control, that makes him need to feel superior to others in some way, and therefore that makes him especially vulnerable to colonialist psychology. At the age of thirty, Nick is still being financed by his father while he tries to figure out what he should do with himself. His summer in New York is just the latest in a series of experiences failing to produce either a promising career or a lasting romance. Nick fears that all he has to look forward to is, as he puts it, "a thinning list of single men to know, a thinning brief-case of enthusiasm, thinning hair" (143; ch. 7). In addition, though Nick comes from the "right" family and the "right" background, apparently he doesn't expect a large inheritance. He needs to find a profession and, while he searches, his family funding goes only so far as to provide a modest cottage and pay his expenses. Certainly, this is no small feat, especially as Nick's expenses include courting Jordan. But given the cultural milieu in which he was raised, he doubtless has had many friends who come from families immensely more wealthy than his. As a member of the cultural elite, Nick knows the importance of gradations in social rank and must therefore be aware that his lack of fortune, relative to his peers, puts him at a social disadvantage. Thus, Nick has at least two important reasons to feel the need to assert his superiority and thereby assert his control. And the othering of ethnic subordinates offers him precisely this feeling.

The novel also helps us understand colonialist psychology from the viewpoint of the colonial subject, the cultural outsider who wants only to be accepted by the cultural elite. Although Gatsby has two important characteristics that place him, geographically, among the cultural elite in the text—he's white and wealthy enough to buy a mansion on Long Island Sound—he has far more in common with the colonial subject. For the culture to which Gatsby aspires, the culture to which Daisy Fay Buchanan belongs, is not his own. Its subtle social codes and gradations of social status are unfamiliar to him, and he can't quite get the hang of them. He is oblivious, for example, to the important social distinction between the upper-crust East Eggers and those who live at "the less fashionable" (9; ch. 1) West Egg, where he resides, just as he is oblivious to the gradations of class among the "menagerie" (114, ch. 6), as Tom calls them, who attend his parties. And it doesn't even seem to occur to Gatsby that a person of Nick's background—a Yale graduate from a socially established family, related to Daisy—might not be interested in selling fake bonds, a criminal enterprise in which Gatsby offers to include him in return for Nick's arranging Gatsby's reunion with Daisy.

In short, Gatsby lacks the proper blood-line, class origin, upbringing, and education for Daisy's set. He has lied and faked his way into her life, both during their initial courtship and again after their reunion. And as a result, Gatsby is a hybrid: a blend of two different cultures. But he's not a hybrid in Homi Bhabha's positive sense of the term as a dynamic, exciting site of cultural potential. Rather, Gatsby is a hybrid in its most conflicted form: his personality is dominated by an endless struggle to rid himself of his own roots, his own identity as a poor boy from a family of "shiftless and unsuccessful farm people" (104; ch. 6) in rural Minnesota. When he tells Nick that his "family all died" (70; ch. 4), the lie carries with it the weight of unconscious psychological desire: Gatsby would like to eradicate all trace of his social origins.

We can see the force of this desire in the excessive quality of Gatsby's mimicry, his elaborate attempt to imitate the dress, speech, behavior, and lifestyle of the culturally privileged. For example, Gatsby fabricated an upper-class family and invented a past that includes an Oxford education; big-game hunting; living "like a young rajah in all the capitals of Europe"; jewel collecting, "chiefly rubies"; and "painting a little, things for myself only" (70; ch. 4). He created a new, more fashionable sounding name for himself. He adopted numerous affectations of upper-class speech and "correct" manners, including calling everyone "old sport" and "excus[ing] himself" from his party guests "with a small bow that included each of us in turn" (53; ch. 3). And he purchased an enormous mansion and many very expensive possessions that he uses for display only. Even Gatsby's blind devotion to the selfish and shallow Daisy can best be explained by her symbolic quality, in Gatsby's eyes, as a princess "[h]igh in a white palace the king's daughter, the golden girl" (127; ch. 7). If Gatsby can win Daisy, then he has proof that he belongs to the cultural elite she represents for him, that he is no longer a poor farm boy, a "Mr. Nobody from Nowhere" (137; ch. 7), as Tom calls him. Clearly, Gatsby is trying to stop being Jimmy Gatz as much as he is trying to become Jay Gatsby. For as his characterization illustrates, mimicry involves not only the laborious attempt to be accepted by a culture different from the one into which one was born but a simultaneous attempt to rid oneself of everything one has identified as other than that culture. Mimicry thus involves the othering of oneself.

Gatsby's characterization also suggests that mimicry is inseparable from unhomeliness, the feeling of belonging nowhere that results from being caught between two cultures. For one wouldn't engage in mimicry if one didn't feel unhomed. Mimicry is an attempt to find a home, psychologically, by finding a culture to which one can feel one belongs. But the conviction of one's own inferiority that produces mimicry also requires one to seek that home in a culture one deems superior to oneself. Therefore, as the portrayal of Gatsby illustrates, mimicry is an attempt to belong that is doomed to failure because, even if one succeeds in adopting the "superior" culture, one's feelings of inferiority will insure that one is never at home in it. Thus Gatsby, who actually succeeds in acquiring the literal home he seeks, the mansion—the "colossal affair by any standard . . . with a tower on one side . . . and a marble swimming pool and more than forty acres of lawn and garden" (9; ch. 1)—does not really occupy his home.

For example, among all the "Marie Antoinette music rooms and Restoration salons . . . [and] period bedrooms swathed in rose and lavender silk . . . [and] dressing rooms and poolrooms, and bathrooms with sunken baths" (96; ch. 5), the only area that shows any signs of Gatsby's occupancy is a small "apartment, a bedroom and a bath and an Adam study" (96; ch. 5). Furthermore, Gatsby doesn't seem to notice the difference between, on the one hand, the well-ordered cleanliness of his home under the care of the trained servants he fires and, on the other hand, the disarray into which it falls at the hands of the non-professional crew supplied him by Wolfshiem: "There was an inexplicable amount of dust everywhere," Nick observes, "and the rooms were musty as though they hadn't been aired for many days" (154–55; ch. 8). Indeed, "[t]he grocery boy reported that the kitchen looked like a pigsty" (120; ch. 7). Neither does Gatsby seem at all perturbed by the prolonged presence of Mr. Klipspringer, evidently a party guest with no place else to go who took it upon himself to stay in one of his host's empty bedrooms. Gatsby doesn't respond to these rather radical alterations in his home because, emotionally, he's not really there. He can't be at home in his home because it's not his home: it's mimicry. And mimicry is too outer-directed to provide any space for one's inner life.

Finally, *The Great Gatsby* reveals, in the character of Tom Buchanan, the detrimental effects of colonialist psychology even on the culturally privileged who are its apparent beneficiaries. Tom is clearly the most culturally privileged character in the novel. Despite his lack of personal refinement, his "ungentlemanly" behavior, he has all the cultural advantages afforded by race, ethnicity, socioeconomic class, gender, family, and education. In addition, his inherited wealth, which he need not lift a finger to maintain, is enormous. "[F]or instance," Nick reports, Tom "brought down a string of polo ponies from Lake Forest. It was hard to realize that a man in my own generation was wealthy enough to do that. . . . [E]ven in college his freedom with money was a matter for reproach" (10; ch. 1).

Tom is also the character who most overtly exhibits the attitudes and behaviors associated with colonialist psychology. For one thing, as we saw earlier, he fervently believes in white supremacy, a colonialist ideology that others nonwhite people in order to justify subordinating them. Paraphrasing the racist *The Rise of the Coloured Empires* by Goddard (a fictional stand-in for *The Rising Tide of Color* by Stoddard),[4] Tom tells Nick, "[W]e're Nordics . . . and we've produced all the things that go to make civilization—oh, science and art and all that" (18; ch. 1), but "if we don't look out the white race will be . . . utterly submerged" by "these other races" (17; ch. 1).

In addition, Tom is a classist, and the belief in the inherent superiority of the upper class is one way in which colonialism justifies the domination of colonized peoples. Indeed, Tom holds everyone in contempt who is beneath him in social class, including "these newly rich people," as he calls those who have acquired their own wealth. He says that "[a] lot of [them] are just big bootleggers" (114; ch. 6). While it is true that a number of people acquired a fortune through bootlegging in the 1920s, the implication here is that people who have not inherited their wealth as Tom has done are not to be trusted. In fact, Tom's mistrust of Gatsby, to whom Tom's comment about the newly rich specifically refers, is the product of his classism. And that mistrust occurs long before Tom learns, to his enormous surprise, that Gatsby is his rival for Daisy's affections.

Tom knows that Gatsby is a West Egger and not a member of his own set, a social distinction made painfully clear to the reader, though apparently not to Gatsby, when Tom and two friends, all on horseback, drop by Gatsby's house one afternoon for something to drink. All three treat Gatsby disdainfully. Tom's friend, Mr. Sloane, doesn't even speak to Gatsby, but just "lounged back haughtily in his chair" (108–09; ch. 6). When Sloane's lady-friend becomes tipsy and invites Gatsby to join them for dinner, Mr. Sloane hurries her outside while Gatsby goes to get his coat, and the three riders depart before Gatsby is able to join them. Tom is outraged that Gatsby doesn't realize he's unwelcome: "'My God, I believe the man's coming,' said Tom. 'Doesn't he know she doesn't want him?'" (109; ch. 6). Tom can't imagine "where in the devil" (110; ch. 1) Daisy could have met Gatsby and writes it off to "women run[ning] around too much these days" and therefore meeting "all kinds of crazy fish" (110; ch. 6). Tom is standing in Gatsby's enormous, lavishly furnished mansion set on a forty-acre estate, and yet he knows, and quite correctly, that Gatsby is his social inferior. Indeed, Gatsby's unawareness of the social distinctions so important to Tom are largely responsible for the mocking references Tom makes to Gatsby's parties, possessions, and probable social origins. For Tom needs everyone to know exactly in what manner he outranks them.

Classism, like racism, is an ideology that others people, a fact illustrated with particular clarity in the language Tom uses when referring to Gatsby. As we have seen, Tom calls Gatsby's parties "menagerie[s]" (114;

ch. 6), that is, collections of animals. He refers to Gatsby's car as a "circus wagon" (128; ch. 7), in other words, something used to transport animals or human "freaks." And he refers to Gatsby as a "crazy fish" (110; ch. 6). Gatsby cannot have fully human status in Tom's eyes because he doesn't have the social rank such a status requires. Surely, Tom's classist othering of Gatsby is also one of the reasons Tom is able to dispose of him without a moment's hesitation when he sends Wilson, armed and crazed, to Gatsby's house, knowing that Wilson intends to murder Gatsby yet taking no action to prevent it.

The connection between classism and colonialist psychology is especially evident in the nature of Tom's womanizing. He doesn't pick on women from his own cultural milieu. He restricts his seductions to working-class women: for example, "one of the chambermaids in the Santa Barbara Hotel" (82; ch. 4), where Tom and Daisy stayed upon returning from their honeymoon; Myrtle Wilson; and the "common but pretty" (112; ch. 6) young woman Tom tries to pick up at Gatsby's party. What seems to attract Tom most to these women is their powerlessness, which augments his own power. He can do what he wants with them. He flagrantly lies to Myrtle. He keeps her at his beck and call. He can even break her nose and get away with it. And the reason he breaks Myrtle's nose— because she dares to say Daisy's name, that is, because she thinks she's as good as Daisy—suggests that Tom sees working-class women as "bad girls," as sexual objects and nothing more, who are in a separate category altogether from "good girls" like his wife and Jordan. Because his mistresses are his social inferiors, he feels they don't deserve the respect reserved for upper-class women. In other words, Tom's classism and sexism are merged, and his womanizing is a form of classist othering. For in terms of Tom's privileged cultural milieu, working-class women are cultural outsiders. That is, Tom's classist victimization of working-class women resembles the white colonial official's racist victimization of women from the indigenous colonized population: both define their prey as "bad girls" and are thereby able to other them, thus relieving themselves of all responsibility toward them as human beings.

Certainly, Myrtle behaves like a colonial subject. She seems to have internalized the same colonialist psychology Tom has. But because she's on the bottom rung of the social hierarchy, that psychology disempowers her and makes her especially vulnerable to Tom: she considers his social superiority such a valuable asset that she will do anything to keep him. We see Myrtle as the colonial subject most clearly during the party at the small, three-room apartment Tom keeps for their trysts, where she engages in her own form of mimicry.

> Mrs. Wilson . . . was now attired in an elaborate afternoon dress of
> cream colored chiffon. . . . With the influence of the dress her per-
> sonality had also undergone a change. . . . Her laughter, her gestures,
> her assertions became more violently affected moment by moment.
> (35; ch. 2)

Behaving as she imagines the very wealthy behave, Myrtle complains
about the elevator boy as if he were her servant, "rais[ing] her eyebrows in
despair at the shiftlessness of the lower orders. 'These people! You have to
keep after them all the time,'" she says (36; ch. 2). Then she "swept into
the kitchen, implying that a dozen chefs awaited her orders there" (36; ch.
2). Clearly, Myrtle behaves in such an artificial manner because she believes that her "real self" isn't good enough, because she feels inferior to
Tom and his social set.

However much freedom and power colonialist psychology affords
Tom, though, it comes at a cost. Besides the obvious spiritual or moral
damage colonialist psychology does to the culturally privileged by facilitating and providing a rationale for unethical behavior, it also can produce a
tormented inner life. This is precisely what it does to Tom Buchanan.

There could be no cultural superiority if there were no cultural inferiority to contrast with it. And no one internalizes this idea more thoroughly than Tom. He behaves as if his social status depended upon
othering everyone "beneath" him and then showing his "superiority"
through some form of aggression. He doesn't merely harbor racist,
classist, and sexist attitudes; as we have seen, he continually and aggressively displays them. And it's the recurrent and petty nature of these displays that suggests the existence of a strong psychological motive.

For example, Tom takes cruel advantage of George Wilson's poverty,
not only by stealing his wife but also by tormenting George about the car
George would like to buy from Tom. George thinks he can re-sell the car
at a profit, which he badly needs, and Tom toys with him repeatedly concerning whether or not he will let George have the vehicle, even offering
to sell him Gatsby's enormous luxury car so that George will have to admit he can't afford it. Indeed, Tom can't even buy a puppy from a poor
old man without insulting him to show that the man has not fooled Tom
about the value of the dog: "Here's your money," Tom snaps as he gives
the man ten dollars; "[g]o and buy ten more dogs with it" (32; ch. 2).
There are many more examples of Tom's unnecessary and open hostility

toward his social inferiors, but the point is that he wouldn't need to display his social superiority so aggressively if he were secure in it.

One explanation for Tom's insecurity is that he is from the Midwest, and therefore he can never have the cultural status that, in his day, belonged only to the wealthy old blue-blood families who had lived in the East since their forebears arrived in America so long ago. He attended Yale and must know, as Fitzgerald painfully knew as a Midwesterner at Princeton, that this is the one kind of cultural superiority he can never have, no matter how many millions he has or how lavishly he lives. In this one way, Tom, himself, is other, a fact that must be especially disconcerting since his recent move East. And I think it is this knowledge, whether it is conscious or unconscious, that makes him feel insecure enough to need to prove his social superiority at every conceivable opportunity.

Nick senses the problem when he says, referring to Tom's comments about *The Rise of the Coloured Empires,* "There was something pathetic in his concentration as if his complacency [self-satisfaction] . . . was not enough to him any more" (18; ch. 1). "Something," Nick adds, "was making him nibble at the edge of stale ideas as if his sturdy physical egotism no longer nourished his peremptory [dictatorial] heart" (25; ch. 1). Nick can't explain Tom's problem, but we can: the colonialist psychology that empowers Tom also undermines his confidence because it simultaneously tells him, "If you're not on top, you're nobody," and heightens his awareness of any way in which he might not be "on top."

As I hope this reading of *The Great Gatsby* makes clear, I'm not suggesting that Fitzgerald's novel can be read as a colonialist allegory, that its characters can be interpreted as symbolic stand-ins for colonialist types the way that characters in, for example, Hawthorne's "Young Goodman Brown" (1835) or "The Minister's Black Veil" (1836) are symbolic stand-ins for abstract moral concepts like good and evil. Rather, I'm suggesting that *The Great Gatsby* reveals the ways in which colonialist psychology, upon which colonialist ideology depends, operates on the home front to sustain the imbalances of cultural power that have characterized America since its inception. For although the founders of this nation broke with Anglo-European political philosophy when they framed the American Constitution, they nevertheless inherited many aspects of Anglo-European cultural philosophy.

Most conspicuously, they inherited the belief that the white race are God's chosen people and the natural rulers of the world. That is, they inherited Anglo-European colonialist ideology, which permitted a small group of small nations—England, France, Spain, Portugal, and the Netherlands—to dominate most of the globe from the mid-eighteenth to the mid-twentieth century and which permitted white Americans, in turn, to dominate the Native American lands we now call the United States of America. An ideology this successful dies hard. And as *The Great Gatsby* illustrates, one reason colonialist ideology is so successful is that it is supported by a complex psychology that strongly influences the way we perceive ourselves and others.

Is colonialist psychology as pervasive a presence in America today as *The Great Gatsby* suggests it was during the 1920s? Certainly, the othering of American citizens is no longer supported by law, as it was in the legal discrimination that subjugated all nonwhite Americans, and many white immigrants, before the Civil Rights movement of the 1960s. And respect for cultural difference is promoted by our government, our media, and our educational system as it has never been before. Surely, these changes constitute a significant improvement.

Yet white-supremacist backlash, for example as witnessed in the proliferation of racist hate groups; the persistence of covert racial discrimination, for example in housing, employment, and education; the othering of the homeless, indeed their virtual erasure from American consciousness and conscience; and all the forms of othering that still flourish in this country today make it clear that America's neo-colonialist enterprises around the globe will be accompanied by versions thereof at home for a long time to come. For colonialist psychology, and the discriminatory ideologies it supports, are part of our historical and cultural legacy, as *The Great Gatsby* illustrates. And this is a reality that will have to be confronted anew by each generation of Americans.

Questions for Further Practice

The following questions are intended as models. They can help you use postcolonial and African American criticism to interpret the literary works to which they refer or other texts of your choice.

Postcolonial Approaches to Other Literary Works

1. Analyze the anti-colonialist agenda of Chinua Achebe's *Things Fall Apart* (1958). In order to accomplish this task, examine the novel's representation of precolonial tribal life in Africa. What is

lost as a result of colonial contact? What are the colonizers' strategies in indoctrinating the native population to their way of thinking? Why are the colonizers so successful?

2. What does Jamaica Kincaid's *The Autobiography of My Mother* (1996) suggest about the social and psychological effects of colonialism on the colonizers (Philip and Moira) and, primarily, on the colonized? Analyze, for example, the problems of corruption, class division, and colonial education as they are revealed in the characterizations of Xuela, the narrator; her father and stepmother; her lover, Roland; and Monsieur and Madame LaBatte. How does Xuela manage to survive psychologically and achieve personal independence and self-confidence?

3. Analyze the themes of unhomeliness and mimicry as they apply to V. S. Naipaul's *The Mimic Men* (1967). How might we say that colonialism has robbed the narrator of a stable (or of any) sense of himself? How does he try to find an identity? Does he ever succeed? Why or why not? How does the narrator's language (word choice, tone, imagery) reveal his emotional distance from his own experience, and what does this add to our understanding of the novel?

4. As we saw earlier, J. M. Coetzee's *Foe* (1988) is considered a postcolonial response to Daniel Defoe's *Robinson Crusoe* (1719). How, exactly, would you say that this is the case? In what ways is *Robinson Crusoe* a colonialist novel, and how does *Foe* undermine that ideology? Note, especially, what Coetzee's novel implies about the slippery nature of narrative, that is, how "one" story can become many different stories, depending on how, for what purpose, and from whose point of view it's told. What does this suggest about the power of stories, especially those that get published and are widely read?

5. What does Mary Shelley's *Frankenstein* (1818) reveal about the ideological and psychological operations of "othering"? For example, how does Shelley's portrayal of the European landed gentry, embodied in Alphonse Frankenstein and his family, represent the rightful "self" in contrast with an alien "other" embodied in, for example, the Arab merchant (among other things, note the contrast between the Arab and his Christian wife), the peasants who raised Elizabeth, the peasants among whom Victor lived while he worked on the female monster, and

the peasants he met after the death of Clerval. In what ways might Safie be viewed as resisting a kind of colonial subjugation? In what ways might she be viewed as seeking it? How should we interpret the monster in this context? Might he be seen as the novel's postcolonial critic, the unhomely "other" who will not accept colonialist domination? In what ways does he not fit this role?

African American Approaches to Other Literary Works

1. In what ways does Toni Morrison's *The Bluest Eye* (1970) participate in the African American literary tradition? For example, you might analyze the novel's anti-racist politics. (Morrison is known for her insights into the psychology of internalized racism.) Or you might analyze its poetics, for example, its orality, its folk motifs, and the ways in which the novel's use of these devices relates to the meaning of the work. Or you might want to argue that Morrison's novel participates more specifically in the tradition of African American women's writing.

2. In his play *The Piano Lesson* (1990), August Wilson sets up a conflict between two recurring African American themes: the importance of cultural heritage and the difficulties of economic survival. Analyze how the play represents and sustains this conflict without letting us resolve it in favor of one side or the other. (Or if you think the play does resolve the conflict, argue for that interpretation instead.) How might you relate Wilson's use of these themes to Houston Baker's observations about the relationship between the spiritual quest and its economic sub-text in African American literature? If you don't think the play quite fits this particular schema of text and sub-text, improvise, as Baker would say, a schema of your own, explaining how yours differs from Baker's.

3. Use Mary Helen Washington's description of recurring character types in African American women's writing—the "suspended woman," the "assimilated woman," and the "emergent woman"— to analyze the female characters in Alice Walker's *The Color Purple* (1982), Zora Neale Hurston's *Their Eyes Were Watching God* (1937) or any other African American work that will lend itself to such a study. Which of these types appear in the text, and how do

they relate to the meaning of the work as a whole? That is, how do these types function in the text to convey some sort of moral or lesson or theme?

4. Compare an African American literary work with a work from another part of the African diaspora in terms of a theme or themes they share. For example, you might analyze Ralph Ellison's *Invisible Man* (1952) and *The Autobiography of My Mother* (1996), by West Indian writer Jamaica Kincaid, in terms of the psychological portraits of their main characters, both of whom narrate their own stories. In what ways are Kincaid's and Ellison's narrators unhomely characters? How is the white supremacist ideology represented in Ellison's novel similar to the colonialist ideology represented in Kincaid's? How might we compare and/or contrast the two narrators in terms of their internalization of resistance to colonialist ideology?

5. Using Toni Morrison's theory of the Africanist presence in white mainstream American literature (the function of black characters, of stories about black people, of representations of black speech, or of images associated with Africa or with blackness), analyze the Africanist presence in a literary text by a white American author. Flannery O'Connor's "The Artificial Nigger" (1955), "Everything that Rises Must Converge" (1961), or "Judgement Day" (1965) might work well for this purpose. Or you might try William Faulkner's "That Evening Sun" (1931) or Kate Chopin's *The Awakening* (1899).

For Further Reading

All of the following works will help you develop your skills as postcolonial and African American critics. Texts listed under "Category I" are written in language accessible to most beginners. Texts listed under "Category II" employ more technical language but are well worth the extra effort that may be required of some students new to the field.

Postcolonial Criticism: Category I

LaCapra, Dominick, ed. *The Bounds of Race: Perspectives on Hegemony and Resistance.* Ithaca: Cornell UP, 1991. (See, especially, Kwame Anthony Appiah's "Out of Africa: Topologies of Nativism," 134–63; Anne McClintock's "'The Very House of Difference': Race, Gender, and the Politics of South African Women's Narrative in

Poppie Nongena," 196–230; Stephen Clingman's "Beyond the Limit: The Social Relations of Madness in Southern African Fiction," 231–54; José Piedra's "Literary Whiteness and the Afro-Hispanic Difference," 278–310; and Satya P. Mohanty's "Drawing the Color Line: Kipling and the Culture of Colonial Rule," 311–43.)

Ashcroft, Bill, Gareth Griffiths, and Helen Tiffin. *The Empire Writes Back: Theory and Practice in Post-Colonial Literatures.* New York: Routledge, 1989.

———, eds. *The Post-Colonial Studies Reader.* New York: Routledge, 1995.

Boehmer, Elleke. *Colonial and Postcolonial Literature: Migrant Metaphors.* New York: Oxford UP, 1995.

Mohanty, Chandra Talpade, Ann Russo, and Lourdes Torres, eds. *Third World Women and the Politics of Feminism.* Bloomington: Indiana UP, 1991.

Tiffin, Helen. "Post-Colonial Literatures and Counter-Discourse." *Kunapipi* 9.3 (1987). 17–34.

Postcolonial Criticism: Category II

Bhabha, Homi K. *The Location of Culture.* New York: Routledge, 1994.

———. *Nation and Narration.* New York: Routledge, 1990.

Braithwaite, Kamau. *The History of the Voice.* 1979. Rpt. *Roots.* Ann Arbor: U of Michigan P, 1993.

Fanon, Franz. *The Wretched of the Earth.* 1961. Trans. Constance Farrington. New York: Grove, 1963.

Harris, Wilson. "History, Fable and Myth in the Caribbean and Guianas." *Caribbean Quarterly* 16.2 (1970): 1–32.

Said, Edward W. *Culture and Imperialism.* New York: Knopf, 1994.

———. *Orientalism.* New York: Pantheon, 1978.

Spivak, Gayatri Chakravorti. *In Other Worlds: Essays in Cultural Politics.* New York: Routledge, 1987.

Taylor, Patrick. *The Narrative of Liberation.* Ithaca: Cornell UP, 1989.

Walcott, Derek. "The Muse of History." *Is Massa Day Dead?: Black Moods in the Caribbean.* Ed. Orde Coombs. New York: Anchor, 1974.

———. "What the Twilight Says: An Overture." *Dream on Monkey Mountain and Other Plays.* New York: Noonday, 1970.

Williams, Patrick, and Laura Chrisman, eds. *Colonial Discourse and Post-colonial Theory: A Reader.* New York: Columbia UP, 1994.

African American Criticism: Category I

Awkward, Michael. *Inspiriting Influences: Tradition, Revision, and Afro-American Literature.* New York: Columbia UP, 1989.

Bell, Bernard W. *The Afro-American Novel and Its Tradition.* Amherst: U of Massachusetts P, 1987.

———. *The Folk Roots of Contemporary Afro-American Poetry.* Detroit: Broadside, 1974.

Gates, Jr., Henry Louis. "African American Criticism." *Redrawing the Boundaries: The Transformation of English and American Literary Studies.* Eds. Stephen

Greenblatt and Giles Gunn. New York: Modern Language Association of America, 1992. 303–19.

———, ed. *Reading Black, Reading Feminist: A Critical Anthology*. New York: Meridian, 1990.

hooks, bell. *Ain't I a Woman: Black Women and Feminism*. Boston: South End Press, 1981.

Hull, Gloria T., Patricia Bell Scott, and Barbara Smith, eds. *All the Women Are White, All the Blacks Are Men, But Some of Us Are Brave: Black Women's Studies*. Old Westbury, New York: The Feminist Press, 1982.

LaCapra, Dominick, ed. *The Bounds of Race: Perspectives on Hegemony and Resistance*. Ithaca: Cornell UP, 1991. (See, especially, Henry Louis Gates, Jr.'s "The Master's Pieces: On Canon Formation and the Afro-American Tradition," 17–38; Hortense J. Spillers's "Moving On Down the Line: Variations on the African-American Sermon," 39–71; Michael Goldfield's "The Color of Politics in the United States: White Supremacy as the Main Explanation for the Peculiarities of American Politics from the Colonial Times to the Present," 104–33; and Françoise Lionnet's "Autoethnography: The An-archic Style of *Dust Tracks on a Road*," 164–95.)

Mitchell, Angelyn, ed. *Within the Circle: An Anthology of African American Literary Criticism from the Harlem Renaissance to the Present*. Durham: Duke UP, 1994.

Morrison, Toni. *Playing in the Dark: Whiteness and the Literary Imagination*. New York: Vintage, 1993.

African American Criticism: Category II

Baker, Jr., Houston A. *Blues, Ideology, and Afro-American Literature: A Vernacular Theory*. Chicago: U of Chicago P, 1984.

Baker, Jr., Houston A., and Patricia Redmond, eds. *Afro-American Literary Study in the 1990s*. Chicago: U of Chicago P, 1989.

Collins, Patricia Hill. *Black Feminist Thought: Knowledge, Consciousness, and the Politics of Empowerment*. New York: Routledge, 1990.

Gates, Jr., Henry Louis. *The Signifying Monkey: A Theory of African-American Literary Criticism*. New York: Oxford UP, 1988.

Nelson, Emmanuel S., ed. *Critical Essays: Gay and Lesbian Writers of Color*. New York: Haworth, 1993.

Gilroy, Paul. *The Black Atlantic: Modernity and Double Consciousness*. Cambridge: Harvard UP, 1993.

Ruoff, A. LaVonne Brown, and Jerry W. Ward, Jr., eds. *Redefining American Literary History*. New York: Modern Language Association of America, 1990.

Notes

1. Today, the words *imperialism* and *colonialism* are often used interchangeably. Before World War II, however, when Britain still had extensive colonial holdings, the distinction between the two terms was fairly clear. Strictly speaking, imperialism is the system of forming and maintaining an empire (a collection of territories under the control of a single ruler) through such means as military conquest, the control of natural resources, the control of world

markets, and colonization. Colonialism (the extension of territorial control through the establishment of colonies) is merely one form of imperialism. In the decades since World War II, however, such concepts as cultural colonization, neo-colonialism, and cultural imperialism—all of which involve the economic and cultural domination of one society by another without the extension of territorial control—have blurred the distinction between the terms *imperialism* and *colonialism*.

2. It is interesting to note that the concept of double consciousness was first articulated in 1903 by African American writer W.E.B. DuBois in *The Souls of Black Folk*.

3. In recent years the term *African American* has largely replaced the earlier *Afro-American*. However, usage is still a matter of personal preference.

4. New York: Scribners, 1920. Cited in "Explanatory Notes," *The Great Gatsby*, p. 208.

Works Cited

Achebe, Chinua. "An Image of Africa: Racism in Conrad's *Heart of Darkness*." *Massachusetts Review* 18 (1977): 782–94. Rpt. in *Hopes and Impediments, Selected Essays*. New York: Anchor, 1989. 1–20.

———. *Morning Yet on Creation Day*. Garden City, New York: Doubleday, 1975.

Baker, Houston. *Blues, Ideology, and Afro-American Literature: A Vernacular Theory*. Chicago: U of Chicago P, 1984.

Bhabha, Homi K. *The Location of Culture*. New York: Routledge, 1994.

Brontë, Charlotte. *Jane Eyre*. 1847. A Norton Critical Edition. Ed. Richard J. Dunn. New York: Norton, 1971.

Christian, Barbara. "The Race for Theory." *Cultural Critique* 6 (1987): 51–63. Excerpted in *The Post-Colonial Studies Reader*. Eds. Bill Ashcroft, Gareth Griffiths, and Helen Tiffin. New York: Routledge, 1995. 457–60.

DuBois, W.E.B. *The Souls of Black Folk: Essays and Sketches*. 1903. New York: Kraus, 1973.

Gates, Jr., Henry Louis. *Figures in Black: Words, Signs, and the "Racial" Self*. New York: Oxford UP, 1987.

———. "The Master's Pieces: On Canon Formation and the Afro-American Tradition." *The Bounds of Race: Perspectives on Hegemony and Resistance*. Ed. Dominick LaCapra. Ithaca: Cornell UP, 1991. 17–38.

———. *The Signifying Monkey: A Theory of African-American Literary Criticism*. New York: Oxford UP, 1988.

Hemingway, Ernest. *To Have and Have Not*. New York: Grosset and Dunlap, 1937.

McClintock, Anne. "The Angel of Progress: Pitfalls of the Term 'Post-colonialism.'" *Social Text* (Spring 1992): 1–15. Rpt. in *Colonial Discourse and Post-Colonial Theory*. Eds. Patrick Williams and Laura Chrisman. New York: Columbia UP, 1994. 291–304.

McDowell, Deborah E. "The Changing Same: Generational Connections and Black Women Novelists." *New Literary History* 18 (1987): 281–302. Rpt. in *Reading Black, Reading Feminist: A Critical Anthology*. Ed. Henry Louis Gates, Jr. New York: Meridian, 1990. 91–115.

Morrison, Toni. *Playing in the Dark: Whiteness and the Literary Imagination*. New York: Vintage, 1993.

Roberts, John W. "The African American Animal Trickster as Hero." *Redefining American Literary History*. Eds. A. LaVonne Brown Ruoff and Jerry W. Ward, Jr. New York: Modern Language Association of America, 1990. 97–114.

Said, Edward W. *Culture and Imperialism*. New York: Knopf, 1994.

———. *Orientalism*. New York: Pantheon, 1978.

Spivak, Gayatri Chakravorty. "Three Women's Texts and a Critique of Imperialism." *Critical Inquiry* 12.1 (1985): 43–61. Excerpted in *The Post-Colonial Studies Reader*. Eds. Bill Ashcroft, Gareth Griffiths, and Helen Tiffin. New York: Routledge, 1995. 269–72.

Tiffin, Helen. "Post-Colonial Literatures and Counter-Discourse." *Kunapipi* 9.3 (1987): 17–34. Excerpted in *The Post-Colonial Studies Reader*. Eds. Bill Ashcroft, Gareth Griffiths, and Helen Tiffin. New York: Routledge, 1995. 95–98.

Washington, Mary Helen, ed. *Black-Eyed Susans: Classic Stories by and about Black Women*. Garden City, New York: Doubleday, 1977.

———. "Teaching Black-Eyed Susans: An Approach to the Study of Black Women Writers." *All the Women Are White, All the Blacks Are Men, But Some of Us Are Brave: Black Women's Studies*. Eds. Gloria T. Hull, Patricia Bell Scott, and Barbara Smith. Old Westbury, New York: The Feminist Press, 1982.

CHAPTER 12

Gaining an Overview

If you've read several of the preceding chapters, you may be feeling a bit overwhelmed both by the amount of information you've consumed and by the various ways in which many critical theories overlap with one another. The following questions are offered, not as a summary of the schools of criticism we've discussed but as a way to organize your thoughts as you reflect upon what you've learned and decide which theories you'd like to pursue further. Certainly, "Some Questions Critics Ask about Literary Texts" and "Questions for Further Practice" (which preceding chapters provide as specific guidelines for applying the critical theories they describe) are more thorough than the brief questions listed below. However, the questions that follow offer you a kind of bird's eye overview of the theories we've studied and, therefore, an opportunity to see more generally the ways in which critical theories both resemble and differ from one another.

Psychoanalytic Criticism—How is the text shaped by its (intentional or unintentional) representation of the psychological desires, needs, and conflicts of its characters (or the psychological desires, needs, and conflicts of its author)?

Marxist Criticism—How is the text shaped by its (intentional or unintentional) representation of capitalism and/or classism and by its embodiment of the ideologies that support or undermine those socioeconomic systems?

Feminist Criticism—How is the text shaped by its (intentional or

unintentional) representation of patriarchal norms and values
and by its embodiment of the ideologies that support or undermine those norms and values?

New Criticism—Is the text a great work of literature? That is, does it
have both organic unity and a theme of universal significance?

Reader-Response Criticism—How do readers make meaning as they
read the text, and what is the relationship of the meaning they
make to the text?

Structuralist Criticism—What is the underlying structural system (for
example, archetypal, modal, or narratological) by which we make
sense of the text?

Deconstructive Criticism—What do we learn about the ideology (or
ideologies) operating in the text by analyzing the text's contradictions rather than by trying to resolve those contradictions into
some overarching theme?

New Historicism—How does the text participate in the interpretation
of history? Specifically, what role does the text play in the circulation of discourses (ways of using language that are associated
with particular ideologies, such as the discourses of liberal
humanism, Christian fundamentalism, or white supremacy)
prevalent in the culture from which the work emerged, and/or
how does the text's role change over the history of its reception?

Cultural Criticism—Especially in regard to working-class cultural
productions (such as popular fiction and movies) and to comparisons of working-class productions with the productions of
so-called "high" culture (such as canonized literature), what
cultural work does the text perform? That is, how does the text
transmit and transform the ideologies that support and/or
undermine the socio-political power structure at the time the text
was produced and/or over the course of its reception?

Lesbian/Gay/Queer Criticism—How is the text shaped by its (intentional or unintentional) representation of lesbian, gay, or queer
sexuality and by its embodiment of the ideologies that support or
undermine heterosexism?

Postcolonial Criticism—How is the text shaped by its (intentional or
unintentional) representation of cultural difference (the ways in
which race, religion, class, gender, sexual orientation, cultural
beliefs, and customs combine to form individual identity) and by

its embodiment of the colonialist and anti-colonialist ideologies
that compete to determine how we perceive that difference?

African American Criticism—How is the text shaped by its (intentional or unintentional) representation of race and by its embodiment of the racist and anti-racist ideologies that compete to
determine how we perceive racial difference?

Although these questions focus on the interpretation of literary texts,
I trust that, by this point, you are fully aware that each theoretical lens
alters the way we perceive ourselves and our world, as well. To cite just
one example, African American criticism, considered in its broadest context, asks us to see what we can learn by examining the ways in which race
(for example, perceptions of racial difference, the history of race in
America, and racism) inform our individual and collective identity; our
interpersonal relationships; our history; and our cultural productions,
including but not limited to literature. Thus, taken together, critical theories enlarge our understanding not only of literary works, though that is a
worthwhile end in itself, but of human experience in general.

I'm sure you've noticed that some of the schools of criticism listed
above are overtly political: their goal is to change society for the better in
some way. Other theories see themselves as apolitical, as removed from
the forces that shape history and politics. A striking example of this kind
of theory is New Criticism, which was the dominant force in literary
studies in the late 1940s and 1950s and which saw itself as occupying a
purely aesthetic realm. However, most critical theorists today recognize
that all critical theories are produced by historical realities and have political implications whether or not their advocates are aware of those realities and implications.

For example, many politically oriented theorists believe that the creation of a purely aesthetic realm of literary analysis is, itself, a political
move that reflects a desire to escape history, a desire to carve out a "safe"
space where one can feel protected from the unpredictable and often
frightening realities of the world. However, a critical practice that ignores
political reality does not thereby remove itself from politics. It merely
protects, however inadvertently, whatever power structure is in place by
drawing our attention away from that power structure. From this perspective, it is not surprising that New Criticism rose to prominence and
that structuralism emerged in the years following World War II, when the
fear of nuclear holocaust was at its height and, therefore, the belief in a
permanent realm of ideas beyond the reach of human events was espe-

cially appealing. Indeed, "apolitical" theories always serve conservative power structures.

One could analyze, in a similar fashion, the historical roots and political implications of any critical theory. Of course, the historical roots and political implications of some critical theories are more obvious than those of others. For example, feminist criticism, African American criticism, and lesbian/gay/queer criticism grew directly out of political movements: respectively, the Women's Liberation, Black Power, and Gay and Lesbian Liberation movements of the late 1960s, although the intellectual roots of all three schools of criticism are as old as the struggle for equality regardless of sex, race, or sexual orientation. Similarly, Marxist criticism is a response to social injustice, as are, in large part, postcolonial, new historical, and cultural criticism.

On the other hand, the political or "apolitical" orientation of psychoanalytic, reader-response, and deconstructive criticism depends entirely upon the individual critic and the purpose for which the theory is used. For example, the psychoanalytic reading of *The Great Gatsby* offered in Chapter Two is "apolitical" (that is, it ignore politics and thus does nothing to alter the political *status quo*) because it focuses on dysfunctional love as an individual, or familial, disorder. Had I, instead, examined the novel's representation of dysfunctional love as a product of modern American culture—perhaps as a product of the intersection of capitalism, patriarchy, and other ideological forces—I would have produced an overtly political psychoanalytic reading (or, depending on how I focused the essay, a psychoanalytically-oriented Marxist or feminist reading).

Similarly, reader-response criticism can function "apolitically" when, for example, it examines how texts elicit particular reading experiences, as we saw in the section on affective stylistics in Chapter Six. Or reader-response criticism can have a political function when, for example, it examines the ideological motives informing the way certain literary works have been read by whole generations of critics. Deconstruction, too, is "apolitical" when it is used to show that the meaning of a text is "undecidable": the text's meaning can't be pinned down and, therefore, the text has no meaning, in the traditional sense of the word. Certainly, if a text has no meaning, it has no politics. In the hands of other practitioners, however, deconstruction can be a powerful political tool when it is used to reveal the ideological contradictions—the hidden politics—operating in a text, as we saw in the deconstructive reading of *The Great Gatsby* offered in Chapter Eight.

In short, the meaning and power of every critical theory depend largely on you. Critical theories are tools in your hands, no more, no less. You can choose one theory and interpret literature through that lens alone, or you can become adept at using two, three, or more theories, even combining the insights they offer as you interpret a single literary work. You might produce, for example, an African American reading that draws on Marxist, psychoanalytic, and feminist concepts in order to interpret the representation of racial difference in a literary work. Or you might produce a feminist reading that draws on postcolonial and reader-response concepts in order to analyze what you consider a recurrent misreading of a literary work written, for example, by a West Indian woman. In fact, it is not unreasonable to argue that, in order to be really proficient at applying some critical theories, it is necessary that you familiarize yourself with the theories upon which they draw. For many Marxist, feminist, postcolonial, African American, and lesbian/gay/queer critics draw upon one another's theoretical frameworks as well as on such theories as psychoanalysis, deconstruction, reader-response theory, and semiotics in order to analyze the myriad forms and processes of oppression and the resistance to oppression.

The theory or theories you choose to use for a particular reading, however, should depend mainly on two factors: (1) your own ability to use the theory and (2) the literary text to which you plan to apply it. For in order to produce a useful reading you need a good fit, both between yourself and the theory you choose and between the theory you choose and the literary text. Not all literary texts lend themselves equally well to all theories. So part of your skill must involve recognizing when to apply which theory. Like any skill worth acquiring, it takes practice. Don't be discouraged by initial difficulties you may encounter. Your violin has to squeak quite a bit before you learn to play Mozart.

And if I may offer one more warning, don't dismiss a theory because you find it has some flaws. It's easy to find fault with critical theories. They all have them. That's part of what it means to be a theory rather than a fact. For example, how can a literary work be its own context, as New Criticism claims it is? Isn't that a logical absurdity, a violation of the definition of context? Or how can psychoanalysis omit or marginalize sociological factors in the creation of the psyche, when the family (which psychoanalysis holds responsible for the formation of the psyche) is itself a sociological entity?

Finding faults in a theory, however, does not necessarily render that theory less helpful for literary interpretation. And if we practice fault-finding too soon in our learning process, we can overlook the enormous usefulness of many theories as our tendency to dismiss them grows, a tendency that is fed, it seems to me, by our understandable desire to feel less intimidated by critical theory. The logic is inviting but very self-defeating: if a critical theory is flawed, then it's not so important that I become proficient at it, and I don't have to worry about my difficulties with it. So I want to urge you very strongly to postpone the "critique mode" for awhile, at least until you have thoroughly familiarized yourself with a range of theories by using them to interpret literature.

Before I send you off on your own to do those readings, however, I'd like to share with you a recent experience that I think reflects both the personal and the political nature of critical theory and literary interpretation. I briefly described my feminist, postcolonial, and queer readings of *The Great Gatsby* to an interested friend who loves to read literature but who knows nothing about critical theory. He immediately asked, "Are any of the theories you use in your textbook in harmony with the novel?" "They all are," I hastened to assure him. "I wouldn't apply a theory to a literary work if it distorted the work," I explained. "No," he said; "I mean, do all the theories find something *wrong* with the novel?"

Then it hit me. He's right! Almost all the theories I used have led me to conclude, in effect, that the novel is ideologically flawed in some way. If I put all these flaws together, I come up with a statement something like this: "*The Great Gatsby* is a classist, sexist, homophobic, racist, colonialist novel that romanticizes the evils of capitalism, glorifies dysfunctional love, and as if that weren't enough, creates an indeterminate reading experience that invites us to project our own beliefs and desires onto the text." Yet *The Great Gatsby* is also one of the most moving and exquisitely written literary works it's ever been my pleasure to read. How can that be?

Perhaps the better question is, How can that not be? Few critics would deny that Fitzgerald had one of the best ears for language ever bestowed upon an American writer or that *The Great Gatsby* is one of the most lyrically beautiful, masterfully crafted works ever produced. At the same time, the novel was written in 1924 by a young white man struggling to be accepted by the upper class and to attain literary recognition that he did not achieve during his lifetime. And if his biographers are to be believed, including those biographers who admire his work and appreciate the difficulties he suffered in life, Fitzgerald was a man of his time who had all the ideological biases that a man of his time could possibly possess. How could these elements not appear in the work that he believed would be his greatest achievement and into which he poured himself so completely? In fact, even had Fitzgerald not shared all the ideological biases that inform his novel, those biases would have appeared in the work in some form because *The Great Gatsby* is a chronicle of the 1920s, of the author's own generation, and Fitzgerald was an extremely accurate observer of human behavior. In short, the times were ideologically flawed even if the author hadn't been.

Yet I didn't really see these flaws as "something wrong with the novel," as my friend put it. I was so excited by my ability to see the appalling ideologies my theories were helping me uncover that I forgot to be appalled by them. Yes, the novel is ideologically appalling, a fact we musn't forget. And the novel is intensely beautiful as well. This is the contradiction I try to sustain as I continue to appreciate both the incomparable artistry of *The Great Gatsby* and the theories that show me the multiple layers of its disquieting subtext. Sustaining that contradiction, in Fitzgerald's novel and in all the literature I read, is, I believe, one of the greatest pleasures that reading through a theoretical lens offers us. It may be an acquired taste. If so, I would be very happy if the book you hold in your hands helped you acquire it.

INDEX